LANDMARK COLLECTOR'S L

HAUNTED WA

A Survey of Welsh Gh

By Richard Holland

The Author

Richard Holland lives in North-East Wales. For 15 years he has been researching and writing about Welsh folklore and collecting details of supernatural encounters in Wales. His previous books include *Supernatural Clwyd; the Folk Tales of North-East Wales* and *Haunted Wales*, both published by Gwasg Carreg Gwalch. His *Wales of the Unexpected* column appears every week in the *North Wales Daily Post*. Richard has taken part in many radio and TV broadcasts on the supernatural, most recently acting as consultant on Teleg Cyf's *Blas y Cynfyd* series for S4C, and he has lectured widely on the subject. His interest in ghosts began at the age of 12, when he was pushed over in an empty room by a poltergeist.

Richard Holland now hosts the website www.hauntedwales.com

Published by

Landmark Publishing Ltd
Ashbourne Hall, Cokayne Ave, Ashbourne, Derbyshire DE6 1EJ England
Tel: (01335) 347349 Fax: (01335) 347303
e-mail: landmark@clara.net
website: www.landmarkpublishing.co.uk

ISBN 1 84306 177 5
© **Richard Holland 2005**

Dedication

This book is Dedicated with thanks to
Messrs Daulby and Lloyd for continual support and frequent bullying.

Photography: Copyright belongs to the author unless otherwise stated
Print: Cromwell Press Ltd, Trowbridge
Design: Mark Titterton
Cover: James Allsopp

Back cover photographs: © Fortean Picture Library

Acknowledgements

Of all those who have contributed to the production of this book, I would particularly like to thank:
the staff at the National Library of Wales, University of Wales, Flintshire Library Service and the North
East Wales Institute for their help and courtesy; Scott Lloyd for valuable advice and tireless practical
support; Alan Daulby for photographic input and for more than 600 miles' worth of driving; Janet and
Colin Bord for encouragement, access to their fantastic library and for illustrations from the Fortean
Picture Library; and everyone at Landmark Publishing.

LANDMARK COLLECTOR'S LIBRARY

HAUNTED WALES

A Survey of Welsh Ghostlore

By Richard Holland

Landmark Publishing

Contents

About this Book	7
A Survey of Welsh Ghostlore	8
The Ghosts of Wales	*8*
Apparitions	9
Weird ladies	9
Phantom horsemen and carriages	10
Phantom armies	10
Animal ghosts	10
The gwyllgi	11
Other weird things	11
Ghosts which appear in many forms	11
Apparitions of living people	11
Invisible ghosts	12
Poltergeists	12
Stone-throwers	12
Other physical effects	13
Indelible marks	13
Omens of death	13
Why do Ghosts Haunt?	14
Violent death	14
Wickedness, wildness or remorse	14
The bonds of concealment	15
Holy ghosts	16
Haunting through choice	16
How to get rid of a Ghost	16
Where the stories come from	17
Edmund 'The Old Prophet' Jones	17
William Howells	18
Wirt Sikes	18
Elias Owen	18
Marie Trevelyan	18
Jonathan Ceredig Davies	19
Honourable mentions	19
Distribution of Stories	20
Authorities Consulted	21
Glossary of Welsh Terms	24
Gazetteer	25
Flintshire	*25*
Broughton (Brychdyn)	25
Halkyn (Helygain)	25
Hawarden (Penarlâg)	25
Llanasa	26
Mancot	26
Mold (Yr Wyddgrug)	26
Nannerch	29
Pontblyddyn	30
Queensferry	30
Rhesycae	31
Wrexham	*32*
Bettisfield	32
Bronington	32
Bwlchgwyn	33
Cymau	33
Glyn Ceiriog	33
Gresford	34
Holt	34
Marford	34
Rossett (Yr Orsedd)	34
Ruabon (Rhiwabon)	35
Wrexham (Wrecsam)	35
Denbighshire	*36*
Bryneglwys	36
Cynwyd	37
Llandegla	37
Llangollen	37
Llangynhafal	39
Llanrhaeadr	40
Llantysilio	40
Llanynys	41
Melin-y-Wig	41
Rhuddlan	42
Ruthin (Rhuthun)	42
St Asaph (Llanelwy)	43
Conwy	*44*
Betws-y-Coed	44
Cerrigydrudion	44
Conwy	45
Llandudno	46
Llanfairfechan	46
Llangernyw	46
Llangwm	47
Llanrwst	47
Llansannan	48
Pentrefoelas	48
Anglesey	*49*
Beaumaris (Biwmaris)	49
Brynteg	50
Holyhead (Caergybi)	50
Llanallgo	50
Llanddeusant	51
Llanddyfnan	51
Llaneilian	52
Llangristiolus	52

Gwynedd 53

Bangor	53
Barmouth (Abermaw)	53
Beddgelert	53
Bethesda	56
Dolgellau	57
Llanegryn	57
Llanfor	57
Llanllechid	58
Llanuwchllyn	59
Llanymawddwy	59
Llithfaen	60
Mynytho	62
Nanhwynan	63
Rhiw	63

Ceredigion 64

Abermeurig	64
Aberystwyth	65
Afon Teifi	66
Blaenporth	66
Borth	67
Devil's Bridge (Pontarfynach)	67
Llanafan	68
Llanbadarn Fawr	69
Llanddewi Brefi	69
Llandre (Llanfihangel Genau'r Glyn)	69
Llandysul	70
Llangunllo/Llangynllo	70
Monachty	70
Pontrhydfendigaid	70
Rhosygarth	70
Swyddffynnon	71
Talybont	71
Troedyraur	72
Ystrad Meurig	72

Pembrokeshire 73

Cilrhedyn	73
Eglwyswrw	74
Glandwr	74
Haverfordwest (Hwlffordd)	74
Letterston	74
Llanychaer	75
Milford Haven (Aberdaugleddau)	75
Narberth	76
Newport	76
Pembroke Dock (Doc Penfro)	77
Pontfaen	78
St David's (Tyddewi)	78
St Dogmaels	79
Stackpole	79
Tangiers	80

Carmarthenshire 81

Carmarthen (Caerfyrddin)	81
Cynwyl Elfed	81
Cynwyl Gaio	82
Henllan Amgoed	82
Llanboidy	82
Llannon	82
Llanybyther	82
Kidwelly (Cidweli)	83
Llanstephan	84
Laugharne	84
Llandeilo	84
Llandovery	85
Llanelli	85
Llanfynydd	85
Llangeler	85
Llangynog	86
Llanpumsaint	86
Llansadwrn	87
Nantgaredig	87
Newchurch	87
Pendine	87
Pontyberem	87
Yscanhir/Yscarhir?	88

Swansea 89

Llanrhidian	89
The Mumbles	89
Pennard	91
Rhossili	91

Neath Port Talbot 92

Aberpergwm	92
Afon Hepste	92
Cwmavon	92
Cymmer	93
Glyncorrwg	93
Glynneath (Glyn-Nedd)	93
Margam	94
Neath (Castell-Nedd)	94
Pontrhydyfen	94
Port Talbot	95
Skewen	96
Tonna	96

Rhondda Cynon Taff 97

Llantrisant	97
Llanwonno	98
Mountain Ash	98
Pontypridd	98
'Rhondda Stonehenge'	99

Bridgend 101

Bridgend (Pen-y-bont ar Ogwr)	101
Bryncethin	101
Llangynwyd	101
Maesteg	103
Merthyr Mawr	104
Newton Nottage	104
Sker	104

Vale of Glamorgan	**106**	*Newport*	**130**
Boverton	106	Bassaleg	130
Colwinston	106	Malpas	130
Cowbridge (Bontfaen)	107	Newport (Casnewydd)	130
Llanmaes	108	Redwick	130
Llanmihangel	108	St Brides Wentlooge	131
Llantwit Major	108	Whitson	131
Llysworney	109	*Monmouthshire*	**132**
Maendy	110		
Ogmore	110	Abergavenny (Y Fenni)	132
St Athan	110	Caerwent	132
St Donat's	111	Llanfihangel Crucorney	133
Southerndown	112	Llangua	133
Swanbridge	113	Llanishen	133
		Magor	134
Cardiff	**115**	Mathern	134
Canton	115	Monmouth (Trefynwy)	134
Cardiff (Caerdydd)	115	Tintern	135
Llandaff	116	Tregare	135
Llanedeyrn	116	Usk	135
Llanishen	117	Wolvesnewton	136
Pentyrch	117	*Powys*	**137**
Roath	117		
Taff's Well (Ffynnon Taf)	117	Abbeycwmhir	137
Tongwynlais	118	Aberedw	137
		Aberhafesp	137
Caerphilly	**119**	Abermule	137
Abercarn	119	Brecon (Aberhonddu)	138
Bedwas	119	Capel y Ffin	138
Bedwellty	120	Disserth	139
Caerphilly	120	Hyssington	139
Crumlyn	121	Kerry	140
Llanbradach	121	Llandysilio	140
Machen	122	Llanerfyl	141
Risca	122	Llanfair Caereinion	141
		Llanfigan (Llanfeugan)	143
Merthyr Tydfil	**123**	Llangattock	144
Merthyr Tydfil	123	Llangunllo	144
		Llangynidr	145
Blaenau Gwent	**124**	Llanidloes	145
Abertillery	124	Llansantffraid	146
Brynithel	124	Llanwddyn	146
Ebbw Vale (Glyn Ebwy)	125	Llanwnog	148
Ebwy Fawr	125	Llanymynech	148
Llanhilleth	126	Llawryglyn	150
		Llywel	151
Torfaen	**126**	Machynlleth	151
Cwmbran	126	Meifod	153
Panteg	127	Mochdre	153
Pontypool	127	Montgomery (Trefaldwyn)	154
Tranch	128	Partrishow (Patricio)	155
Trevethin	129	Rhayader	155
		Trelystan	155
		Welshpool (Y Trallwng)	156
		Ystradgynlais	157

About this Book

Everyday, it seems, someone somewhere in Wales sees an apparition or experiences some other ghostly phenomenon. It is a frightfully haunted country. If I had decided to include every single ghost sighting in *Haunted Wales*, it would have had to run to several volumes; indeed it may never have been completed.

I have therefore limited myself mainly to accounts of ghost sightings which appear in the literature pre-dating the Second World War. This has enabled me to trace back to their original sources ghost stories which have appeared in more recent books and which have been elaborated upon by careless authors more concerned with telling a story than recording an event as reported. The work of some modern authors is very muddy, as I have discovered to my own cost. An early book of mine, *Haunted Clwyd*, published in 1992, contains errors which I compounded from modern sources, and this is a shame, because the original versions have proved just as interesting.

The reader may be surprised that certain well-known ghost stories are missing from *Haunted Wales*. This is because I have been unable to find an early source and the only modern version is one I am wary of. The reader can be assured that every report of every story which appears in *Haunted Wales* is a true reflection of the original source and that no extraneous detail has been incorporated into it. Each story is footnoted so that readers can check out the early version or versions for themselves.

Any reported speech used in the stories has been taken directly from the original text. For this reason many of the Welsh words which appear in my text are in 'old Welsh'; I have maintained the spellings used in the sources. Individual Welsh words which may be unfamiliar to the reader, such as *bwgan* or *yspryd*, I have italicised. However, I have not continued this style in names incorporating them, such as Bwgan yr Hafod or Yspryd Cynon, because I felt this would tend towards unnecessarily italicising every Welsh name or phrase which appears.

Haunted Wales was intended to be the definitive guide to Welsh ghostlore. In this I hope it almost succeeds. However, the material was so much more extensive than I anticipated that, for reasons of publishing viability, I had to satisfy myself with English language sources. No doubt there is still a quota of stories to be rediscovered among the Welsh language works of the period. However, I trust that these are comparatively few, since so many Welsh language sources were used and in some cases carefully translated by writers such as Elias Owen and J Ceredig Davies.

Haunted Wales is in two sections. Firstly, there is a survey of Welsh ghostlore, discussing the types of ghosts and the common themes of ghost stories from Wales. This section also includes brief biographies of the most often quoted folklorists, since I considered it important for the reader to be familiar with the sources of these stories. A familiarisation with the original writers also goes a long way to understanding the rather uneven distribution of the stories – the geography of haunted Wales.

The second section is a gazetteer of Welsh ghosts and is the main content of *Haunted Wales*. Here are the ghost stories themselves, arranged county by modern county so that the reader will be able to quickly learn which ghosts haunt his own neighbourhood.

I would stress that although the following stories are of some age, the majority will be new to the reader, for many have not appeared in print since their original publication, in some cases more than two hundred years ago. I hope they will all serve to intrigue, fascinate and perhaps even frighten you.

As Wirt Sikes put it in the year 1880:

'The phantoms of the Welsh spirit-world are always picturesque; they are often ghastly ... but besides, they are instructive to him whose purpose in studying is, to know.'

A Survey of Welsh Ghostlore

The Ghosts of Wales

'... more ghosts and goblins I think were prevalent in Wales than in England or any other country.'

So wrote researcher William Howells way back in 1831. And I believe he was right. Wales is a fearfully haunted place. The country abounds in castles and mansions, ancient churches, lonely lanes and crossroads, even bare mountainsides, all of which can boast a resident spook. The ghosts of Wales are of great age, their manners and appearance hinting at beliefs older than the oldest books and suggesting that it is a place of particular magic and spiritual power. And they are bold and memorable, striking of appearance, forceful in character, terrifying – even dangerous.

Wales is not content with the forlorn nuns, shadowy monks and vaguely glimpsed Victorian ladies or men in ruffs which linger in the haunted houses of its English neighbours. Here we have a more exciting roster which includes, to quote but a few: headless horses, phantom pigs and raging bulls; creatures which are half-human and half-dog; wailing monsters with bright, staring eyes; huge creatures with long, curling tongues; bat-winged ladies with claws and fangs; and mysterious glowing lights which prophesy doom.

Welsh ghosts are not shy. They will go out of their way to announce their presence by creating an unearthly din of bangs and crashes, or by lighting up the whole house with an ethereal glow. They often have a purpose and will accost unfortunate mortals to do their bidding, putting them to great inconvenience and brooking no refusal. Many have suffered greatly at the hands of a spirit whom they have ignored or insulted.

In Welsh folklore ghosts and goblins are largely indistinguishable and most of the words used to name them are interchangeable. The most common is *bwgan*, which has the same root as the English 'boggart' and 'bogey'. The word is used to denote any frightening and inexplicable presence or apparition, particularly one that is grotesque, disruptive or malignant. *Bwbach* suggests a less alarming entity, a harmless spook. The common suffix has given

us 'Boo!'. *Ellyll*, the Welsh equivalent of 'elf', may also be used to denote a ghost, as at the Ffynnon yr Ellyllon, or 'Goblin Well', near Mold, which was haunted by the apparition of a headless woman. *Bwci* and its variant *pwca* are used for mischievous ghosts and goblins – 'sprite' might be a good translation. The words are used in naming specific goblins of local tradition, such as the Bwci Bo or Pwca Trwyn, both of which haunted particular areas of Glamorganshire and whose names were used to frighten children. The only Welsh word exclusively used for a ghost rather than a goblin is *yspryd*, which means 'spirit'. A glossary of such terms can be found on page 24.

This nomenclature reflects the fact that the boundaries between ghostlore and fairylore are narrow. One of the earliest collectors of supernatural encounters in Wales, Edmund Jones, made no distinction between ghosts and fairies in his book of 1780; to him they were all apparitions of God's divine purpose. The White or Green Ladies of tradition (see below) certainly behave like ghosts but their choice of haunts – beside rivers, on mountainsides and in the vicinity of sacred springs, for example – has led to interpretations that they might be nature spirits, or surviving memories of local pagan goddesses. In the past, the strange disturbances which today we assign to a 'poltergeist' were as likely to have been blamed on a mischievous fairy as they were on the presence of an evil spirit. Welsh ghostlore is peopled with many grotesques which are neither ghost nor fairy, such as the Banshee-like *Gwrach y Rhybin* ('Hag of the Mist') or the *cannwyll corff* ('corpse candle').

There is a curious difference between the way ghosts are reported today and how they were often reported in the past. Today writers tend to be concerned with the identity of a ghost; if it appears as a man in a top hat or a woman in a long, flowing dress, who is it 'the ghost of'? Modern ghost literature frequently refers to the idea that apparitions are playbacks – like those on a video tape – of people and incidents which have occurred in the past. The implication is that each ghost reflects a precise personality or event peculiar to it. There are many examples of a particular person haunting a particular place in Wales (the Norman baron FitzHamon haunting Newport Castle, the poet Dylan Thomas haunting Laugharne in Carmarthenshire, for example) but in traditional Welsh ghostlore such a tidy connection between personality and location is does not always exist.

For example, J Ceredig Davies notes in 1911 that a spot near Ystrad Meurig in Ceredigion had become haunted because an old woman had been murdered there. However, the resulting apparition was not that of the victim. On the contrary, the ghost which now manifested at the murder site took on at least two very different forms – that of a man on horseback and on other occasions that of a cat. The same author,

in referring to a haunting at Llanbadarn Fawr, consistently refers to the ghost as a 'he', but later refers to it as a lady in a white dress! The inference is that a ghost has neither sex nor any other human identity, it is merely a thing or an effect, a force outside human familiarity or understanding. This, no doubt, is why the word *bwgan* has such a nebulous definition.

Very broadly speaking, ghosts can be arranged into two types – those that are seen and those that are not seen. Visual ghosts are called apparitions and there are many kinds. Those that are not seen are often associated with poltergeist activity, more of which later. In addition there is a range of phenomena closely associated with ghostlore, the death omens or *Tolaeth*. There now follows a brief description of the main types of Welsh ghost.

Apparitions

Apparitions take many forms. A 'simple apparition' might be the aforementioned figure of a monk, or a woman in Victorian dress; some fleeting, silent image. The apparition may be the mute record of some incident in history, usually a tragedy, or it might be anonymous, some forgotten person whose impression has somehow remained behind in the place where he or she lived. These are, of course, the most uninteresting kind of ghost, and make up the majority of today's modern sightings. Far more interesting are those ghosts which interact with the living, speaking to them, asking them to perform some function for them, or simply going out of their way to frighten them silly. Here then is a breakdown of the types of apparition which have commonly occurred in Wales.

Weird ladies

The White Ladies, Green Ladies, Grey Ladies and Ladies in Black of Welsh ghost tradition share much in common, indeed the only thing they do not share is their taste in clothes. Their colourful names derive from the colour of gown they choose to wear. The White Lady is sometimes referred to affectionately by her Welsh name, *Ladi Wen*. Often she is no more than a 'simple apparition', a lovely but dejected figure seen wandering about the grounds of a venerable mansion or the ramparts of a ruined castle. On other occasions there is a reason for her haunting and she will approach a person (usually

a man), or wait until he approaches her, to explain the reason for her presence. In Glamorganshire she often requires the kindness of a mortal to help free her spirit from the earth. Fortunately, more often than not, she is of fair appearance, which helps her to allay any supernatural fear on the part of the person she approaches.

Grey Ladies, of course, wear grey. In England this is usually because in life the lady was a nun, accustomed to wearing a grey habit, but in Wales phantom nuns are comparatively rare (as, indeed, are phantom monks, also common over the border). Grey Ladies are usually quiet haunters, but may have had violent pasts. The Grey Lady of Ruthin Castle in Denbighshire, for example, was an axe murderess.

The mournful appearance of ladies in black may hint at a past tragedy associated with their haunting. The lady who haunted Pwll Helyg in Rhondda Cynon Taff, for example, wore black because she was in mourning for her lost husband – and her lost jewels. However, their sombre clothing is often of no particular relevance and they go about their business in much the same way as their cousins, the White, Grey and Green Ladies.

The most striking of the lot are the latter variety. Green is a colour associated with the fairies and the Green Ladies almost always choose to haunt open areas of the countryside, such as riverbanks and hillsides. They are benign, beautiful, intelligent and are usually seen in the daytime. White Ladies, too, often appear during the day. Old healing wells are especially favoured by the Weird Ladies, which hints at a possible pagan origin. One Green Lady used to appear beside the eye-well in Marcross in old Glamorganshire and watched as people performed an age-old healing ceremony there.[1] The White Lady of the Goblin Well in Mold cheerfully admitted to having her head cut off in a sacrifice!

One exception to the charming appearance of these spirits is the Green Lady of Caerphilly Castle. She is more goblin than ghost – diminutive in size but possessed of a huge head and enormous eyes.

Phantom horsemen and carriages

Phantoms on horseback come in two classes, each equally mysterious. The first type spend their time charging up and down dark rural lanes and frightening benighted travellers. The reason for this behaviour is usually obscure and the tragedy or crisis which originally spurred their desperate flight has been long forgotten. The second variety are quiet, shadowy figures, who silently ride up behind a traveller and then keep abreast with him for an unnerving period of time, never uttering a word – then they vanish as unexpectedly as they arrived. In the case of an incident which took place near Llanuwchllyn, in Gwynedd, this sudden appearance was of great benefit to the witness, for the horseman's presence scared off a ruffian who had been intent on robbing him.

Some aristocratic ghosts prefer the comfort of riding around in their own carriages. Wicked Lady Matthias, of Stackpole in Pembrokeshire, for example, trundles about in a carriage pulled by headless horses and driven by a headless coachman. Juan White, a weird, witch-like spirit, rode her carriage along impossibly narrow and rocky tracks on the mountainous border of Powys and Blaenau Gwent. Often these phantom carriages are assigned to no one in particular and still follow routes they would have used when on the mortal plane – sometimes they are seen to crash, recalling a tragedy of the pre-motorised past.

Phantom armies

On a few occasions great hosts of ghosts have been seen, armed as if for battle. At Rhewl, Denbighshire, these were known to be the angry spirits of a defeated company of Welsh soldiers. In other cases, however, the army's appearance has been a one-off event and its origin entirely inexplicable to the onlookers. In the case of the phantom armies seen on different occasions in the 17th century at Montgomery in Powys and Bwlchgwyn, Wrexham, the ghosts were assumed to be some sort of 'forewarninge' of trouble to come in the future rather than an apparition of some event that had occurred in the past. However, in neither case were these fears founded and the visions remain as mysterious today as they were to the crowds of astonished witnesses more than 300 years ago.

Animal ghosts

It is not just the spirits of humans which return from oblivion; those of animals do, too. They are usually of the domestic variety. Dogs are the most common, perhaps because of their closer association with humankind. When the ghost of the haughty Madam Godolphin used to appear at Llansantffraid in Powys, she would always be accompanied by her little pet dog; perhaps it did not wish to leave its mistress alone in the afterlife. Equally loyal were the dogs said to haunt a path called Gallows Way in Vale of Glamorgan, for it is thought that they were the pets of criminals who had been hanged here.

Obviously, one cannot have phantom horsemen and carriages without having the phantom horses to go with them, but occasionally an equine apparition will appear on its own. The favourite horse of a 17th century mariner used to manifest in a field near Cardiff, and a dark lane near the Shropshire border was haunted by a frantically galloping white horse with 'great blood clots' on its shoulders.

Phantom pigs, too, are not unknown, and they are always black in colour. There are also a few records of spectral cats. Near Monmouth there is a ghostly cow which appears in the early morning quietly chewing its cud and looking just as solid and comfortable as its fellows. The ghost of an entire flock of sheep was seen at Bedwellty in Caerphilly.

Stranger animal ghosts are also on record. A phantom panther was once said to pad about the corridors of St Donat's Castle in Vale of Glamorgan. From Powys there are several stories of spirits manifesting in the form of gigantic, angry bulls. A breed apart, however, are the so-called Dogs of Darkness, or *gwyllgi*, described below.

The gwyllgi

Gwyllgi is a Welsh word used by some writers, including Charles Redwood in 1839, to describe a particular kind of horror which haunted lonely lanes and crossroads at night.[2] The word 'gwyll' can be variously used to mean 'darkness', 'twilight', 'fairy' or, in modern usage, 'wild'. 'Gi' is the mutation of 'ci', the Welsh word for dog. Usually these creatures resemble huge hounds of the mastiff variety and they are often described as being the size of a calf. Sometimes they resemble a calf more than they do a dog. Most often they are black in colour and sometimes they have shaggy pelts and glaring eyes. Sometimes they are silent, and will pad along just behind, or alongside, some night-bound traveller, but they have also been known to set up a hideous and nerve-jangling howl.

There are many examples of this sort of apparition from Wales. However, there are also variants. In Neath Port Talbot, they were blood red in colour and were known to appear early on Sunday mornings as well as at night. Individual spooks showed a variety of imaginative features, but canine characteristics are always present. The ghost of Llysworney in Vale of Glamorgan, for example, had the head and shoulders of a human being but the 'body and limbs like those of a large, bright-spotted dog'. Gwyllgi of the more common mastiff breed have also been reported from England – in East Anglia, for example, where the apparition is called Black Shuck, and in northern England where it is known as Padfoot, Trash or Shriker.[3]

Many English phrases are used to describe the gwyllgi, such as 'Hounds of Hell' or 'Dogs of Darkness'. An old farmer of Cynwyd, Denbighshire, who actually encountered one of the beasts, gave it the lavish name of 'The Black Hound of Destiny'.

Other weird things

A 'miscellaneous' section under 'Apparitions' must also appear, for there are many strange examples, weirder even than the gwyllgi. Edmund Jones (see below), writing in 1780, recorded many grotesque apparitions unlike any others in Welsh ghostlore. They include giant ghosts, impossibly tall and thin ghosts, ghosts without limbs, or with improperly formed heads, or with hideously long tongues, and ghosts which crawled along on all fours or which rolled over and over like Catherine wheels. Either Mr Jones had a particularly vivid and gruesome imagination, or

his friends and neighbours did – or South Wales was a place where one would hardly dare venture out at night two and a quarter centuries ago.

To Jones's grotesque corpus can be added others, such as the strange birdlike thing that would screech in misery from the tree-tops at the Faenol estate in Gwynedd and the horrible, wailing figure with glowing eyes which terrified a poacher in the Gloddaeth woods near Llandudno, Conwy.

Many ghosts appear in a more nebulous form. A bwgan may be no more than a vaguely man-sized glowing light. One such was the Ysbryd Bryn-glas which regularly appeared beside a lane leading to Bryn-glas Hall in Powys. It waited every night so that it could intone a message of doom to the squire as he staggered home from the pub. Perhaps the vaguest of all was another Powys ghost, the Ysbryd Cefn Yspytty, of Llanwddyn, which appeared 'as alternate light and darkness'.

Ghosts would often appear as a ball or wheel of fire. The wheels of fire which were seen to roll down a hill at Llansannan, Conwy, and down the River Colwyn in Gwynedd, each recalled the site of a murder. These spectral fires could be vast; one at Risca, in Caerphilly, was 'as large as a small field'.

Ghosts which appear in many forms

Previously I have mentioned the haunting at Ystrad Meurig where the ghost of a cat and the ghost of a man on horseback were both considered to be one and the same bwgan. Some spooks were credited with the ability to take many forms. At Llangwm, Conwy, for example, Ysbryd Ystrad Fawr could manifest as a spectral fire, or as a gwyllgi or, uniquely, 'like a turkey with his tail spread out like a spinning wheel'. Among a roster of ghosts collected by the vicar of Llanwddyn in Powys there is an Ysbryd Fedwddu which had 'sometimes the appearance of a human without a head, a beautiful horse with a rider, a large bull and as a greyhound'. Elsewhere in his list he describes an Ysbryd Ceunant Croesau as being 'visible in all shapes'.

Apparitions of living people

Sometimes the ghosts of people are seen even when they are not dead. In Wales the apparition of a person who is still alive is called a lledrith. For a person to see their own ghost was considered extremely unlucky, a foreteller of misfortune, even of death.[4] But in many other cases such a phenomenon seems to have been taken as a curiosity lacking any special significance. The grandfather of Ceredig Davies, a Mr Evans, once appeared as a *lledrith*. While he was away in Aberystwyth for the day, his apparition was seen wandering around his farm at Llanddewi Brefi. When told of the event he shrugged it off with the words: 'To see the spirit of a living man is not a bad sign.' He meant that if his spirit had been seen after his death it might have meant his spirit had been unable to find peace, was perhaps in hell. Here is an intriguing implication that the spirit is somehow separate from the mind and body and can function independently of either.

Davies records many other examples of the *lledrith* from Mid Wales, but I include only one or two in *Haunted Wales*, for lack of space. However, I do include a striking example from Beaumaris, Anglesey, and one other, a famous case dating from the 17th century in which a young wife in Gower is tormented by the apparition of her dissolute husband.

Invisible ghosts

Many ghosts never show themselves. The sound of footsteps echoing around an empty corridor or up and down a fine old staircase without any visible agent to account for them is a common feature of haunted houses. Other examples of invisible ghosts include the barking of dogs heard at Colwinston, Vale of Glamorgan, and the whinnying of a frantic horse at Dolgellau, Gwynedd, both of which record horrible tragedies at the spots where they are heard. Ghostly smells have also been noted. This may be the elusive whiff of perfume worn by a long departed lady or, as at Llanasa, Flintshire, something more specific and more significant.

Disembodied voices are particularly eerie. At Cymau, Wrexham, a woman distinctly heard a voice crying 'Pray for my soul' right under her bedroom window, and a pool of water at Beddgelert, Gwynedd, became known as 'The Lake of the Maiden's Cries' on account of the wailing of the spirit haunting the spot. Inexplicable noises were often believed to warn of an approaching death (see 'Omens of death' below) and are associated with poltergeists.

Poltergeists

Numerous books and films of modern times have made the term 'poltergeist' a familiar one. The word is German and broadly translates as 'noisy ghost'. Phenomena associated with poltergeist activity include inexplicable bangs and crashes and the sounds of furniture moving about or items breaking, even though nothing is found afterwards to have been disturbed. In addition objects may actually move or be thrown about and the spook can be by turns mischievous and witty in its doings, or downright nasty, resorting to pinching and slapping individuals in the household or dousing them with water. Often it focuses its attention on just one person in the house, usually a young female servant. It is rare for poltergeists to cause actual physical harm but they can be dangerously destructive nonetheless. An unfortunate family at Llangunllo in Powys watched their house being systematically destroyed by an invisible entity, and it was eventually burned to the ground.

In most poltergeist cases the spirit remains invisible, but in some instances, a long time after the initial onset of the disturbances, apparitions begin to appear or disembodied voices are heard claiming to be the spirit. The so-called Pwca Trwyn, haunting a farmhouse by that name, enjoyed many chats with the household and even announced its eventual departure. The Bwgan yr Hafod which caused havoc in a grand old house in Ceredigion once appeared as a beautiful woman and on other occasions as a friendly pig!

Stone-throwers

The throwing of stones is a popular pastime of poltergeists. The Pwca Trwyn, for example, once pelted a man who had offended it with a hail of rocks, none of which missed their target, although they successfully avoided all the people who were trying to protect him. Nevertheless, there appears to be a strain of poltergeist whose sole manifestation is the throwing of stones. Elias Owen refers to a 'dangerous spirit' at a place called Caellwyngrydd which would stone people as they passed along the road, and John Jones, an elderly informant of Ceredig Davies, referred to a ghost at Pontrhydfendigaid, Ceredigion, 'which was engaged in the dangerous game of stone-throwing'. Dangerous, indeed, it could be – a family at Llanllechid, Gwynedd, were driven out of their home by an entity which hurled heavy boulders around the house.

Davies records an intriguing incident which took place at Mydroilyn, Ceredigion, in the

1840s or 50s. One night a Mr Stephens saw the spirit of a neighbour (still living but presumably at home in bed) standing in a field and throwing stones 'with all his might'. Even more oddly, the field was described as one in which 'stones were not to be found'.[5] What link is there, I wonder, to this odd behaviour and the examples we have of stones appearing out of nowhere and bombarding houses?

Other physical effects

In some hauntings a person can feel themselves touched by a ghost, or experience some sort of physical presence quite different to those experienced in poltergeist cases. In the Cymau case, for example, a member of the family awoke to feel a hand pressing down on his chest. Captain Alldridge, commander of the haunted HMS *Asp*, wrote: 'I was awoke from my sleep by a hand, to all sensations, being placed on my leg outside the bedclothes ... on one occasion as I lay wide awake a hand was placed on my forehead.'

In Carmarthen a far more dramatic form of physical haunting took place – a youth was brutally beaten by the spirit of a recently deceased farmer for trespassing on his field.

Indelible marks

At a house in Meifod, Powys, two marks were pointed out in a haunted room which were supposedly those left behind by the bloodstained boots of a murderer. Such 'indelible bloodstains' – which no amount of washing will remove – are common staples of ghostlore throughout the British Isles. A variant on the theme is the 'Robber's Grave' in Montgomery churchyard. For years no grass would grow on this grave, where lies the body of a man wrongfully executed for highway robbery. This bald patch of ground was a silent testament to the man's innocence.

Omens of death

Tolaeth is a Welsh word for a phenomenon in which mysterious noises warn of coming misfortune, usually death. By extension it has been used to encompass a whole host of supernatural omens. The word has no equivalent in English, although Ceredig Davies ponders whether it may have any relation to 'toll', as in the tolling of a bell.[6] It is more likely that it is related to *teulu*, the Welsh word for family, for these were seen as domestic spooks, of personal significance, and *teulu*, or as Davies spells it, *toili*, is also used for certain of these portents. The existence of the *Tolaeth* was said to have been brought about by the prayers of St David, who felt it was kinder that his flock should have some warning of their coming demise, so that they might better prepare themselves for the afterlife.[7]

Tales of the *Tolaeth* were probably the most common of those told by Welsh firesides and there are many of them. So many are there and so similar are the stories, that I have included only a representative sample in *Haunted Wales*. There follows an outline of those varieties of *Tolaeth* which the reader will come across:

Corpse candle (*cannwyll corff*) – The corpse candle is a small glowing light which hovers about the room of a dying person or which is seen at a spot where someone is doomed to die. Often they are seen traversing the countryside at dead of night, following the course to the churchyard or burial ground which will later be taken by a funeral.

Phantom funeral (*teulu, toili, anghladd* or *drychiolaeth*)[8] – These are exact facsimiles of real funeral processions that are seen processing towards a burial ground, following the route which will later be taken by the real funeral party. These complicated apparitions are so accurate that faces can be recognised in the crowd and minor details noticed again when the genuine funeral takes place. Sometimes the funeral is not seen but the sounds of its procession, including hymns, are heard instead. It is not wise to stand in the way of a phantom funeral, because the apparitions are capable of badly jostling and trampling the unwary – they may even drag along the unfortunate witness for the length of their journey.

Tolaeth – The *tolaeth* proper are inexplicable bangs and crashes which are heard in the house of someone about to die. They can be quite specific. A collier at Maesteg, Bridgend, heard a crowd of people come to the door and then barge into his sitting room. Although he could see nobody, the room seemed full of people and he could hear confused talking and the bustle of men moving about. The next evening, a fellow miner who lived in the house was killed by a fall in the mine. His body was brought in by a crowd of men and the sounds they made exactly corresponded to those heard the night before.[9] Carpenters commonly reported hearing the knocking and sawing associated with the manufacture of a coffin coming from their empty workshop on the night before a death in the community.[10]

Cyhiraeth – The *Cyhiraeth* was a 'crying' spirit which could be heard wailing inside or outside the house of a dying person, or meandering down the streets of a village before an outbreak of disease. The spirit also made its home on the seashore where its shrieks of despair would warn of a forthcoming shipwreck. An excellent description of the *Cyhiraeth*, courtesy of a countryman of the 18th century, can be found under Llannon, Carmarthenshire.

Gwrach y Rhibyn – The name translates approximately as 'Hag of the Mists', or, as Charles Redwood has it, 'Hag of the Mountain Dribble'. Although, as her name implies, she was considered a spirit of the mountains, the *Gwrach y Rhibyn* was just as at home patrolling ruined castles, ancient manor houses and the occasional unlucky village. She was a hideous creature, boasting fangs, claws and bat-like wings and her appearance was a warning of death, usually in some important family. She, too, was often heard to wail and in some stories seems synonymous with the *Cyhiraeth*. The similarity of both spirits with the famous Banshee of Irish folklore is obvious. A gruesome, first-hand account of a sighting of the *Gwrach y Rhibyn* comes from Llandaff, Cardiff. Its appearance in this urban setting is particularly unnerving.

Church spirits – It was a common belief in rural Wales that if one visited the churchyard at midnight on Hallowe'en and hid in the church porch, one could hear a mournful voice intoning the names of all those parishioners doomed to die in the coming year. This could prove risky – for many people heard their own names being read out! At Llangernyw, Conwy, this mysterious spirit was called the Angelystor. Uniquely, at Llangynwyd, Bridgend, the spirit visited on the night of New Year's Eve.

Why do Ghosts Haunt?

Ghosts haunt the mortal plane and bother the living either because they want to or because certain laws compel them to. The most common reasons for hauntings, and those which will feature in most of the stories in this book, are explored below.

Violent death

A person who has been murdered, suffered a fatal accident or who has committed suicide may find they cannot pass on into the afterlife and instead hang around the place of their death as a ghost. Spiritualists might claim the reason for this is that the shock of their sudden death has left them confused or unprepared for the spirit world; I do not believe that such a suggestion exists in folklore, however.

In the case of murder, a soul may cry out for justice, may even wish to expose the murderer. In past times suicide was considered a sin and the superstitious believed that their spirits would walk after death. In the days when burial was denied in consecrated ground, suicides would be buried at crossroads, sometimes face down or staked down to confuse them and prevent them from wandering. The soul of any body buried in unconsecrated ground was likely to haunt the spot where it was buried, the unexpected discovery of a skeleton ending a haunting which may have been a mystery to the neighbourhood for years (see, for example, Boverton and Llanmaes, in Vale of Glamorgan, and Tintern, Monmouthshire).

Wickedness, wildness or remorse

Sometimes a spirit is simply too wicked to go to heaven and is doomed to remain behind on the earth as a kind of penance. The spirit of Charles Lewis, a tanner, haunted Disserth in Powys because he had been in the habit of cheating his neighbours in business deals. John, a steward of Hawarden Castle in Flintshire, remained on the mortal plane because all his life he had been 'an absolute tyrant' to his underlings. Wickedness and remorse often go hand-in-hand with such hauntings.

Members of the wicked aristocracy are often doomed to a continued existence on earth, but it is sometimes uncertain whether it is their sin which is keeping them from 'passing over' or the simple fact that their wild spirits refuse to rest. 'Old Tamberlain' was, despite his name, still a youngster when he died in 1839, his dissipated habits being a contributory factor in his demise. After his earthly death, his spirit enjoyed charging about the neighbourhood of his former home at Llanymawddwy, Gwynedd, on the phantom of a favourite horse and playing pranks on the locals. There seems to be no reason for this behaviour other than – if you'll pardon the pun – high spirits. Similarly over-exuberant personalities include the inveterate gambler Lady Prendergrast, of Beddgelert, and the tyrannical Madam Godolphin, of Llansantffraid, in Powys.

The bonds of concealment

In the days when life in the Welsh countryside was a hand-to-mouth existence and all the agricultural folk lived in varying degrees of poverty, it is natural to presume that the selfish concealment of money, or any other valuables, for one's own use would be greatly frowned upon. I believe that it is this taboo which has led to so many Welsh ghost stories following the same theme – that hidden valuables bind the concealer's spirit to the earth until those valuables are discovered.

To take a typical example: at Neath in Neath Port Talbot, a brave servant girl stayed behind from church one Sunday to face out the ghost known to be haunting a certain room in the house where she worked. When the apparition of an elderly gentleman strode into the room, she pertly asked it its business, and it replied that she should inform her master that if he would lift up a particular flagstone in the dairy, he would find under it a pot of gold. Once this had been removed, the ghost assured the girl that he would haunt the house no longer.

Although money and gold are the norm, almost anything can be considered 'treasure' in such a story. A ghost may haunt because of the existence of a single coin stashed away, or because of a hoard of old iron, a rusty tool, even some wool, and in one case a mildewed Bible. The important thing is that the item was hidden for later use but remained concealed because of the owner's death.

A spirit bound to the earth for this reason will often go to considerable trouble to ensure that the treasure is found and its release assured. Often it will cause bangs and crashes about the house, or illuminate it with an unearthly light. It may approach mortals directly, as in the case of the Green Lady of Pentyrch, Cardiff, who begged two men to claim her gold for themselves, thereby freeing her. But the men disbelieved the ghost, even though her slippers were coated with gold dust, and she vanished, wailing in despair.

A spirit desperate for release may single out one person to perform the task of unearthing the valuables and will pester them unmercifully until they agree to do so. Sometimes this person is a friend or neighbour of the spirit but just as frequently it is someone unknown to them. The ghost which tormented a servant girl at Maendy in Vale of Glamorgan told her – when she finally plucked up the courage to speak to it – that it had been waiting for her to help it since 'before she was born'. In these latter cases, the spirit always waits until it is spoken to, and usually only when a holy name is invoked, before explaining its presence.

Regrettably, in very many of these cases, the gold cannot be kept by the person coming to the aid of the ghost; it must be disposed of so that it is of no use to anyone. Usually the money must be thrown into a body of water. In south Glamorganshire this is invariably the River Ogmore, further north the confluence of the rivers Rhondda and Taff. Elsewhere any sizeable lake or pool will do. If a river is chosen, it is imperative the money is thrown downstream – people throwing it upstream by mistake are likely to be severely punished by the angry ghost. This depositing of valuables in rivers and lakes reminds one of the offerings made in similar bodies of water by the prehistoric Celts. Perhaps there is some ancient religious significance to these stories, something in the nature of a ritual sacrifice.

The further north we travel in Wales the less frequent these stories become. However, it seems the case that in North Wales it is more usual for the mortal who recovers the treasure to be allowed to keep it for himself.

In order to facilitate the removal and disposal of the treasure, the spirit often employs the power of flight to transport its helper to the place of concealment and afterwards to the chosen lake or river. According to the parson of Boverton in the Vale of Glamorgan, a kind of aerial taxi service was undertaken by one particular spook, the Bwca-Bo, and it was he who transported all the mortals on behalf of the other spirits.[11] On other occasions the spirit would accompany the helper on foot, but the journey would seem shorter and less arduous than expected. In either case both spirit and helper would be invisible to people they passed. The spirit also had the power to impart abnormal strength to its chosen mortal, so that boulders could be easily lifted and heavy chests of gold comfortably carried.

Holy ghosts

Some apparitions seem to have come into existence due to divine influences. The minister whose life was probably saved by the sudden appearance of a phantom horseman at Llanuwchllyn (mentioned above) was convinced he had been rescued through 'a special interference of Providence'. Another preacher travelling about the country had an even more dramatic experience of this sort when a 'gigantic figure' appeared before him in the road at Meifod, Powys, and intoned: 'For your life go back.' It later turned out highwaymen had been waiting to rob him.

At Machen in Caerphilly a lout who harboured the intention of ravishing a young woman was foiled in his foul purpose by an increasingly bizarre parade of apparitions which sprang up before them as they promenaded about the countryside. Near Aberystwyth, Ceredigion, a young man of a religious turn of mind was similarly accosted by apparitions, including those of a headless horse and 'an innumerable number of mice', because he had broken the Fifth Commandment by failing to observe the Sabbath. This was a common reason for ghosts to appear. The *Gwyllgi* in particular made it their duty to frighten revellers returning from pubs on Sunday night. The result, we are assured by writers like Edmund Jones, is that they were shocked into a life of piety and sobriety.

Haunting through choice

Finally we must consider those ghosts which haunt the living because they *want to*. Mischievous poltergeists and those wild and wicked personalities described above may fall into this category. The creepy clergyman of Broughton, Flintshire, seemed to have a purpose to his haunting. He made a habit of startling young courting couples, presumably because he disapproved of their behaviour. The Squire of Foelas at Pentrefoelas, in Conwy, returned to guard his orchard. If the celebrated Ladies of Llangollen really do haunt their former home, it might be presumed they do so because they were happy there, and still enjoy a visit. This presumption could be made of many of the quieter ghosts who haunt the grand old houses of Wales.

How to get rid of a Ghost

Among the most common ghost stories of Wales are those describing the removal of a troublesome spook. The ceremony employed for this purpose is called an exorcism, or, in the parlance of our forefathers, 'ghost laying'. Laying a ghost involved first pacifying the *bwgan*, then imposing upon it a term of imprisonment, during which time it would be unable to haunt the living.

The whole process could prove a real struggle. Typically the ghost would show its aggravation by manifesting in terrible and frightening forms, usually those of large and fierce animals, in an attempt to intimidate the ghost-layer. However, this worthy gentleman would always have taken the precaution of first drawing round himself a protective circle through which ghosts cannot pass, and through prayer, incantation and sheer nerve he would wear down the spook so that it would appear successively less and less alarming. Eventually it would have been reduced to a harmless fly or spider, and this the exorcist would then imprison. A bottle or a small box was most commonly employed, but goose-quills or the Holy Book itself might be used instead, and the *bwgan* would buzz about impotently inside while the exorcist decided what to do with it.

Often the ghost would be banished to Egypt or to the Red Sea, a punishment with a Biblical flavour about it. More often the ghost, still inside its little prison, would be interred somewhere locally, usually in a body of water. Water may have been seen as something literally 'not of this earth', which is why it was suitable both for imprisoning spirits and as a repository of ghost treasure. Burial under bridges was another popular choice. Bridges (and stiles and crossroads) were seen as symbolic of the spirit world in that they belong to no place, rather they are connectors of places. Bridges which crossed watercourses were, of course, doubly popular.

The exorcism was often a kind of bargain with the *bwgan*. There could be some considerable wrangling over the length of the imprisonment. The experienced exorcist would seek to keep this as vague as possible. Dic Spot, a well-known character of 18th century Oswestry, laid the troublesome Ysbryd Cynon under a stone in the river at Llanwddyn, Powys, with the injunctions that it should remain there until the river dried up or the water had worked its way between the stone and the dry land. Unfortunately, when the Llyn Vyrnwy reservoir was under construction, both injunctions came to pass, which caused great consternation among the locals!

In other cases, an imposition would be placed upon the ghost; it would be allotted some task to perform which should prove either impossible or so time-consuming as to do away with any fear of it haunting again. The Bwgan yr Hafod, for example, was commanded to chip away a fathom of rock 'with an ounce hammer and a tin-tack' and a 'dangerous Spirit' banished to the Red Sea was allowed to return to its former home at Caellwyngrydd, Gwynedd, by the length of one barleycorn a year.

Many people set themselves up as jobbing exorcists. The aforementioned Dic Spot was one such, and a Nonconformist minister of Denbighshire, the Rev Griffiths, was frequently called upon to perform this service. Every region of Wales seemed to have its own *Dyn Hysbys* (Wise Man) or *Gwrag Hysbys* (Wise Witch) skilled in the dark arts – and when all else failed, one could always resort to the local vicar! However, a family at Barmouth found they were able to quell their own poltergeist merely by making more noise than *it* did. A fascinating first-hand account of an exorcism by a ghost-layer can be found under Beddgelert, Gwynedd.

Where the stories come from

To locate the ghost stories which make up *Haunted Wales* I have trawled through many 'old volumes of forgotten lore' and dusty periodicals. The compilation of a book such as this would certainly have been impossible without the hard work of many other researchers writing long before me. I have acknowledged these writers frequently and have enjoyed quoting from them, sometimes extensively, to give a flavour of their own styles and to prevent the reader from becoming jaded with my own clumsy prose. It is important then that I give some background to these authors, not only to provide a clear provenance for the stories, but also to familiarise the reader with some names which will crop up again and again in the forthcoming pages.

Edmund 'The Old Prophet' Jones

Edmund Jones was a Nonconformist preacher who was born and lived all his life in the region of South Wales now called Torfaen. His fiery personality, visionary outlook and ranting preaching style earned him the nickname 'The Old Prophet'. Jones was possessed of a passion for all things supernatural. For him a disbelief in the existence of ghosts was tantamount to blasphemy, his argument being that apparitions were earthly manifestations of God's power. Indeed he argued, in the most politically incorrect manner, that: 'They are chiefly women and men of weak and womanish understandings, who speak against the accounts of spirits and apparitions.'

In 1780 he set out to convince people of this by writing a book, *A Relation of the Apparitions of Spirits in the County of Monmouth and the Principality of Wales*, in which, in one slim volume, he gathered together an extraordinary collection of allegedly true, and contemporary, encounters with ghosts and goblins. Its premise was not unique; other Nonconformists of the period shared his views and had done for a while: in 1691, for example, Richard Baxter wrote a similar book, *The Certainty of the World of Spirits* (which contains a classic account of a haunting on the Gower peninsula in Swansea).

What makes Jones's book particularly fascinating is that most of the stories have been related to the author by the witnesses themselves. Jones takes pains to assure the reader of the reliability and honesty of his sources, and yet the ghosts described are far and away the most bizarre and horrible ever recorded from Wales.

In addition to *Apparitions of Spirits*, Jones collected similar stories as part of a history of his home parish of Aberystruth, published in 1779, and there are two manuscripts of unpublished material held at the National Library of Wales. Stories from these sources have also been included.

A catalogue entry at the NLW states that an early edition of *Apparitions of Spirits* was published in 1767 but there is no other evidence for the existence of this book and certainly no copy survives today; I suspect this is a mistake. In his recent compilation of Jones's work, *The Appearance of Evil*, Prof John Harvey theorises that one of the NLW manuscripts (he seems to be unaware of the existence of the other) actually forms the body of the enigmatic book of 1767, but in this he is mistaken, since several of the stories contained in this manuscript are clearly stated by Jones as having been told to him in years after this supposed date of publication.[12]

In *The Appearance of Evil*, Prof Harvey has done an excellent job in modernising Jones's erratic spelling, especially of place names, and this has helped me enormously in *Haunted Wales*. However, I have referenced the original sources rather than Prof Harvey's book because in the latter these sources have become confused: Harvey has rearranged and renumbered the stories and he has made errors in his attribution of them. Ten stories which feature in the unpublished manuscript are referenced by Harvey as belonging to the book of 1780 – and vice versa.

The definitive compilation of Edmund Jones's supernatural writings is yet to be undertaken – as one of our earliest sources of Welsh folk belief, he certainly deserves more careful treatment.

William Howells

The attitude of our next author, William Howells, to the ghost stories he collected couldn't have been more different to that of the 'Old Prophet' Jones. Howells wrote: 'I firmly credit that persons of fearful dispositions have created most of the ghosts themselves.' This statement (and the one I quote at the top of this Survey) comes from his book *Cambrian Superstitions*, which was published in 1831, in answer to an advertisement which appeared in the *Carmarthen Journal* for a lengthy work on Welsh folklore. The prize was twenty guineas and a medal.

Howells was aged just nineteen when *Cambrian Superstitions* was published. The youth's cocky prose style grates at times and his own disbelief in the subject matter tends him to use as many words scorning the perceived absurdity of the tales as he does on the tales themselves, but we can at least be grateful that such an early collection of ghost stories was made. Most of Howells's stories come from Carmarthenshire, a county which Edmund Jones found equally rich in material.

Wirt Sikes

Fifty years passed by before the next major work on Welsh folklore appeared. This was *British Goblins*, published in 1880 by the then American Consul for Wales, the extraordinarily-named Wirt Sikes. Sikes took great pleasure in his adopted home, and was intrigued by the customs and beliefs of its people. Helped to some extent by a Glamorganshire antiquarian by the name of T H Thomas (who also provided the book's attractive illustrations), Sikes spent some time chatting with the locals on the subject of their superstitions but otherwise borrowed largely from Howells and Jones. His writing style is more appealing than either of his predecessors, however, and he is eminently quotable.

Elias Owen

Like William Howells before him, the Rev Elias Owen began his study as part of a competition – Owen's essay on Welsh folklore won the prize at the 1887 National Eisteddfod. Nearly ten years later he expanded this essay into one of the best books on the subject, his *Welsh Folk-Lore* (1896). Owen's book is important because not only does it show real scholarship but it contains unique material collected by himself and personal correspondents, usually fellow clergymen. *Welsh Folk-Lore* also helps to redress the imbalance of sources which focused on South Wales. Owen was a vicar in Denbighshire and later in Montgomeryshire, and his sources show this bias. Owen was a tireless collector of traditions, superstitions and customs from his native land. As well as *Welsh Folk-Lore* he contributed a mass of invaluable material to periodicals, especially *Bye-gones* and the *Montgomeryshire Collections*.

Marie Trevelyan

Late in life Emma Mary Thomas, whose bardic name was Marie Trevelyan[13], published *Folk-Lore and Folk-Stories of Wales* (1909), a bumper collection of legends which include several classic ghost stories. Many of these stories she collected – or possibly invented – herself, others she stated as having been collected by her late father. Previous books by Trevelyan, *Glimpses of Welsh Life and Character* (1893) and *From Snowdon to the Sea* (1894) contained ghost stories, but told in a more honestly fictionalised manner.

Folk-Lore and Folk-Stories of Wales was Trevelyan's attempt at a serious book on the subject. Her failing in this regard is that she is extremely vague about her sources, using a series of symbols to indicate whether they came from such shadowy characters as travelling preachers and family retainers. In one or two cases I have caught Trevelyan out, noting that certain tales she claims to have heard firsthand actually appeared some years earlier in other written sources, such as *Archaeologia Cambrensis*.

The author is also equally vague about precise locations. The latter has meant that several stories have been left out of *Haunted Wales*, because their provenance was no more precise than, say, 'a farmhouse in South Wales'. The vast majority of the stories she presents are set in her home county of Glamorganshire and its neighbours.

Increasing doubt has been placed on Trevelyan's scholarship in recent years[14], but *Folk-Lore and Folk-Stories of Wales* remains a standard work and has enjoyed an excellent reputation for many years. Trevelyan's stories therefore have a place in *Haunted Wales*, and it must be confessed that she boasts a particularly fine prose style, which has tempted me to quote her versions in full more than a few times. My personal belief is that most of Trevelyan's ghost stories are genuine but she forgot where she heard most of them – her wish to prove herself a scholar encouraged her to suppress this fact.

Jonathan Ceredig Davies

Our final major source of ghostlore from Wales is *Folk-Lore of West and Mid-Wales* by Jonathan Ceredig Davies, published in 1911. Davies, like Elias Owen, was a clergyman and spent many valuable hours recording tales from the countryfolk of his native Cardiganshire (Ceredigion). Previously, the adventurous Rev Davies had been a minister at the Welsh colony in Patagonia and at a rough mining community in Australia. Because he collected these stories himself, many are unique to his book and some were told to him by the witness or a close friend or relative of the witness. This, and the fact that his area of interest – Ceredigion, northern Pembrokeshire and northern Carmarthenshire – went otherwise unregarded by folklorists, makes *Folk-Lore of West and Mid-Wales* a valuable book.

Honourable mentions

I cannot acknowledge every writer here (except, of course, in the bibliography) but there are a few who deserve a brief mention. T Gwynn Jones, the Denbighshire folklorist, included several ghost stories in his excellent *Welsh Folk Tales* of 1930. Unfortunately, constraints made on him by his publisher meant that he had to keep every story brief, thus limiting their usefulness for inclusion in *Haunted Wales*. Charles Wilkins, in his *Tales and Sketches of Wales*, published in 1875, is the source of many well-known legends which have since been retold freely. He has brought his own imagination to bear and written them up in a romanticised manner, but his ghost stories appear to have been told to him personally, which makes them interesting. His is a comparatively early book on the subject.

Charles Redwood contributed many stories in his *The Vale of Glamorgan*, published way back in 1839. The accounts are all local to this area, which he knew intimately. Equally limited in terms of place are the works of father and son T C Evans and Frederick Evans, who both wrote histories of their home parish of Llangynwyd in Glamorganshire. The elder collected some superb stories into his history of 1887, and Frederick added one or two more in his volume published in 1912. D Rhys Phillips and Martin Phillips (also father and son, I wonder?) did the same duty by their home area of Neath Port Talbot. Another excellent localised collection, this time from North Wales, can be found in *Beddgelert: Its Facts, Fairies and Folklore* compiled by D E Jenkins in 1899, using material gathered by antiquarian William Jones. More recently Fred Hando and Stephen Clarke gathered stories from Monmouthshire and Gwent and Roy Palmer has provided two scholarly works on the folklore of (old) Monmouthshire and Radnorshire. The husband and wife team of Mr and Mrs Hall also deserve a mention for their exhaustive *A Book of South Wales*, published 1861. Not only does it contain one or two good stories, it also boasts some marvellous engravings, a few of which I gladly reproduce in this book.

Finally I must acknowledge the fertile ground provided by the editors and contributors of the many antiquarian journals of Wales, in particular the *Cambrian Quarterly*, *Cambrian Journal*, *Archaeologia Cambrensis* (perhaps surprisingly) and, most productive of all, the extraordinary *Bye-gones*, whose publishing heyday was between 1871 and the First World War.

It will be apparent from a glance at the Contents page that some counties are made up of far more pages than others. If *Haunted Wales* was a collection of modern ghost sightings we might expect to find that most of them took place in our towns and cities. This is simply because more people live there (and there is therefore more chance of a ghost being seen by one of them) and more people have died there (and there is therefore more chance of them 'returning' as a ghost). However, the old ghost stories of Wales are concentrated in the rural areas. There appears to me to be only one reason for this – that the people who collected the stories did so in the countryside, not in the towns.

The reason one county in Wales is possessed of more ghost stories than another is not that it is actually more haunted, but that a keen folklorist happened to live there and took the trouble to write them down. The modern unitary authority of Vale of Glamorgan, for example, has far more spooky stories than any other county of comparable size, more indeed than some that are larger. Why? Because Marie Trevelyan, one of the keenest and most prolific writers on Welsh folklore, happened to live in Llantwit Major, and she also had access to the folk tale collections of her father and the work of Charles Redwood, who lived in a nearby village.

Powys boasts the largest 'chapter' in this book, partly because it is by far the largest county in Wales, but also because the Rev Elias Owen, author of *Welsh Folklore* (1896), was a Montgomeryshire man and the area benefited from several active antiquarian societies and the folklore-rich journal *Bye-gones*.

A few counties are disappointingly barren of ghost stories. In part this is because I decided to adopt modern boundaries, and some of the new unitary authorities are very small. In the case of the bustling regions of Rhondda Cynon Taff and Merthyr Tydfil, which became industrialised very early on, I believe the indigenous culture and its folklore was lost before the Victorian interest in collecting folk tales became established. I have no explanation as to why Anglesey (Ynys Mon), such a magical island and such a bastion of Welsh culture, should be so bereft of traditional ghostlore – unless that it simply keeps its secrets better.

[1] Trevelyan, 1909, p. 204.
[2] Redwood, 1839, p. 40.
[3] Hole, 1950, pp.152 and 154.
[4] Owen, 1896, p. 303.
[5] Davies, 1911, p. 164.
[6] Ibid, p. 209.
[7] Jones, 1780, quoted by Hall, 1861, p. 465.
[8] The latter two terms are from Owen, 1896, p. 301.
[9] Evans, 1887, p. 171.
[10] Owen, 1896, p. 303.
[11] Redwood, 1839, p. 301.
[12] The manuscript in the National Library of Wales is catalogued as NLW MS16161B. For two examples as to why it could not date from 1767, see p. 5 ('This story was related to me by M H himself in 1772') and p. 10 ('About Michaelmas in the year 1773...')
[13] Brooks, 1987, p. 143.
[14] See for example Ronald Hutton's *Stations of the Sun*, Oxford University Press, p. 420.

Authorities Consulted

Anglesey Antiquarian Society and Field Club Transactions (1913-present)

Anonymous, *Welsh Legends*, J Badcock, 1802

Anonymous, 'Ceubren yr Ellyll or The Bride of Nant Gwytheyrn', *Cambrian Quarterly*, Vol. III (1831), pp. 467-86

Archaeologia Cambrensis (1846-present)

Armstrong, G.H., 'The Strange Tales of Plas Teg', *Country Quest,* October 1977, p. 29

Back, I.D., *The Story of Mancot*, Mancot WI, 1970

Baring-Gould, Sabine, *A Book of South Wales*, Methuen, 1905

Barnwell, E.L., 'Alignments in Wales', *Archaeologia Cambrensis* (1868), pp.169-79

Baxter, Richard, *The Certainty of the World of Spirits etc*, London, 1691

Bennett, Ernest, *Apparitions and Haunted Houses*, Faber & Faber, 1939

Bezant Lowe, Walter, *Llansannan: Its History and Associations*, 1915

Bradley, A.G., *Highways and Byways in North Wales*, MacMillan & Co, 1919

Brooks, J.A., *Ghosts and Legends of Wales*, Jarrold, 1987

Bye-Gones (1871-1939)

Cambrian Journal (1854-64)

Cambrian Quarterly (1829-33)

Clarke, Stephen, *Ghosts of Monmouth*, Monmouth, 1965/6

Clough, M.B., *Scenes and Stories Little Known*, Mold, 1861

Coulter, Stan, *The Rhewl*, Corwen, 1986

Country Quest (1960-present)

Croker, Thomas Crofton, *Fairy Legends and Traditions of the South of Ireland*, Vol 3 (1828)

Cymmrodorion, Transactions of the Honourable Society of ... (1890-present)

Davies, Jonathan Ceredig, *Folk-Lore of West and Mid-Wales*, Aberystwyth, 1911

Ellis, Bryn, *The History of Halkyn Mountain*, Gwasg Helygain, 1998

Evans, Leslie A., *Margam Abbey*, Port Talbot, 1958

Evans, C.J.O., *Glamorgan*, Cardiff, revised edition 1943

Evans, Frederick, *Tir Iarll*, 1912

Evans, T. C., 'Folklore of Glamorgan', *Transactions of the National Eisteddfod at Aberdare*, 1885, pp. 216-35 – *History of Llangynwyd Parish*, 1887

Evans, Thomas Henry, 'History of the Parish of Llanwddyn', *Montgomeryshire Collections,* Vol. VII (1874), pp. 65-116

Evans Wentz, W.Y., *Fairy Faith in Celtic Countries*, Oxford University Press, 1911

Fewtrell, John, 'Parochial History of Llanymynech', *Montgomeryshire Collections* Vol. XII, (1879), pp. 361-412

Flintshire Historical Society Transactions (1911-present)

Gascoigne, Russell, *The Haunting of Glamorgan and Gwent*, Gwasg Carreg Gwalch, 1993

Giraldus Cambrensis, *The Journey Through Wales/The Description of Wales*, 1191, translated by Lewis Thorpe, Penguin, 1978

Gittins, Edward, 'A Parochial History of Llanfair Caereinion', *Montgomeryshire Collections* Vol.XII, (1884), pp. 321-30

Halifax, Lord, *Further Stories from Lord Halifax's Ghost Book*, Geoffrey Bles, 1937

Hall, S.C. and A.M., *A Book of South Wales*, Virtue & Co, 1861

Hallam, Jack, *The Ghosts' Who's Who*, David & Charles, 1977

Hando, Fred J., *The Pleasant Land of Gwent*, R H Johns, 1944

– *Journeys in Gwent*, R H Johns, 1951

– *Out and About in Monmouthshire*, R H Johns, 1958

– *Here and There in Monmouthshire*, R H Johns, 1964

Harris, Mary Corbett, 'Legends and Folklore of Llanfacreth Parish', *Journal of Merioneth Historical and Record Society*, Vol 5, (1965-8), pp. 9-20

Harvey, John, *The Appearance of Evil*, University of Wales Press, 2003

Hippisley-Coxe, Antony D., *Haunted Britain*, Hutchinson, 1973

H.L.J., 'Early Inscribed Stones of Wales', *Archaeologia Cambrensis* (1860), pp. 128-36

Hole, Christina, *Haunted England*, Batsford, revised edition, 1950

Holland, Richard, *Supernatural Clwyd; The Folk Tales of North-East Wales*, Gwasg Carreg Gwalch, 1989

– *Haunted Clwyd*, Gwasg Carreg Gwalch, 1992

– *Bye-Gones*, Gwasg Carreg Gwalch, 1992

Howells, William, *Cambrian Superstitions*, Longman & Co, 1831

Ingham, John, *Haunted Homes and Family Legends,* 1904 (1961 rpt)

Jarman, S.G., *Rossett and Marford Past and Present*, Wrexham, 1904

Jenkins, D.E. (using material collected by William Jones), *Beddgelert: Its Facts, Fairies and Folk-Lore*, Llewelyn Jenkins, 1899

John, Brian, *Pembrokeshire Folk Tales*, Greencroft Books, 1991

Jones, Edmund, *A Relation of the Apparitions of Spirits in the County of Monmouth and the Principality of Wales etc*, 1780

Jones, Francis, *The Holy Wells of Wales*, Cardiff 1954

Jones, Moses Glyn & Roberts, Norman, *Bwgan Pant-y-Wennol*, Pwllheli, 1986.

Jones, T. Gwynn, *Welsh Folklore and Folk Custom*, Methuen, 1930

Laws, Edward, *The History of Little England Beyond Wales*, 1888

Leather, Ella Mary, *The Folk-Lore of Herefordshire*, Jakeman and Carver, 1912

Lloyd, J. Y. W., *History of Powys Fadog* , Vol 1 (1881), Vol 3 (1882), Vol 5 (1885) & Vol 6 (1887)

Longrigg, G.H., *Legends of the Dee*, Liverpool, 1901

Madoc-Jones, Geraint, 'Lest We Forget: Youthful Memories of Beaumaris Grammar School', *Anglesey Antiquarian Society and Field Club Transactions* (1971), pp. 130-9

Marshall, Lady, 'The Hawarden Castle Ghost, A Legendary Ballad', *Cambrian Journal*, Vol.III (1856), pp. 357-60

Martin, T.P., 'Oystermouth Castle', *Archaeologia Cambrensis,* (1887), pp. 182-92

Mavor, Elizabeth, *The Ladies of Llangollen*, Penguin, 1973

Montgomeryshire Collections (1868-present)

Motley, James, *Tales of the Cymry*, Llanelli, 1848

Morgan, Alun, *Legends of Porthcawl and the Glamorgan Coast*, 1974

Morgan, J.J., *Awelais ac a Welais*, Vol 2, 1949

Moss, Fletcher, *The Fourth Book of Pilgrimages to Old Homes*, Didsbury, 1908

O.J., 'Local Traditions, Anglesey', *Archaeologia Cambrensis* (1850), pp. 145-6

Owen, D. Edmondes, 'Pre-Reformation Survivals in Radnorshire', *Transactions of the Honourable Society of Cymmrodorion* (1910-11).

Owen, Edward, 'The Incised Stones of Caernarvonshire', *Archaeologia Cambrensis*, (1864), pp. 315-20

Owen, Elias, 'Folk-Lore, Superstitions, or What-Not in Montgomeryshire and Elsewhere', *Montogomeryshire Collections*, Vol.XVI (1883), pp. 131-60

 – *Welsh Folk-Lore*, Woodall, Minshall & Co., 1896

 – 'Montgomeryshire Folk-Lore', *Montgomeryshire Collections*, Vol.XXIX (1896), pp. 68-74

Palmer, Roy, *The Folklore of (Old) Monmouthshire*, Logaston Press, 1998

 – *The Folklore of Radnorshire*, Logaston Press, 2001

Pennant, Thomas, *A Tour In Wales*, Two Vols, 1784

Phillips, D. Rhys, *The History of the Vale of Neath*, Swansea, 1925

Phillips, Edgar, *Edmund Jones, The Old Prophet*, Robert Hale, 1959

Phillips, Martin, *The Folklore of the Afan and Margam District*, Guardian Press, 1933

Pritchard, W., 'Anglesey Folklore', *Anglesey Antiquarian Society and Field Club Transactions* (1914), pp. 35-70

Reader's Digest, *Folklore, Myths and Legends of Britain*, 1973

Redwood, Charles, *The Vale of Glamorgan, Scenes and Tales Among the Welsh*, Saunders & Otley, London, 1839

Rhys, John, *Celtic Folklore*, Two Vols, Clarendon Press, 1901

Rhys, Morgan, 'Unpublished Traditions of Glamorganshire', *Cambrian Journal*, Vol. II (1855), pp. 68-72

Shanahan, Margaret R., 'Ghosts of Glamorgan', *Port Talbot Historical Society Transactions*, (1963), pp. 32-44

Sikes, Wirt, *British Goblins*, Sampson Low, 1880

Sikes, Wirt, *Rambles and Studies in Old South Wales*, Sampson Low, 1881

Simpson, Jacqueline, *Folklore of the Welsh Border*, Batsford, 1976

Thomas, D., Chwedlau a Thraddodiadau Gwynedd, published in *Y Gordofigion*, 1870, pp. 94-128

Thomas, T. H., *Some Folk-Lore of South Wales*, Cardiff, n.d. (1904?)

Townshend of Raynham, Marchioness, and ffoulkes, Maud, *True Ghost Stories*, Hutchinson & Co, 1936

Trevelyan, Marie, *Glimpses of Welsh Life and Character*, John Hogg, 1893

 – *From Snowdon To The Sea*, John Hogg, 1894

 – *Folk-Lore and Folk-Stories of Wales*, Elliott Stock, 1909

 – *Llantwit Major*, Newport, 1910

Underwood, Peter, *Ghosts of Wales*, Christopher Davies, 1978, (Corgi paperback edition, 1980)

Vaughan, H.F.J., 'Oswestry, Ancient and Modern, and its Local Families', *Archaeolgia Cambrensis* (1885), pp. 97-119

Vincent, Henry J., 'Caerau in the Parish of Dogmells', *Archaeologia Cambrensis* (1864), pp. 299-314

Wilkins, Charles, *Tales and Sketches of Wales*, Cardiff, 1879

Williams, J.G., 'Witchcraft in Seventeenth Century Flintshire (Part I)', *Flintshire Historical Society Transactions*, Vol.26 (1973-4), pp. 16-37

Willams, Lucy, 'The Development of Holyhead', *Anglesey Antiquarian Society and Field Club Transactions* (1950), pp. 54-62

Glossary of Welsh and Unfamiliar Terms

Bwbach	A ghost.
Bwci	A goblin; occasionally used to mean an apparition.
Bwgan	A word which encompasses a variety of grotesque, alarming or trouble some ghosts, including those which cannot be seen.
Canwyll corff	A corpse candle (qv).
Corpse candle	A ball or taper of light which warns of a coming death.
Cyhiraeth	An invisible entity which cries or wails to warn of a coming death or other calamity.
Dog of Darkness	A frightening apparition usually associated with lonely lanes and cross roads. Often it resembles an enormous black hound, but can incorporate cow-like features, and occasionally human features. In Welsh, *Gwyllgi*.
Dyn Hysbys	A 'wise man'. A countryman skilled in magic.
Ellyll	A goblin. More properly an elf. Sometimes used to mean a ghost. Plural is *ellyllon*.
Ffynnon	A spring or well.
Ghost-layer	An exorcist. See 'lay/laid'.
Green Lady	A fairy-like female apparition dressed entirely in green.
Grey Lady	A female apparition dressed entirely in grey.
Gwrach y Rhibyn	'Hag of the Mists'. A female apparition whose appearance acts as a death omen. She is often hideous to look upon and may wail like the *Cyhiraeth*. A breed of *Gwrach y Rhibyn* haunts the high hills where they may lead travellers astray.
Gwrag Hysbys	A 'wise witch'. A countrywoman skilled in magic.
Gwyllgi	A Dog of Darkness (qv)
Holy well	A spring with a connection to a saint and whose waters are believed to possess extraordinary healing properties.
Lady in Black	A female apparition dressed in black or otherwise sombre or mournful apparel.
Lay / laid	To lay a ghost is to exorcise it. After a successful exorcism, the ghost is said to have been 'laid'.
Lledrith	The apparition of a living person.
Phantom funeral	A funeral procession seen or heard in advance of a real funeral taking place.
Poltergeist	A German word referring to an invisible, noisy and mischievous or destructive ghost.
Pwca	A fairy or goblin which haunts houses or which leads travellers astray.
Revenant	A French word meaning 'the returned'. A spirit visiting the earth after bodily death.
Stone-thrower	A ghost whose sole form of manifestation is the unpleasant habit of throwing rocks about.
Teulu / Toili	A phantom funeral (qv).
Tolaeth	A mysterious sound warning of a coming death. Any supernatural omen of death, especially a phantom funeral (qv).
White Lady	An apparition, appearing as a woman dressed entirely in white.
Yspryd	A spirit.

Gazetteer

Flintshire

Broughton (Brychdyn)

Some years ago a woman now living in Buckley told me about an extraordinary ghost which haunted the neighbourhood of Broughton and which terrified her parents and her aunt and uncle during the early 1930s. In those days the favourite place for courting couples to promenade was the Old Warren, a lonely and wooded stretch of road which was conveniently dark and unfrequented in the evening. One night my correspondent's parents, then young and yet to marry, were enjoying each other's company in the Old Warren when they were startled by something swooping down upon them. It was the apparition of a very tall man dressed in black, with a cape, and 'an old-fashioned clergyman's hat' upon his head. He glided past and cast upon the terrified young couple a highly disapproving look, which upset them greatly.

Some time later the creepy clergyman also appeared to my correspondent's aunt and her future husband. The boy had a motorbike which he had propped up against a wall as they said goodnight. But then – 'The same apparition glided past and the bike's light went off and on, off and on. They jumped on the bike and rode away!'

Asking around the neighbourhood, they learnt that the ghost was that of an old rector from one of the local churches and that others had seen him, too. Today the Old Warren is even less frequented. Since a modern trunk road was built, the Old Warren has become a dead end, leading nowhere, and has subsequently become even more overgrown. This can hardly have diminished its suitability for couples seeking privacy – and it is therefore even more likely to attract the unwanted attentions of this phantom prude![1]

Halkyn (Helygain)

Bryn Ellis, in compiling his excellent *The History of Halkyn Mountain*, uncovered the following snippet about a ghost with arsonist tendencies. It comes from the *Flintshire Observer* of October 8th, 1880:

'Some of the people of Halkyn are much exercised at present respecting the doings of a reputed ghost who is said to have shown such a strong liking for fire, especially that of an incendiary character, that it has made either five or six attempts to fire the stackyard of one of the farmers in the parish. Strangely enough the ghost does not stalk forth at dead of night, the hour when ghosts are reputed to hold high revelry, but at "early morn and dewy eve" and fortunately its mischievous pranks have been each time discovered in time to prevent serious loss. Possibly in the course of a short time a charm may be found that will lay the spirit and prevent its too liberal indulgence in frolics over other people's goods.'[2]

Hawarden (Penarlâg)

Once upon a time, possibly in the 1740s but details are vague, a ghost was seen in the laundry at Hawarden Castle. A 'misty form' resembling that of a deceased steward called John drifted past several maid-servants, driving them into hysterics. John had been an unpopular bully during life, an absolute tyrant to those he considered his inferior, so this may explain their extreme reactions.

Lady Marshall, who learnt of the incident from a 90-year-old servant whose mother had been one of the maids, wrote it up in the form of a whimsical ballad. The ballad is very long but the story very slight, and it took some time to dissect it from Lady Marshall's intentionally rococo language and shamelessly bad rhymes. We learn the staff were very distressed –

'And they, for want of public ghost inspector,
Resolved to lay the case before the Rector.'
(You get the idea!)

The rector told them they were all 'tomfools', so instead the servants sought out the services of a sympathetic priest, who agreed to perform the rites of exorcism.

The ghost was duly conjured up among the sheets and smalls in the laundry, and John-as-was told the priest that 'after so much wrong' performed by him on his fellows, his spirit was unable to find a resting place. He did not explain why, of all places, he chose to haunt the laundry, and on being told 'he must be laid', he begged that it be in somewhere more salubrious. Initially he suggested his spirit be conjured into a crow (which seems somewhat less salubrious to me) but the priest rejected this idea because he thought it might lead to 'mischief'. So, John then suggested he be turned into a harmless leaf, but the priest also disapproved of this plan. He argued that an unfortunate cow might chance to eat the leaf – and the cow become possessed! Finally, John agreed to be secured inside a block of granite. This was done, the stone buried, and John's spirit no longer troubled the living.[3]

Llanasa

Through the course of this book there will be many accounts of visual ghosts, or apparitions, and a great many of spooky noises; phantom smells, however, are comparatively rare. Near Llanasa there were (perhaps still are) a couple of cottages haunted by an aroma which, though pleasant enough to smell, actually recalled a foul murder. It was said that many, many years ago two children were done away with here and their bodies concealed under a bed of thyme in the garden. By 1891, when this story was recorded by folklorist Elias Owen, a strong smell of thyme would sometimes still be smelt by passers-by, even though it had been a very long time (no pun intended) since the herb was grown there.

I was unable to find the name of these cottages, Yr-ardd-ddu, on the 1:25,000 map. Owen states that they stood on the road to Penyffordd and another place I was unable to locate, Pen-y-Glasdir. Possibly this places them in the vicinity of Glan-yr-Afon (birthplace of the playwright Emlyn Williams). A local person may be able to find them, or the ruin of them – perhaps they are still identifiable by the lingering smell of thyme...[4]

Mancot

Deiniol's Ash, now called Ash Farm, was the old manor house of Mancot. Here, in the early 18th century, there lived the Cratchley family, who had a feud with the Glynne family of Broadlanes, a nearby mansion which was later converted into Hawarden's 'Castle'. In true Romeo and Juliet style, a young member of the Glynne family fell in love with a daughter of the house of Cratchley. William and Rebecca tried to keep their love a secret but inevitably they were discovered, and the relationship brutally ended when William was packed off on the 'Grand Tour'. Poor Rebecca was heartbroken and waited long years in vain for her beloved's return. Sadly, he died in Europe and she never saw him again. Her forlorn spirit is said to still haunt Deiniol's Ash[5] and this belief is largely supported by the following sighting of an apparition which took place here in 1935.

A group of young women were on their way to a New Year's dance in Hawarden when they saw the insubstantial figure of a girl, which they immediately recognised as a ghost, emerging from the gateway leading to Ash Farm. Much to their dismay, the ghost began to approach them down the lane, but before it reached them it vanished. The women were so frightened they dropped their handbags in the road and ran home. A young man had to prove his valour a short while later by retrieving their things – the girls absolutely refused to pass that way again that night.[6]

Mold (Yr Wyddgrug)

One of the most famous ghost stories from Wales is that of the Golden Spectre of Goblin Hill. Its fame is due largely to the fact that the ghost is authenticated not just by witnesses' testimony but also by a real, solid artefact which survives today – and which just happens to be one of the prize possessions of the British Museum. Goblin Hill, or to give it its correct Welsh name Bryn yr Ellyllon, rises to the east of Mold in an area of the town called Pentre. As a child I lived in a house on its summit, but no one I knew called the place Bryn yr Ellyllon, for that name went out of fashion in the 19th century, long after the 'goblin' itself had ceased to appear.

On the left-hand side of the hill, as one leaves Mold, a stone plaque has been fixed to a wall, commemorating an important archaeological discovery. Near the plaque there was once a prominent mound called the Tomen. On October 11th, 1833, Mr John Langford, who rented the field, ordered that the mound be levelled and the stones composing it be taken to fill in a hole by the side of the road. In the base of the mound the labourers came across a *cist*, or slab-lined grave, and in this grave they uncovered the largest piece of prehistoric goldwork ever found in Europe. The so-called 'Mold Cape' is an exquisitely ornamented sheet of gold which would have fitted round the shoulders of the Bronze Age chieftain or priest whose crumbling bones were interred here. Initially its value wasn't recognised, and it was thrown to one side. When someone noticed it was made of gold, however, something of a free-for-all took place and chunks of it were ripped off, and taken away as souvenirs, the result being that it survives today in a sadly mutilated form.

Prior to the opening of the ancient grave, the area around the Tomen, and indeed the Tomen itself, were the haunt of a ghost called the Brenin yr Allt, or King of the Hillside. He was described as taking the appearance of a man of huge stature – a man who was seen to be 'glittering and shining in gold'! John Langford was well aware of the stories of the Golden Spectre and made a point of visiting an old lady named Nancy who claimed to have seen it fourteen years previously while fetching home his cows one moonlit night. Nancy was delighted to learn that the 'ghost was raised' and her story substantiated.

A keen student of local history and folklore, Angharad Llwyd, learnt of other sightings of the Golden Spectre. She heard that in about the year 1810, 'a female was leading her drunken husband through the Goblyn field, when they saw the Golden Spectre standing on the Tommen, which scared the woman into fits and the man into sobriety'. She also learnt of a dressmaker who had seen the ghost in 1828 and who had been left 'crazed' by the experience.[7]

That Bryn-yr-Ellyllon was a famously haunted spot is evident from a letter by a man who actually saw the open grave and the golden cape soon after its discovery. His memory of the ghost is quite different to those supplied by Mr Langford and Miss Llwyd, but then he was only a boy of thirteen at the time, and his letter was written sixty-eight years after the event. He wrote:

'I certainly heard it rumoured a year or two before 1833 that Bryn yr Ellyllon and Cae'r Yspryd [Field of the Ghost] were haunted as well as the adjacent main road by an apparition – "A Headless Warrior riding a grey horse." You may imagine the excitement which arose when something was found. In the afternoon I and many others, young and old, saw the Corselet doubled up and somewhat damaged, and placed in a [wheel-] barrow, where it was the "observed of all observers". The great lesson I learned from that discovery was that through a labyrinth of old ghost stories, miracles, poetry, and legend there is more real history than we

have yet comprehended.'[8]

Another story which supports the presence of the ghost is that of a woman who encountered it three years before the grave was discovered:

'In 1830 a respectable woman was returning home on horseback on a fine summer's evening, after having finished her marketing at Mold. When she came near the tumulus she perceived some of the trees in a wood on the opposite side of the road to be illumined, as we see the blades of grass to be lit up by the phosphoric light of a glow-worm. As she looked intently on this phenomenon, she perceived an apparition of unusual size, and clothed with a suit of golden armour, emerge from the wood, and approaching, cross the road, and disappear in the tumulus. She was so struck by this extraordinary occurrence that she determined to return to Mold and tell the circumstance to the then vicar, the Rev C B Clough. This gentleman wrote down what she told him, and got three other respectable persons to witness it.'

Given the date of the sighting, this tale is compelling – it is evidence that the Golden Spectre was a real phenomenon, and that *vice versa* the gold cape is evidence of the existence of a ghost! However, this story didn't find print until 1885, more than thirty years after the cape was found. It would be an exciting find indeed should the woman's witnessed testimony ever come to light.[9]

A mile or so outside Mold, on the road to Gwernaffield, there once existed an old well which, like Tomen yr Ellyllon, was destroyed by road works. This was the equally haunted Ffynnon Ellyllon, or Goblin Well. In 1861, a Mrs Clough recounted a tale of the Goblin Well in a tiny, pink-bound book called *Scenes and Stories Little Known*.[10] Unfortunately, she chose to tell her tale, and the others in the book, in the same manner as Lady Marshall at Hawarden – in the form of very poor verse. This seems to have been a bad habit among the mid-Victorians, for I have been forced to grimace my way through many other rotten poems of the period to extract (rather like teeth) the legends contained within them. But on with the story.

As the name suggests, the Goblin Well had an eerie reputation, one that was sufficient to impel most people to avoid it after dark. One young man, however, had no choice but to walk past it night after night, for he lived in Gwernaffield and his girlfriend lived in Mold. The lady was the hostess of a public house Mrs

Clough calls the *Fish*, and John would invariably spend his evenings there, feasting his eyes on his beloved while simultaneously feasting on her onion stew and ale. At eleven o'clock, she would gently eject him with the stern reminder not to forget to say a prayer as he passed the haunted well. One night, as he stumbled drunkenly home, he forgot the warning and was startled by the sudden appearance of 'a lady bright ... arrayed in white'.

The woman begged that she might accompany John up the hill, for she was afraid of the spirits 'in their midnight revelry'. It seemed a reasonable request and John bowed politely in acknowledgement, but he couldn't help feeling there was something uncanny about his new companion. The Lady in White wore a hood over her head (a 'snowy mantilla of satin rare', no less) and her face was entirely hidden in its dark enclosure. With a thrill of fear, John peered in and saw those fears confirmed – the woman had no face! There was no head under the hood!

'See, here is my beautiful head!' cried the lady, and she pulled aside her mantle to reveal it, tucked in traditional style under one arm, its long hair trailing to her feet. Before John could run away from this nightmarish apparition, the detached head ordered him to stay, or suffer unpleasant consequences. John stayed put and the spirit exercised some sort of charm over him, Lamia-like, so that he found himself now rather taken with her than otherwise. The spirit explained she had been dead for hundreds of years and was doomed to walk at night until a youth could be found brave enough to help her. She continued that there was 'a precious store of sparkling gems, and of golden ore' buried near the well, all of which could be his if he were to return on the following midnight, suitably equipped with pick and shovel. All she wanted from the treasure was a necklace – one that would re-attach her head.

'Aye,' she continued, 'no more will it tumble off when set,

In its ancient place on my shoulders, wet
With the blood of the sacrifice shed.'

John readily agreed to this and promised to help in any way he could. But just then an evening breeze made John sneeze (yes, that's another of Mrs Clough's rhymes!) and he automatically followed it with a 'Heaven keep me!' At those unintentionally uttered holy words, the spirit's spell was broken and John came out

of his trance. The first thing he saw was the look of fury on the face of the severed head, and it was quite enough to convince him to end this weird conversation at once.

'Heaven help and forgive me now!' he cried, and: 'Heaven send thee to thy place!'

The White Lady vanished in a spark of flame and poor John ran like fury for his bed, half out of his wits with terror. Once inside his door he flung himself into bed, clutching a charm of rowan wood.[11] He never visited the *Fish* again and continued his suit with its hostess from a safe distance. Mrs Clough adds that the adventure took place twenty years before the writing of her book, that is to say about 1840. She states that the story was 'exactly as related', only the names of the hero and the pub had been changed. The *Fish* is therefore likely to have been the *Dolphin*, which stands opposite Mold parish church near the top of the road which leads to Gwernaffield.[12]

The story is a rare example from North Wales of a type we will come across *ad nauseam* from the southernmost counties of Wales, that of a spirit appearing as a White Lady and bound to the earth by the presence of buried treasure. What is especially interesting is the reference to the lady having been beheaded as a sacrifice. It is impossible now to know how much of the tale is from Mrs Clough's imagination and how much is genuine tradition, but there is no doubt that the severed head was of mystical significance to the ancient Celts and that skulls were kept at sacred wells elsewhere in Wales, where they were used as drinking vessels. It is possible that the White Lady of the Goblin Well was a folk memory of its ancient guardian spirit. The Grey Lady of Nannerch may have had a similar origin, and we shall encounter another supernatural severed head at Rhesycae.

Opposite the celebrated Clwyd Theatr Cymru, there is a popular pub restaurant named the *Glas Fryn*. Back in the days when this was a private home, sometime in the 1920s or 30s, the Rev J J Morgan was passing by this way one bright night, after preaching at Northop. As he strode down the hill – a rather lonely one in those days – he noticed a young couple sitting on the stile over the path which led to Glas Fryn. The young man was just in the act of putting his arm round the girl's shoulders, as if in an embrace – but then the Rev Morgan saw the blade of a knife flashing in the moonlight! Before he could react, the man had plunged the

28

knife through the girl's long, blonde hair and into her neck, right up to the hilt. The girl let out an unearthly scream, and the appalled minister rushed over, only to find that both figures had vanished. No story ever came to light to explain this shocking vision.[13]

Nannerch

Moel Arthur is one of many hillforts which guard the passes through the natural defensive barrier of the Clwydian Range of hills on the Flintshire-Denbighshire border. That it is named after the legendary Welsh hero is a real possibility, for tales of Arthur's exploits in the region are numerous, and another hillfort which faces Moel Arthur from the east bears the name Caer Afallwch, intriguingly similar to the Welsh name for Avalon, the king's final resting place. A fabulous treasure was said to be buried on Moel Arthur, but it was protected by a guardian spirit, as Marie Trevelyan explains in her *Folk-Lore and Folk-Tales of Wales*:

'A woman robed in grey formerly used to frequent a spot on Moel Arthur, overlooking the Vale of Clwyd. Under a rock near which the grey lady was chiefly seen, treasure was concealed in an iron chest with a ring handle. People said that the place of concealment was illuminated by a supernatural light. Occasionally in the evening, or soon after dawn men dug for this treasure; but their efforts were rewarded with fearful noises, and they were driven away by thunder, lightning and rainstorms. One man found the grey lady beckoning to him as he ascended with pickaxe and shovel. He went to her, and she gave him some peas in a pod, and whispered, "Go home." He did so, and the peas turned to gold in his pocket.'[14]

A woman in black haunts the road leading to the *Royal Oak* pub near the village. I was alerted to the existence of the ghost by Mr Alan Williams, who had actually seen it. He told me he and a friend had been walking to the pub one evening when the woman stepped out in front of him, apparently from the hedge. He muttered a word of apology and then realised the woman was nowhere to be seen – and he then learnt that his friend hadn't seen her at all. Mr Williams described the woman as wearing a full black gown and that she had her head bowed and hidden by a hood; possibly she was reading a book. He asked me whether I knew anything about the ghost. I admitted that I didn't but I was determined to find out more, so I published Mr Williams's story in a weekly column I was writing at the time in a local newspaper.

I had an excellent response from readers, proving that Mr Williams's ghost was well-known locally. We learnt that she had been seen in the 1950s by the village police constable. His widow wrote: 'One winter's night, when on duty, he was walking towards the Wheeler Hill when suddenly this lady walked towards him, then suddenly vanished into the hedge. He shone his powerful torch, called out something, but there was not a sight or sound of anyone. Her attire was ... rather Victorian, wearing head gear.'

Subsequent letters revealed the Lady in Black was a ghost of some antiquity. Another correspondent wrote to say she had been seen by his father just after the end of the First World War when he was cycling home from work: 'A lady dressed in long, Victorian clothes, but whose face was hidden, suddenly stepped out in front of him. He swerved so violently that he fell off his machine, but when he turned round, the lady had completely vanished.'

The earliest record I received dated a sighting of her to 1904, and I am indebted to the 75-year-old reader who wrote to me for having such a sharp memory. She recalled her father telling her that when he was a young man he and some companions had taken the pony and trap to a party one night, but was warned by *his* father to return home in good time to avoid the ghost – which suggests her presence was known about as long ago as the 19th century. The youth ignored his father's warning and as he passed the haunted spot his horse suddenly 'made an awful noise and bolted'.

'Coming towards them was a white mist and as they went forward a great chill came over them and then it vanished. Looking round they saw this woman in a flowing cloak go into the hedge. The horse never stopped galloping until it got home to the stable, and it was covered with sweat and lather and was frightened to death.'

It was exciting to be able to substantiate a modern ghost sighting in this way. It is a good example of why I believe in ghosts; I feel sure Mr Williams had no knowledge of this ghost until he encountered it, and I have no reason to doubt the veracity of my correspondents either. Mr Williams carried out some research of his own and he spoke to a Holywell resident who recalled a story about a woman being killed at this spot on her way to church. Mr Williams conjectured that she may have been reading her Bible and been struck by a horse or carriage as she stepped into the road.

One reader of my column furnished the information that there used to be a little gate at the place where the ghost appeared (now there is nothing more than a length of anonymous hedgerow) and that this led to a cottage, the ruins of which could still be seen in the 1930s. A few stones and the suggestion of a garden are visible today. This, presumably, was the home of the mysterious Lady in Black. Perhaps it was abandoned after she began to haunt the place. If her costume really does date from the late Victorian era, the fact that she appeared as long ago as 1904 suggests she must have begun her hauntings very shortly after her death.[15]

Pontblyddyn

Plas Teg, or the Fair Mansion, is Flintshire's most celebrated haunted house. The ghost story of Plas Teg is very well known but I have been unable to find any reference to it which predates the 1960s. Legend has it that a girl was drowned in a well while trying to hide her jewels in it – the gems were needed to finance an elopement with a young neighbour and to save her from a forced marriage with someone far less desirable.[16] It has all the hallmarks of being a genuine, traditional tale, but the cliched plot of star-crossed lovers is also an easy one to invent.

There is no doubt in my mind that Plas Teg deserves its haunted reputation, however. I had an eerie experience here myself when I inexplicably found myself drawn into a room which I afterwards learnt from the owners was the room they knew to be haunted, although it was not the one usually pointed out as such to visitors. A man I knew, an accountant, lodged in the house for a few months and used to feel a sinister presence in his room. One night something invisible sat on his bed![17]

The dual carriageway which runs past Plas Teg is also haunted. Many drivers have swerved to avoid the figure of a woman which suddenly crosses the road in front of them; one woman went so far as to phone the police, convinced she had run someone over. A friend of mine saw quite a different apparition while idling in traffic – the semi-transparent image of a knight in armour trotting peacefully down the central reservation.[18]

Queensferry

'Call it ghost or what you will, still I assure you that which I am going to relate is what really did take place, and much as I was, and am, a sceptic in ghost stories, I must confess myself completely at a loss to account by natural causes for that which did actually occur.' So wrote Captain Alldridge about the eerie happenings which took place on board HMS *Asp* one year as he sailed it around Wales. The earliest manifestations of the haunting took place while the *Asp* was in use as a surveying vessel around the mouth of the River Dee.

When Capt Alldridge took possession of the *Asp* in 1850, it was in dock in need of repairs. The superintendent of the dockyard warned him: 'Your ship is said to be haunted and I don't know if you will get any of the dockyard men to work on her.' Capt Alldridge thought this absurd and for a few days at least he was proved correct. However, before the week was out, the shipwrights came to him en masse and begged him 'to give the vessel up as she was haunted and could never bring anything but ill-luck'. It took a long time before the repairs were finally completed and the *Asp* able to carry out its duties in the Dee. It didn't take long, however, for the ship's commander to learn there was something in the ghost stories after all.

One evening shortly after the *Asp* had begun operations, Capt Alldridge and another officer heard strange noises coming from a cabin known as the 'after' or 'ladies' cabin. This cabin faced the captain's own and was separated from it by no more than the companion ladder. It therefore should have been impossible for anyone to get into the ladies cabin without being seen by the occupants of the captain's cabin. The sounds they heard resembled 'such as would be caused by a drunken man or a person staggering about' but on investigation, the cabin was found to be disconcertingly empty.

'After this evening,' wrote Alldridge, 'the noises became very frequent, varying in kind and in degree. Sometimes it was as though the seats and lockers were banged about, sometimes it sounded as though decanters and tumblers were being clashed together.'

One night the *Asp* was moored opposite Church Quay at Queensferry and Alldridge and his fellow officer had taken the opportunity to visit a friend in the town for tea. They returned at ten o'clock, just in time for Alldridge to hear someone rush from the ladies cabin into his own cabin. Quickly he climbed the companion ladder and once there, drew his sword and handed it to the officer, who had followed close behind.

'Stand still, I think I have caught the ghost,' whispered Alldridge, still convinced the disturbances were caused by some intruder. 'Allow no one to pass you; if anyone attempts to escape cut him down.'

The captain then crept into his cabin and struck a light, fully prepared to tackle with some unwelcome visitor – but once again he was to be frustrated. There was no one there. He recalled: 'Nothing could I find to account for the noises I had heard, though I declare solemnly that never did I feel more certain of anything in my life than that I should find a man there. So there was nothing to be done but to repeat for the hundredth time, "Well, it is the ghost again!"'

The disturbances continued unabated: 'Often when lying in my bed at night have I heard noises close to me as though my drawers were being opened and shut, the top of my washing stand being raised and banged down again, and a bed which stood on the opposite side of my cabin, pulled about; while of an evening I often heard while sitting in my cabin a noise as though a percussion cap were snapped close to my head [ie a very loud bang!]; also very often (and I say it with godly and reverential fear) I have been sensible of the presence of something invisible about me, and could have put my hand, so to say, on it, or the spot where I felt it was; and all this occurred, strange to say, without my feeling in the least alarmed or caring about it, except so far that I could not understand or account for what I felt and heard.'

Unfortunately, this level-headedness on the part of the captain was not shared by the crew. Some while later the haunting took on a new aspect, one which so terrified the crew that many jumped ship! One sailor 'fell down with fright', another 'went into violent convulsions'. The reason was that, no longer content with making anonymous noises in the cabins, the ghost now began to show itself and on one occasion actually spoke to a crewman. The ghost was no longer something the commander of the *Asp* could ignore. But to find out what happened next and to learn in what form the apparition appeared, we will have to follow the ship on its course south, to Pembroke Dock, where the story ends (see page 77).[19]

Rhesycae

Wardley Hall, Bettiscombe Hall, Burton Agnes Hall – dotted round the British Isles are a number of old manor houses which each boast a most unusual artefact, a human skull. The skulls are kept as a kind of totem or fetish and no matter what legend has been invented to explain their presence, one factor remains the same; that they should on no account be taken from the building, or the result will be a fearful haunting. In Wales, there is only one such haunted skull, that belonging to Ffagnallt Hall, now a farm, which is situated near Rhesycae on Halkyn Mountain.

The legend of the skull is that it belonged to one Dafydd, a Welsh prince during the reign of Henry I. Dafydd came to Ffagnallt as a fugitive from English injustice, seeking shelter with his sister, who was mistress of the house. Unfortunately for Dafydd, his brother-in-law was more interested in gold than family honour and poisoned the prince so that he could claim the bounty. Before he died, Dafydd cursed the treacherous lord and said that his dying wish was that his head should remain forever more at Ffagnallt as a reminder of the cowardly deed. After his death, his head was struck from his body and taken to Chester, or perhaps to London, where it was put on display. Dafydd's heartbroken sister left her cruel and cowardly husband to suffer the fate of her brother's curse. This followed swiftly and in an especially bizarre and undignified way – he was trampled to death by his own cows! After his demise, the skull of his victim was stolen from the English and brought reverently back to Ffagnallt, where it has remained ever since.

The skull is kept in a glass-fronted box on the mantelpiece of what used to be the great hall of the house. It is very small, indeed child-sized, and there is very little of it left, just the upper forepart showing eyebrow ridges and the top of the nasal cavity. The reason for its fragmentary state may be explained by the story recorded by Mrs Clough in her *Scenes and Stories Little Known* of 1861. At the time her story took place – perhaps two or three decades prior to publication – the skull was kept on top of a bookcase in 'an earthen cup'. The maid employed at Ffagnallt was forbidden to touch the skull, even to dust it, a fact which seemed very unfair to her when one day she was chastised for the filthy state of the books below it. It was apparent to the maid that it was the dusty old relic, all spun round with spiders' webs, which was the cause of the dirt, so in a fit of pique after her telling-off, she took the skull and threw it in the duck-pond.

That night a 'wild shriek' sounded through Ffagnallt Farm, startling everyone out of their slumber. There came another shriek and, seeking its source, the farmer and his wife were astonished to see, splashing about in the pond, 'a bending form in white ... moaning in deadly fear'. It was Anne, the maid. As they hurried to help her, she moaned: 'The Dead Man's curse hath come on me'. Then they saw that she was tightly clutching the skull, or what remained of it. They helped her back into the house and, with 'weak trembling hand', she replaced the skull in its accustomed place and then fainted away. After she had recovered, she explained she had been awoken in the night 'by fingers dripping wet ... and shadowy forms around her couch', which forced her to retrieve the venerated relic from where she had so unceremoniously chucked it.[20]

[1] Personal communication with author.
[2] Ellis, 1998, p. 224.
[3] Marshall, 1856.
[4] *Bye-Gones*, September 1891, p. 172.
[5] Back, 1970, p. 6.
[6] Personal communication with author, 1988.
[7] Davies, Ellis, 1949, pp. 256-63.
[8] *Bye-Gones*, May, 1901, p. 98.
[9] Lloyd, 1885, p. 247.
[10] Mrs Clough was the wife of the vicar of Mold supposedly visited by the woman who saw the Golden Spectre of Bryn yr Ellyllon in 1830.
[11] See Jones, T G, 1930, pp. 29, 141 and 175 for the use of rowan wood as a protection against ghosts and fairies.
[12] Clough, 1861, p. 24.
[13] Morgan, J J, 1949.
[14] Trevelyan, 1909, p.196, See also *Bye-Gones*, January 1877, p. 181.
[15] Personal correspondence with the author.
[16] Armstrong, 1977, p. 29.
[17] Personal communication with the author.
[18] Personal communication with the author.
[19] Davies, J C, 1911, pp. 169-71, quoting letter by Capt Alldridge dated March 15, 1867, and reproduced in the *Pembroke County Guardian* of Feb 16, 1901.
[20] Clough, 1861, p. 75.

Wrexham

Bettisfield

In 1762 a contributor to the venerable *Gentleman's Magazine* recorded that Bettisfield Hall was haunted. The Hall had been partly destroyed by a fire some years previously, and the writer said that after this unhappy event, the spirit of one Madam Ffowler set about 'troubling the house'. The family called in a 'magician' who exorcised the spirit. He did this by trapping it in a bottle, which he then sank in a nearby pond. The writer continues:

'There she remained until the pond was mudded, when the inquisitive men must needs draw the cork, when out, with a whiz, comes something like a humble bee, which makes straight for Llys Bedydd [Bettisfield Hall], and in her flight assumes the appearance of Madam Ffowler. Warned by experience, she troubles them no more.'[1]

Trapping spirits in bottles and sinking them in bodies of water was a common form of exorcism, as we shall see. For one example, see Llanidloes, Powys.

Bronington

Like many other clergymen, the Rev Matthew Henry Lee, vicar of Hanmer in the 1880s, kept a preacher's book in which he kept a note of church finances, sermons he had read and other minutiae of the administration of his parish.

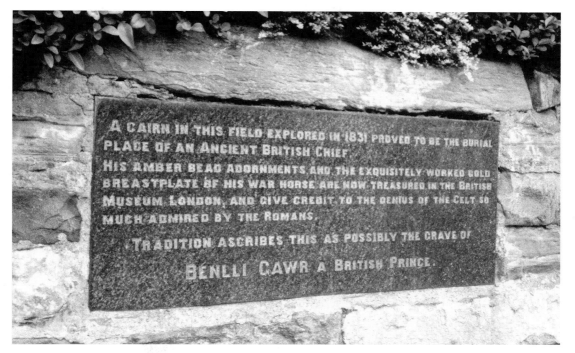

Mold, Flintshire: This plaque, with its inaccurate legend, marks the site of a Bronze Age cairn which was haunted by the prehistoric chieftain buried here.

Broughton, Flintshire: Courting couples have been terrorised by the apparition of a disapproving clergyman in the wood-bound lane known as the Old Warren.

Nannerch, Flintshire: The ramparts of the Iron Age hillfort on Moel Arthur are patrolled by a Grey Lady.

Pontblyddyn, Flintshire: Many have had strange experiences both inside and outside Plas Teg, but the ghost story belonging to the house may be a modern invention. Picture: Fortean Picture Library

Holt, Wrexham: Two children were drowned in the River Dee below this handsome medieval bridge and their piteous cries can still be heard.

Marford, Wrexham: Cottages with crosses fixed to the walls and windows which have been made in the shape of crosses – all to keep at bay the vengeful spirit of Lady Margaret Blackbourne. Picture: Fortean Picture Library

Tied him down and proceeded to search the House.

Llantysilio, Denbighshire: Mysterious voices were heard to emanate from this church one cold night, prophesying the doom of the local squire.

Llangynhafal, Denbighshire: This picture from a book published in 1919 illustrates the story of a robbery at the old house of Plas Draw which later led to its being haunted. Picture: Fortean Picture Library

Llandegla, Denbighshire: An angry poltergeist was trapped under this little bridge by Griffiths the ghost-layer.

Llangollen, Denbighshire: Beautiful but unearthly voices have been heard coming from the ruins of Valle Crucis Abbey. Picture: Fortean Picture Library

Llangollen, Denbighshire: In the 1930s Dr Mary Gordon had a lengthy chat with the spirits of the long-dead Ladies of Llangollen in their former home, Plas Newydd. Picture: Fortean Picture Library

Rhuddlan, Denbighshire: The demonic Warrior Knight of the Blood Red Plume and the Princess Erilda are the ghosts of Rhuddlan Castle. Below the castle is the River Clwyd, into which the demon dragged his hapless victim. Picture: Fortean Picture Library

Llanrhaeadr, Denbighshire: The restless spirit of the wicked David Salisbury has been seen galloping round this charming village on a white horse.

Llandudno, Conwy: A ghastly spectre with 'eyes burning like fire' terrified a poacher in Gloddaeth Woods.

Betws y Coed, Conwy: In the deepest pool below the Swallow Falls, the spirit of the unpopular Sir John Wynne is 'purged, spouted upon and purified'.
Picture: Fortean Picture Library

(Above) Cerrigydrudion, Conwy: An evil spirit once took possession of the church at Cerrig, and had to be dragged out by two mighty oxen.

(Right) Llangwm, Conwy: So many ambushed travellers were murdered in the steep wooded valley below Pont Glyn-diffwys that it was said to be crowded with anguished souls. This engraving of the once celebrated beauty spot was made by Gastineau in the 1820s.
Picture: Fortean Picture Library

(Right) Llangernyw, Conwy: The two prehistoric standing stones in Llangernyw churchyard indicate that this has been a sacred site for millennia. Every Hallowe'en the church would be visited by a spirit called the 'Angel-ystor', which would recite the names of parishioners doomed to die during the coming year.

Brynteg, Anglesey: Gwyn Llewellyn revisits the Cadair y Bwgan, or Goblin's Chair. Now almost forgotten and half-buried in a hedge, this lump of rock was once a source of dread, believed to be the haunt of a malicious ghost. Picture: Michael Bayley Hughes

Llanddyfnan, Anglesey: The eerie Lon y Bwbach (Ghost Lane) was haunted by an invisible presence which particularly affected horses.

(Left) Llaneilian, Anglesey: Somewhere in the neighbourhood of Llaneilian church, a preacher, the Rev Hughes, was accosted by a spirit which appeared as a greyhound in 'an artificial circle on the ground'. The neighbouring farm has the suggestive name of Corn Ellyll, which translates as Horn of the Elf or Goblin. Could this originally have been Cor Ellyll – Goblin's Circle – and have been the site of the Rev Hughes' adventure?

(Below) Llyn Gwynant, Gwynedd: This lake became the reluctant resting places of many troublesome spirits, banished beneath its waters by local ghost-layers.

(Above) **Llanddeusant, Anglesey:** A noisy poltergeist once made life a misery for the household at Clwchdernog.

LlamTrwsgwl, Gwynedd: The Stumbling Leap across the River Conwy as photographed in about the year 1899 (left) and by the author in 2004 (above). The site is now entirely overgrown and home of a water board station. The deep pool where a young bride-to-be met her tragic end is in the foreground of the old picture and hidden from view to the left of my picture. It is now almost impossible to photograph!

Beddgelert, Gwynedd: David Pritchard, landlord of the Goat Hotel, returned from the dead and began to pace about the village. In Beddgelert churchyard his spirit told a former servant about some gold coins he had hidden some years previously.

Llanfor, Gwynedd: The old church at Llanfor – today only the tower with its beard of ivy is original – became the home of an unwelcome guest, a mischievous ghost wearing a tricorn hat.

Llanuwchllyn, Gwynedd: When preacher the Rev John Jones departed the inn at Llanuwchllyn, his footsteps were dogged by a would-be robber. The robber was deterred by the sudden appearance of a phantom horseman.

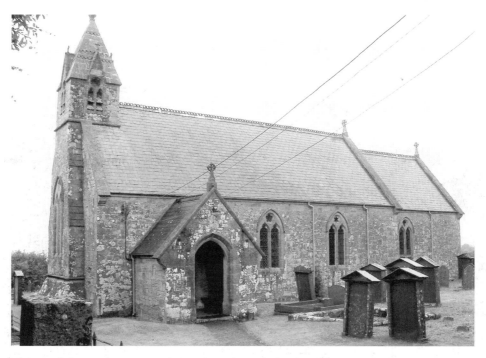

Blaenporth, Ceredigion: 'White Mary', the resident ghost of Blaenporth, woke up a farmer to tell him that the communion cup had just been stolen from the church. She then ordered him to go after the thief – and was even able to say in which inn he was sleeping.

Rhosygarth, Ceredigion: A gwyllgi, one of the terrible Welsh 'Dogs of Darkness', was seen on the road which runs through Rhos-y-Garth.

Llandre, Ceredigion: A young maidservant at Glanfred farm became rich overnight – thanks to a ghost.

Talybont, Ceredigion: At the handsome mansion of Penpompren a servant was tormented by a poltergeist which particularly enjoyed throwing water at him. A Dyn Hysbys, or Cunning Man, was called in to exorcise it.

Borth, Ceredigion: The popular sands at Borth were once considered 'demon haunted ground'. The agonised shriek of a murdered sea captain echoed down the generations as a curse followed the descendants of the murderer.

Ystrad Meurig, Ceredigion: One night a horseman with hooves instead of feet silently followed a frightened young man down this track across the Rhosmeherin moor.

Ystrad Meurig, Ceredigion: With a deafening crash, the devilish horseman of Rhosmeherin suddenly vanished at this crossroads.

Swyddffynnon, Ceredigion: The old Post Office is a quaint feature of this village, where, in the 19th century, a woman saw an apparition which proved to be an omen of a future tragedy.

But there are one or two rather more interesting entries in Rev Lee's book. Scribbled on the margin of one page is the address of the fledgling Psychical Research Society and elsewhere details of local encounters with the supernatural. In addition to some eerie experiences had at Cymau (see below), there is the following careful record of a ghost sighting at Bronington:

'George Metcalf of Moss Lane (leading to Cuckoo's Nook) in Bronington, who was born about 1821, told me on Friday September 19th 1884, that as he was going to Welsh Coals in 1844 August [sic] he saw before him in the Wrexham Road, where the Pandy Toll Bar afterwards stood, the figure of a woman in a light-coloured dress, with a Tuscan bonnet, and some broad ribbon which fell upon the left shoulder and waved in the wind. She held up her dress with her right hand, and wore low black shoes. He intended asking her to ride in the cart, and taking his eyes off her for a moment to hasten the horses, she was nowhere to be seen. This happened about 4.30 am.'[2]

Bwlchgwyn

In September, 1602, an extraordinary and frightening vision was seen at Nant-y-Ffrith, a steeply sided wooded valley. Here is contemporary chronologer Robert Parry's account of the event:

'About this time was seane about Nant-y-Ffrith ... in the edge of the eveninge to a number of 2 or 3 thousande armed men a hors backe with banners displayed marchinge in warlike maner where as indeed there was no such thinge but some apparition of forewarninge of likelyhoode. And yet that was verefyed by 8 or ixen persons some of them credyte that all iontly saw the same.'

The 'forewarninge' never came to pass, no army later marched that way, and the reason for the awe-inspiring apparition has never been explained. Perhaps it was the ghost of some forgotten medieval campaign. A similar phantom army of obscure origin was seen later that century at Montgomery, in Powys.[3]

Cymau

When a Mr Butler landed a job as engineer in the Fron ironworks in 1886, he looked for a house to rent. In the short-term he installed his wife at Old Cymau Hall – a house which turned out to be badly haunted. On her first night in the house, his wife was woken up by a tapping on her window. As she blinked in the darkness, she heard a mournful voice call up from below: 'Pray for my soul!' This chilling request was repeated many times, over and over, as poor Mrs Butler hid her head under the bed-clothes. It is a pity she was too frightened to accede to the miserable spirit's request, for the performance was repeated the following night. On this occasion she was able to mutter a prayer for the benefit of the tormented soul, and the voice was silenced. Afterwards, Mrs Butler learnt that a man had committed suicide below her window not long before she moved in.

A week after this unpleasant experience, the Butlers moved down the road to New Cymau Hall, now Cymau Farm. But if Mrs Butler now expected a quieter night's sleep, she was sadly mistaken – her unlucky husband had chosen another haunted house to live in! Once again some invisible entity disturbed their rest. Mr Butler woke up one night to feel a hand pressing down on his chest. On another occasion Mrs Butler was startled by an urgent knocking on her bedroom door – her mother, who occupied the room adjoining, heard a knocking on her door at precisely the same moment. They both rushed out and met in the corridor, equally bemused and a little frightened. Rev Henry Lee (see Bronington), who took down their statements, noted that in later years other people suffered uncanny experiences in this room.[4]

Glyn Ceiriog

The lonely and lovely valley of the Ceiriog now forms a kind of rural leg for the largely industrial and suburban new county of Wrexham. Here in 1700 a most extraordinary character was born. His name was John Edwards and although he was by trade a weaver, he was also a poet, a translator – and a necromancer! He was known by the name of Sion y Potiau (or 'John the Tippler'). He left his home village for the alien world of London, where he lived with a bookseller for about seven years. Here he 'acquired knowledge more than the common about Glyn Ceiriog'.

After his return he settled down in a cottage by a yew tree a short way above the church. Among his orthodox achievements were the composition of an ode on Llangollen Church and a Welsh translation of *Pilgrim's Progress*. Less orthodox was the naming of his sons – Cain and Abel. But it was his command over the spirit world which most impressed the residents of

Glyn Ceiriog. 'John Edwards, like most of the old bookmen of his time, had often to do with ghosts,' to quote one historian. It was said that, like Shakespeare's Owen Glendower, Edwards was able to 'call spirits from the vasty deep'. He used these spirits to carry him about. It was said that an apparition had often been seen transporting Edwards from his cottage door and over a steep glen called Nant y Weniar. The ghost would place Edwards gently down on the other side of the mountain. An old piece of doggerel has survived:

'The ghost of Allt y Badau
'Used to poke Sion the Potiau.'

I feel I must leave the meaning of the word 'poke' in this context for my discerning readers to decide for themselves.[5]

Gresford

A Marford builder, Mr William Davies, who died at the age of 91 in 1874, used to enjoy a good constitutional of an evening. Sometimes he would be accompanied on his walks by a Mr Williams, of the Old Parsonage, Gresford. Late one evening they were returning in the direction of Gresford and had reached the bottom of Little Acton Hill, near a cottage called the Bluebell, which had once been a pub. Ahead of them in the gloom they saw approaching them a lady dressed in white.

'Now you will catch it,' quipped Mr Davies to his friend, 'here is Mrs Williams coming to meet you.'

But the white figure 'vanished in the darkness'. Horrible to relate, when Mr Williams arrived at the Old Parsonage, he found his wife hanging by the neck and quite dead.[6]

Holt

Two young boys, heirs to important estates in North Wales during the reign of Edward I, were drowned in the freezing waters below the medieval bridge at Holt by their guardians, John, Earl Warren, and Roger Mortimer of Wigmore. The two lords, far from being punished for their cruel deed, were rewarded with vast chunks of the land the boys were to have inherited:

'And now when at midnight the wayfarer goes
From Farndon to Holt, and the River Dee flows
Beneath the old bridge in full flood to the sea,
He hears, it is stated, as clear as can be,
The agonised cries of the murdered young boys
Above all the river's tumultuous noise.'[7]

Thomas Pennant, writing in 1784, said the memory of the murder had been recorded 'under the fable of two young fairies, who had been destroyed in that manner, and in the same place'.[8] Another variant on the story is suggested by a poem on Holt Bridge published in 1832, for it refers to two 'daughters' who were drowned.[9]

Marford

It has been alleged that the quaint architecture of Marford village owes something of its design to the perambulations of a ghost. The old estate cottages and the village inn are all ornamented with crosses and shapes representing the 'evil eye', many in the form of windows. It has been said that these were incorporated into the walls of the cottages to ward off one 'Lady Blackbird' who haunted the village. An early account of the ghost says that she was a lady murdered in Pant Wood and that she used to walk in the direction of Trevalyan at nearby Rossett. She was eventually exorcised – or 'laid' as the terminology has it – by 'an eminent divine'.[10]

Later versions of the story are more elaborate, and say that Lady Blackbird was, in life, one Margaret Blackbourne, murdered in her home, Rofft Hall, by her cruel husband in the early years of the 18th century. Shortly after her death, her husband remarried, a cue for her angry spirit to rise from her tomb and make its way to Rofft Hall to disturb the peace of the less than happy couple. En route she would pause at every cottage window and tap on the glass to let the terrified occupants know she was abroad. It took seven ministers with bell, book and candle to lay her tormented spirit, but the cruciform windows still seemed a wise precaution to the nervous villagers.[11]

Rossett (Yr Orsedd)

The attractive and rather exclusive village of Rossett was at one time shunned by its neighbours. The reason for this was a grisly gibbet erected on the green, from which there dangled a half-corrupted corpse. So horrid was this emblem of death that it blighted the community, to the extent that farmers found that their wares were boycotted at market. The corpse was that of a man called Jeffrey who had severely assaulted and left for dead a farm labourer near Gresford. The man recovered and testified against Jeffrey, who was arrested and hanged at Ruthin. His body was brought to

Rossett and gibbeted for all to see.

The villagers, especially the farmers from whom no one would buy, grew very resentful of Jeffrey's ghastly presence and they decided to rid themselves of him. At dead of night, a gang got together and brought down from the gibbet the gruesome remains. Jeffrey was buried on the village green – and may still be there. Since his bones were buried in unconsecrated ground, it is no surprise to learn that his spirit began to stalk the village. This had its uses. All it required to bring in recalcitrant children after dusk was a reminder that 'Old Jeffrey will have you', and in they'd come![12]

It would appear that the gibbet on which Jeffrey's body was hung was dismantled once its function had come to an end. Part of it went into the construction of an outbuilding at the *Golden Lion* in the village. When I visited the pub in 1994, the manager very kindly let me examine the outbuildings. In one of them I found an old, blackened beam across the ceiling, out of which jutted a square, iron 'hook', which may well have served to suspend a body. I found, too, that Jeffrey himself was not forgotten, that a story still prevailed that he haunted the inn's former stables.[13]

Ruabon (Rhiwabon)

A man had a very strange adventure one night while walking through Ruabon. His nephew told the story to the folklorist Marie Trevelyan, who recorded it in her book *Folk-Lore and Folk-Stories of Wales*, published in 1909:

'In the twilight of a bitterly cold day in December he was hurrying homeward, when not far from the parish church, his progress was obstructed by what appeared to be in the growing twilight a funeral procession. He could distinctly see the bier, the coffin on it, the mourners, and others following. In order to let the procession pass my uncle stood aside, and then he saw the well-known faces of a doctor and a tradesman who lived in Ruabon. The people were singing but he could not distinguish the words, although he was familiar with the tune. But presently he observed that the funeral passed the church instead of going into it. Impelled by curiosity, he followed the funeral, which vanished when it reached a house not far from the church. Much impressed with what he saw, he hastened home and told his wife of the vision he had witnessed.

'About six weeks later my uncle happened to be in Ruabon in the twilight, and a funeral procession passed the spot where he had seen the phantom mourners. Curiously, the real funeral passed the church, and halted at the house he had seen in his vision. In the procession the doctor and tradesman were seen as before. The body was that of a person who had died in the South of England, and was conveyed to the house of the deceased, there to remain until the next day. This explained the remarkable circumstance of a funeral in the late twilight.'[14]

What this man had experienced was a phantom funeral, one of the many supernatural death omens which make up the Welsh tradition of the 'Tolaeth'. Many other people, until the early years of the 20th century at least, reported very similar encounters, more commonly in South Wales than in the north.

Wrexham (Wrecsam)

A gruesome tale centres on Borras Hall, a few miles outside the town. When I met the owners in 1991, they assured me the yarn was an old one but they had no reason to believe that there was any truth in it. It follows a traditional pattern, however, and I suspect it is of some antiquity. The protagonist is a cruel squire – something of a cliché in old ghost stories – a man of drunken temper, who enjoyed ill-treating his servants and taking advantage of the prettier maids. His favourite pastime, however, was fox-hunting.

One day, when he was out riding to hounds, he paused on a ridge commanding a fine view of his estate and watched with satisfaction as the pack snarled and slobbered in a frenzy below him. Suddenly, his horse was startled by something invisible, it kicked and shied and threw the Squire of Borras out of the saddle. He plummeted down the hill and crashed through the branches of a tree with such violence that his head was struck from his body! The head bumped and rolled right under the noses of the slavering hounds – *who wasted no time in gobbling it up*.[15]

(For a story of a man sharing a similar fate, see Colwinston, Vale of Glamorgan.)

[1] Lloyd, 1882, p. 367, quoting a 1762 edition of *Gentleman's Magazine*. Lloyd learnt of the inclusion of this ghost story in the magazine from the Rev M H Lee (see Bronington).

[2] Preacher's book of Rev M H Lee, kept at Clwyd Record Office, Hawarden, seen 1991.

[3] Williams, J. G. (1973-4), p. 21, quoting from NLW Plas Nantglyn MS.I, f.28.

[4] Preacher's book of Rev M H Lee, kept at Clwyd Record Office, Hawarden, seen 1991.

[5] *Bye-Gones*, December 1890, p. 520.

[6] Ibid, February 5, 1902, p. 282.

[7] Longrigg, 1901, p. 13.

[8] Pennant, 1784, Vol. I, p. 217.

[9] *Cambrian Quarterly*, 1832, p. 238.

[10] Jarman, 1904, p. 18.

[11] *Country Quest*, November 1984, pp. 18-19.

[12] *Bye-Gones*, July 1902, p. 393.

[13] Personal communication with the author, April 1994.

[14] Trevelyan, 1909, p. 185.

[15] Personal communication with the author, 1991.

Denbighshire

Bryneglwys

One of the most interesting characters in the folklore of North Wales is a certain Mr Griffiths, mentioned by Elias Owen and other authors as having been active in Denbighshire in about the first half of the 19th century. Details are lacking, but Mr Griffiths certainly seems to have been a real person, a Nonconformist minister who had his home at Graianrhyd, near Llanarmon-yn-Iâl. According to the stories, Mr Griffiths was an exorcist.

Griffiths was a kind of specialist pest exterminator, his expertise ridding the home of bothersome poltergeists, rather than the usual rats or cockroaches. Elias Owen heard of two examples of his work at Bryneglwys. At Ffrith farm a poltergeist made a nuisance of itself in the dairy and kitchens, smashing the pots and pans and throwing 'filthy matter' into the milk to spoil the cheese. The farmer offered a reward of £5 (a hefty sum in those days) to anyone who could rid him of it. An aged priest had a go at exorcising it one Sunday afternoon, but the poltergeist showed its contempt for him by waving a woman's bonnet in his face.

Mr Griffiths was invited to try next and the first thing he did was to entice the *bwgan* into the barn. Perhaps he chose the barn because it afforded him plenty of room, or perhaps because it enabled him to carry out his work without too many distractions (the farrago with the priest had drawn quite a crowd of curious spectators). Whatever the reason, as soon as he was inside, the exorcist drew a protective circle on the floor and stood inside it. This was just as well, because the *bwgan* had transformed itself into a lion! It snarled and clawed the air in an attempt to intimidate Mr Griffiths, but could not enter the charmed circle to harm him.

Mr Griffiths told the spirit that he would take no notice unless it changed itself into something less fierce. A show-off like all poltergeists, it obliged by changing itself into a big dog. This too the minister objected to and at last he had persuaded it to become nothing more formidable than a fly. Quick as a flash, Griffiths trapped the 'fly' inside his tobacco box and this he took away, with the poltergeist, no doubt, buzzing furiously but impotently inside.[1]

On another occasion Mr Griffiths was called to Tymawr farm, which was plagued by an angry spirit which pinched the servant girls all day and all night, making their lives a misery. The reason for this visitation seemed to be related to a call made on the farm by a beggar, whose plea for food had been met with jeers of scorn and nothing else. As the vagrant left the farm still hungry, he said over his shoulder: 'You shall repent your conduct to me.' Shortly afterwards the invisible attacks on the heartless servants began, and went on for day after day, until they 'were tired of their lives'. This time the friendly neighbourhood exorcist succeeded in coaxing the spirit into the form of a spider, which was snapped up, like the other one, into his tobacco box. This Mr Griffiths carried triumphantly away, perhaps to add to his collection.[2]

Cynwyd

A former sergeant in the Denbighshire Yeomanry, Edward Jones, had an unnerving experience one night when he was returning home from the fair at Cynwyd. He was crossing the moors on horseback when he realised he was being followed by a *gwyllgi*, one of the horrible Dogs of Darkness which patrol many a lonely Welsh road. Jones called it the 'Black Hound of Destiny' and said that it was 'a beast of fearsome visage and blood-shot eye'. The creature followed 'just astern of him ready for the spring, but never quite achieving the awaited climax as in the horrible, cold sweat anguish of a nightmare'. It seems they had quite a chase across the moorland until Jones reached his farm, Cyrchynan Uchaf.

As an aside I may mention that Jones also claimed another encounter with the supernatural. He told how 'he had seen the "little folk" or "the fairies" in a mischievous mood remove all the slates from the roof of one of his buildings in the dead of night with much noise and fury, and how by the morning all of the slates had been replaced'.[3]

Llandegla

At Llandegla we learn of the further exploits of Griffiths, the Graianrhyd ghost layer. The charming Old Rectory in the village had become afflicted with a troublesome poltergeist and Griffiths was sent for. It took him a great deal of time to overcome the spirit, for night after night it appeared to him in some terrible form. At length, however, it took the shape of a harmless fly, possibly worn down by Griffiths' prayers and indomitable will. Quickly, Mr Griffiths shut up the phantom fly in a little box, and this he carried with all haste to the river which flows below the village. Here he splashed about until he found a big stone under the water. Under this stone he secured the box containing the buzzing *bwgan*. The spirit would remain trapped, pronounced Mr Griffiths, until the top of a little tree growing nearby had reached the height of the bridge over the stream.

For many years, the local children would trim the branches of this tree to prevent the prophecy coming true, and so ensure that the spirit remained in its watery prison. Today, however, all the trees by the bridge are taller than it, so we must assume this custom was abandoned as the Llandegla schoolchildren grew more 'sophisticated' with each succeeding generation. And we must also assume that, as a result, the spirit has long since escaped...[4]

On the Mold Road between Llandegla and Rhydtalog there is a place named Boncyn y Porthman, or in English, Grazier's or Drover's Bank. For many years it was considered haunted. Wagoners hated to pass the Boncyn at night because something unseen to them would spook their horses and it was with great difficulty that they could be made to continue on their way. Sometimes a sudden and intense darkness would fall all around and a high wind would spring up. By the time they'd got past, the horses would be 'all of a perspiration'.

One evening something even more sinister occurred at Boncyn y Porthman. A farmer returning home rather late from Chester market saw a man approaching him through the gloom. This man, whose appearance he never saw clearly, suddenly pulled him from his horse and proceeded to beat him up most severely. So violent was the attack that the farmer passed out. When he came to, he found that contrary to his expectation, he had not been robbed; all his money was safe. For this reason, and perhaps for others he was unable to express, the farmer came to the conclusion that this was no living man who had assaulted him but some kind of spirit.

In the 18th century a grazier was robbed and murdered at Boncyn y Porthman, an incident which may have explained the haunting, as well as the name. However, there is another intriguing fact about this place. In 1890, many years after the farmer's assault, some roadmen clearing stones here accidentally uncovered a prehistoric grave containing a small urn and part of a skeleton.[5]

Was the farmer attacked by some sort of madman, or was it a spirit as he supposed? Was his experience some strange echo of the murder of another man, or could the weird manifestations at Boncyn y Porthman have been somehow linked to the ancient burial site? We shall, of course, never know, but I, for one, am grateful that every time I pass this place, as I often do after visiting friends, I do so in my car and at some speed!

Llangollen

Marie Trevelyan, in her *From Snowdon To The Sea*, has two characters, itinerant preachers, discussing ghost stories. The accounts are written in a fictionalised way, but Trevelyan was keen to be seen as a collector of genuine folk tales, so it is probable that the stories are not purely fiction, but the dressed-up accounts of real experiences. For the first of these stories, we encounter the two ministers as they descend into the 'Vale of the Cross' at Llangollen.

One misty morning, so early that the moon, rather than the sun, is still shining down upon it, Robert Owen and Richard Rhys are walking past the romantic ruins of medieval Valle Crucis Abbey when they hear the sound of someone singing in Latin. They realise that it is coming from the ruins, and entranced but fearful of disturbing the singer, they tiptoe into the Abbey so that they can listen all the better. Owen catches 'a glimpse ... of the long and somewhat broad shadow, apparently of a man', but he and Rhys, anxious not to be seen, retire to a secluded corner, where they are hidden from view (and where, therefore, they cannot see the singer). They listen enraptured to the *Dies Irae* as it echoes around the marble walls and shattered casements gleaming in the moonlight. The *Dies Irae* is followed by the *De Profundis*, at first in Latin and then, as a finale, in English:

> 'Out of the depths have I cried to thee, O Lord.
> 'Lord, hear my voice...'

Then the 'wonderful and melodious voice' ceases and to their amazement the two preachers realise that it is now full morning and sunlight is flooding the Abbey ruins. They have an appointment with a third preacher and his brother in Llangollen and, realising they are likely to be late for the dog-cart which was to take them the remainder of their journey, they delay no further but hurry on their way. They discover they are *three hours late* for their appointment and their friend and the cart has gone without them. They curse themselves for their folly – but later learn there has been a fatal accident; the horse drawing the cart bolted and their friend is badly injured and his brother killed. If they had not stopped to listen to the extraordinary singing in Valle Crucis Abbey, they may have been killed, as well.[6]

The ghostly music of Valle Crucis has been heard more recently. In 2003 I spoke to a Liverpudlian lady, now living in Helsby, who recalled staying at the campsite next to the Abbey in August, 1950. Having ventured into Llangollen for a drink, she and her friend took a short-cut back from town which brought them to the road opposite the ruin. It was about 10.30pm.

'I could hear beautiful music, singing like a choir, and an organ, coming from Valle Crucis,' she remembered. Her friend couldn't hear anything and assumed she was imagining it. Why would anyone be playing music in a ruin at that time of night, she wanted to know.

'No one would believe I'd heard anything and the next day we went to have a look around,' she continued. 'But when I was there I had another strange experience. We went up these stairs into the only room left with a ceiling on it, the old reading room we were told it used to be, and when I was coming back down I had this horrible feeling. I went quite funny and I caught my friend by the arm and I said I felt like something tragic had happened. It was very strange. But I can never get the memory of that beautiful music and that beautiful singing out of my head.'

A few years later my informant read a letter in the *Liverpool Echo* from a man whose bicycle had broken down opposite Valle Crucis Abbey and he, too, heard singing coming from the ruin. But he was the only one able to do so; his companion could hear nothing.[7]

A similar but even more vivid experience was had by a Wrexham lady, who wrote to tell me about it: 'Walking one night on the road opposite Valle Crucis with my aunt, we stopped to peer through the darkness to the Abbey. I was amazed to see in front of the Abbey the ground light up in a large circle of the most dazzling light – apparently emanating from the ground. In the middle of the circle there was some kind of golden object, several feet high, and walking about quite a number of human figures, garbed in wonderful golden costumes with golden kind of helmets on their heads.

'I had never seen such a radiant scene. I said to my aunt: "Isn't it wonderful – everything in that shining, golden light. It must be some kind of pageant they are putting on." I couldn't believe it when she replied: "What light? What pageant? It's all dark." [For] some seconds the wonderful scene went on, but she couldn't see it. Then it finished as suddenly as it had come.'[8]

On this occasion no sound was heard, the vision was silent. Perhaps the music heard by others accompanies the ceremony described by my correspondent, but it is rarely seen.

In the 1930s a Dr Mary Gordon decided to

make a pilgrimage to Valle Crucis, a place she had not seen for fifty-six years. Whilst staying with Carl Jung, the great psychologist, she had a vivid dream about the old abbey and Jung, a firm believer in the power of dreams, urged her to return to the place to find out what it was all about. In the event it was not Valle Crucis but Plas Newydd which proved significant to Dr Gordon.

Plas Newydd is the show house of Llangollen. It was built in 1778 by two aristocratic ladies who deserted their native Ireland so they could live together in the manner they chose without the interference of their families. Lady Eleanor Butler and Sarah Ponsonby lived at Plas Newydd for the rest of their lives, raising bemused eyebrows for their adoption of masculine dress and their refusal to marry men, largely considered a woman's sole role in life in those days. However, their wit and excellent hospitality won them many celebrated friends, including the Duke of Wellington and William Wordsworth, and they became minor celebrities in their own right, known forever more as the 'Ladies of Llangollen'.

On her visit to Plas Newydd, Dr Gordon 'became immediately and intensely aware of two presences, whom she at once took to be the Ladies'. She had had no great interest in the Ladies of Llangollen before, but now intrigued, she spent some time researching their lives, and revisited the house eight months later. She no longer felt the presences at the house but, as she walked up the Bache, a walk which had been popular with Butler and Ponsonby, she saw 'sitting by the hill path and outlined against the strong sunlight, two figures whom she recognised instantly. They were wearing light blue linen habits and fine muslin shirts, and they were sitting so still that it seemed to the Doctor that they must have been asleep for some considerable time'.

Dr Gordon shyly approached the quaint figures. She spoke to them – and they replied! A rendezvous was agreed, that Dr Gordon and the two ghostly Ladies should meet at Plas Newydd at nine o'clock that night. The house was uninhabited and in the care of the local council in those days, so Dr Gordon – in her seventies – had to force an entrance and clamber in through a window. In the library she was joined by the spirits firstly of Lady Eleanor and then of Sarah Ponsonby. They enjoyed a long and varied conversation until it was interrupted by the coming dawn, the fruits of which Dr Gordon wrote down in a book, *The Flight of the Wild Goose*, a kind of fictional biography based on their lives as described by the spirits of the Ladies themselves.[9]

According to Jack Hallam in his *Ghost's Who's Who*, the quaint figures of the Ladies of Llangollen reappear on Christmas Eve, but, ironically, their apparitions can only be seen by men.[10]

Llangynhafal

During the reign of the second King George there lived at the manor house of Plas Draw a miserly squire. He was possessed of a great many valuables, more than the average country farmer of his generation, and these gave him as much worry as they did pleasure. In his old age the squire became housebound, unable to ride around the grounds as had been his daily habit but forced instead to stay put in a favourite armchair. Unknown to anyone else, however, he had had a secret compartment made in the base of this armchair, inside which he had hidden his most highly prized possessions. All day long he would sit on his valuables 'with much deliberation and contentment of mind'.

One fateful Sunday evening, however, his contentment was smashed when a gang of robbers broke in. One of them was a former servant who had fallen in with the house-breakers while in London and whose account of the quantity of silver plate available at Plas Draw, and the isolated situation of the old house, had tempted them to make such a lengthy journey. The ex-servant suggested a Sunday afternoon as the ideal time to mount the raid, because most of the staff were at church. However, there was one fact of which this clever man was in ignorance – the unusual hiding place of the treasure. The first thing the gang did after silencing the servants was to tie up the squire, who was protesting their intentions with great indignation. They bound him to his chair to keep him still, entirely unaware that the sought-after silver was right there beneath him!

Unable to find what they were after, but afraid to linger too long, the disappointed ruffians took what they could immediately lay their hands on and scarpered. A small child had seen their arrival, however, and had scampered to the church to tell the congregation what was happening. The villagers were soon in hot pursuit of the robbers and were shortly joined by several young bloods who, on hearing the alarm, did the sensible thing and got ready their horses. They pursued the gang all the way back to London, never quite catching up with them but able to make inquiries which resulted in their swift arrests. The gang was brought back to Denbigh and there hanged.

The ghost of Plas Draw records this exciting event, although the ghost itself is far from dramatic. It is the forlorn, silent spirit of the former servant, who flits from room to room at dead of night, filled with remorse for his treachery.[11]

Llanrhaeadr

Griffiths the ghost layer, who was always on the look-out for restless spooks, saw one one night near the village of Llanrhaeadr. He recognised it as the spirit of David Salisbury, a member of an important local family, who 'had given considerable trouble to the living, long after his remains had been laid in the grave' (his death was in the 1820s). Griffiths said he saw Salisbury 'mounted upon a white horse, galloping over hedges and ditches in the middle of the night, and had heard his "terrible groans".' Salisbury made these groans, Griffiths believed, because of 'the weight of sin troubling the unhappy soul', and he concluded that his riding round and round in this aimless manner was a form of punishment for his misspent life. Once upon a time there existed a ballad called *Yspryd Dafydd Salbri (The Ghost of David Salisbury)* which gave an account of the history of the apparition, but this now seems to have been lost.[12]

Llantysilio

The Rev John Simon, 'a well-known preacher in the Vale of Llangollen', told the following story to his son, Rev John Simon Jr, who then related it in the 1892 Christmas edition of the *Methodist Recorder*. One night a man had been awoken from his bed by a 'mysterious person' who was standing in his room and silently beckoning to him. He followed the spirit – for such it must have been – through the night air to the little church of Llantysilio, which is situated on a rise above the River Dee, some miles from the village. To his surprise, he saw that the church was open and all lit up with 'a ghostly light'. He heard voices within the church denouncing the local squire. They said that the squire would not die a natural death and that when he did die

Llantysilio Hall would be claimed by a stranger, a man who had no legal right to it. Here was news indeed!

The next morning, the villagers were gathered in the churchyard, listening to the man's fantastic story. Rev John Simon Sr was present that morning and his son remembers how he used to describe 'the solemn conclave under the yew trees and the profound discussions of the rustic sages'. The whole thing would have been dismissed as a dream – but the prophecy came true. The squire remained hale and hearty for some time – 'not one penny worse for ghostly denunciation', as the Rev Simon puts it – but then, one day, while in the cellar decanting wine, he cut his hand severely on a broken bottle; the wound would not heal, he grew ill, and shortly thereafter he died.

On the day of his funeral, a man, presumed to be a friend of the squire, but one unknown in the neighbourhood, presented himself at the Hall to take part in the ceremony. However, when the cortège set out for the church, the stranger was not to be seen among the followers. When the ceremony was over and the unlucky squire laid to rest, the villagers returned to the Hall – only to find it locked and bolted against them. The stranger had taken possession. He claimed he was the legal owner of the Hall, because he had won it while gambling with the late squire. The estate, relates Mr Simon, 'was thrown into Chancery, remaining there for many long years'.[13]

A possible sequel to this event was recorded by a correspondent of *Bye-gones*. He refers to some problem over Llantysilio Hall, which involved the fact that the squire's will could not be found. The above incident would certainly make the finding of such a will of paramount importance. One night an old woman in Oswestry had a dream that the will had been put into the coffin with the squire. This fired the imagination of the locals and one 'cold, dismal night in Autumn' a gang of men crept to Llantysilio Church with a view to exhuming the late squire. They dug with some haste, for they were afraid of being caught in the act of grave-robbing. Just as they were lifting the coffin out of the ground, however, 'some unearthly noise was heard' which so alarmed them that they all downed spades and ran off. Not surprisingly, some of them had to appear in court for the sacrilege – whether the missing will was ever found is not recorded.[14]

Two years after the *Methodist Recorder* published the story of the cursed squire, Marie Trevelyan published a romanticised version of it in *From Snowdon To The Sea*. In this version she names the man who overheard the prophecy as 'Robin Ddu, a tailor of Llangollen who was acquainted with the black arts'.[15]

Llanynys

Llanynys' name, which translates as Island Church, seems an odd one for a village in the Vale of Clwyd. But in times past the land around Llanynys was marshy and liable to flood. The church really was situated on an island of sorts. Today the winding lanes which lead to Llanynys pass over many little bridges and the fields are criss-crossed with streams and dykes. Centuries ago, an exciseman found himself benighted in this treacherous country and became increasingly afraid that he would unwittingly lead his horse into a bog. He was very glad, therefore, when he made out the shape of a house in the darkness, for he urgently needed shelter.

Unfortunately, the tenant of the house, which was called Ty Felin, turned out to be an unfriendly individual, who made it clear that the traveller should seek shelter elsewhere. He argued that the only spare room he had was haunted, but this the exciseman took as an excuse and he insisted on bedding down there. At last he had his own way, and prepared to settle down for a night's rest.

He'd hardly put his head down, however, when in walked a man, a Jew, who started to wander aimlessly around the room. The officer jumped up to ask him his business, but the stranger promptly left. More than a little curious, the exciseman followed, just in time to see the Jew leave the house and make his way out into the darkness. He gave chase, but soon lost sight of him. Greatly puzzled, the sleepy man returned to his bed. And in walked the Jew again! So sudden was his appearance, that the excise officer began to suspect what the reader has already guessed – that the room was haunted after all. Again he followed the silent man out into the yard, and again he vanished. The sequence was repeated a third time, but on this occasion the excise officer took careful note of where the apparition vanished, and this place he hastily marked with a stick. This seemed to satisfy the restless spirit, for it was seen no more that night.

The next morning, the officer continued on his interrupted journey, but he soon returned to Ty Felin, this time accompanied by a policeman. Together they investigated the spot in the yard still marked by his stick and here they uncovered a well. And in the well, there was a corpse. It didn't take long for the two officers of the law to force a confession from the surly tenant of Ty Felin. He admitted that the corpse was that of a travelling Jew, a seller of jewellery, who had once lodged with him. He had murdered the Jew and cast his body in the well. No wonder he had tried to prevent the exciseman from sleeping in the haunted room – for 'murder will out'. His victim's spirit had returned to condemn him to the gallows.[16]

Melin-y-Wig

A Mr John Roberts, who lived in this out-of-the-way village in the 19th century, used to enjoy the comfortable habit of smoking a quiet pipe at the end of the day after the rest of the household had gone up to bed. Often he liked to 'take a peep into the night' to keep himself amused while he did so and on this occasion, as he was standing outside his front door, his attention was drawn by a small light in the distance, shining in a place where he knew there was no house. He peered at it in some curiosity and then realised that it was moving, coming slowly along the road from Bettws Gwerfil Goch. From time to time, Roberts would lose sight of it as it disappeared into a dip in the road or became obscured by trees or hedges, but slowly and inexorably the light came on.

Roberts became very intrigued. At first he thought the light might be caused by a lantern, but he couldn't understand why anyone would be walking that lonely road at that time of night. He realised that his curiosity would soon be satisfied, however, for the road passed right by his house. Sure enough, the mysterious light approached and Roberts saw that it more resembled the glow of a candle than that of a lantern but never mind how hard he stared, he was unable to see anyone holding such a thing. Imagine his shock when, instead of passing by his house, it suddenly turned into the lane leading to his own home and began coming up his garden path!

In a sudden fear, Roberts jumped back into his house and hastily shut the door. But the light brooked no such refusal – it entered *through the locked door*. It then floated up to the ceiling, where it hovered a little while before vanishing. John Roberts went to bed greatly perplexed. The next morning he discovered that his servant man had died during the night. The dead man's room was directly above the spot where the weird light had been floating. Roberts would now have recognised the mysterious spark as having been a corpse candle, one of the *Tolaeth* apparitions, come to warn of the servant's demise.[17]

Rhuddlan

Welsh Legends, published in 1802 by J Badcock, is credited with being the earliest book of Welsh folk tales. It is a lurid collection told in a grotesquely over-emphasised gothic prose but makes fascinating reading. One of the most dramatic of the legends centres on Rhuddlan Castle. Erilda, Princess of North Wales, is betrothed to the Prince of South Wales. Their marriage is expected to unite Wales, to bring peace to the country. However, shortly before the date of the ceremony Erilda has an adventure. She is thrown from her horse while out hunting and she becomes lost in a fog-bound wood. She is rescued from her predicament by a stranger, a knight in black armour with a crimson plume on his helmet. He introduces himself as Wertwold, 'The Warrior Knight of the Blood Red Plume'.

Carrying in his arms the fainting princess, the Warrior Knight is accorded a hero's welcome when he brings her home to her frantic father. Erilda is carried to her bed-chamber and a feast is prepared in Wertwold's honour. However, although the strange knight shows every courtesy to his host and courtiers, he refuses to eat anything and avoids answering any questions about himself. At length, he asks to take his leave of the princess, and in her chamber he presses a gold ring into her hand, telling her that should she ever need him again, she should hold the ring and call his name – he shall hear her. Then he leaves Rhuddlan Castle, as much of an enigma as when he arrived.

From that moment Erilda finds she is unable to get the Warrior Knight of the Blood Red Plume out of her mind, indeed she has fallen passionately in love with the dark stranger. At last, on the night before her wedding to the Prince of South Wales, Erilda clasps Wertwold's ring to her bosom and, almost unconsciously, whispers his name. In an instant, Wertwold magically appears before her. He wastes no time in proposing to Erilda, but, understanding her duty only too well, she tearfully refuses him. Wertwold insists, and tells her that he is 'cursed' and that the only way his curse can be lifted is for him to marry a girl of pure spirit. After much romantic interchange, Erilda, afraid yet elated, finally agrees to marry the Warrior Knight.

The couple escape by Erilda's window but as they pass through the gateway, they are spotted by a sentry, who raises the alarm. The Warrior Knight urges Erilda to hurry and presses into her hands a dagger for protection. Pursued by men from the castle, they make a dash for the River Clwyd, where Wertwold says he has a boat moored. Just as they reach the river's edge, a hand grasps Erilda's shoulder. In a panic she turns and stabs her pursuer with the dagger given to her by Wertwold. In horror she realises she has slain her own father! It is only now that the ill-fated Erilda discovers the very dreadful error she has made...

The Warrior Knight of the Blood Red Plume laughs scornfully at the poor girl's despair, pointing out that since her father would have suffered long years of agony at the knowledge of her treachery, why should she grieve that she has brought about a swifter end for him? He then tells her that far from loving her, he is incapable of love, that he is 'an agent of the Infernal' – a demon. By spoiling the union between North and South Wales he has assured continued conflict and misery, as was his sole purpose. And then, before Erilda's appalled eyes, Wertwold beings to change, to reveal his true inhuman form. He becomes a big, scaly monster! The demon stabs the princess through the heart with a trident, and then tosses her body contemptuously into the river. Its evil plan completed, the hideous creature then sinks below the surface of the water.

Ever after, claims the anonymous author of *Welsh Legends*, the spirit of the remorseful Erilda haunted Rhuddlan Castle, her terrified form seen running through the ruins, pursued by the phantom of the devilish Warrior Knight of the Blood Red Plume.[18]

Ruthin (Rhuthun)

One of the terrible Dogs of Darkness (see Cynwyd) was seen near the town by the grandmother of folklorist T Gwynn Jones. Jones writes: 'My grandmother declared that as she and my grandfather were riding on horseback from Ruthin one evening, in passing a roadside house, the nag suddenly shied and pressed to the hedge. At the moment a very tall mastiff was passing on the other side. My grandfather, who rode behind, saw nothing and his horse had not been startled. They had just come to live in the district and only got to know afterwards that the house had the reputation of being haunted.' Unfortunately Jones does not tell us the precise location of the haunted house.[19]

The better known ghost of Ruthin haunts the castle behind the attractive Victorian hotel of the same name. She is the Grey Lady, who is said to have killed a rival in love with an axe in the 15th century or thereabouts. Unfortunately, like other well-known ghost stories, this is another which seems to have only been recorded in recent times and its antiquity is therefore in doubt. A pile of stones hidden away in a corner of the battlements is pointed out as 'the Grey Lady's grave' and although this may be a fabrication of comparatively modern times, it does suggest the tale has some age to it.[20]

St Asaph (Llanelwy)

Of all the interesting documents to be preserved in the local archives, perhaps the most intriguing (for me) is a letter dated Christmas, 1812, and written by the farmer of Bodeugan, near St Asaph. The subject of the letter is innocuous enough; the tenant farmer, Robert Roberts, is apologising to his landlord for not being able to send him any geese that year. But it's the reason he gives that makes this such a rare and compelling document. For during December, 1812, Bodeugan Farm had been plagued by a poltergeist. I shall allow Mr Roberts to explain matters in his own words (although his punctuation is largely non-existent):

'On the 1st Day of December at night Something began to break the windows by throwing stones and coals and other materials and did so the night following ... the day after it began again in the day time especially in the dairy to throw down the pots containing churning milk and breaking them to pieces and great many other earthenware and throwing cans and other things at us, but that night it was so terrible that the women left the house and went to a neighbour's house ... it threw stones bricks and the

like that they had no quiet to milk by throwing dung upon them ... from noon a Thursday till Monday nothing was felt and it began on Monday the second time threw water and glasses at us that we were so wet as we had been in a river, and shifting many other things...'

For some reason the spook then left the house alone for ten days. But on Christmas Eve it returned, 'more dangerous' than before. It kicked and pinched the servants and threw their bedclothes on the floor, and then the servants along with them. Roberts said that it had 'done great deal of damage' and that his poor wife had become ill with the terror of it all. Although I have confidently asserted that it was 'a poltergeist' which caused all this upset, the idea of a ghost being responsible did not occur to Roberts himself. His belief was that 'some malicious person or persons had been with some of the conjurers', which proves that witchcraft was still being openly practised in North-East Wales at this time.

The landlord's response to this extraordinary letter was to ask two friends of his to investigate on his behalf. These were a Mr Hughes and a Mr Lloyd, the latter curate at Llandrillo. In the dairy they caught one of the servant girls throwing a potato and then a pepper-pot. The girl vehemently denied throwing either article, but the two men went away convinced she was the cause of the disturbances. However, Mr Roberts's father-in-law later wrote to say that he was certain of her innocence, and the two men did agree 'that the Ghost might have made use of her hands to throw things'. This is very interesting; not only does it show that the idea of a ghost had now entered the minds of the Bodeugan household, but Hughes and Lloyd had been perceptive enough to recognise a phenomenon that has been reported in recent poltergeist cases, that people involved in such hauntings often contribute without their conscious knowledge.

Unfortunately, there is no further correspondence in the archives, so we will never know whether this was a true haunting or just some elaborate prank. However, it remains one of the most important items in the records of haunted Wales, a rare, first-hand account of some considerable age.[21]

[1] Owen, 1896, p. 196.
[2] Ibid 195.
[3] *Bye-Gones*, January 16, 1929, p. 74.
[4] Owen, 1896, p. 199.
[5] *Bye-Gones*, August 1890, p. 439.
[6] Trevelyan, 1894, p. 96.
[7] Personal communication with author, 2002.
[8] Ibid, 1989.
[9] Mavor, 1973, pp. 208-210. Original source *The Flight of the Wild Goose* by Mary Gordon (Hogarth 1936).
[10] Hallam, 1977, pp. 107-8.
[11] Bradley, p. 127.
[12] *Bye-Gones*, May, 1877, p. 211.
[13] Ibid, December 1892, p. 463.
[14] Ibid, Jan 2, 1907, p.1.
[15] Trevelyan, 1894, p. 13.
[16] Owen, 1896, p. 198.
[17] Ibid, p. 300.
[18] Anon, 1802.
[19] Jones, T G, 1930, p. 46.
[20] Personal communication to author from Ruthin Castle, 1987.
[21] Clwyd County Council archives (Hawarden), item D/BC/911. Last seen 1988.

Conwy

Betws-y-Coed

The Swallow Falls has been a magnet for tourists since tourism was invented. The boiling waters of the plunging River Llugwy are certainly impressive, and it is no surprise to find they are inspirers of legend. Below the falls, whose proper Welsh name is Rhaeadr y Wenol, there is a deep pool where the waters swirl, surging together before continuing their inexorable push down the valley. This mini-maelstrom traps more than twigs and carelessly discarded cola cans in its vortex, for it is the prison, too, of an earthbound spirit, the soul of Sir John Wynne of Gwydir (see Llanrwst). It is claimed that Sir John, MP for Carnarvonshire in 1596, led such a cruel and oppressive regime against the people of his constituency that his soul was doomed to remain at the bottom of the pool until... well, Doomsday.

Elias Owen was 'grieved' to learn of this legend, for, after all, Wynne was a fellow writer, author of 'the interesting and valuable' *History of the Gwydir Family*. A later edition of this book defends its author with the words: 'Being shrewd and successful in his dealings, people were led to believe he oppressed them'. Owen quotes from Yorke's *Tribes of Wales*:

'It is the superstition ... to this day that the Spirit of the old gentleman lies under the great waterfall ... there to be punished, purged, spouted upon and purified from the foul deeds done in his days of nature.'[1]

Cerrigydrudion

A well-attested story from the 19th century concerns a Dr Davies, of Cerrigydrudion, who previously had always scoffed at tales of the supernatural. Dr Davies was woken up one bitter winter's night by someone under his bedroom window shouting up that he was needed at a farm called Craigeirchan. Now, this farm was three miles away and was only accessible by trudging up a long, muddy track. It was not a journey Dr Davies cared to make on such a nasty night, so he remained under the bedclothes, listening expectantly but hopeful that the person would go away. But again the voice called up and again it urged him to go to Craigeirchan. So Dr Davies dragged himself out of bed and opened his window. He looked down, shivering in the sudden blast of cold air, but he could not see anyone. Had he been dreaming? Shaking his head, he stumped back to bed – but again he heard the shout.

Fully awake now, Dr Davies hurried to the window and called down into the darkness that he was on his way. It took him a little while to dress himself and then saddle his horse, so he was not surprised when, on his journey to Craigeirchan farm, he didn't see anyone. The

44

voice had belonged to a young man, and Welsh farm lads are fleet of foot on their own terrain. Nor was he surprised to see, when Craigeirchan came into view, that the farmhouse was lit up, as this confirmed that there was some crisis and the family were up and about in consequence. The family, however, were very surprised to see *him*. The pregnant wife of the house had suddenly gone into labour a short while before, and the doctor's services were indeed urgently needed; in fact it transpired that he was instrumental in saving the lives of both mother and baby. *But no one had been sent from the farm to fetch him...*[2]

A much older story tells how Cerrigydrudion Church became possessed of an evil spirit. The fiend's hideous face could be seen grinning out of the windows, even in broad daylight, and the people became too frightened to walk past the church, let alone worship there. At length they consulted a Dyn Hysbys (Wise Man) as to how to remove their unwanted guest. He told them that the only things powerful and resilient enough to force the spirit out were the Ychen Bannog, a pair of gigantic long-horned oxen which lived wild on the slopes of Bron Bannog, a nearby mountain whose peak is crowned by an outcrop of rock resembling the horns of a bull.

The evil spirit was ejected from the church (presumably by prayer, although the legend does not say) and then attached, struggling violently, to a sledge chained to the oxen's yoke. Unfazed by their sulphurous new burden, the Ychen Bannog, goaded on by the villagers, began to make their stolid way towards a lake a few miles away. It was a long and tiresome journey. The fiend did all it could to prevent its departure and the oxen made slow progress, the sledge leaving great furrows in the soil. The final hurdle was a crag of rock overlooking the lake and here the Ychen Bannog's hooves dug so deeply into the rock that their impression could still be seen centuries later (this crag is near the farm which featured in our previous story). At last, they came to the edge of the lake, but because the spirit 'would not yield', everything – evil spirit, sledge and oxen – disappeared under the water, never to be seen again. The lake ever afterwards was called Llyn Dau Ychen (Lake of the Two Oxen).[3]

Conwy

Ty Mawr is a fascinating showplace, a rare example of a Tudor town-house with many original features. There is a persistent legend attached to Ty Mawr, claimed to date from the 16th century. However, this is another which close examination reveals might be a 'legend' of modern times.

The story has it that while the master of the house was away, his heavily pregnant wife missed her footing on a dark staircase and fell, dragging her first child, a toddler, with her. Mother and child, both mortally ill, were carried to the Lantern Room which overlooks the courtyard. In the meantime, a servant was sent to fetch the doctor. The usual physician being absent, however, he was obliged to find another, and this proved to be a young and inexperienced locum named Dr Dic. Dr Dic hurried to the house but after a swift examination, he declared that there was nothing he could do to save the unfortunate woman. In a fit of panic and dread, the elderly housekeeper in charge of Ty Mawr fled from the room, but locked it behind her, trapping Dr Dic inside. Presumably, she wanted to avoid the brunt of her master's wrath on his return by having the hapless young doctor explain the tragedy. What thoughts went through Dr Dic's mind as he watched his patients die can only be imagined. He must have been infected by something of the housekeeper's fear.

Sometime later, the master of the house came home and, on hearing of the accident, rushed to the Lantern Room. Here he found his wife and child lying cold and dead. Of Dr Dic, however, there was no sign. The door was still locked and the windows were fastened. Perhaps he had climbed up the chimney as the only means of escape – or he had died in the attempt. At any rate, he was never seen again. The ghost of the grieving husband and father is said to still be heard in the Lantern Room, his heavy tread echoing on the floorboards as he continues an endless search for the missing doctor whom he blamed for the tragedy.[4]

The origin of this dramatic tale is something of a mystery. Peter Underwood states that it was told to members of the British Medical Association by the first curator of the house, a Mr John Furness.[5] However, it is an odd fact that when Cheshire historian Fletcher Moss visited Ty Mawr in 1908, and was shown round the house by Mr Furness – who was an old friend of his – no mention was made of the ghost, even though Moss, while looking up the chimney to examine a secret passage, complained about the lack of records 'or even legends' regarding it. Did Mr Furness take the hint and later invent a legend?[6]

Llandudno

The woods around Gloddaeth Hall, now a teaching establishment, are all that remain of a primeval forest which once spread over much of what is now Conwy. One night a man from Rhyl, Thomas Davies, entered these woods intent on capturing some foxes whose den he had found earlier that day. Farmers considered foxes vermin and paid good money to anyone who reduced their population. For this reason Davies climbed an oak tree overlooking the den and settled down in its branches to wait for the chance to trap them. But in the event, it was Davies who was trapped – by a malevolent, unearthly being! Davies told his frightening tale to the Rev Owen Jones, vicar of Pentrefoelas, who then passed it on to his friend and fellow clergyman, the folklorist Elias Owen. The following is from Elias Owen's account:

'Davies had taken his seat on a bough opposite the fox's den, when he heard a horrible scream in the direction of the sea, which apparently was that of a man in distress, and the sound uttered was "Oh, Oh". But, as the sound was a far way off, he felt disinclined to heed it, for he did not think it incumbent on him to ascertain the cause of the distressing utterance. He therefore did not leave his seat on the tree. But the cry of anguish, every now and again, reached his ears, and evidently, it was approaching the tree on which Davies sat. Nearer and nearer came the dismal "Oh! Oh!" and with its approach, the night became pitch dark, and now the "Oh! Oh! Oh!" was only a few yards off, but nothing could be seen in consequence of the deep darkness.

'The sounds, however, ceased, but a horrible sight was presented to the frightened man's view. There he saw before him a nude being with eyes burning like fire, and these glittering balls were directed towards him. The awful being was only a dozen or so yards off. And now it crouched, and now it stood erect, but never for a single instant withdrew its terrible eyes from the miserable man in the tree, who would have fallen to the ground were it not for the protecting boughs.'

Davies froze with fear. He had his gun, but could not rouse himself to use it. It was as if he was hypnotised by the thing's glowing eyes. He would shut his own eyes, trying to block out the dreadful sight, but, as if compelled, the lids would drag apart and those 'burning orbs' would fix on him again. The unfortunate man passed the whole night in a state of extreme tension, wondering when the creature would finally spring upon him, as it so often threatened to do. At about 4 o'clock in the morning, he heard a cock crow from a nearby farm, heralding the coming dawn. This time when Davies opened his eyes, he saw that the entity had vanished. His ordeal was over.[7]

Llanfairfechan

The hills above Llanfairfechan are littered with prehistoric monuments, such as cairns, hut circles and standing stones. One tumbled down old cairn bore the name Carnedd-ddew, which translates as the 'Cairn of the Idol'. This name apparently predates the following story, which just shows how accurate these old Welsh names can be.

In the 1720s one Paul Parry, of Rhiwla, Llanfairfechan, was working near the Carnedd-ddew when he picked up – an idol! There is no description of it unfortunately, but that it was prehistoric seems more than likely. Archaeology was probably not Parry's strong suit, but what did attract him was that the idol appeared to be made out of gold – and he wasted no time in getting it home. Ancient sites do not enjoy being disturbed, however, and as soon as the mysterious object was under Parry's roof, his house 'was immediately haunted'. To end the disturbances, Parry threw the relic away, but where to is not recorded (and it would be very interesting to know).

This story was taken down in 1864, the informant being Paul Parry's grandson. This Mr Parry was convinced of the truth of his grandfather's finding the idol but doubted very much whether the ghost was real. He supposes that the spook was 'a shrewd neighbour, who made a more profitable bargain of the idol than his grandfather did'.[8]

Llangernyw

The pretty little church of Llangernyw stands on very ancient ground indeed. Beside it are two Bronze Age standing stones, ornamented by early Christian crosses, scratched there at some later – though still antiquated – date. Elsewhere in the churchyard is a venerable yew tree which botanists claim to be the oldest living thing in Wales, believed to have been already standing when the prehistoric inhabitants erected their sacred stones.

Perhaps the antiquity of the site explains the

existence of a mysterious spirit, called Angelystor, which visited the church every Hallowe'en. On this Night of the Dead, the voice of Angelystor could be heard from the direction of the altar intoning the names of all those of the parish who were doomed to die during the coming year. The curious would settle themselves under the east window at midnight to satisfy themselves that they were not among those listed.

One fateful Hallowe'en night a tailor, who fancied himself as a bit of a wit, drunkenly announced that he was going to prove that Angelystor was a myth. Ignoring the warnings of his friends, the tailor, whose name was Sion Robert, left the pub and weaved his inebriated way to the church. Smirking, he leant his ear to the east window and promptly heard a grim and sonorous voice announce: 'Sion ap Robert!' Sion's heart was clutched with fear and he blurted out, 'Hold! Hold! I am not quite ready.' But, ready or not, Sion Robert died that year.[9]

Llangwm

Ystrad Fawr farm was once haunted by a shape-shifting entity, which was capable of appearing in many strange and startling guises. It was described in an essay on the folklore of North West Wales by D Thomas, of Llanfachraeth, the relevant passage later translated into English by Elias Owen:

'There was a ghost at Ystrad Fawr, near Llangwm, that was in the habit of appearing like a turkey with his tail spread out like a spinning wheel. At other times he appeared in the wood, when the trees would seem as if they were on fire, again he would assume the shape of a large dog gnawing a bone.'

The latter two appearances tally with the descriptions of certain apparitions encountered in South Wales (see Risca, Caerphilly, for example). Perhaps Ysbryd Ystrad Fawr was also responsible for the weird experience had by a man who one night saw an old lady in traditional Welsh costume sitting on a heap of stones near Llangwm. He bid her good night but she made him no answer. Instead she rose to her feet and began to walk away down the road, but as she did so, she swelled up like a balloon, growing bigger and bigger with every step until she completely filled the road!

This expansive lady was seen near the hamlet of Tynant, on an old stone bridge called Pont Glyn-diffwys. Glyn-diffwys is a dramatic gorge through which the River Alwen bubbles and foams. The modern A5 passes close by, but this formerly celebrated beauty spot is now all but forgotten. Once upon a time, long before the A5 existed, this gorge formed part of the route travellers took when making their way from North West Wales into England (and back again, of course). Unfortunately, its secluded position combined with its steep, enclosed sides shrouded in thick vegetation made Glyn-diffwys an ideal place for bandits to make ambush on the unwary. Many a solitary traveller met his end here and it was once said that at night the gorge was literally crowded with the ghosts of murdered men.[10]

Llanrwst

A scholarly article discussing family history in an old edition of *Archaeologia Cambrensis* makes unexpected mention of a ghost. Unfortunately, it is little more than a mention. The scene is ancient Maenan Hall, two miles north of Llanrwst, which for generations was the seat of the Kyffin family. The hall is haunted by Sir Thomas Kyffin, 'whose rest is said to have been broken by his having, in a fit of rage, caused the death of a boy. He was a learned man and a lawyer of considerable eminence, but having one of the usual characteristics of the British race, a hot and violent temper.'[11]

Almost as brief is the mention made by Elias Owen, in his *Welsh Folk-Lore*, of a layer of ghosts, a man named Gruffydd Jones, of Cilhaul. This worthy trapped the spirit of one Abel Jones, of Henblas, in a bottle, which he then buried in a 'gors' near Llanrwst. Owen continues:

'This Gruffydd Jones had great trouble at Hafod Ucha between Llanrwst and Conway, to lay a Spirit. He began in the afternoon, and worked hard the whole night and the next day to lay the Spirit, but he succeeded in overcoming a part only of the Spirit. He was nearly dead from exhaustion and want of food before he could even master a portion of the Spirit. This preceding is a singular tale, for it teaches that Spirits are divisible. A portion of this Spirit, repute says, is still at large, whilst a part is undergoing purification.'[12]

Between Llanrwst and Llangernyw there is a small lake called Chwythlyn. Once upon a time, two young lovers who were returning one night from a fair lost their way in the mist, so decided to bed down beside the lake and wait for morning. Their sleep was disturbed, however, 'by a great noise, as of men fighting, shouting and groaning, which continued till daylight'. They could not see anything to account for the gruesome sounds. The weird experience had tragic consequences for the young couple, for after it they began to suffer from increasing ill health, and both died within a year.[13]

Llansannan

'The unusual configuration of the Llansannan neighbourhood tends to the creation of and transmission of folk tales and ghost stories, and especially so as the district is seldom visited by the ordinary traveller.'

So wrote W Bezant Lowe in 1915. I am not sure what he means by 'unusual configuration', unless it is the steep, secluded river valleys which cut through the otherwise relentless moorland.

Bezant Lowe refers to 'the Ghost of Dyffryn Aled' that appeared, like the Ghost of Ystrad Fawr above, 'in all shapes and forms'. This tendency to place a number of apparitions under the auspices of one ghost is interesting, for modern writers, including myself, would be inclined to list them separately. Indeed, since they appeared in different places as well as different guises, I shall do so.

The first ghost was of a 'tall, smart young lady' who used to appear during the hour after midnight at some saw mills near the Plas of Dyffryn Aled. She would walk silently alongside any solitary traveller making their way past the mills, disappearing as abruptly as she appeared. She would never show herself if there was more than one person present.

A phantom coach-and-four would appear at midnight outside Plas Newydd and would then take the lanes 'at full speed' past the saw mills, Dol Las and Berllan until it reached Dyffryn Aled. It was an impressive sight – 'lamps were lit, and ... a driver in full livery sat on the box, and on the back seat the guard, blowing his horn'. A doctor who, in the 1890s, used to care for the family at Dyffryn Aled, said that he had seen this coach parked outside the hall on several occasions.

The grimmest ghost of all used to appear in the house itself. It manifested as a corpse in a coffin, supposedly that of a former squire, Pierce Wynn Yorke. The ghost of a corpse strikes me as very unusual and possibly unique.[14]

A strange and dramatic spectre was often seen in the vicinity of Pribwll. It appeared as a wheel of fire, which rolled 'with great force' down a steep slope. Bezant Lowe explains its origin in this way:

'About a hundred years ago [ie circa 1815], there lived at Pribwll farm a man named Thomas; he was a cattle-dealer, and used to go to England to sell his cattle, and, as he was coming back one time with a large sum of money in his pocket, he suddenly disappeared. He was seen riding through the village on a white pony, and soon afterwards, the white pony was seen grazing in the fields of Pen Cefn Aled, but riderless. Thomas's relatives concluded that the man had been killed for the sake of the money he had in his pocket, and that he had been buried in the bottom of the valley, where the wheel of fire stopped.'

In Pribwll house itself there were supposedly to be found indelible bloodstains, but Mr Lowe dismisses these as simply due to the geology of the stone on which they could be seen.[15]

Pentrefoelas

After the squire of the estate of Foelas died, two workmen decided to take advantage of his absence to scrump some apples from his orchard. They shinned up a likely looking tree, gathered up some fruit and then turned to climb down again. Their hearts froze when they saw below them the familiar three-cornered shape of the deceased squire's hat – and beneath that the deceased squire himself! Even death had not prevented the late Squire of Foelas from keeping a watchful eye over his property. The apple thieves leapt down and ran as fast as they could out of the orchard, leaving the squire's ghost nonchalantly leaning up against the tree.

As soon as they had quit the orchard, the two men ran without stopping to nearby Bryn Coch, but were appalled to see that the ghost had preceded them – there was the squire in the lane, leaning on his stick and quietly regarding them. The two frightened men again took to their heels and safely made it home, but neither dared steal anything from the orchard again.[16]

Between Pentrefoelas and Cerrigydrudion, near Cernioge Mawr farm, an unusual ghost used to be seen. This was a black sow, which would emerge from a ruin and then follow people down the road. People who didn't enjoy being pursued by a phantom pig might lash out at it with their stick, but the stick would pass right through, and the *bwbach* would come on, undeterred.[17]

1. Owen, 1896, p. 211, possibly from Thomas, 1870, p. 107.
2. Ibid, p. 294.
3. Ibid, p. 132.
4. Brooks, 1987, p. 130.
5. Underwood, 1978, p. 58.
6. Moss, 1908, p. 184.
7. Owen, 1896, p. 193.
8. Owen, Edward, 1864, p. 318.
9. Owen, 1896, p. 170.
10. Ibid p. 197, quoting Thomas, 1870, p. 106.
11. Vaughan, 1885, p. 111.
12. Owen, 1896, p. 211, probably from Thomas, 1870, p. 107.
13. Jones, T G, 1930, p. 106.
14. Bezant Lowe, 1915, p. 114.
15. Ibid, p. 115.
16. Owen, 1896, p. 200.
17. Jones, T G, 1930, p. 47.

Anglesey

Beaumaris (Biwmaris)

The venerable Beaumaris Grammar School was popularly believed to be haunted by its founder, Mr David Hughes. A young girl called Enid Madoc-Jones saw his ghost while sleeping in a bedroom on the top floor of the School House. It was early one morning and she suddenly woke up to see 'a ghostly figure' standing by her bed. She did the obvious thing and immediately hid her head under the bedclothes. When she had plucked up enough courage to take a peek, she saw the apparition moving away. Some time after this, she heard that a girl who had slept in the room next to hers had once 'experienced the eerie feeling of ghostly hands pressing on her'.

Many years later, when she was a teacher herself, Enid met an 'old boy' named Gwyn Pritchard, who brought up the subject of David Hughes's ghost himself. He said he and some school-fellows had seen it one evening when they were standing in the doorway of the Big School, next to the main entrance. He said they saw 'a queer apparition coming towards them', at the sight of which they immediately scarpered! As they ran, they caught a glimpse of the ghost vanishing through the wall into the boarders' dining room.[1]

Henllys Hall, now a hotel not far from Beaumaris, was once haunted by a White Lady who disappeared once she had disclosed the site of some hidden treasure. She may have been the same apparition which haunted the countryside roundabout and was known by the name of the White Lady of the Gate.[2]

A man named Roberts found himself the centre of an extraordinary incident when he was a young draper's assistant in Beaumaris in the 1840s. Roberts's lodgings were some way from the shop, but his strict master only allowed him half an hour for lunch; it didn't matter what time he left, he had to be back at work no later than half past twelve.

'One day he was late and while hastily swallowing his meal ... he looked up and saw the clock pointed to *half past* twelve! He was thunderstruck, and with the fear of his master before him, all but lost consciousness, and was indeed in a dazed state for some minutes, as was noticed by those at the table. Shaking this off by an effort he again looked at the clock, and to his relief and astonishment saw that the hands only pointed to a *quarter past* twelve! Then he finished his dinner, and returned to the shop at the appointed time.

'There he was told that at a *quarter past* twelve he had returned to the shop – had put up his hat, moved about in an absent manner, had been scolded; and had thereupon put on his hat again and walked out! Several persons corroborated this story; whilst on the other hand his aunt [who had been seated at the table with him during lunch] was positive that although, at that moment, he had fallen into a strange fit of abstraction, he had never left the table.'[3]

Apparitions of people still living do not appear to have been that uncommon. In Wales they were sometimes referred to as a *Lledrith* and many writers suggest that they were omens of death, but this is not borne out by the actual accounts.

Brynteg

A few miles from Brynteg, along the road to Maenaddwyn, there is a strange boulder with a round depression, or 'scoop' taken out of it. The stone is called the Cadair-y-bwgan, or 'Haunted Chair'. W Pritchard, who wrote an article on folklore for the Anglesey Antiquarian Society in 1914, describes the *bwgan* as 'a terrible phantom' which 'used to visit the farm houses of the neighbourhood, always with some malevolent purpose, such as befouling the dairies, causing the cows to with-hold their milk, overturning the milk pails, and even bringing the animals under baleful influences. After becoming tired of tormenting the farmers and others, he would retire to his chair on the roadside to the great terror of the passers by.'[4]

Native of Anglesey, broadcaster Gwyn Llewellyn, was able to pinpoint the location of the stone for me (W Pritchard had been very vague) and informed me that in his young days the stone was known by the variant name Cadair Wgan. He said that it sits on an earthen bank bordering the road and that it is still there now, although entirely overgrown. He saw it many times in his youth and his father, when a boy himself, had an eerie experience while passing by it. Mr Llewellyn senior had been walking his bicycle up the hill, which is very steep here, when 'something like a tornado' rushed out from the direction of the Cadair Wgan and under the wheels of the bike. It was all the boy could do to stop it being toppled over. Although he didn't see anything supernatural, and heard only a rushing noise, he was convinced it was a manifestation of the *bwgan* itself and in later years enjoyed telling the story to his son whenever they had occasion to pass the mysterious rock.[5]

Holyhead (Caergybi)

On the shore north of the fort is the Cei, a landing place first used by the Romans. Near here, on the Longford Road, was an inn called the Plas Newydd, which was better known in the 19th century as 'the English House'. It earned this nickname because it stood on the route used by the carriages from England and English people tended to put up here before embarking for Ireland. For many years, it had a resident poltergeist.[6] Outside the town, a farm called Cerrig Llech was also known to be haunted.[7]

Llanallgo

Bwgan y Parciau (the Parciau Ghost) used to haunt the neighbourhood of Llanallgo. According to W Pritchard, in his article on folklore for the Anglesey Antiquarian Society, this was believed to be the spirit of a 17th century gentleman named Sir John Bodvel.[8] Pritchard offers no further information in his article but a letter in response to my *Wales of the Unexpected* column in the *North Wales Daily Post* helped shed further light on him.

An 84-year-old reader, Mrs Griffith, repeated to me a very old family ghost story. It had been told to Mrs Griffith by her grandmother, who had heard it from her own mother, who in turn had heard it from *her grandmother* – and it was this lady who had seen the ghost. The incident happened when she was a little girl, living at Marian Glas, near Llanallgo.

Mrs Griffith writes that the girl 'was standing in the doorway with her mother and a visitor who was about to leave, when her mother said to the visitor: "I wouldn't go just yet". Just then, "The Marian", as it was called, lit up and a white horse and rider appeared – and the rider had cloven hoofs.'

Mrs Griffith recalls that the spook was known by the name of 'John Bodvol' (as she spells it) and that her ancestor's sighting was certainly not the only one. She adds: 'A midwife was walking along a country lane, having attended a mother-to-be, when she heard the clatter of hoofs coming beside her. It stopped beside her, and the rider asked if she wanted a lift. She noticed his cloven hoofs and refused.'[9]

After I'd printed Mrs Griffith's letter in my column, I received a helpful e-mail from writer Dafydd Meirion, who was researching a book on Welsh pirates. He told me the ghost was that of John Wyn ap Hugh, of Bodvel, near Pwllheli. A notorious pirate himself, he turned Ynys Enlli (Bardsey Island), which he owned, into 'a pirate haven'.

Mr Meirion's e-mail added that John Bodvel was believed to have buried treasure at Marian Glas. It might be the existence of this treasure which has bound Bodvel's spirit to the earth, or perhaps his haunting is the result simply of his wickedness in life, like that of David Salisbury at Llanrhaeadr in Denbighshire.[10]

The roaming spirit of a pirate may not be the only weird inhabitant of Llanallgo. In his article, W Pritchard states that the area around the village was also well known for 'strange howlings in the air'. He adds: 'To all appearance, they moved from place to place in the neighbourhood with great rapidity; as if there were two or three or more responding to each other.' [11]

Llanddeusant

A farmhouse called Clwchdyrnog was haunted by a troublesome spirit which no one dared approach. During the night it would make a terrible racket, banging doors, overturning the furniture, smashing crockery and ripping material – but the next morning all would be found in its proper place and undamaged. A servant named Modryb (Aunt) Sian, from Llanerchymedd, heard the ghost in her room soon after arriving at Clwchdyrnog. It made a noise like 'the rending of a garment'. Refusing to be frightened, Sian cried out into the darkness: 'Rend a yard for me!' The *bwgan* heard her and in response 'a great noise of rending was heard above, around, and everywhere, and lasted for the greater part of the night.' Sian regretted teasing the ghost and regretted going to work at Clwchdyrnog at all. She handed in her notice the next day and returned at once to Llanerchymedd. [12]

Elias Owen records how the raucous hauntings finally came to an end. One night the *bwgan* began to create its usual din in a room where a widower named Hughes was courting one of the farm's servants. Hughes was greatly frightened but summoned up the courage to ask the spirit why it was troubling the house. After a series of questions and answers, the *bwgan* at last informed Hughes and his girl: 'There are treasures hidden on the south side of Ffynnon Wen, which belong to, and are to be given to, the nine months old child in this house: when this is done, I will never disturb this house anymore.'

The next day, having been given detailed instructions as to where to dig for the treasure, Hughes took a spade to the spot near the spring indicated, and soon he had uncovered a chest crammed with gold and silver and other valuables. These he handed over to the child's parents, who placed them in trust until he came of age. This satisfied the noisy spirit and it was never heard from again. [13]

Llanddyfnan

The lord of Plas Llanddyfnan during the Civil War was a Mr Griffiths and he had an illegitimate son who 'made himself rather prominent as a loyalist'. When the Parliamentarian forces began to cut a swathe through the island, this younger Griffiths thought it wise to avoid them. Unfortunately, a little way from Llanddyfnan, he was overtaken as he tried to make his escape and there 'cruelly murdered'. Murdered souls do not rest easy, certainly not in the minds of superstitious countryfolk in the 17th century, and it was not long before the lane where Griffiths met his end earned a haunted reputation, and it became known by the name of Lon y Bwbach, or 'Lane of the Spook'. [14]

Although it is natural to suppose the lane was haunted by the murdered man, another suggestion has it that the hauntings were carried out by the spirits of the murderers 'doing penance'. [15]

A correspondent of J Y W Lloyd, author of *History of Powys Fadog* and a bit of a fan of ghost stories, informed him that the ghost of the lane had nothing to do with the cruel murder of young Griffiths. She said that it was the shade of a Lady Gwenllian. She went on to explain that the nature of the hauntings was both unusual and specific. Lon y Bwbach had a weird effect on animals; horses would suddenly become distressed and would fall down in the lane in a fit. Human eyes were never able to see whatever it was the horses saw, however. [16]

The OS map still names this track 'Lon y Bwbach' and an eerie spot it is, too. In truth I visited it on a very gloomy day in which a grey pall with constant rain had fallen on Anglesey, so I did not find it hard to imagine it the haunt of ghosts. I walked about half its length; gnarly thorn bushes and sticky mud, as well as the drizzle, soon defeated my enthusiasm but this was enough to see that in its day it must have been a well-used route. Mature trees and the remains of a stone wall line its length. Lon y Bwbach reminded me very much of Washington Irving's Sleepy Hollow.

J Y W Lloyd's lady correspondent also informed him about a haunted house named 'Plas Tref...n' on Anglesey. I have not yet identified Plas Tref...n, so include it here. The ghost of the house was that of 'a naval officer of high rank', an ancestor of the family then living at the Plas (ie in 1881). One night a 'Mildred T' (all the names have been disguised, unfortunately) woke in the haunted room to see 'an old man at the foot of her bed, leaning with both hands on a twisted stick'. She closed her eyes, offered up a prayer, and when she looked again, saw the ghost pass through a door without opening it. The next morning she told her hosts what she had seen – and when she was shown a portrait of the naval officer she was so struck by its resemblance to the ghost that she nearly fainted away with the shock.

Plas Tref...n was also possessed of another phenomenon. This was described as 'a glorious effulgence of brilliant light' which on occasions was known to illuminate the biggest bedroom in the house. Anyone who saw it was struck with an almost religious awe by the experience.[17]

Llaneilian

The Rev Mr Hughes, a popular clergyman of the 18th century, was riding from Amlwch to Llaneilian one evening when he came upon 'an artificial circle upon the ground'. Maybe this was some sort of stone circle, or perhaps a fairy ring, no one can now be sure, but whatever it was – it was haunted. Poor Mr Hughes was attacked by what appeared to be a large grey-hound. The unearthly creature jumped up and knocked him from his horse. Somehow he managed to get away and continue on his journey, but when he passed that way again the following night, the same thing happened.

Not one to be afraid of ghosts, even ones in the shape of big dogs, Mr Thomas approached the circle on a third occasion, but this time on foot. Sure enough, there in the circle's centre he could see the spectral greyhound, but this time he noticed that it was chained. Careful to keep beyond its reach, Mr Thomas cautiously approached the spirit and asked it: 'Why troublest thou those that pass by?' Its reply was that when alive (and a man, not a greyhound) it had hidden some money under a stone and now it could not rest. This is not an uncommon cause of restlessness among the dead, but the amount of money concerned was extraordinarily small – one groat, or fourpence! However, the coin was intended as a gift to St Eilian's Church and he had pretended at the time that he had lost it, to avoid paying. Understanding the spirit's trouble, Mr Hughes now willingly agreed to retrieve the groat and hand it over to the church. Once he had done so, the chained spirit was set free.[18]

Llangristiolus

A miserable miser of Llangristiolus used to think of nothing but money. One night he was awoken by a stranger, who told him he knew where he could get his hands on a hidden store of cash. He said it was under a stone in a field near Trefeilir, but he had little time to spare, so if he wanted it he had better come at once. The miser hurried into his clothes and followed the suspiciously generous stranger all the way to Trefeilir – once there, however, the moon shone on his new friend and he saw 'that he was no man at all but some other kind of being'. Not only that, but there was a suggestion of 'sulphur fumes' about the stranger, which convinced the miser that he 'had some connection with the lower regions'! The miser ran back home as fast as his legs could carry him and we may hope that after his devilish adventure, he began to mend his ways.[19]

[1] Madoc-Jones, 1971, p. 137.

[2] Pritchard, 1914, p. 41.

[3] Owen, 1896, p. 293, quoting from *Fortnightly Review* 1883. The same summary, quoting the same source, appears in *Bye-Gones*, April 1883.

[4] Pritchard, 1914, p. 40.

[5] Personal communication with the author from Gwyn Llewellyn. My thanks to Michael Bayley Hughes for alerting me to the 'Lon Cadair Bwgan' and for putting me in touch with Mr Llewellyn.

[6] Williams, Lucy, 1950, p. 62.

[7] Ibid, p. 54.

[8] Pritchard, 1914, p. 43

[9] Personal communication with author, November 2004

[10] Personal communication with author, November 2004

[11] Pritchard, 1914, p. 43

[12] Ibid.

[13] Owen, 1896, p. 202.

[14] O J, 1850, p. 146. Also OS map Explorer 263.

[15] Lloyd, 1887, p. 212.

[16] Lloyd, 1881, p. 243. Lloyd forgot about the ghost of Lady Gwenllian when he made the suggestion regarding the spirits of the murderers six years later (note 11).

[17] Lloyd, 1881, pp. 243-4.

[18] Jones, Edmund, 1780, p. 44. See also Sikes, 1880, p. 168.

[19] Pritchard, 1914, p. 41.

Bangor

The thousands of people who flock to the Faenol estate to enjoy the music festivals held there may be in danger of encountering a very weird ghost. It sits in the branches of trees 'in the shape of a large bird' and screeches at passers-by. In a shrill voice it utters the following cry:

> 'Gwae! gwae! imi erioed
> Ro'i bwyall mewn troed
> I dori coed y Faenol!'

In English this translates as:

> 'Woe! woe's me that I ever put
> A handle to my axe
> To fell the trees of Faenol!'

The tradition was that this is the spirit of a man who was executed for unlawfully cutting down trees on the estate.[1]

Barmouth (Abermaw)

In the June 1892, edition of *Folk-lore* there appeared the following fascinating account of a poltergeist. It is especially interesting because it indicates a way in which it might be possible to rid the house of such an unwelcome guest.

'About 1842, the house of a relation of mine at Barmouth was haunted by noises, as if all the crockery in the cupboards and on the shelves were breaking, and other noises in different places which could not be accounted for. This went on for many weeks. A well-known con-jurer and exorcist was sent for, but he failed to put a stop to the disturbance, which got so bad at last that all the family – parents, children and maids – left the house one night for refuge at the house of a relation who lived near. But as soon as they arrived there similar noises commenced in the corner cupboard of that house.

'Then, from mere bravado, the children said they would make as much noise as the spirit, so they got sticks and hammered the floors and doors and tables and tin kettles &c until the spirit-noise in the corner cupboard ceased, and for some time after. I was often told by them they made a regular Bedlam, merely from bra-vado, to drown the noises of the spirit. The spirit, or whatever it was, never disturbed them after that night; they returned to their own house next morning, and never heard a repeti-tion of the noises.'[2]

It is interesting that it is a common supersti-tion worldwide that the creating of loud noises drives away evil spirits. In Tibet, for example, an annual ceremony involves the monks and villagers crashing huge cymbals to keep the community safe from the attentions of demons.

Beddgelert

Lady Prendergrast was Maid of Honour to Caroline, Queen of George II, and at one time was the richest heiress of her day. But she 'squandered and gambled all her possessions away' and it is said that she died a beggar in a poor-house in Shropshire. She was a wild woman and such a wild spirit was unlikely to rest peaceful in its grave. She took to haunting a place called Gwernydd in Beddgelert parish. Sometimes she appeared riding a horse and sometimes she was seen rattling about in her carriage. Morus Roberts, the farmer of Croesor Bach, had a terrifying and very physical en-counter with Lady Prendergrast when he was returning home from Penmorfa late one night.

'When he got near Gwernydd it suddenly became so dark that that he could not see his hand ... all at once a lady came up, galloping on horseback, and taking hold of him by the collar carried him on her steed away through the air. He knew nothing more until in the morning he awoke to find himself safe at home, but in a very weak state, and there was such a peculiar smell on his clothes that his wife had to boil them in a strong solution of soda, and then put them on a blackthorn hedge, where they had to be left for a long time.'[3]

The terrible pong was probably that of sul-phur, also called brimstone, the same substance smelt by the miser of Llangristiolus, Anglesey. The same stench is recorded after encounters with ghosts at Rhiw (see below) and Llanwddyn, Powys. There is something devilish about the smell of brimstone!

The most famous story of Beddgelert is that of Gelert, the hound who rescues a baby from a hungry wolf, only to be blamed for devouring it himself. The 'legend' is believed by some to have been invented in the 18th century by David Pritchard, the owner of the Goat Hotel, as a way of bringing in tourists. If so, it worked! Pritchard was certainly an intelligent and capa-ble man. He expanded the hotel and turned the stony and marshy land around it into a very profitable farm. By the time of his death, he had achieved considerable wealth. Whether or not he was the creator of the Gelert legend, it is amusing to learn that he himself became part of the local folklore – soon after his death, he became a ghost!

His apparition was seen coming out of the bar, pottering about the stables, idling in his fields 'with his hands in his trouser-pockets', and even strutting about the roads and lanes at night. One evening Hwlyn, an aged labourer on the farm, saw his former master outside the cow-shed. The apparition wandered off in the direction of the church and old Hwlyn followed it. He caught up with the ghost in the church porch, where he found it leaning against the door.

'Well master,' asked Hwlyn, 'what has induced you to wander about in this fashion?'

Replied the ghost: 'Hwlyn, I'm glad to see thee, because my bones could not rest in their grave. Go and tell Alice tomorrow to raise up the hearthstone of the bar-room, and she will find there a hundred guineas, two of which she must give thee.'

Hwlyn took the message to Pritchard's widow and the guineas were soon found. Two, of course, went to the loyal old labourer who had the courage to talk to the ghost.[4]

We have two men to thank for most of the ghost stories from Beddgelert. Local legends were collected by William Jones, who contributed to the Welsh language periodical *Y Brython*. Jones's Beddgelert stories were translated, and added to, by D E Jenkins, who then wrote a book called *Beddgelert: Its Facts, Fairies and Folk-lore*, which he published in 1899. Among the stories which appear in the book is the account of a phantom carriage which later turned out to be the exact replica of one which brought a fatally ill man to the Bettws Hotel and various weird encounters in the Aberglaslyn Pass. In the Pass – one of the most celebrated beauty spots in Snowdonia – night-bound travellers reported being frightened by a phantom horseman, 'a figure of fire', and a Dog of Darkness 'the size of a year-old calf'. The Pass was also well known as the haunt of a White Lady who had died in an accident here and always appeared to warn others of impending disasters. In the 19th century a white rock was pointed out to tourists as 'the White Lady' and, at a distance, it apparently looked quite spooky.[5]

A mile or two north of Beddgelert there is a place called variously Llam Trwsgl, the 'Clumsy Leap', or Llam Trosgol, 'Leap over the Colwyn' (the modern map erroneously names it Llan Trwsgl). Here the River Colwyn passes through a narrow cleft in the rock, three or four feet wide, before plunging into a deep, dark pool. Jenkins reproduces a picture of Llam Trwsgl in his book on Beddgelert. In his day its banks were bare of all but heather and its narrowness encouraged people (youths mainly) to jump over the river. But it was a dangerous place to lose one's footing, because if you fell into it, its slippery sides made it almost impossible to get back out again. Today the banks of Llam Trwsgl are overgrown with small trees and other foliage and no one would be able to jump across it, even if they were foolhardy enough to try. Although the local Water Authority have now built a little station here and created a small weir, the deep, silent green pool still possesses an eerie atmosphere and when I visited it in the spring of 2004, I had no trouble imagining it to be haunted. Here is the story of Llam Trwsgwl:

A young man from Pennant who had enjoyed a long engagement with a girl from the Colwyn valley met another girl in his own neighbourhood, one who proved so fascinating that he decided to break it all off with his first love. However, he was afraid to do so, not only because it would bring shame on his own family but because he feared real, physical retribution from *her* family. His solution to his difficulty was a cruel and cowardly one. On the afternoon before the wedding day, he went round to his fiancée's house, all smiles and bearing presents, and then asked his excited bride-to-be to accompany him on a walk. They walked to Llam Trwsgl. At the jumping place, the youth reached out for the girl's hands as if to make the leap together. She smilingly obliged – but then he pushed her headlong into the foaming waters of the pool! The river was in flood and the poor girl didn't have a chance. Her murderer didn't even have the courage to wait and see if his cruel deed was successful, instead he ran away.

Not surprisingly, the pool in the River Colwyn afterwards became haunted by the spirit of his victim. Some people passing this way by night saw 'a beautiful young woman rising out of the pool half naked, her dripping hair hanging down her white shoulders', others saw 'a stately maid walking about ... clad in rustling silk'. On other occasions a ball or wheel of fire was seen flaming down the river. Most often, however, nothing was seen but the lonely spot shrilled with the heartrending cries of the murdered girl. For this reason, the pool became known as the Llyn-Nad-y-Forwyn, which Jenkins translates as 'Pool of the Shrill Cries of the Maiden'.

Despite its apparent isolation, the way past the pool would frequently be used by farmers returning from Caernarfon market. If they had to pass that way at night, they would wait in the tavern at Bettws Garmon to make sure they had company! Fortunately, 'a stout-hearted old Christian from Nanmor' had the courage to speak to the spirit on one of her rare appearances by the pool. She was then able to tell her tragic story, and was able to go to her rest. The haunting was over. Whether her murderer was still alive and therefore punished as a result of the ghost's evidence, is not recorded.[6]

(T Gwynn Jones, in his *Welsh Folklore and Folk Custom,* published in 1930, uses a source which places Llyn-Nad-y-Forwyn on the Lleyn.[7] Elias Owen in his *Welsh Folk-Lore* of 1896, vaguely refers to it as being somewhere in 'old Carnarvonshire' but confirms that the River Colwyn flows through it. However, he describes it as a lake.[8] The translation of Llyn as a pool in a river rather than as a lake is not unheard of – see, for example, Llanfor, below – and the precise local knowledge offered in Jenkins's *Beddgelert,* published in 1899, convinces me that the location he gives is the right one.)

Hafod Lwyfog is an ancient mansion standing near the head of the spectacular Gwynant valley. For some time in the early years of the 19th century it was possessed of a poltergeist which wreaked havoc among the family of Sion Roland. Initially, it made its presence known in the usual way, by making an appalling and mysterious din about the place – 'one night it seemed as if the ghost were throwing the milk pans about the floor; another night it seemed to be enjoying a clog-dance to the sound of some harp strings'. It had a habit of lifting up the servants' beds and letting them down with a loud bang. It performed the same unkind trick on an itinerant tailor and his apprentice who were staying the night. It got under the bed, lifted it up, dropped it again and then pulled the quilt off. The tailor tried to hang onto it, but to no avail. The same thing happened with the blanket, and then the mattress, so that the two men were thrown into the middle of the floor.

Naturally, this sort of behaviour made every-one very tired and irritable. One servant man, trying to get some much delayed sleep, heard the ghost enter the room and he shouted at it: 'Let me see thy face, thou old coward!' In retaliation, something invisible squeezed the man's leg so hard that he started shouting for quite another reason; after this treatment the man was unable to move for a whole fortnight. At length, a Pwllheli man came to Hafod Lwyfog and proved able to defeat the poltergeist. He banished it to the bottom of Llyn Gwynen (today called Llyn Gwynant).[9]

One cannot help wondering whether, instead of being laid to rest, these poltergeists don't just find themselves alternative accommodation. The noisy *bwgan* of Hafod Lwyfog is very similar to that which haunted nearby Plas Gwynant. This grand house can be found further down Nant Gwynant, sheltered by some woods just off the main road. Its superb setting made it keenly fought over by would-be tenants – but few of them stayed long. The owner of Plas Gwynant, a man named Vawdrey, stayed in the house intending to disprove its haunted reputation, but came away dismayed. He and his servant both heard footsteps tramping round the house and on one occasion they heard a knocking on the door made by an invisible hand. When they opened the door, something blew out their candle and they both heard distinctly the sounds of two men entering the room. When the candle was relit, there was no one to be seen.

Eighteen months after this experiment, one of Mr Vawdrey's maids got married, so he offered her free accommodation in Plas Gwynant. By this time, no one would stay at the house, and he hoped that the residence of the maid and her husband would convince prospective tenants there was nothing to be afraid of. This venture had tragic consequences, however. The ghost was 'exceedingly troublesome' to the young couple and one night the girl saw 'something very strange', something she could not describe, outside the front door. The apparition literally frightened the life out of her – she fell ill and a few months later she was dead.

A faithful Christian, one Griffith ap Rhisiart, was the next person to risk sleeping in Plas Gwynant. Having joined Mr Vawdrey's staff and hearing about the ghost, he offered to stay in the house to see if he could put an end to the haunting. The *bwgan* wasted no time in convincing Mr ap Rhisiart of his presence. It 'tramped the floors and stairs as if in wooden clogs, threw open the doors with a clash, and dragged the bed and bedclothes all over the room'. Mr ap Rhisiart refused to be perturbed, lay down on the floor and announced to the disordered room: 'Well, it matters little whether one sleeps on the floor or in his bed, as long as he does sleep.' The ghost 'grew weary' of trying to annoy its adversary and soon all was quiet again.

The haunting at Plas Gwynant seemed to be at an end and the house was taken over by a respectable sporting gentleman, who lived there for many years undisturbed. In the 1850s it was lived in by the theologian and historian Prof J A Froude. Prof Froude experienced no disturbances during his tenancy, either. Perhaps the spook moved on to Erw (see below).[10]

One of the most important stories in *Beddgelert: Its Facts, Fairies and Folk-lore* is the first-hand account of an exorcism by a practising ghostlayer, whose name, disappointingly, Jenkins withholds. The exorcist described what happened when he struggled with a spirit at a farm called Erw. Firstly, he explained that it was essential to determine the correct 'grade' of the ghost, so that you knew how to deal with it. Ignorance of the grade could prove fatal, he said. He told Jenkins that the Erw ghost was 'an awful ghost, one of the worst that I ever heard of'. The way he tackled it appears to tally with the technique employed by other exorcists, such as Griffiths of Denbighshire:

'I at once consulted the oracles, and after satisfying myself with regard to the ghost and its strength, I promised to go and put it down. One evening – I shall never forget it – I went thither, and entered the house; I then made the mystical circle on the floor with salt, and drew the image of the cross in its centre. Then I entered the circle myself and stood between the arms of the cross in the customary way, reading the usual charm passage. Almost instantly the door is flung back, and some hideous creature, not unlike a huge tiger, enters, gnashing its terrible teeth at me. It then turned around the circle, as much as to say, "I have got thee now."

'I immediately perceived that I had mistaken its grade, and that I had used too low a summons. But I stood like steel before him, showing not the slightest bit of fear, and ordered him to withdraw in the name of the cross on which I stood, or else that I would curse him with endless torture. He stood unmoved, and there we remained for a long time staring at one another, until at last I could see him gradually withdrawing. I then instantly changed one word in the charm passage, and he came back, licking the floor like a dog before his master.

'I pronounced his sentence and sacrificed him to the bottom of Llyn Du; and while there is water in that lake he will never come forth to trouble any one again. That was the last spirit with which I had to do, or will have to do. If I had betrayed the least bit of fear, or if I had taken my eye off for the quarter of a second, I would have been done for.'[11]

Bethesda

Frightening though they often undoubtedly are, it's best to stand your ground when approached by a ghost, because good can sometimes come of the encounter. As we have previously seen, if a person who has hidden some valuables dies before reclaiming them, their spirit is likely to remain restless. On occasions, such a spirit, fed up with lingering, will actively seek out someone to pass the booty onto. After all, they have truly learnt through personal experience that 'you can't take it with you'.

One Betty Jones had just such a 'generous spirit' haunting her shop in Twr, Bethesda. Unfortunately, she was too nervous to do anything about it. Her shop was situated in a grand old building which had been the home, in the 17th century, of an eminent divine by the name of Dr John Williams. Dr Williams had enjoyed or otherwise a life of considerable ups and downs before retiring to Bethesda. He'd been incarcerated in the Tower of London for perjury, then released and made Archbishop of York, then given the charge of fortifying Conwy Castle during the Great Rebellion, only to be compelled to give it up to an army of Roundheads. By rights the poor man should have been good and tired after all that excitement, but alas his spirit could not rest. The reason for this was that a great deal of money, which he had put aside for a rainy day, still remained buried in Betty's garden.

His ghost appeared to a startled Betty and showed her where to dig, but her natural timidity got the better of her and she fainted away. From then on she absolutely refused to have anything to do with the ghost and its gold. She even had an argument with it, the spirit begging her to release it by making herself wealthy... but to no avail. Betty never dug for the treasure. It was found years later by a man and his son while making alterations to the property.[12]

A note in an 1856 edition of *Archaeologia Cambrensis* places Twr in the neighbourhood of the Penrhyn Slate Quarries. It appears to have been a ruin even then, and I suspect its site has now been entirely quarried away. This version of the story is somewhat different:

'A new tenant, on taking possession of this house, was sadly troubled with the nocturnal visits of the spiritual stranger; who, however, contrived to intimate to the man of flesh and blood, that if a certain sum of money were deposited in a particular place, he should be troubled no more. The man was fool enough to place the money there, and laid the ghost accordingly.'[13]

The Rev Elias Owen briefly mentions a spirit of Caellwyngrydd and the only place I have located bearing this name is at Bethesda. Of the *yspryd*, he says:

'This was a dangerous Spirit. People passing along the road were stoned by it; its work was always mischievous and hurtful. At last it was exorcised and sent far away to the Red Sea, but it was permitted to return the length of a barley corn every year towards its lost home.'[14]

Dolgellau

Nannau Park, a few miles north-east of the town, was once ornamented with an old oak tree, whose blasted appearance was claimed to have been made not by lightning, but by malevolent spirits. This 'tree of ghostly dread' must be very long gone, for as far back as 1831 William Howells, the 19-year-old author of *Cambrian Superstitions*, referred to it as 'not now standing'. He states that 'in days of yore, a huge giant was discovered in the tree, grasping a ponderous sword and shield' and that some time after this discovery it was 'supposed to have been blown down by the ysbrydion (spirits)'. Nonetheless, the site where it stood was supposedly 'still viewed with dread' by what the rather pompous young author charmingly refers to as 'the superstitious peasants'.

The Rev Elias Owen seems to confirm this, however, more than 30 years later, when, in 1896, he published his *Welsh Folk-Lore*. He gives the name 'Ceubren yr Ellyll (Hollow Tree of the Hobgoblin)' to the oak and expands on its legend: 'Tradition says that it was within the trunk of this tree that Owen Glyndwr buried his cousin, Howel Sele, who fell a victim to the superior strength and skill of his relative.' He adds that 'ever after that sad occurrence, the place was troubled, sounds proceeded out of the tree, and fire hovered over it'.[15]

Llanegryn

A very annoying *bwgan* haunted a farm at this village north of Tywyn. It enjoyed a kind of alfresco poltergeist activity, taking delight in snatching up the neatly gathered together sheaves at harvest time and then scattering them all over the fields. The spook was laid by the curate of the parish, a Mr Williams, who held a religious service in Latin after surrounding himself with twelve big candles. An eye-witness to the exorcism recalled it in 1880: 'I was just a boy at the time and staying at the house, and I and some other boys got up secretly from our beds in the night, and through some cracks in a panel beheld there the clergyman reading to himself and laying the ghost; and the ghost was not known to be troublesome afterwards.'[16]

Llanfor

The church at Llanfor was once haunted by a gentlemanly apparition in a three-cocked hat. He would stand up during the service, much to the alarm of the congregation, and at night he would illuminate the building with an unearthly glow. He had another trick, of spinning the staves between the railings of the gallery round and round like spindles, 'although they were fast in their sockets'. Sometimes he would be seen outside the church, on one occasion taking a healthy constitutional up the hill of Moelyllan.

'Although harmless,' writes Elias Owen, 'he was a great terror to the neighbourhood.' It wasn't long before he was being referred to as 'the Evil Spirit'.

The church was abandoned, and services were held instead in a neighbouring pub (very sensible, in my opinion). The parish books, however, were stored in a coffer in the church and no one, not even, we must assume, the preacher himself, was prepared to retrieve them. At length, the landlady of the pub summoned up the courage and she lit a candle and boldly entered the portal. As soon as she had done so, the ghost blew out her light, plunging her into darkness. She lit another candle; this too was extinguished. Rather than return for another light, the brave woman groped her way through the darkness until she found the coffer. She returned to the public house, her arms laden with books, and the 'Evil Spirit' left her unmolested.

Nevertheless, such a state of affairs could hardly be tolerated for long, and 'two gentlemen skilled in divination' were hired to remove the squatter. The ghost layers spent an afternoon conversing with the spirit, and they made an appointment with him later that night – all very civilised. Unfortunately, as is so often the way with tradesmen, they arrived later than agreed and the spirit was made furious by the delay. After a great struggle of wills, they compelled the spirit to take the form of a cockerel and they carried him on horseback to the River Dee, stopping by a pool in the river called Llyn-y-Geulan-Goch. God was clearly on their side, because the horse made the journey from the church to the pool – which was two fields away – in just two leaps.

There followed another mighty battle of wills in order to compel the Evil Spirit to enter the water and so be laid to rest, but at last he agreed to do so, provided his tormentors lay face down on the ground while he did so. This they did, and the spirit, making a splash, disappeared beneath the surface, never to be heard of again. Tradition had it that the horse which carried the spirit left the mark of its hoof on a stone by the riverside. Parallels with the story of the ejection of an evil spirit from Cerrigydrudion Church (see Conwy) are obvious.

Elias Owen consulted various authorities as to this tale and gathered several variants. The version above he learnt from a Mr R Roberts, a native of Bala, who had himself heard it from his grandmother. This venerable lady was born in 1744 but even to her it was a legend, its origin obscure. Mr Roberts told Owen that he had never seen the stone bearing the horse's hoof, nor had anyone he knew. According to Ann Hughes, an elderly woman who lived in a cottage near Llanfor Rectory, the Evil Spirit was heard but not seen by the people. He used to patrol a lane leading from Rhiwlas to the church, 'making a great noise, as if dragging after him chains, or wheeling a wheelbarrow'. At night, as well as illuminating the church, he would make it resound with bangs and crashes, as though he were 'engaged in manual labour'.

According to this version of the story it was the parson in the company of another man who laid the spirit. They were seen to enter the church one night and to come back out in the company of a third man. These three held a consultation in a parlour of the nearby pub, the parson giving strict instruction that no one should pry into the affair. One drinker did have the temerity to peek through the keyhole, but only had enough time to see that there were indeed three individuals in the room, before the parson spotted him and assured the household that if anyone else looked through the keyhole, 'their plans would be frustrated'.

Ann Hughes agreed that the spirit was laid in Llyn-y-Geulan-Goch, but she added a further detail. A candle was lighted in the church at the time of the exorcism and the spirit was bound to remain in his watery gaol while it remained burning. She said that it was hidden somewhere in the church and presumed that it was still alight, as the spirit had shown no signs of escaping.

A third version of the legend is recorded in an essay by D Thomas, a précis of which Elias Owen provides in his *Welsh Folk-Lore*. In this version 'a man' and 'a friend' borrowed a mare and rode into the church, bringing the Evil Spirit out on the animal's back in the form of a pig. An old woman who witnessed this cried out: 'Duw anwyl! Mochyn yn yr Eglwys (Good God! A pig in the Church)'. 'On hearing these words,' continues Owen, 'the pig became exceedingly fierce, because the silence had been broken, and because God's name had been used, and in his anger he snatched up both the man and the mare, and threw them right over the Church to the other side, and there is a mark to this day on a grave stone of the horse's hoof on the spot where she lit.'

This tantrum was a vain effort on the part of the Evil Spirit, for in this version, too, he finds himself imprisoned beneath the waters of Llyn-y-Geulan-Goch. The horse rather suffered in her valiant efforts to bring him there: 'So much did the poor animal perspire whilst carrying him, that, although the distance was only a quarter of a mile, she lost all her hair.'[17]

Llanllechid

A malevolent poltergeist made life a misery for a family at Llanllechid, a few miles north of Bethesda, in or about the year 1758. This spook's particular trick was stone throwing, a trick in which many modern poltergeists have shown themselves adept. In most modern cases, however, the stones, though apparently being thrown with some force, do no harm, their collision feeling no more than a gentle tap. Indeed, it is usually the case that the stones, expertly aimed, fail to strike anyone. Not so at Llanllechid. If anyone was unlucky enough to get in the way, they were hurt. This was extremely dangerous because some of the missiles weighed up to 27lbs! Most of the stones seemed to come from the river which flowed behind the farmhouse, for they were all worn smooth. Sometimes they appeared inside the house and were chucked from one room to another.

A party of clergymen who came over from Bangor to pray down the spirit were also pelted with rocks and had to beat a hasty retreat. After this, the unfortunate family gave up. They abandoned their home to the poltergeist.[18]

One wonders what relationship this entity had with the stone-thrower of Caellwyngrydd mentioned under Bethesda, above.

Llanuwchllyn

The oddly named Wirt Sikes, who was the United States Consul for Wales for many years, took a great interest in the folklore of his adopted home and published a fascinating book on the subject in 1880, *British Goblins*. It is a book we will hear more of as we travel further south, for Mr Sikes lived in Cardiff and on the whole limited his study to those counties most accessible to him. The following adventure, however, took place in old Meirionethshire, along the Bala to Machynlleth road.

The Rev John Jones, of Holywell in Flintshire, was travelling this road alone one day when he found himself ambushed by a man whose intent was undoubtedly to rob him. Mr Jones had glimpsed this man on a couple of occasions running in a crouching manner behind the roadside hedges, keeping pace with his horse. In his hand was a murderous-looking sickle. Mr Jones recalled meeting the man the previous evening at the inn at Llanuwchllyn and he also recalled that at this inn he had unwittingly revealed his watch and his purse.

Warning bells were now sounding in Mr Jones's head but it was too late to take any action – he was nearing a place where a gate crossed the road, and here he saw the man conceal himself. The hedge was now at its thickest, not only offering a hiding place for his probable assailant but also shielding any wrongdoing from any habitation that might be nearby. Mr Jones slowed his horse to a halt and considered what to do. He knew he was alone on the road.

Should he turn back? He bowed his head and offered up a silent prayer for guidance. Whilst he was doing so, his horse, impatient at the delay, took the initiative and trotted forward...

'I clutched the reins, which I had let fall on his neck, when, happening to turn my eyes, I saw, to my utter astonishment, that I was no longer alone: there, by my side, I beheld a horseman in a dark dress, mounted on a white steed. In intense amazement I gazed upon him. Where could he have come from? He appeared as suddenly as if he had sprung from the earth; he must have been riding behind and have overtaken me, and yet I had not heard the slightest sound. It was mysterious, inexplicable; but joy overcame my feelings of wonder, and I began at once to address my companion. I asked him if he had seen any one, and then described to him what had taken place, and how relieved I felt by his sudden appearance. He made no reply, and on looking at his face he seemed paying but slight attention to my words, but continued intently gazing in the direction of the gate, now about a quarter of a mile ahead. I followed his gaze, and saw the reaper emerge from his concealment and run across a field to our left, resheathing his sickle as he hurried along. He had evidently seen that I was no longer alone, and had relinquished his intended attempt.'

Mr Jones offered up a phrase of pious thanks for his deliverance, to which the stranger murmured 'Amen'. But this was the only word Mr Jones heard him speak, for a moment later he vanished! Mr Jones's head was a whirl. At first he thought he must have imagined the other rider, but then he remembered that the would-be robber had seen him, too.

'What could I then believe but that ... in the mysterious horseman I had a special interference of Providence, by which I was delivered from a position of extreme danger?'[19]

Llanymawddwy

Yr Hen Damberlain was the name of the ghost which tramped about Victorian Llanymawddwy. In life he was James Thomas Tamberlain, the son of a rector and something of a wild character. To quote one old writer: 'He was rather notorious in his admiration of the fair sex; and judging from his frequent visits to the Llanymawddwy public houses he was uncommonly thirsty.'

Not surprisingly, he died young, his afterlife nickname of Hen Damberlain (Old Tamberlain) being therefore something of a misnomer. After his death (which took place in 1839), Tamberlain's spirit proved as restless as the living man, and it began to haunt the family home of Bryn and the roads around. He would be seen riding 'the ghost of a very valuable white horse he once possessed', and enjoyed playing pranks on the mortal parishioners. In time, though, he grew weary and spoke of his cares to a man named David Jones, who lived at a place called Pen-yr-erw. Having unburdened his conscience, he then told Jones to lie face down on the ground while he disappeared. Jones lifted his head a little too soon and saw Tamberlain vanishing 'in the shape of a volume of fire'.

Poor David Jones, who was ever after known as Deio yr Ysbryd (Davy of the Ghost), never knew good health after this encounter. He also refused to divulge the nature of the conversation he had had with Yr Hen Damberlain. The ghost himself, now also known by the appellation Bwgan y Bryn, made fewer and fewer appearances in the district and on the occasions when he did appear proved less troublesome. He has not been seen for many a long year.[20]

Llithfaen

Rising high above Llithfaen in the south-west and Trefor to the north-east are the three mountains called collectively Yr Eifl, or as they are known in English, The Rivals. One of these mountains boasts a strange apparition, apparently that of a wizard. Marie Trevelyan records his presence in her book, *Folk-Lore and Folk Stories of Wales*, which was published in 1909:

'Among the mountains called The Rivals in North Wales is the beetling and furrowed Craig Ddu, with its almost black rocky surface and inaccessible sides rising sheer against the sky. In the 18th century people said that the apparition of an old man with long white hair and flowing beard used formerly to be seen wandering down the valley, and pausing to mutter unknown words beside the Craig Ddu. Sounds of strange music were heard, and magic signs were made by the old man.'

It is very tempting to consider this the ghost of the greatest wizard of them all, Merlin (more correctly Merddyn), for Gwynedd was one of his main stamping grounds. As an addendum to this intriguing story, Trevelyan states: 'If anybody fell asleep in the shadow of Craig Ddu he would sleep for ever, and be carried away by unseen hands, so that his resting-place could not be known.'[21]

Nant Gwytheyrn, a lovely and lonely valley near the seashore, provides the ideal setting for a classic tale of doomed love. The story was told in high literary style between the pages of the *Cambrian Quarterly* in 1831, but took place more than a century before the publication of this august journal. It opens on the morning of June 4th, one year in the early 18th century. Two young country people, very much in love, are to be married the next day. The young lovers are out walking, when Rhys pauses by an oak tree and boldly carves in its bark the legend: 'Margaret, married June 5th'. He turns to his beloved, expecting her to be pleased with this show of affection, but instead Margaret is struck with a superstitious dread.

'Oh but if we never *should* be married, Rhys Bach!' she cries. 'I do not like that writing on the tree, indeed, indeed!'

'Not married!' laughs Rhys. 'And it is only tomorrow we are to be, my girl!'

'Ah! there are so many things do happen when we do promise ourselves so much.' Alas for poor Margaret – her premonition is proved all too horribly true!

June 5th proved a glorious day for a wedding, warm, sunny and bright and full of promise. A little cottage had been furnished for the couple's use and decked out in flowers to welcome them on their return from church. The ceremony was to take place that morning, but beforehand a time-honoured custom was to be played out. The young men of the valley had gathered to seek out Margaret after she had left her father's house and to bring her as a willing captive to her future husband's arms. It was Margaret's duty to evade her pursuers with a pretty show of reluctance. However, neither she nor Rhys approved of this game, and between them they had agreed to meet behind the church, Margaret intending to avoid the gang of youths by using an obscure path over the mountain. Unfortunately, she heard their approach much sooner than she anticipated, so she quickly hid herself in a haystack, hoping they would pass by, and so affording her a clear run to the mountain path. The unnamed author's description of the scene when the boys spot Margaret's little white foot peeping out of the hay is very charming:

'A shout from her pursuers told her she was betrayed. Up sprung grasses and buttercups and clover flowers; and the fair apparition of some wood nymph, or such Arcadian phantasy, stood dropping flowers; stood a moment, half fearful, half wishful to be caught, darted back a smile like a sun flash at her pursuers, then bounded away...'

The youths hared after Margaret but she had a good start on them, and shortly reached the mountain path she had chosen to reach the church and the arms of her adoring Rhys. Soon they lost sight of her behind the hill – and that was the last time the unfortunate young girl was ever seen alive. Margaret never arrived at the church; but her pursuers arrived there and were mystified at having missed her. She was not at her father's house, as the increasingly frantic Rhys had half hoped, nor, when he ran back, was she now at last waiting for him by the altar. It was as if she had vanished from the earth:

'All that night lights were seen moving in every direction, and voices heard calling her name, re-echoed by the hills, and only answered by the owls, or some fishers lying off the land's edge, who thought themselves called to from the shore; all possible and impossible places were explored in vain; every brambled hollow below, and every natural quarry in the fractured rocks above – all in vain!'

Rhys's growing dread for his missing bride as day wore into night and then into day again is more easily imagined than described. His sister took the initiative of climbing up to the hovel of a Gwrag Hysbys, or Wise Woman – 'a melancholy woman, whose strange lonely life, and partial insanity, made her the sybil of the country' – to see whether some supernatural means might be employed to find the vanished girl.

'Will she be found?' was the first question asked of the Gwrag Hysbys.

'Yes,' was the brief reply.

'Who shall find her? And how and where shall we search?' – but the old woman merely shook her head.

'Will the bridegroom find his bride again?' came the next desperate question.

'Yes.'

'On earth or in heaven?'

'On earth.'

'Thank God! But when? Oh when?'

'When a light from heaven shall show her to him: search no more; heaven itself shall find her out, and face to face they shall stand by its light.'

And with this obscure and comfortless prediction, Rhys's sister had to be content. But the prophecy took a long time in its fulfilling and Rhys, already in a state of shock, became more

and more deranged as days became weeks and weeks became months without any sign of his beloved Margaret, alive or dead. Even the finding of her corpse may have provided some relief for the man, but without even the melancholy comfort of a burial, with this appalling mystery of her disappearance preying on his mind and nerves, he became all but insane. He began to wander the mountains like a Merlin, or a Lancelot, or a Nebuchadnezzar, more animal than man. Into the pretty little house he and his lost bride were to share, 'he never entered more, nor would allow an article to be removed, or repair to be done; so it stood, death silent, in all its ghostliness of decaying finery, till the strong winds from the sea stripped off the thatch, and damps made the whitened walls green as the sods without – till, at last, the owl and the bat made it their haunt as a ruin, and the fox and the wild cat by turns littered and howled in the marriage-bed.'

Long years passed. Our story comes to its climax one noon-day in the late summer of 1728. Although it was noon, a 'murky gloom' had gathered over the mountains from the sea, darkening the day to a premature night and bringing with it warning of an approaching thunderstorm. Through this sudden twilight, Rhys's sister, hurrying home to avoid the expected downpour, caught sight of her tragic brother sitting up on a promontory overlooking the sea. He was under an old oak tree, which 'standing high and lonely as it did ... was a mark for thunder, and had been twice struck by lightning' It was not a safe place to be sitting in a storm! His sister hastened to Rhys's side and embraced him fondly, urging him to come away. But the demented man refused to leave. He stared up at the threatening clouds and told her that he felt no fear, for he had already suffered an 'eternal storm' in his heart to which this one was 'a very calm'. He roared up at the tumultuous heavens, calling upon God to free him from his misery, and at that moment –

'The shock of a lightning-strike ... prostrated him at the foot of the tree: a dreadful rushing noise, as of splitting ice, astounded his sister: and opening her eyes again after the flash, to see the cause, a sight struck her soul that made them close again in faintness. The trunk was rent from top to bottom, laying open the tree's inward hollowness, unknown before; and through the fissure appeared an upright skeleton, the grim skull-face greened by damps to the appearance of lichoned stone, the ribbed cage of what had been a snowy bosom, hung still with black shreds, the remains of dress, and flesh, and sinews, now indistinguishable from each other! The arm-bones, even still inextricably wedged in the cavity, told the tale of a frightful death.'

Desperate to meet her lover as promised, and to avoid capture by the pursuing gang of youths, Margaret had climbed up the tree and, finding it hollow, slid into its interior and had here become trapped in the manner in which 'boys had frequently lost their lives in chimnies'. The shock was too much for poor Rhys: 'With body shivering, teeth chattering, eye dilating with horror, the thunder-stricken man only pointed ghostlike, and smiled on his sister such an indescribable smile, as conveyed to [his sister], more than words or shrieks, the strangely mixed horror and pleasure of their meeting again – and meeting thus!'

His sister could only watch appalled as Rhys bent to kiss the skeleton of his lost bride, but 'before his lips and the lipless half-circle of snowy teeth met, he sank down, and never spoke again. The distortion of that hideous smile remained on his corpse face, frozen there by death, and there stayed, even when one coffin received him and her whose loss had made youth age, and his very life a death.'

The tragic couple were buried side by side and so the story ends – or not quite, for this is, after all, a collection of ghost stories:

'The fatal tree, as long as its shattered trunk remained standing, was known as the "Ceubren yr Ellyll", "The Spirit's Hollow Tree"; for there was often seen by fishermen, in a moonlight midnight, as they awaited morning in their boats on a calm sea, an apparition of dry bones, frightfully mimicking the actions of life, the white skull rounded with the mockery of wild flowers which had garlanded the hair of the lost bride that morning, and the bony arms raised often to the teeth rapidly, as if in the rage of hunger. Such a figure (they said), magnified by mists, that passing, enveloped it as in a shroud, would stand for hours on the round brink of the promontory.

'Others had seen in the last of twilight, two figures, hand in hand, the skeleton bride and wild-man bridegroom, as they called the spectres; he with his beard, long hair, and nails like talons, fixing his stony eyes, and she her eyeless sockets, on the calm sky and silvered clouds, as

if still scowling dumb complaint against the heavens, which had been to them so merciless. Nor would ever bird, except the owl and the foul cormorant, it was believed, alight on the boughs, nor any animal rest under the shade of that black thunderstricken ruin of a tree – the grave of love – the ghastly Ceubren yr Ellyll.'[22]

This gothic horror follows a traditional theme among ghost stories, that of the skeleton bride. Possibly this is why it was ignored by the Victorian folklorists. The story appeared anonymously but was stated as being from a soon to be published (in 1831) book called 'The Welsh Decameron'. I have been unable to trace this book, however, and wonder whether indeed it was ever produced. I have included the story because the fact that the location, the names of the protagonists and even the date are specified, strongly implies that it was a tradition genuinely heard by the author. Also, I thoroughly enjoyed reading and repeating the over-ripe prose!

Mynytho

A poltergeist is alleged to have haunted a house named Pant-y-Wennol (or Pantywenol), at Mynytho, near Abersoch, in the 1860s. The 'Bwgan Pant-y-Wennol' became something of a cause célèbre, but there are doubts as to whether the haunting was real or a malicious hoax. This is what the *Caernarvon & Denbigh Herald* of May 29th, 1866, had to say about it:

'THE PANTYWENOL GHOST – Certain doings have for some time been the almost universal theme of conversation in the neighbourhood. Most wonderful deeds were said to be performed at Pantywenol and many people actually believed that the devil or some of his commissioners had taken possession, but for what purpose was a mystery, the only work done being the cutting up of other people's clothes, no article of apparel was safe. At length the Police took the matter up and succeeded in tracing the act to the daughter of the poor woman which resulted in her being apprehended and bound over to keep the peace. It is rumoured that this young woman instituted these ghostly proceedings for the express purpose of frightening her mother away, purposing to take possession of the house herself.'[23]

An excellent study of this alleged haunting has been made by Moses Glyn Jones and Norman Roberts (*Bwgan Pant-y-Wennol*, Pwllheli, 1986).

Nanhwynan

At Nanhwynan in old Caernarvonshire a farmer's spirit could not rest after he was dead. The reason? When alive he happened to find a mildewed Bible in a ruined chapel and decided to keep it. His ghost wandered about his former home until someone spoke to him, and then he told them his trouble. The Bible was returned to the ruin and the farmer was seen no more.[24]

Rhiw

In 1936 a book of *True Ghost Stories* was compiled by Marchioness Townshend of Raynham and her friend Maude M C ffoulkes. This was one of two 'society' ghost books published that year – the other was the more famous *Lord Halifax's Ghost Book*. Like Lord Halifax, the Marchioness and Maude invited pals from the upper social circle to send in true accounts of eerie experiences, and in this way produced a volume which contained much original material. *True Ghost Stories* contains two stories from Wales. The first on our list was submitted by the Hon. Mrs Greville Nugent and concerns a house which she locates near Pwllheli and names 'Plas-yu-Rhiw'. This is a mis-spelling of 'Plas-yn-Rhiw', a beautiful old mansion now in the care of the National Trust, which can be found down at the tip of the Lleyn peninsula, overlooking Porth Neigwl ('Hell's Mouth'). Here follows Mrs Nugent's story, the spelling corrected:

'In the summer of 1892, I was staying with my friend the late Lady Strickland, at an old manor house called "Plas-yn-Rhiw", near Pwllheli. I was the only visitor, and one night Lady Strickland and I sat up so late playing cards that it was long past midnight when we prepared to go to bed. In view of what happened, I should mention that the servants of "Plas-yn-Rhiw" (who had all gone to bed long before) slept in another wing, and as they used the back staircase to go to their rooms, *no one but ourselves could possibly be using the front staircase at that hour.* [Mrs Nugent's italics]

'The old house was in absolute stillness, and the moonlight lay in pools of silver on the oak staircase. My bedroom, on the first floor, faced the landing, and Lady Strickland, who slept on the floor above me, was just in the act of lighting her candle from mine, when we heard heavy footsteps coming upstairs from the hall. The steps were slow and hesitating, apparently those of an old man, and they were accompa-nied by the sound of laboured breathing, punctuated by various degrees of coughing.

'"Who's that coming upstairs?"

'There was no reply – we looked over the balusters, but although the coughing and wheezing came nearer and nearer, we saw no one. By this time we were too scared to move, our candlesticks fell to the ground, and we clung to each other in fear of the unknown. The steps paused for a moment beside us, as if the unseen owner of the feet had stopped to take breath. He then continued his upwards progress, until the coughing gradually died away and we heard no more.

'I implored my hostess not to go up to her bedroom, but to share mine, or any other on the first floor, but she refused, saying: "I have some Holy Water in my room, and with spiritual protection I fear nothing."'

Lady Strickland asked discreetly round the neighbourhood and discovered that Plas-yn-Rhiw had once been owned by 'an old reprobate squire, who drank himself to death' and was told that his earth-bound spirit occasionally returned, 'vainly trying to obtain some gratifi-cation for his ceaseless thirst'.[25]

Not far from Plas-yn-Rhiw there is another fine, medieval manor house. This is Gelliwig. An evil spirit once took possession of Gelliwig and Williams, a parson, was called in to exorcise it. He had a terrible struggle. He tried to lay the *yspryd* in a hole bored into a beam in the house (firmly stopped up, of course), but there was some argument as to how long its imprisonment was to last. Williams argued for fifty years but the spirit agreed to only ten. At length they settled on twenty years. Since this story was first recorded in 1908, the period of its 'sentence' is now irrelevant – we may be sure that the spirit has since escaped to cause mischief elsewhere. After his battle with the *bwgan*, Williams was somewhat the worse for wear: 'his clothes were in tatters and he was so evil-smelling that he had to be carefully washed with soft soap.'[26]

And finally, J Y W Lloyd, in his *History of Powys Fadog*, recounts a ghost story of some pathos which occurred somewhere unspecified on the Lleyn. A young member of the landed gentry had an affair with a woman 'in a lower grade of life than his own'. Alas, he abandoned her and within a year she was dead. He then courted another young lady and the date was set for their wedding. Shortly before that date, however, the young man fell mortally ill. His fiancee, sitting by his bedside, suddenly saw the apparition of the jilted woman, dressed in white and carrying a baby in her arms. The man could see her, too – he ordered the apparition away. But she stood glaring at him from the side of the bed. Appalled, he turned his head away and cried out: 'O Dduw! Gwared fi rhag yr ysprydion tywyllwch!' (Oh God! Deliver me from the spirits of darkness!) and immediately died.[27]

[1] *Bye-Gones*, January 1893, p. 3.
[2] Ibid, June 1892, p. 332.
[3] Ibid, Sept 1905, p. 129.
[4] Jenkins, 1899, p. 77.
[5] Ibid, pp. 316-7.
[6] Ibid, p. 149.
[7] Jones, T G, 1930, p. 34.
[8] Owen, 1896, p. 209, possibly quoting from Thomas, 1870, p. 108.
[9] Jenkins, 1899, p. 285.
[10] Ibid, p. 238.
[11] Ibid, p. 76.
[12] Underwood, 1978, p. 24, taken from *Notes and Queries*, no date given, told by Aneurin Williams.
[13] *Archaeologia Cambrensis* (1856), p. 185.
[14] Owen, 1896, p. 214.
[15] Howells, 1831, p. 96, and also Owen, 1896, p. 191. Owen may have been quoting from Thomas, 1870, p. 110.
[16] *Bye-Gones*, February, 1880, p. 13.
[17] Owen, 1896, p. 162.
[18] Jones, Edmund, 1780, p. 45. See also Sikes, 1880, p. 180.
[19] Sikes, 1880, p. 174.
[20] *Bye-Gones*, January, 1894, p. 267.
[21] Trevelyan, 1909, p. 138.
[22] Anon, 1831, pp 467-86.
[23] Quoted by Jones & Roberts, 1986, p. 29.
[24] Jones, T G, 1930, p. 35.
[25] Townshend, 1936, p. 266.
[26] Jones, T G, 1930, p. 44.
[27] Lloyd, 1881, p. 229.

Ceredigion

Abermeurig

This wonderful old mansion – now a stylish B&B – is situated on the banks of the Afon Aeron north-west of Llangybi, near Talsarn and Trefilan.

In 1846 there lived at Abermeurig a wealthy doctor named Rogers. Dr Rogers was a good-hearted soul and, thanks to a sizeable independent income, was in the habit of treating the poor for free. Among his servants were two brothers, John and Davydd Davies, who possessed a great deal of loyalty and affection for their master. Dr Rogers was fond of them, too, especially the younger brother, Davydd. It seems the good doctor couldn't bear to be parted from Davydd. He cared for him enough to want him to do well in life and at his own expense apprenticed him to a saddler in Lampeter. But six weeks later,

'finding he could not get on without Davydd', the boy returned to Abermeurig. A year later, Dr Rogers made a second attempt, and sent Davydd to a carpenter – with the same result. As the recorder of this affecting history has it: 'He took him back, as the young man was breaking his heart to go back to his master, and would not learn his trade; for it appears that neither could live without the other.'

Now we come to the tragic events which led to a haunting. One fine summer morning, when Dr Rogers's daughters were visiting, the doctor set out to the high mountain of Pen Dychryd to see a sick friend who lived near there. As summer days in Wales will sometimes do, the weather suddenly turned: 'It became intensely dark; and a terrific storm of thunder and forked lightning, with a deluge of rain, burst on the mountains and the Vale of Aeron.'

Young Davydd braved the storm and found his master returning from his errand – but, horror of horrors, Dr Rogers was struck by lightning! The frantic Davydd enlisted the aid of the farmer of nearby Pen yr Heol and they managed to get the stricken man on his horse again. But things were only to get worse:

'The river Aeron rose so suddenly that it overflowed the whole valley, and rushing with impetuous fury, undermined the churchyard of Nantgynllo, carried the coffins out to sea, and overflowed the road. The farmer tried to persuade Dr Rogers not to attempt to go through the torrent, but he would not listen; and Davydd said that if they went they would certainly be drowned. The farmer then tried to prevent Davydd from going with his master, but he answered: "If my master loses his life, I will lose my life with him, and will not forsake him."

'They both started, and the foaming flood swept the unfortunate doctor and his devoted servant into the raging torrent. The doctor fell from his horse, but his foot stuck in the stirrup, which Davydd perceiving, he threw himself off his horse, for he was a good swimmer, and endeavoured to save his master; and eventually caught hold of the horse's tail, but was soon obliged to let go, and was carried by the torrent to the bank, on which stood a house with a pump close to it, and he managed to catch hold of the handle, by which he held on, till the river undermined the house, and the falling stones struck the poor young fellow on the head and killed him.'

Dr Rogers also lost his life. His body was found some hours later, but that of Davydd was carried for four miles down the river and became entangled in debris beneath a bridge called Pont Breinant. A Captain Lewis of Llantyr had a dream in which he saw the body in this very place, and because of this it was found and recovered.

But this is not the end of the supernatural events. Poor John Davies was left distraught after the loss of his brother and his master, and he grieved for both with equal intensity. One night soon after the tragedy, he heard Dr Rogers's footsteps and the creaking of his boots coming up the stairs. John listened with growing dread as the door creaked open – and then the apparition of Dr Rogers came to his bedside. The ghost looked down and said: 'John, you must not cry and grieve for me any more,

for I am very happy.' Then he left. John, who was greatly upset, heard the noise of the door being shut as the apparition left.[1]

Aberystwyth

A headless dog haunted Pen Parcau, near Aberystwyth. The strange legend behind the ghost was that the dog had once belonged to a giant. The giant was riding at a desperate pace to help his beleaguered father. One hand held the reins of his horse, the other the leash of his faithful hound. He rode so fast, however, that the poor dog couldn't keep up. It was dragged along behind until – its head was pulled off. Afterwards it was doomed to haunt the land on which it had made its fatal run. The story originally appeared in a collection of manuscripts made in the 16th century.[2]

At a house called Crugiau the apparition of a lady used to appear. A Miss Ellis told T Gwynn Jones that a young girl saw the ghost while playing the piano here. When she finished playing, the girl turned to the other people in the room and asked who the old lady was. On being told that there was no one, she replied: 'There was a lady in old-fashioned dress sitting there all the time I was playing.'[3]

From an old Welsh book called *Ysten Sioned*, comes the following tragic tale (as rendered by J Ceredig Davies):

'About seventy years ago [ie 1840] a young French sailor at Aberystwyth in Cardiganshire, had fallen in love with a servant maid in that town, and she with him. One evening, when this young woman was preparing to go to bed she heard her lover calling to her by her name. It was a bright moonlight night, and when she went to the door there she saw the young man approaching and offering his hand to her; but to her great surprise he disappeared again without speaking a single word. Soon after this, news came to the town that a ship from Aberystwyth got lost on the coast of Spain, and that amongst others of the crew, who were drowned, was the young Frenchman. The young woman discovered that her lover was drowned on the Spanish Coast in the very same hour that she saw his apparition at Aberystwyth!'[4]

A young man of a very religious turn of mind had a bizarre and frightening series of adventures while trying to get home to a place called Penrhiw at Aberystwyth. William Davies had been working in England for a few weeks and hoped to get home in time to help his father in reaping his field first thing Monday morning. But he was delayed and still some miles from Aber by Sunday evening, and his conscience began to prick him that he should be in church or chapel. However, he was determined to press on.

When he reached Llanfihangel-y-Creuddyn, he guiltily hid from view until all the villagers, some of whom he knew, had gone to their respective places of worship. Then he continued on his journey by taking a short-cut through a field. And it was at this point that weird things began to happen:

'He had not proceeded far through the barley field before he found himself surrounded by a large number of small pigs. He was not much struck by this, though he thought it strange that so many pigs should be allowed to wander about on the Sabbath Day. The pigs, however, came up to him, grunted and scampered away. Before he had traversed the barley field he saw approaching him an innumerable number of mice, and these, too, surrounded him, only, however, to stare at him and disappear.'

Davies hurried out of the field in some consternation. He saw on the pathway ahead a large greyhound. He watched it anxiously to see what it might do – 'but suddenly it vanished out of sight'. Now Davies was 'thoroughly frightened' and convinced that the animals were in fact apparitions, sent to punish him for breaking the Sabbath. Full of regret, but now miles from anywhere, the man went on. Three miles further on, having passed through Llanilar without incident, his nerves began to steady. But there was worse to come. He saw something approaching him at high speed down the highway. He stood horror-struck until it was almost upon him and then he saw that it was a headless horse! He only just had time to jump out of its way into a ditch as the horrible thing thundered past. This happened close to the house of Tan'rallt, but he was too ashamed to go in and seek shelter, so he pressed on, conscious of the fact that he was only a few miles now from home. *But there was still worse to come.*

As he came in sight of home, he considered the quickest way to safety, and recalled that there was a gap in the hedge which separated the properties of Tan'rallt and Penrhiw. This he headed for as fast as he possibly could manage – only to find his way impeded by the most bizarre phantom of all, 'a lady, lying at full length, and immovable, and stopping up the gap entirely'. This last apparition was too much

for Davies and he screamed and then fainted. As soon as he awoke, he fell on his knees in supplication and at the top of his voice prayed for pardon for his sinful breaking of the Sabbath. And in this position, his parents, who had heard the commotion, found him.

A clergyman friend, the Rector of Llangynog in Montgomeryshire, later tried to convince Davies that the whole adventure had been down to 'his imagination working on a nervous temperament', but Davies insisted for the rest of his days that it was no hallucination, but a punishment for his having broken the Fourth Commandment.[5] Many other horrible spectres, such as the Dogs of Darkness, appeared to Sabbath-breakers, especially those who frequented alehouses. (See, for example, Risca, Caerphilly.)

Afon Teifi

Along the banks of the River Teifi, 'when the May flowers were in bloom', a very charming lady dressed all in green used to make her appearance.

'Her dark hair was plaited with long switches, and bound with bands of gold,' Marie Trevelyan informs us. 'She wore a golden girdle, from which was suspended a bunch of golden keys.'

Her home was a mound near the river and, despite her rather royal appearance, she seems to have lived the simple life. Two farmers once watched her as she washed her hands and face in the river and on another occasion they saw her filling a tub with water and carrying it back to her mound. The tub was a posh one, though, for the staves were held together by hoops of gold. No one had the courage to speak to her but the belief was that there was treasure hidden in the mound and it was the Green Lady's duty to guard it.[6]

Blaenporth

An extraordinary tale of a White Lady solving a crime is told from Blaenporth. One midnight the farmer who lived at Tan-yr-Eglwys near the church was woken by a knocking at the door. He called out: 'Who's there?' and got a surprising answer: 'Mair Wen of Blaenporth – the silver communion cup has been stolen from the church.'

Mair Wen – White Mary – was the local ghost. The spirit begged the farmer to go and retrieve the stolen cup. She knew exactly where it was – stuffed under the waistcoat of some lout who was asleep on a couch in a Cardigan pub. Well, the farmer could hardly ignore such a plea, and as fast as he could he saddled up his horse and rode the few miles into town to search for the sacrilegious thief. He soon found him, fast asleep where Mair Wen said he would be. On being awoken, the wretch stood up, and the silver cup fell out onto the floor. The farmer did not wait for any arguments, he snatched the treasure up and ran back to his horse, which he then set galloping back to Blaenporth. The communion cup was soon in its rightful place again.

In gratitude this 'good spirit or guardian angel of Blaenporth Church', as Ceredig Davies refers to her, told the farmer that the church bell would toll three times before his death, and the deaths of all his descendants 'until the ninth generation'. Davies said that this prophecy came true, so that in former times Blaenporth had its very own Tolaeth.

'I wonder,' pondered the folklorist, 'if the word "Tolaeth" is derived from toll?'[7]

Borth

Centuries ago a Portuguese ship came to grief on the Borth sands. The local fishermen discovered the wreck at first light and began looting everything with great gusto. Keeping an eye out for the coastguard, they boarded the ship, believing the crew to be drowned. On deck, however, they were startled to find one man still alive – the captain, 'who had kept his place, guarding his ship to the last'. He glared at them from the mast and, though too weak to speak due to the ordeal he had suffered, it was clear that he condemned their behaviour. Just then, the frightened fishermen heard the thudding of the hooves of the approaching coastguards' steeds, and in a panic killed this witness of their looting and threw his body into the sea – having first stripped him of his gold and jewellery.

The result of this cowardly deed was a curse on the family of the man who struck the fatal blow; he and six others all perished at sea. The bay itself was also said to be cursed, and considered 'demon haunted ground'. The horrible shriek of the doomed captain echoed down the ages as a reminder of his murder.

In 1839 this eldritch sound was heard on the night that the last of the murderer's line was extinguished. The young man, a Mr R——, had been preparing to use the ferry across the Dyfi, but he failed to reappear after entering the sandhills which fringe the bay. His riderless horse, dripping wet, returned home at dawn.

The young man's body was found weeks later, washed up on a distant beach. It was believed he was murdered in error by a gang who mistook him for another man preparing to cross the ferry, one who was known to be in possession of a good deal of money.[8]

Devil's Bridge (Pontarfynach)

The legend of this spectacular construction is well-known. The Evil One agreed to build the bridge, provided he could claim the soul of the first living thing to cross it. This turned out to be a hapless dog, sent across by the old woman with whom Satan had struck the deal.

Near Devil's Bridge there was an important house named Hafod Uchtryd which was celebrated not only for its grandeur and its beautiful location but also for its poltergeist, the Bwgan yr Hafod. The house was still haunted when T Gwynn Jones wrote about it in 1930, but twenty years later it had been pulled down, another of the 'great lost houses of Wales'. Its site is now covered by a caravan site.

According to Jones, the Bwgan yr Hafod first made its appearance in 1751 and returned to plague the house in 1759. It was by turns helpful or irritating, gentle or violent. When it was in a useful mood it would 'carry stones, vessels and other articles about the house and hand various tools to persons according to their crafts'. Usually, though, it was mischievous, and liked to show off its power but without causing any harm, as these examples testify:

'A hall table, as much as four men could lift, would be turned feet upwards, knocked against the ceiling, instantly replaced. When the mistress called for a tub with oatmeal, it was thrown on to the table without spilling a grain. Potatoes in a basket ready for boiling jumped out one after the other to the ceiling, no more to be seen until they returned into the basket, "as you have seen maggots jump out of a cheese in hot weather". A company of fifteen being in a room shut close, the hearth was filled with stones. A person put his foot on one stone to keep it secure. All the stones, including the one under the man's foot, were removed to the other end of the room.'

The *bwgan* had a sense of humour: 'The master's great coat would be put about a chair and buttoned up, two or three pieces of peat placed on top for a neck and a hat a-top of that. When the old man hit them down in a passion, the buttons would open and the coat be thrown after him.'

It could be gentle – 'a piece of delf ware came gently on to a person's plate' – but when a clergyman annoyed it, it became violent, and the parson 'had his head broken till the blood ran'. This is a very rare case of a poltergeist doing someone actual physical harm; usually they do no more than pinch, or slap or splash with water.

As is so often the case with poltergeists, the Bwgan yr Hafod evolved over the years, and when it returned to the house in 1759 it had developed a voice and a physical appearance. It would laugh and shout and 'kiss women in the dark'. Then it appeared as 'a beautiful woman wanting to be kissed'! On another occasion it took the form of a pig and 'rubbed against the master and mistress'. Jones took this information from an 18th century manuscript.[9]

Charles Wilkins, writing in 1879, said that the bwgan's main haunt was the stables. 'If Mr Johnes [the owner] wanted a horse saddled quickly, the moment it was done, everything would be taken off by invisible hands. Busy stablemen would get lumps of turf thrown at them, and they would be obliged to run away in fear and trembling, and when they returned it was to find everything in disorder – combs and brushes lying about in all sorts of places, harness piled in a heap, and, in fact, just such a condition of things as one might expect from the hands of a practical joker.'

Wilkins says that the grand house was razed to the ground by fire, although whether this was by the machinations of the poltergeist was unclear. What was certain, though, is that the fire hadn't rid the place of its doings, for it continued to sport among the ruins. Mr Johnes did not want to rebuild Hafod with the poltergeist still in residence so he engaged a graduate of Oxford, who had recently moved to the area, to exorcise it. The exorcism took the form we have seen previously carried out by Griffiths of Denbighshire and by the anonymous ghostlayer of Beddgelert in Gwynedd. The conjurer drew an enchanted circle around him and commanded the bwgan to appear, which it did in various alarming guises, such as a bull and a bulldog. After a time, it was compelled to take the form of a fly, which the wizard snapped up in his Holy Book (or possibly book of spells). At last, the bwgan was trapped by this injunction: that 'he should betake himself to Devil's Bridge, and there with an ounce hammer and a tin tack cut off a fathom of the rock'.[10]

Ceredig Davies, writing in 1911, adds that despite this injunction 'there is a rumour throughout the whole of North Cardiganshire, that Hafod is still haunted'.[11] As we have seen, T Gwynn Jones believed the house still possessed its ghost in 1930. I wonder whether the caravan site is haunted?

Llanafan

Near Pont Llanafan, where there is a pool popular with anglers, there was once a home for 'retired pirates'. These defunct buccaneers hid some booty somewhere near the bridge, and this led to it becoming haunted. The ghost was seen in the early 1900s, but there are no details of the sighting. Perhaps the treasure is still there. [12]

J Ceredig Davies was informed of the Pont Llanafan ghost by a man named John Jones, who was 95 when the author published his Folk-Tales of West and Mid-Wales in 1911. Mr Jones provided Ceredig Davies with many of his stories, including this next one, regarding a farmer who lived near the bridge and was 'continually molested by a mischievous ghost day and night'.

Poor Edwards – for that was the farmer's name – suffered a great deal of inconvenience due to the poltergeist. It would throw stones down the chimney, put ashes in the milk and make a ruckus in the barn; it was always 'meddling with something'. On one occasion, Edwards spent a day trying to put up a new fence round his field, but the entity 'kept with him all day, and threw down both the fence and the gate'. Eventually, the harassed farmer cried out in exasperation: 'Yn enw Duw, paham yr wyt yn fy aflonyddi o hyd? (In the name of God, why do you trouble me continually?)' As is so often the case, buried treasure was the reason and, although Edwards kept close counsel after the event, it was understood by his neighbours that he was directed to an old wall near his house, wherein he found a considerable sum of money. He used the stones from the wall to build a new house and 'greatly prospered' unhampered by the presence of the spirit.

When Ceredig Davies mentioned this story to a friend who lived at Pontrhydfendigaid, his wife confirmed that it was true and that she had received '£500 of the Ghost's money'. She was a descendant or near relation of Mr Edwards.[13]

Llanbadarn Fawr

A noisy ghost disturbed the peace of the family at Broginin, an ancient farmhouse located in Llanbadarn Fawr parish and six miles from Aberystwyth. The ghost would clump about the house at night, stomping up and down stairs and wandering in and out of the rooms, slamming the doors as it went. Obviously it was seeking some attention, and when making a lot of noise failed, it would also illuminate 'the whole house at once with a gleaming light, and the next moment [vanish] as suddenly as he came, leaving behind him utter darkness'.

It is interesting that Ceredig Davies, who described the ghost, should refer to it as a 'he', because the author then goes on to say that it was seen walking across the farmyard 'appearing as a tall handsome lady attired in a lustring white dress, and her face covered by a silken veil'! This is the only transvestite White Lady I have on record. He/she was a bit of a drama queen, too, for having caught the attention of some young men in the farmyard, she 'suddenly disappeared in a ball of fire'. In all other respects the ghost behaved much as other White Ladies, her trouble being the usual one of hidden treasure:

'One Sunday evening ... about the beginning of winter ... all the family as usual had gone to chapel, except the servant maid, who did not feel well, and her lover came to keep her company. Naturally, the young man and the young woman began to talk about the ghost, and Evan (for that was the young man's name) laughed, and boasted what he was going to do should the disturber appear. But the next moment, without the least notice, a lady in her white dress stood right in the middle of the room, with her face uncovered, and her brown curly hair down over her shoulders. She held in one hand a comb and the other a roll of paper, but she did not whisper a word.

'The servant maid, and her young man who had just been boasting shuddered in terror, and dared not move or utter a word. The "lady" walked round the apartment several times; then suddenly stood; and having opened the door through which she had entered without opening, beckoned the young man to follow her. As he dared not disobey, he followed her up stairs, into a dark back room, but which was now lighted up in some mysterious way. With her finger she pointed out a particular corner under the low roof, at which place the young man with his trembling hand found some hard parcel carefully tied in an old woollen stocking. When he opened it he found it full of money, and at the same moment the "White Lady" vanished and never disturbed the house again.'

There is no explanation offered as to why the ghost should have been handling 'a comb and a roll of paper' when it appeared. Perhaps it had been at its ablutions when the opportunity to seek help from the young man presented itself.[14]

Llanddewi Brefi

One morning Mr John Evans, of Gogoyan, set off from Llanddewi to Aberystwyth, about twenty miles away. Early the same afternoon, one of Mr Evans's servants was surprised to see him pottering about in the field he was busy ploughing. He wondered what he was doing there and why he had returned from Aber so early. The truth was, he hadn't returned at all – and didn't do till many hours later, after dark. The astonished servant told him what he had seen, but Mr Evans wasn't too concerned.

'Well,' he said, 'if you saw me, you only saw my spirit, for I have been away all day; now to see the spirit of a living man is not a bad sign.'[15]

This Mr John Evans was the grandfather of J Ceredig Davies. Experiences similar to this one, involving different people, were also reported by Davies as having taken place at Llandysul and Llanrhystud.

Llandre
(Llanfihangel Genau'r Glyn)

There is a treasure legend attached to a house named Glanfred, which John Ceredig Davies spells 'Glanfread'. The story goes that one Christmas holidays the young nieces of the owner of the house came to stay and one night decided to play cards, inviting the housemaid to join them. They played until very late and it began to grow cold, the fire having almost gone out. The housemaid (of course) went outside to collect some firewood, but took a very long time about it. When she did eventually return, she passed out on the floor!

The next morning the housemaid was asked what had happened while she had been outside but she refused to tell them. This made the owner of the house very angry – and he threatened her with his gun, telling her that he'd shoot her unless she told! Still she refused and not very long after she married her boyfriend, a farm servant, and they bought a very large farm. This caused great consternation in the neighbourhood – how could two poor servants afford such a property? The general consensus of opinion was that she had been directed to some hoard by a ghost the night she fainted. Perhaps treasure was known to be hidden somewhere about Glanfred, which is why the owner became so aggressive when he learnt of his housemaid's strange behaviour.[16]

(Ceredig Davies also informs us that Glanfred was the birthplace of one of the most famous of Welsh antiquarians, the celebrated Edward Llwyd, author of *Archaeologia Britannica*, which was published in the 17th century.)[17]

Llandysul

Near Llandysul there is a pool in the River Teifi which bore the name, in translation, 'The Pool of the Harper'. It earned its name because an old harper was drowned there long ago. If you can find this pool and sit on the river bank on a fine summer afternoon, you may hear the sound of a harp playing among the swirling waters, the musician's spirit undaunted despite his watery grave.[18]

In the early years of the 19th century, a Mrs D Thomas, of Llanfair, lost her daughter, causing her great heartbreak. It was said she 'bewailed her loss day and night'. But one day, when she was out in the potato field, the spirit of her dead daughter appeared before her and glared at her 'with severe looks'.

'Don't cry after me,' she said, 'for I am in a much better place.'[19]

It is recorded that there was once 'a well-known haunted spot' in the neighbourhood of Pontshan, and it was haunted by 'a ghost' – neither very useful bits of information, but the one short account which remains about it does contain an interesting detail. A man walking past the haunted spot one night saw the ghost by the roadside, so he immediately pulled out his knife and the spook vanished at the sight of it. It is unlikely the ghost was afraid of physical injury from the blade, so what frightened it off? Cold iron or steel was often used as a defence against fairies and it appears to have had the same effect on this *bwgan*.[20] Edmund Jones describes the drawing of a knife to ward off fairy magic in his *A Relation of Apparitions*, a fact noted by T Gwynn Jones in his *Welsh Folklore and Folk Custom*.[21] Here we have

another example of the cross-over between Welsh fairylore and ghostlore, as discussed in the introduction.

Llangunllo/Llangynllo

This parish – both spellings seem correct – is situated three and a half miles north-east of Newcastle Emlyn on the way to Lampeter. Here, at Gernos, a White Lady used to be seen. Tradition had it that she was a young woman put to death by the Romans.[22]

Monachty

The grand mansion of Monachty near Aberaeron was haunted in the first half of the 19th century. A man named James Jones was brought up in the neighbourhood of Monachty at that period and he recalled being terrified as a small boy that the ghost would come and get him when he was in his bed. The spook was said to be 'so small that it could go through even the eye of a needle', and there was no way little James would be able to stop up all the cracks in his father's tumbledown cottage!

The people of Monachty called in some students from Ystrad Meurig College to lay the ghost. This they did, dooming the spirit to cut away at a rock near Llanrhystud, presumably with some tiny instrument to make the task last forever.[23] (Having studied the prospectuses of all the colleges in Wales, I am disappointed to report that none of them now hold courses in Exorcism or Ghost Laying, not even as a night class...)

Pontrhydfendigaid

'Old John Jones', who was an important source of stories for J Ceredig Davies (such as that from Rhosygarth, below), lived at this charmingly named village (it translates as Bridge of the Blessed Ford). Mr Jones told the folklorist that a nearby farm was haunted by a ghost which was 'engaged in the dangerous game of stone-throwing to the great discomfort of the family'. The farm was located somewhere along the road to Tregaron.[24]

Rhosygarth

The *gwyllgi*, the Dog of Darkness of Welsh legend, is often described as a hound as big as a calf. The *gwyllgi* which haunted Rhosygarth, a village on the A485 south of Aberystwyth, was more cow-like than most, only its head resembling that of a dog. One witness was a Mr Hughes, of Pantyddafad, who was riding by Rhosygarth one night when he spotted the weird creature crossing the road in front of him. He often spoke of his experience and one of his servants, John Jones – later of Pontrhydfendigaid – recalled it many years later when asked for local ghost stories by Ceredig Davies.[25]

Swyddffynnon

In this little community north of Tregaron there once lived a lady named Mrs Evans. One evening she had a terrible fright. A neighbour, a Mr Edwards, on calling to see her, found her sitting in an armchair 'greatly depressed'. He asked her the matter and she told him that she had seen a ghost in her home and it had upset her very much.

She had noticed a light coming from an unoccupied bedroom at the far end of the house but had hardly had time to ponder on the matter when she saw a tall, dark man with a long beard, a complete stranger to her, enter the house. She clearly observed him take off his hat and place it on a table, pull off his gloves and throw them in the hat, and then place his riding whip across the hat's brim, before entering the lit-up room. He had carried out this performance without uttering a single word.

So astonished was Mrs Evans that it appears she did nothing to investigate the reason why this strange man had entered her home. Elias Owen, who heard the account from Mr Edwards's son, does not make the reason for this clear, but I suspect that the lady had already picked up on the atmosphere of the supernatural and had recognised the stranger as an apparition rather than a living intruder. At any rate, she waited without interfering until the bearded man came back out of the room, collect his things and leave the house. As soon as he had left, she noticed the light had gone out in the room, and that was the end of the adventure.

A while later, an explanation for this apparition became apparent. Mrs Evans was expecting a baby but her pregnancy went wrong and she became very ill. As there was some fear for Mrs Evans's safety and she lived in so out-of-the-way a place, Mr Edwards – presumably in the absence of Mr Evans – agreed to ride over to Aberystwyth to fetch a doctor. Unfortunately, when he arrived, he discovered that the town's two doctors were both absent. But he was informed at his inn that a physician from London happened to be staying nearby, so this gentleman's services were requested. On hearing of the seriousness of the case, the London doctor agreed to accompany Mr Edwards back to Swyddffynnon, and they rode back as rapidly as their horses could carry them.

It will be no surprise to the perceptive reader that this doctor happened to be tall and dark and that he had a long beard, but it did momentarily startle Mr Edwards when, on entering the house, he saw him take off his hat and place it on a table, pull off his gloves and throw them in the hat, and then place his riding whip across the hat's brim, just as Mrs Evans had described. He then observed that there was now a light in the unoccupied room which had featured in Mrs Evans's vision. It transpired that Mrs Evans had suffered a miscarriage – and the stillborn baby had been placed in this room by solicitous servants.

The tale does not end entirely tragically, however. Although the London doctor had arrived too late to save the child, he was in time to save the mother, and Mrs Evans lived for many long years after this strangely prophesied crisis.[26]

Talybont

Penpompren, a large house near this village in northern Ceredigion, was once plagued by a troublesome poltergeist which focused its unwelcome attentions on the head servant. This unfortunate individual had no peace, for whenever he went out after dark, the *bwgan* would be sure to follow him; its particular trick was throwing water in the servant's face. At last the victim of this supernatural prankster sought out a *Dyn Hysbys*, or Cunning Man, to help him. The *Dyn Hysbys* accompanied the servant to Penpompren and carried out an exorcism, by which he conjured the spirit into the form of an insect, which he then trapped inside a bottle. Having securely corked it, the Cunning Man then threw the bottle under a nearby bridge, and no more was heard from it.[27] Many other spirits have been buried under Welsh bridges (see, for example, Llandegla, Denbighshire and Llanidloes, Powys).

A pathetic little ghost, testament to a secret tragedy, haunted a place called Allt y Crib in the neighbourhood of Talybont. In the 1850s the body of a tiny baby was found hidden in a mineshaft. The locals guessed who the mother was and a rumour got about that both she and her family were haunted by the infant's pitiful spirit. If so, they were not the only people to see it, for the child also wandered Allt y Crib, 'and its bitter crying disturbed the whole neighbourhood, till many timid people were afraid to go out after dark'. For decades afterwards the hole where the baby was found was called Shaft y Plentyn (Child's Shaft).[28]

Troedyraur

At the other end of the county, a few miles from Newcastle Emlyn, another child's ghost was seen. This little apparition always appeared dressed in yellow, earning it the name Bwci Melyn Bach y Cwm, or Little Yellow Spook of the Valley. The use of the word Bwci, frequently used to describe a goblin or mischievous fairy, implies that this ghost was of some antiquity.[29]

Ystrad Meurig

There are two interesting examples of travellers encountering spectres in the vicinity of this village, which is north of Tregaron. The first concerns an old couple named Shon and Shan, who lived in a cottage at Ynysfach. Shon was late returning home from work one night and, convinced that he had waylaid himself in a pub owned by a friend of his, Shan went out to fetch him. But Shon was not there (indeed the story does not tell us what happened to Shon, so we must presume that he eventually turned up of his own accord). Downhearted, Shan left the Tyngraig alehouse and began to make her way back to Ynysfach.

'It was a cloudless moonlight night, almost as light as day, but the road was lonely and the hour late, and when she had walked some distance, to her great terror, she noticed a ghost in the field making his way nearer and nearer to her till at last the strange object came to the hedge on the roadside quite close to her. Frightened as she was, she struck the ghost with the strong walking-stick which she held in her hand, saying "D——l! thou shalt follow me no longer." When Shan struck the ghost her walking-stick went right through the head of the thing, but she did not "feel" that it touched anything. It was like striking a fog; but the spirit vanished into nothing, and Shan walked on. The ghost was now invisible, but the old woman "felt" that it still followed her, though she could not see it; but when she was crossing a brook she became aware that her pursuer left her.'[30]

Near Ystrad Meurig, a desolate open place called Rhosmeherin had a fearfully haunted reputation. A 'poor old woman' had been murdered here, and this, the locals believed, had given rise to the haunting. However, the apparition which manifested itself here did not, as might be supposed, take the form of the murdered woman – it appeared in the shape of a cat. A young man encountered this phantom pussy in a tree one night, and struck out at it, causing it to vanish 'in a blazing fire'. This same young man met another ghost – or perhaps the same one in a different guise – on another occasion at Rhosmeherin. Here is his story:

'I was going home one evening from my work from Ros y Wlad, and had to go through Rhosmeherin. I heard the sound of a horse coming after me. I jumped [to] one side to make room for him to pass; but when he came opposite to me he did not go forward a single pace faster than myself. When I went on slowly, he went slowly; when I went fast, he went fast. "Good night," said I at last, but no answer. Then I said it was a very fine night, but the gentleman on horseback did not seem to take any notice of what I said. I was beginning to perspire and almost ready to fall down with fright, hoping to get rid of him, as I now perceived that he was the Devil himself appearing in the form of a gentleman.

'On we went along the dark narrow lane till we came to the turnpike road, when it became a little lighter, which gave me courage to turn my eyes and see what kind of a man he was. The horse looked like a soldier's horse, a splendid one, and his feet like the feet of a calf, without any shoes under them, and the feet of the gentleman in the stirrups were also like the feet of a calf. My courage failed me to look what his head and body were like.

'On we went till we came to the cross-road. I had heard many a time that a ghost leaves everybody there. Well, to the cross road we came. But ah! I heard the sound of the ground as if it were going to rend, and the heavens going to fall upon my head; and in this sound I lost sight of him. How he went away I know not, nor the direction he went.'[31]

A horseman with cloven hooves for feet certainly sounds very devilish – no doubt 'the direction he went' was down!

[1] Lloyd, 1887, pp. 460-462. Nantgynllo is now spelt Nantcwnlle.

[2] Jones, T G, 1930, p. 47.

[3] Ibid, p. 39.

[4] Davies, 1911, p. 212 quoting from *Ysten Sioned*, no date given, by D Silvan Evans and John Jones.

[5] Owen, 1896, p. 153.

[6] Trevelyan, 1909, p. 205.

[7] Davies, 1911, p. 209.

[8] Clough, 1861, p. 56.

[9] Jones, T G, 1930, p. 40.

[10] Wilkins, 1879, p. 16.

[11] Davies, 1911, p. 190.

[12] Ibid, p. 154.

[13] Ibid.

[14] Ibid, p. 153.

[15] Ibid, p. 163.

[16] Ibid, p. 155.

[17] Ibid, p. 177.

[18] Ibid, p. 174.

[19] Ibid, p. 165.

[20] Ibid, p. 188.

[21] Jones, Edmund, 1780. See also Jones, T G, 1930, p. 68.

[22] *Bye-Gones*, September 1912, p. 270.

[23] Davies, 1911, p. 190.

[24] Ibid, p. 150.

[25] Ibid, p. 182.

[26] Owen, 1896, p. 296.

[27] Davies, 1911, p. 189.

[28] Ibid, p. 166.

[29] Ibid

[30] Ibid, p. 192.

[31] Ibid, p. 173-4, translating from *Ystraeon y Gwyll* by D Lledrod Davies, 1893.

Pembrokeshire

Cilrhedyn

An especially weird example of the *Tolaeth*, or omen of death, was reported by William Howells as having taken place at Cilrhedyn some years before the publication of his book *Cambrian Superstitions*, in 1831.

One Hallowe'en night some young women decided to perform a time-honoured custom to determine the identities of their future husbands. The ladies hung their 'chemises' up on a line, and then settled back to enjoy the evening. They believed that at some point during the night they would see the apparition of a spouse-to-be approach the dangling undergarments, touch one, and therefore make his choice. One of the flesh-and-blood contenders for the young women's affections, having heard of their plan, invited himself along to join the fun. He even went so far as to hang his shirt upon the line alongside the chemises, a tacit invitation, no doubt, for one of the girls to choose *him*.

Such levity proved fatal, however. The Dark Powers of the Pembrokeshire countryside took their revenge. Neither man nor woman approached the garments, instead a floating coffin was seen! The grim spectre flew across the room and touched the young man's shirt. Everyone was extremely upset, but the youth bravely laughed it off, persuading himself it was a dream. One night not long after, however, he went out to buy some tobacco from a shop and fell off a wooden bridge into the river, 'and was discovered a corpse in the morning'.[1]

Eglwyswrw

At a place called Yet Wen, Pen'rallt, near Eglwyswrw, a very unusual ghost was seen – a white cat. The local people believed this inoffensive-looking creature was actually His Satanic Majesty in disguise. One night an old woman passing Yet Wen called out: 'Come out, you devil!' and the white cat appeared, although what happened next is not recorded. Sometimes the more traditional White Lady was seen instead of the cat, but she was regarded with an equal suspicion of hellfire.[2]

White cats may have been associated with the afterlife. A clerical friend of the folklorist Elias Owen was once approached by a man who was concerned that his recently deceased brother had gone to hell. He explained that he had seen a white cat descending the trunk of a tree near his brother's home and believed that it represented his brother's soul. It was the fact that the cat was coming down the tree that concerned him; if it had been climbing up, he would have presumed his brother was bound for heaven.[3]

Glandwr

A very sober and respectable clergyman, one Rev John Griffiths, had an experience with a phantom funeral which convinced him of the reality of the death omens, a belief he had previously considered ignorant and possibly ungodly. He had been riding back to Glandwr one night in a narrow lane when his horse suddenly shied. He was unable to see what could have possibly startled the mare, so he urged it on. To his surprise, she reared aside as if frightened of something and when, in his irritation at the beast's irrational behaviour, he dug in his spurs, she promptly leapt over a hedge! Astounded by the animal's behaviour, and a little shaken, Rev Griffiths dismounted and led his recalcitrant mount back into the lane. Although he was still unable to see anything untoward, his ears picked up a sound. Soon he was able to distinctly hear footsteps treading down the road, although there was no human agency visible to account for them.

Swallowing hard, the reverend gentleman realised that what he was experiencing was very similar to the sorts of superstitious accounts he had often declaimed against in the pulpit. Determined to satisfy himself that this was indeed the case, he followed the footsteps. They led him to *his own chapel*, and seemed to gather together in a corner of the burial ground at-

tached to it before fading away. When, in the course of the following week, a real funeral procession made its way to the chapel, for a burial in precisely the spot where the footsteps had led, Rev Griffiths was big enough to own his mistake and never more ridiculed such phenomena in his sermons.[4]

Haverfordwest (Hwlffordd)

According to Mr and Mrs Hall, in their enjoyable and beautifully illustrated *A Book of South Wales*, published in 1861: 'Under the Monument Arch of Old Havorfordwest Bridge … a spirit has been laid for a thousand years; at the expiration of that time … it will again be free to roam the earth and be a trouble to mortals.'[5]

A *gwyllgi* haunts the road to Pembroke Dock. In 1920, a Mr J W Phillips wrote to *Archaeologia Cambrensis* (of all things) to tell them that he had seen the apparition twice and that he knew of five other people who had seen it. He described it as a 'large black creature' about the size of a St Bernard dog 'but its head and forequarters were more like a goat's or a calf's and it had short horns'. Mr Phillips said it appeared near a house called 'Woodbyne', about two miles south of Haverfordwest. He added that on the first occasion, he got a really good look at the creature because it was a bright, moonlit night and he was only a couple of yards away from it.[6]

Nearby Prendergrast was also haunted. Edward Laws, in his *History of Little England Beyond Wales* (1888) states that a deceased member of the Stepney family was known to walk in the village long after his body had been confined to its grave.[7]

Letterston

A man called one evening at an inn and stayed some time, refreshing himself. It was after dark when he gathered himself up to continue on his journey. The landlord became agitated when he saw the stranger was about to depart and hurried to inform him that the road was haunted. He said the ghost was heard to cry out: 'The days are long and the nights are cold to wait for Noe.'

'O, I am the man sought for,' said the traveller, unperturbed, and he went out into the night. Neither the ghost nor the stranger with the peculiar surname of Noe were heard of again. John Ceredig Davies was informed by an elderly woman that this incident took place at Letterston, south of Fishguard.[8]

Ceredig Davies refers to another story with a similar plot, but the action of which he is only able to place 'in a certain part of West Wales'. It might just as well appear here. The story concerns a room in a farmhouse which was haunted by a spirit which could be heard to complain in a mournful voice: 'Hir yw'r dydd, a hir yw'r nos, a hir yw aros Arawn (Long is the day and long is the night, long is waiting for Arawn).' No one could use the room and it was kept shut for a very long time.

One cold evening a stranger was welcomed in to warm himself at the fire, and the family treated him to supper, too. He asked whether he could have lodging for the night, but he was regretfully informed that there was only one spare room – and it was haunted. No matter, said the man, and begged to be allowed to stay. Since he had been fairly warned, the family acceded to his request. Later, in the conversation that followed, they were amazed to learn that his name was none other than Arawn. Arawn went to bed in the haunted chamber as agreed and the spirit was quiet for the first time in ages. Imagine the family's surprise when they called on Arawn the next day and found him gone! The ghost, too, was never heard of again.[9]

The name of the stranger is an interesting detail in this story, for, in Welsh fairylore, the king of the fairies is sometimes named Arawn, and this suggests there may have been something otherworldly about the traveller. The name 'Noe' in the previous tale seems strangely anonymous, too. For another legend of this type, see Kidwelly, Carmarthenshire.

Llanychaer

Llanychaer belongs to the little parish of Llanllawer south-east of Fishguard. Near here there is a field called Parc-y-Marw (Field of the Dead) in which there is a line of prehistoric 'pillar stones' parallel to the road. This stone row had a strong reputation for being haunted. An antiquarian investigating the stones in 1868 heard all about the White Lady who frequented the ancient site:

'A lady, clad all in white, appears to those who are rash enough to walk that way by night; and so ancient is this tradition, which is still firmly believed, that a short distance before the stones commence, a foot-path, by long use now become public, turns across the fields to the left, making a detour of nearly a mile before it leads again into the road.' The historian also uncovered a tradition 'of a desperate battle fought on the spot, among the pillar stones themselves, as if the possession of them were said to have been the sole object of the combatants'.[10]

Twenty years later, Edward Laws, in his *The History of Little England Beyond Wales* describes the ghost, not as a gentle White Lady, but as a 'nameless pre-historic hopgoblin'! He, too, notes the footpath diverted round the stones.[11]

Milford Haven (Aberdaugleddau)

A Mr Pavin Phillips had a very weird experience in Milford in 1854. He had returned home after an absence of a few years and took a stroll round the churchyard. Here he came across a handsome tomb, enclosed in railings, covering the grave of a local dignitary who had died in Mr Phillips' absence. After his stroll, Mr Phillips happened to mention the tomb to his father. But his father said there was no such tomb – lack of funds had prevented it. Mr Phillips, naturally, refused to believe this but on being taken back to the graveyard, he was astonished to find nothing more than a simple green mound in the spot where he had seen the tomb. Two years later, relatives of the deceased man got together sufficient money to build a more lasting memorial to his name – and it matched exactly the tomb Mr Phillips had seen.[12]

Mr Phillips, who related his experience in the July, 1858 edition of *Notes & Queries*, also gives details of Tolaeth apparitions, seen by himself and others. His tales are neatly summarised in John Ingham's classic *Haunted Homes and Family Legends* of 1904.

William Howells tells an amusing story of a man named David of Pille, who chose as his bedchamber none other than the charnel house of the church. This morbid habit upset the villagers so much that they decided to give him a fright in the hope that it would break him of it. One night, after a few pints, some of the young men covered themselves with sheets and crept up to David's gruesome billet intending to terrify him with their less than convincing disguises.

They ought to have known it would take more than a few drunks going 'whoo! whoo!' to alarm a man who regularly bedded down with skeletons. Far from being terrified, David let out a roar of rage and cried out: 'Oh! You are devils sure enough, and I am David of Pille, so here's towards you!' At which point he started bunging lumps of masonry at the would-be spooks and they quickly *bwganed* off. Unfortunately, though they were unable to put the wind up the fearless David of Pille, they did frighten the life out of a young man who had been courting a maiden in a quiet corner of the churchyard. He was on his way home when he stumbled upon the fleeing 'phantoms' running through the tombstones and the shock killed him!

David retired to his rest in peace but it seems that some time after this black comedy he saw a *real* ghost, for, although he would not say exactly what he had seen, his indomitable spirit had been broken and he would never venture out after dark again.[13]

Expert on Pembrokeshire folk tales, Brian John, identifies Pille as Pill, near Milford Haven.[14]

Narberth

The *gwyllgi* are often described as being the size of 'a shaggy black calf'. The animal which appeared near a brook at Narberth early in the 19th century really does seem to have been a black calf, however. There was something unearthly about it, so much so that the locals believed it was the Devil in disguise. One night two men caught it and dragged it back to a stable, where they imprisoned it. The next morning, however, it was nowhere to be seen.[15]

On their tour of South Wales in the year 1860 or thereabouts, Mr and Mrs Hall heard of a Narberth man who was pestered by a ghost: 'He used to be so haunted and tormented that his life became a burden. He feared to go to bed; he could procure no rest. When he did, the spirit would approach, call upon him by name, and compel him to leave his room. He could hear, but it was only a shadow he beheld. At one time he slept between two farm lads, but they were no protection to him. At a certain hour he would be called. He would quake with fear, but he must rise. At last he was bold enough to interrogate the apparition, and to follow it to a place where it is supposed treasures were hidden. Afterwards he was not disturbed.'[16]

Newport

Between Newport and Cilgwyn stands the ancient manor house of Trewern. This house held a strange secret, one which did a lot of good to a humble Baptist minister lodging there. The house 'had been haunted as long as anyone could remember. Strange noises were often heard in it, dishes would dance about of their own accord, and sometimes a lady dressed in silk appeared.' Attempts to exorcise the spirit failed and in the end no one was prepared to live there, except the minister and his servants.

Things continued like this for a while, but then the minister began to act strangely. He would take regular trips to London, not an easy or inexpensive journey from West Wales in the first half of the 19th century, and a surprising one for a humble preacher to make. And then, suddenly, he moved out of Trewern, and not because he had been scared away by the ghost, but because he had become mysteriously and unexpectedly rich! He bought up Brithdir Mawr, the farm to which Trewern once belonged, and lived in luxury there for many years. It was said that on his death he left an estate worth a substantial £50,000. But how had he acquired this wealth? What was the meaning behind his solitary trips to London? These were the questions his neighbours asked themselves, for here there was a very real mystery.

The answer came when one of the minister's servants lay dying and he wished to unburden his soul. He spoke about the days, and more significantly the nights, spent in haunted Trewern. He said that one night the ghost – he called it 'the Devil' – approached his master and told him that 'there was an image of great value walled up in the room over the main entrance to the manor'. The minister went searching, and he uncovered an ancient idol made of gold. No one knows what this image was – there are two traditions on that subject, that it either dated from the time of the druids, or that it represented a Christian saint. Being a Baptist, the minister would have had no religious feelings for an idol, even a Christian one, and unfortunately, he had no archaeological sensibilities either. The result was that he dismantled the image, piece by piece, and cautiously banked the gold in London over a long period of time. The servants were sworn to secrecy and lived in comparative luxury along with their master. The finding of the treasure also had the benefit of ending the hauntings at Trewern.[17]

This curious story appeared in *The Fairy Faith in Celtic Countries* by Evans Wentz but was also hinted at in John Ceredig Davies's *Folk-Lore of West and Mid-Wales*; both these books were published in 1911. Neither author names the hero of the adventure, but the community of people who live and work at Brithdir Mawr today have not been so coy, for their website reveals him to have been the Rev David

George, and they say he is recorded as living at Brithdir Mawr in the 1871 census. Wentz heard of the legend from a local gentleman 'who lived within sight of the farm' and was shown the recess in Trewern where the idol was supposedly found.

Davies said the story was well-known in the neighbourhood, adding that he spoke to several people who 'vouched for the truth of the fact'. However, in the accounts he heard, the hidden treasure was no mysterious idol but gold hidden during the Civil War. This version is supported by the compilers of the Brithdir Mawr website, who provide the further detail that the treasure belonged to the Warren family, who were resident during the 1640s. The time of Cromwell encouraged many great families to hide their valuables, so this version is the more believable, if not the most intriguing, of the two.[18]

Pembroke Dock (Doc Penfro)

It is at Pembroke Dock that the story of the haunted ship, HMS *Asp*, which we began at Queensferry in Flintshire, reaches its conclusion. The commander of the *Asp*, Captain Alldridge, had been warned the ship was haunted when he collected it from the dockyard where it was undergoing repairs and subsequent incidents on board had all but convinced him there was indeed some supernatural agency at work. As the following events play out, however, Alldridge will learn he really does have the command of a haunted ship – as well as an hysterical and mutinous crew.

While the *Asp* lay at anchor one night, Alldridge was awoken by the quartermaster in a very excitable state. He begged the captain to come up on deck and see to the lookout man, who had rushed down from his position in terror because he had seen a ghost. Alldridge was furious at having been woken up on what seemed such an absurd pretext and he angrily told the quartermaster to send the lookout man back up on deck and to 'keep him there till daybreak'. But this task was not so simple. The lookout man was so terrified that, when they tried to compel him to return to his post, he 'went into violent convulsions'. Capt Alldridge had to take the watch that night.

The apparition that had finally made its appearance on board the *Asp* now began to manifest often, and always in the same form. It appeared as 'the transparent figure of a lady pointing with her finger up to Heaven'. The lookout man was only the first to see this dramatic figure.

The tension on board ship was keyed up another notch one Sunday afternoon. The *Asp* was lying in the river opposite the village of Lawrenny. The captain and crew were ashore, leaving just one man on board the haunted ship, the captain's steward. This man was descending the ladder leading from the captain's cabin when he 'was spoken to by an unseen voice'. He was so startled that he fell off the ladder, and when Capt Alldridge saw him later, he 'found his appearance so altered that I really scarcely knew him!' Alldridge continued: 'He begged to be allowed his discharge and to be landed as soon as possible, to which I felt obliged to consent as he could not be persuaded to remain on board for the night.'

Capt Alldridge's problems were just beginning: 'During the years that I commanded the *Asp* I lost many of my men who ran away on being refused their discharge, and a great many others I felt forced to let go, so great was their fear... For many years I endeavoured to ridicule the affair as I was often put to considerable inconvenience by the loss of hands, but to no purpose.'

It must have been difficult for the captain to look his men in the eye when ridiculing their stories, for his own cabin was fearfully haunted as well...

'One night,' Alldridge recalled, 'I was awoke from my sleep by a hand, to all sensations, being placed on my leg outside the bedclothes. I lay still for a moment to satisfy myself of the truth of what I felt, and then grabbed at it, but caught nothing. I rang my bell for the quartermaster to come with his lantern, but found nothing. This occurred to me several times, but on one occasion as I lay wide awake a hand was placed on my forehead. If a man's hair stood on end mine did then.'

He added: 'I believe that when the officers went out of the vessel after dark none of the crew would have ventured into the cabin on any account' – proving that tales of the captain's own eerie experiences had got about.

Things finally came to a head in 1857 when the *Asp*, in need of repairs, was put alongside the dockyard wall at Pembroke. On the very first night the apparition made its appearance. A sentry stationed near the ship saw 'a lady mount the paddle box holding up her hand towards Heaven. She then stepped on shore and came along the path towards him.' The sentry brought up his musket and, in time-honoured fashion, demanded 'Who goes there?' But the 'lady' walked right through his musket! In terror, the man dropped his gun and ran for the guard house.

Another sentry had witnessed all this and fired off his musket to arouse the guard. Meanwhile, the ghost glided past a third sentry and entered the overgrown churchyard of Pembroke Dock's old parish church. He watched as it climbed onto the top of a tomb and then, as it had done so often before, it pointed dramatically to Heaven. Then it vanished. The sergeant of the guard, with all his company behind him, rushed to discover the cause of the disturbance, and, writes Capt Alldridge: 'The fright of the sentries all along the Dockyard wall was so great that none would remain at their post unless they were doubled, which they were.'

Unfortunately, Alldridge does not record the name on the grave the ghost mounted, which is a pity because it must have been significant, for this final dramatic appearance proved to be the apparition's last. The mysterious lady had now found peace. So, too, therefore, had the *Asp*; after years of frightening manifestations, the ghost was never to be seen again and there were no more unearthly noises to disturb the rest of the captain or the sanity of the crew.

But to his credit, Capt Alldridge did not let the matter rest there. He continued to make inquiries to discover the cause of the phenomena which had plagued his ship. At last he learnt of an incident which might have explained it. I give it in his own words: 'Some years previously to my having her, the *Asp* had been engaged as a mail packet between Port Patrick and Donaghadee. After one of her trips, the passengers having all disembarked, the stewardess on going to the ladies' cabin found a beautiful girl with her throat cut lying in one of the sleeping berths quite dead! How she came by her death no one could tell and, though, of course, strict investigations were commenced, neither who she was or where she came from or anything about her was ever discovered. The circumstances gave rise to much talk, and the vessel was remanded by the authorities, and she was not used again until handed over to me for surveying service.'[19]

This certainly seems to indicate a case of a restless spirit seeking justice. What would have been learnt if anyone had had the courage to speak to the 'lady'? And what was it she said to the steward when he was alone on the ship? Alas, we shall never know.

Pontfaen

Arguably the commonest of all apparitions reported from Wales was the *canwyll corff*, or 'corpse candle', seen even more frequently than the ubiquitous phantom funeral. The following example is a classic account, containing all the usual elements associated with such stories. It also includes another form of *Tolaeth*, ominous and mysterious noises.

Morris Griffith, a schoolmaster at Pontfaen, was returning home one night when he noticed a very bright, red light, standing out clearly in the darkness. Griffith, who had never believed in such things, realised that it was an example of what was usually described as a corpse candle, so he decided to follow it, to see what he might learn of the phenomenon. It led him a fair distance but at last approached Llanferch-Llawddog churchyard. It hovered in one place near the church for about a quarter of an hour, then went into the church itself. Griffith waited a little while, then saw the light re-emerge and hover over a certain point in the graveyard. Then it vanished.

Griffith assumed this was the end of his adventure, but a few days later, about noon, he was teaching his class when they were startled by a great, thundering noise which sounded overhead. Griffith rushed upstairs but could find nothing to account for the din. This, like the *canwyll corff*, proved to be a sad omen. One of his pupils, the son of a Mr Higgon, died. The carpenter who was to make the coffin went to fetch the boards of wood, which he stored in the garret under the school-house's roof. The sound he made, clattering about with these boards, was identical to that the teacher and his class had previously heard. Not only that, but when Griffith took part in the boy's funeral procession, he realised that the route they were taking was exactly the same as that taken by the corpse candle he had followed. The procession came to a halt for about fifteen minutes while they negotiated some flooded ground – in the same place the light had waited. The boy's grave was situated where he had seen the light finally vanish.[20]

St David's (Tyddewi)

Giraldus Cambrensis, the 12th century journalist, records that the first Bishop of St David's to eat meat – thus abandoning the traditional healthy fare of fish and vegetables – was a Bishop Morgeneu and that his wicked indulgence did not go unpunished. In the year 999 St

David's suffered a real emergency – it was attacked by Danish pirates and Bishop Morgeneu was killed. On the night of his death, Morgeneu's spirit appeared to a colleague in Ireland. Pointing out his horrible wounds, the apparition said: 'Because I ate flesh, I am become flesh.'[21]

St Dogmaels

The ruin of St Dogmael's Abbey on Cardigan Bay is a popular tourist attraction. In the nearby parish church can be found the so-called Sagranus Stone which was instrumental in helping to decipher the ancient Ogham writing, a kind of note-form using cuts or slashes down the edge of stone monuments. The Ogham inscription was accompanied by one crudely engraved in Latin, showing that the stone was erected as a memorial to someone called Sagranus. It dates from the 6th century.

Before it found its home in the church, it stood in the abbey ruins but this was only after it had been rescued by a Victorian antiquarian, the Rev H J Vincent. Prior to Mr Vincent taking an interest, the Sagranus Stone had been used as a gate-post and then as a bridge over a stream. It was during its career as a bridge that the stone became associated with a ghost. It was said that at midnight a White Lady would walk across it.

'This was fortunate, perhaps, that this should have been the case,' writes the stone's discoverer in 1860, 'for the superstitious feeling of the neighbours not only tended to preserve it from injury – no man nor woman touched it willingly after dark – but this very tradition, added to its peculiar form, probably led to its ultimate rescue.'

It helped, too, that the stone had been placed face down, so the ornamentation didn't suffer any more wear than that accomplished by the weather. The Rev Vincent discovered the stone some time after its service as a haunted bridge; it was 'covered with a thick coat of whitewash, in the wall adjoining his house'. After he had acquired it, and cleaned it up, it stood for a time 'amid mounting ivy against a mossy, fern-growing bank in his own beautiful garden'. Vincent was happy to relocate the Sagranus Stone to the parish church so that others could enjoy it, too.[22]

Two White Ladies haunted the neighbourhood of Caerau, in St Dogmaels parish. One used to appear in a field in which 'groaning' had also been heard at dead of night. The other used to hang about a crossroads called Bwlch Pant-y-Groes at midnight.[23]

In or around the year 1804, a man was busy cutting a hedge between Pant-y-Groes and Trefas, when a mysterious old man approached him. The sage informed him that there was a subterranean passage which led from Caerau to Pentre Ifan and that if he were to dig at a certain place he would find 'two hundred murk'. By murk, he probably meant marks, which were currency during the Middle Ages. It's not known whether the hedge-cutter investigated the strange man's claim, but a similar one was made to a ploughboy on another occasion, and this proved fruitless. A female apparition informed the ploughboy that 'ten murk' were hidden under the threshold of a place called Caerau Back. Many people gathered round when the cottage which stood on this site was taken down, but neither murks nor marks were found.[24]

Stackpole

Only the beautiful gardens and some of the elegant outbuildings remain of the important manor house of Stackpole Court, formerly the home of the Earls of Cawdor. Giraldus Cambrensis recorded a legend of the much earlier Norman manor, then owned by one Sir Elidyr de Stackpole. Sir Elidyr unwittingly hired a 'demon steward', a man of loose morals who appeared to be able to read people's minds and who was discovered having secret meetings with his fellow demons down by an old mill. When told to leave Stackpole Court, he owned up to being the son of 'an incubus' who had copulated with his mother while disguised as her husband. In this he shared a similar parentage with such Welsh celebrities as Merlin and King Arthur, but this fact didn't help him keep his job.[25]

In later years the neighbourhood of Stackpole Court became haunted by one Lady Mathias, who rode about in a spectral coach boasting two headless horses driven by a headless coachman. Lady Mathias, too, was headless. According to Edward Laws, writing in 1888, the coach used to travel to nearby Sampson Cross Roads from Tenby, but Ceredig Davies claims that it was also seen trundling around Stackpole's grounds. The parson of nearby St Patrox exorcised this ostentatious lady, dooming her to empty a pond with a cockleshell. Now neither she nor her transport are ever seen, neither at Stackpole nor on the Tenby Road.[26]

Tangiers

For our final foray into Pembrokeshire, I must confess that I am not certain the location I have chosen is the right one. Edmund Jones, 'The Old Prophet', was the first to recount the following story, in his book *A Relation of Apparitions of Spirits*, published in 1780. A condensed version appeared a century later in *British Goblins* by Wirt Sikes, and this version was quoted verbatim in 1911 by Jonathan Ceredig Davies. Unfortunately, none of these authors name a town or village near where the adventure occurred. The scene is a field called Cot's Moor in which were to be found two standing stones called the Devil's Nags. The only name which corresponds is Cottes Moor to the west of the Tangiers Business Park, but any trace of the Devil's Nags appears to have been lost forever.

In the 1780 version of this story, the hero is named by his initials only, 'D W', but Wirt Sikes identifies him as Mr David Walter, 'a religious man'. Mr Walter, for so shall we call him, was walking past the above-mentioned Devil's Nags when some invisible thing suddenly threw him over the hedge! The next time Mr Walter had to pass that way he took the precaution of taking with him 'a strong fighting Mastiff Dog'. But the thing that haunted the Devil's Nags was ready for him; suddenly Mr Walter saw another mastiff approaching, 'a dog more terrible than any he had ever seen'. Even the fierce dog he had brought with him was overawed by the terrible hound and could not be made to go near it. In desperation, Mr Walter scrabbled on the floor for a rock he could throw at the dog, but then he stood amazed as a ring of fire erupted around it, and he knew then that he was face to face with 'one of the Infernal Dogs of Hell'. Through the flames, Mr Walter saw the terrible fangs grinning at him and also noticed that it had a white tail and a white 'snip' down its nose.[27]

Mr Walter survived this ghastly encounter, but he said he suffered ill-health ever afterwards. The unlucky fellow had another experience with an unearthly thing which also caused him great upset. He'd gone for a walk one evening when he saw 'the likeness of a man' some distance away but apparently following him. The figure seemed to lack arms and – equally suspicious, apparently – it wasn't wearing a hat. The weird thing walked round and round Mr Walter several times, but always kept its distance. At first he thought it was someone who had lost their way, and he spoke to the figure but received no answer. And then a great and unaccountable terror seized him, such 'that he scarcely knew where he was' and he hurried away on his journey. He staggered up a hill and, turning to see if the weird thing was still following him, saw instead a ball of fire. By the time he got home, he was close to fainting, but they gave him some cordial which 'recovered him from his trembling'.[28]

(There is one other possible location for the above encounters. Ceredig Davies refers to a place called 'Nag's Head' in his introduction to the story.[29] There is no village called Nag's Head but there is a well-known inn of that name at Abercych near the borders of Ceredigion and Carmarthenshire. Most of the stories Davies tells in his *Folk-Lore of West and Mid-Wales* are set in Ceredigion or northern Carmarthenshire. He relates comparatively few from Pembrokeshire, and most of those are from the northern part of the county. This location would also tally with the researches of Edmund Jones and Wirt Sikes, who seldom cast their nets further west than Carmarthenshire.)

1 Howells, 1831, p. 62.
2 Davies, 1911, p. 181.
3 *Bye-Gones*, November 1894, pp. 473-4. Contribution by Elias Owen.
4 Howells, 1831, p. 63.
5 Hall, 1861, p. 466.
6 *Archaeologia Cambrensis* (1920), p. 190.
7 Laws, 1888, p. 413.
8 Davies, 1911, p. 160.
9 Ibid.
10 Barnwell, 1868, p. 177.
11 Laws, 1888, p. 413.
12 Ingham, pp. 168-72, quoting *Notes & Queries*, July 1858.
13 Howells, William, 1831, p. 20.
14 John, 1991, p. 107.

[15] Sikes, 1880, p. 198.
[16] Hall, 1861, p. 466.
[17] Evans Wentz, 1911, p. 156.
[18] Davies, 1911, p. 156. See also www.brithdirmawr.com/php.htm (Last accessed, July 18, 2004).
[19] Davies, 1911, p. 171.
[20] Jones, Edmund, 1767, p. 80. See also Sikes, 1880, p. 243.
[21] Giraldus, p. 163.
[22] *Archaeologia Cambrensis* (1859) p. 338. See also H L J, p. 129.
[23] Vincent, 1864, p. 305.
[24] Ibid.
[25] Giraldus, p. 154.
[26] Davies, 1911, p. 191.
[27] Jones, Edmund, 1780, p. 76. See also Sikes, 1880, p. 170.
[28] Jones, Edmund, 1780, p. 77.
[29] Davies, 1911, p. 181.

Carmarthenshire

Carmarthen (Caerfyrddin)

Back in the days of horse and cart, before the roads were tarmacked and roaring with traffic, a ghost used to terrify travellers along what is now the busy A40 out of Carmarthen. Near Johnstown (once St John's Town) an apparition would appear every night along this road and it was no ordinary ghost – it was the ghost of a witch!

Unfortunately, I have no more information to give you regarding this interesting spook, for its existence was recorded way back in 1831 and dismissed with some sarcasm by the 19-year-old author of *Cambrian Superstitions*, William Howells. Howells does say, however, that the appearance of this ghostly crone was a fact 'pretty generally known' by the people of Carmarthen and that it had manifested itself up until at least a year or two before the publication of his book. Possibly the witch has herself been frightened away by the numbers of cars and lorries which hurtle along the road, or today's travellers are simply moving too fast to see her.[1]

A man who had his home in Water Street in the town was one evening passing by the old paper mill which stood on the outskirts of Carmarthen when he noticed standing in a hedge something 'clad in white and about the size of a boy of twelve'. A scoffer at things supernatural, the man boldly approached it to get a better look, but it moved away. He followed it, but it continued to move away until he found that he had been led into the middle of a field. Here the apparition suddenly vanished. The shock of this, rather than the shock of seeing the thing in the first place, upset the man so much that when he got home to Water Street he 'fell down insensible'.[2]

Another brief but interesting account from young William Howells's book concerns a trespasser who was physically attacked by an angry spirit. As he crossed a meadow near Carmarthen he was startled to suddenly see before him the irascible farmer who – prior to his recent death – had owned the field. The furious phantom began to beat the trespasser on the back with a big stick – 'in such an unmerciful manner, that he was obliged to scamper off'.

'Between fright and the efficacy of the drubbing,' writes Howells, 'he was under the necessity of keeping to his bed for several days.'[3]

Cynwyl Elfed

Cynwyl Elfed is probably the 'Conwil parish' referred to by William Howells as the location of the haunted farm of Ysgol Goch. The farm was frequently disturbed by noises at night resembling the crashing of pewter plates and its front door would unexpectedly fly open as if by the hand or boot of an invisible visitor. On many occasions the door would refuse to stay closed even if an iron bar was fixed against it. This strange activity seemed to be linked to the form of 'a genteel personage in black' who one evening strode boldly into the farmhouse, hung up his three-cornered hat on a peg and then entered another room. Shrieks from the farmer's daughter who had witnessed this unexpected entrance roused the household, but the stranger was nowhere to be seen – and his hat had vanished, too![4]

Cynwyl Gaio

Francis Jones, in his *The Holy Wells of Wales*, tells a strange tale from this parish. Here there is, or was, to be found a healing well named Ffynnon Gwenno. Gwenno was a woman who, having resorted to the soothing waters, then foolishly decided to explore a nearby cave, hidden beneath a lofty crag. This cave was taboo in the neighbourhood and the crag 'had always been the prescribed limit to the devotees of the well'. It is no wonder the locals were cautious, for it seems that the crag and cave were the abode of mysterious spirits. Gwenno paid for her curiosity – as she passed under the crag, the spirits took her and she was never seen alive again. Her ghost, however, was often seen on stormy nights and when the moon was full, hovering over the crag, which was ever afterwards known as Clochty Gwenno.[5]

Henllan Amgoed

An unfortunate young man named Reynold decided one night – after a few beers too many – to put to the test a legend he had often heard. The legend ran thus: 'If any person watched in any church porch for a night, they would see those that would be buried that year come in at the church to be buried.' However, Reynold, who lived at the little community of Henllan Amgoed, chose not to visit a church, but instead the meeting-house, reasoning that since this was next to a burial ground, it would do just as well. He sat in the cold, gloomy porch for some considerable time, and his curiosity was at last rewarded (if rewarded is quite the right word).

He did not see a procession of the dead, as the legend promised, nor even a single apparition; instead a thick mist approached him, darkening the night air around him still further and filling him with dread. The terrified Reynold stumbled out of the porch, narrowly avoiding this atmosphere of evil, and lost no time in getting safely home. Once within his own door, however, he discovered something startling and rather horrible – on the side of his head which had been nearest the mysterious mist, his hair had been turned completely white! This aberration remained all the rest of his days, a constant reminder to him not to meddle again with things supernatural.[6]

Llanboidy

A blacksmith, one William John, was riding somewhat drunkenly home one evening when he saw ahead of him, flickering down the lane, a *canwyll corff* ('corpse candle'). Feeling emboldened by booze, he rode up to it, intending to block its way. But he got a fright when he saw that the candle was being held in the fingers of a corpse which 'dreadfully grinned at him' as it lay on its bier. Before he had time to react, John was knocked off his horse by something invisible. He was left insensible in the road and confined to his bed for some weeks after. While he was so laid up, the woman whose corpse he had seen died, and her body was taken along the route taken by the *canwyll corff*.[7]

Llannon

The hundred of Ynys Celyn, in which Llannon resides, was the spiritual home of the *Cyhiraeth*, or crying spirit. This spirit would moan and groan loudly in the dark to warn of the death of anyone living in the district, or even of those who were born there but now lived in other parts. The *Cyhiraeth* was heard elsewhere in Wales but its home seemed to be here, possibly because Llannon is the church of Non, who was the mother of St David, and it was the prayers of St David which had brought death portents such as the *Cyhiraeth*, the phantom funeral and the corpse candle into existence.[8]

An old fellow named Joshua Coslet heard the *Cyhiraeth* at Llannon and gave a wonderful description of its sound and habits to the Prophet Jones, who wrote it up in his *A Relation of Apparitions etc*. Calling it the 'king of terrors', he said: 'That it is a doleful disagreeable sound heard before the deaths of many, and most apt to be heard before foul weather; the voice resembles the groaning of sick persons who are to die; heard at first at a distance, then comes nearer, and the last near at hand; so that it is a three-fold warning of death. Sometimes when it cries very loud, it bears the resemblance of one crying who is troubled with a stitch. If it meets any hindrance in the way, it seems to groan louder.'[9]

Llanybyther

A 'sober, sensible man' who lived in a roadside house in Llanybyther parish once heard the *Cyhiraeth* outside his window. It had a 'disagreeable horrid sounding voice ... very terrible and impressive on the mind and memory' and it uttered these words: 'Woolach! Woolach!' The Rev Edmund Jones, who usually has an explanation for everything, however odd, admitted that 'Woolach! Woolach!' are 'strange words of no signification', but, since a funeral passed that way soon after, it can at least be admitted that the *Cyhiraeth* was doing its job, even if nobody could understand what it was going on about.[10]

Kidwelly (Cidweli)

There are two very interesting ghost legends attached to Kidwelly, both dating from the period of the Norman occupation and both featuring beautiful but doomed heroines.

Firstly, we have Gwenllian, lovely wife of a 12th century Prince of South Wales, Gruffydd ap Rhys ap Tudor. Gwenllian proved both brave and resourceful when the Normans began to advance on Gruffydd's castle at Kidwelly. As chance would have it, the Prince was absent, so Gwenllian and her young sons took up arms against the invader themselves. Alas, their efforts ended in disaster. Gwenllian was captured by the Norman commander, Maurice de Londres, who promptly had her beheaded. It's a tragic story, but even more tragic is the way the tale degenerated over the years until, as a ghost, brave Gwenllian became almost a figure of fun. The legend is not unlike that of the Goblin Well at Mold (Flintshire).

In the 18th and early years of the 19th centuries, Gwenllian's spirit could often be seen wandering about on the heights of Mynydd-y-Garreg, in a field still called in those days Maes Gwenllian, because it was here that she was beheaded all those many years ago. Gwenllian was always seen to be robed in grey, with a hood pulled up over her head. A man who on one occasion unexpectedly met her face-to-face declared that indeed she had no face at all and that the hood was there as a kind of disguise, hiding the fact her head was actually missing. At last a kind-hearted old gentleman commanded the Grey Lady to tell him, 'in the name of the Deity and Jesus Christ', what it was she wanted there.

'Alas!' she answered, 'I cannot rest until I find my head. Help me search for it.'

For three nights in succession, the good old soul helped her search, but in vain. On the third night he found a round stone which happened to resemble a skull and this he handed over to Gwenllian. It was enough for her. She hid the stone under her robe and hurried away off the mountain, never to be seen again.[11]

Now for the equally lovely and equally tragic Nest. Unlike Gwenllian, this lady welcomed the Norman invaders – or one of them, at least, Sir Walter Mansel, with whom she was in love. Since Nest was the daughter of the then Lord of Kidwelly, Sir Elirdir Ddu, this may have been awkward. More awkward, though, was the fact that Sir Elirdir's niece, the equally beautiful but jealous Gwladys, was also in love with Sir Walter. And just to complicate matters further, Sir Elirdir's son, Griffith, was in love with Gwladys, but she didn't care a farthing for him. Oh dear.

This pressure cooker of a situation erupted after Sir Elirdir left home to join the Crusades, having first strongly hinted to Sir Walter that it was better if he didn't court his daughter while he was away. Sir Walter was not so easily put off, though, a fact which not only irked Nest's brother but also infuriated the scorned Gwladys. Even though she had in her turn scorned Griffith, this did not prevent her from using him as an instrument of her revenge. Griffith was in charge of the castle after the departure of Sir Elirdir and it was his duty to prevent his sister from seeing the handsome Norman knight. Gwladys had made it her business to spy on Nest and Sir Walter and knew that their favoured trysting place was a bridge over the river Gwendraeth. She worked on Griffith's loyalty to his father and informed him of the lovers' meeting place. At last, the desperate young prince hired a villain named Merig Maneg to murder the Norman.

Merig hid in a reed-bed near Pont-y-Gwendraeth and prepared an ambush for Sir Walter. Nest arrived on the bridge first, anxiously waiting for her lover. When he arrived, she crossed to meet him, only to see him dispatched by the villainous Merig. An arrow came whistling out of the reeds, piercing Sir Walter's side. Then Merig leapt onto the bridge and hurled the mortally wounded knight into the churning waters of the river below. Giving 'a wild shriek of despair', the horrified Nest then leapt in after her lover, and the treacherous current swept both of them to their deaths.

Not surprisingly, Nest's spirit did not rest after her tragic demise, and she returned to haunt the murderer Merig. She told him that her suicide doomed her to walk the earth until such time that a member of her family married a member of the Mansel family. Until that union occurred she would appear on Pont-y-Gwendraeth to give warning of the death of any of the descendants of Sir Elidir Ddu. The bridge soon became known as Pont-yr-Yspryd-Gwyn, the Bridge of the White Ghost and, it was said, for generations a white shape occasionally appeared, giving utterance to 'a wild unearthly shriek' before vanishing.

This legend of Kidwelly Castle was first recounted in an 1879 volume called *Tales and Sketches of Wales*, by Charles Wilkins. At the end of the story Wilkins vouches for its truth by describing an experience which befell a man in the 18th century:

'In 1775, Mr Rhys, a lineal descendant of Rhys Ddu, of Kidwelly Castle, a magistrate, was returning one evening from Quarter Sessions when he was startled by seeing a white figure flit rapidly across the Bridge, and disappear over it into the water. His horse refused to go on. Mr Rhys thought of the Ghost Story and prediction and riding towards Kidwelly, noticed a large crowd and heard that a shocking murder had been committed upon a poor old woman. He entered the cottage and discovered a small portion of a man's coat sleeve lying upon the bed. By inquiry, he found it belonged to "Will Maneg". Will was arrested, confessed, and was hanged on Pembrey mountain, while as still further to strengthen the prediction, Mr Rhys was informed that day of the death of his brother Arthur, of the Royal Navy, who was drowned at sea; and also of his wife's mother's death, Lady Mansel, of Iscoed, who was burnt to death at Kidwelly.'[12]

Elsewhere in the neighbourhood of Kidwelly there is a haunted well. In 1971, Mr Kemmis Buckley, an authority on holy wells in South Wales, wrote an article which drew attention to Pistyll Teilo, a remote fountain to be found in the bottom of a gorge, reachable only by a craggy path. This article can be found among the back issues of *Source*, a periodical devoted to sacred springs, all of which have been reproduced on a Bath University website. Quoting Mr Buckley:

'It is said that a ghost haunts this pistyll and cries in pitiful tones: "It is long and cold and tiresome to wait for the descendants of Wil Wattar." To this day natives of this district prefer not to walk by night along the road which skirts this ravine; and one can only assume that this is because of the ghostly voice which is supposed to come from the bottom of the cwm.'

The identity of Wil Wattar was a mystery, and remained so in 1994, when Mr Buckley updated his article with the words: 'So far as I am aware the descendants of Wil Wattar have not yet arrived at Pistyll Teilo: had they done so, I would surely have been told by one of the patrons of the *Prince of Wales*, Mynydd y Garreg, the inn at the head of this haunted gorge.'[13]

One is reminded of the tales of 'Noe' and 'Arawn' from Pembrokeshire (see Letterston in that county).

Llanstephan

T Gwynn Jones mentions a ghost story to be found in a 15th or 16th century manuscript, making it one of the earliest in Wales:

'The mother of Thomas ap Llywelyn ap Ywain, lord of Iskoed, was Annas, daughter of Tomas ap Robinod, constable of Llanstephan Castle. This Robinod came, with 21 knights on white steeds, to invade Korrws ... On the way ... he was met by the ghost of Gruffudd ap R ap Ph[ylip] Vychan ... who was nicknamed Gruffudd Corr y Gryngrair, and his ghost killed Robinod on the road.'

A ghost which can kill a living warrior is an awesome thing indeed. I wonder what happened when Robinod was dead? Did he, too, become a ghost and did he then go seeking revenge on the ghost of Gruffudd? In some Valhalla of the Welsh, they might be fighting still. [14]

Laugharne

On a lane leading from Laugharne Castle to the village there is a hollow named Pant-y-Madog which is one of the many stamping grounds of the *Gwyllgi*. This is an extremely noisy example of the breed, however. When a young woman named Rebecca Adams encountered it one night, it sat down and 'set up such a scream, so horrible, so loud, and so strong, that she thought the earth moved under her'.[15]

Llandeilo

Derwydd Mansion, near Llandeilo, has a long and interesting history. King John stayed here in 1210 and Henry, Earl of Richmond (later Henry VII) was entertained in the house before the Battle of Bosworth in 1485. The owner of the house in Henry's time was Sir Rhys ap Thomas, who accompanied the Earl to Bosworth and who was later made a Knight of the Garter for his loyalty. It is the so-called Sir John ap Rhys Room which is reputed to be haunted. The haunter, however, is not Sir John, but a lady, Gwen Vaughan. It is polite to call her 'a lady' but apparently she only shows herself to unmarried men, so perhaps she is not that much of a lady![16]

Llandovery

The spirit of a young man who had died two years before accosted a friend of his, Morgan Prytherch, and demanded that he recover a purse of money hidden in a certain room of the farmhouse in which he slept and then throw it into the river at Llandovery. Prytherch promised to do as he was bid, but on the night agreed upon to do the deed the ghost was aggrieved to find him tucked up in bed in the barn. The angry spirit sternly summoned Prytherch to follow, and in his confusion the youth put on his shoes rather haphazardly – one was polished, the other dirty. Then he followed his deceased chum out of the barn to the farmhouse. There were several people in the room hiding the treasure, but it was apparent that none was aware of his presence, nor that of his unearthly companion. The money was therefore recovered without incident.

There followed a lengthy journey to the river, but at length Prytherch was able to fulfil his promise. He threw the purse into the water and, where it sank, he saw a flame flare up on the surface. Then all was still. The spirit asked Prytherch whether he would like his company on the return journey, too, but the young man had had enough excitement for one night, and politely declined. He was left alone.

It took him at least an hour to walk home, but at last he reached the comfortable barn and began to pull off his shoes to get ready for bed. He then noticed that they were in precisely the same condition as when he had left two hours previously. One was quite grubby, the other spotless and polished – and yet he had just tramped across a riverbank and down some very muddy lanes. He wondered whether a supernatural agency had carried him home after all.[17]

Llanelli

Referring to *Old Llanelly* by John Innes, J Ceredig Davies tells of three phantom ladies who haunted the old mansions of the town. Llanelly House 'probably had had ghosts for it is certain that spirits haunt there even now,' according to Mr Innes, who also states that Old Stradey House was the haunt of a Lady Mansel (of the same family as the doomed Sir Walter of Kidwelly, see above). More interesting is the mysterious ghost of Stepney Mansion; not only was 'the rustling brocade' of her gown heard sweeping down an empty corridor, but during the night she 'played upon an organ built up in one of the thick walls' – surely

the only ghost outside of fiction to do so.[18]

On January 27th, 1868, sixteen ships were wrecked in one night on the coast around Llanelli. The next morning, 'from Whitford Sker to Burry Holms the shore was strewn with seaman's clothes, broken spars, shattered hulls of stranded vessels, sails, carpenters' tools, vast quantities of coal, and corpses'. On the evening of the tragedy, the rector of the parish, Rev D J Davies, was in the church ready for choir practice when he heard something that sent a thrill of horror through him:

'Suddenly, an indescribable scream of terror was heard in the churchyard, as of one in the last extremity of mortal fear,' he said. 'I immediately ran out to see what was the matter, and saw a young lad, whom I knew very well, standing in the middle of the walk, not far from the porch, with his face not only blanched, but actually distorted with fright. "What is the matter, my lad?" I asked. "Oh!" he replied, "I saw a man without his hat come and look in through the window." I brought the poor terrified lad into the church, where he remained some little time before he came to himself. It was currently believed that what he saw was the apparition of one of the poor seamen who was drowned, as it was just about the time when the wreck took place.'[19]

Llanfynydd

In the 1850s a house called Alltisaf was troubled by a *Bwbach* which manifested itself in all manner of animal shapes, including those of a pig, a hare and a mouse. The spook was exorcised by Harries of Cwrtycadno, described by Ceredig Davies as 'a celebrated wizard'. Unfortunately he furnishes no further details of what was undoubtedly an interesting case.[20]

Llangeler

One day some children were playing in the grounds of an estate in Llangeler parish, where their father was employed, when they came across some little cakes on the ground. Of course, being children, these morsels were very tempting, but just as they were about to put them in their mouths, the spirit of their dead mother appeared before them, crying: 'My dear children, don't eat those cakes for there is poison in them!' When this story got about, the children's stepmother found herself suspected by all her neighbours of planning to do away with them.[21]

On May 21st, 1719, an extremely powerful and dangerous poltergeist began to plague a farm at Llangeler. J Ceredig Davies presents a detailed account of this *Bwgan's* activities in his *Folk-Lore of West and Mid-Wales*, having translated it from an old book in Welsh entitled *Golwg ar y Byd ('Look at the World')*, by the Rev D Lewis, vicar of Llangattwg, Glamorganshire, and printed at Carmarthen in 1725. The incidents were therefore still fresh when first taken down. Here is Ceredig Davies's translation:

'On Thursday in Whitsun week, at eight in the morning, the thrashing began (at a farm) and at the same time he (the spirit) began to throw stones. At first it was one of the men who were thrashing that noticed a stone descending on the thrashing floor. The second stone fell on the leg of the housemaid, wounding her; and after this, very shortly, they filled the thrashing floor and the place around. The men who were thrashing gave up their work, and went to see who were throwing them, but could see no one.

Friday – The servant maid in the garden was struck three times. Several of the children were struck till they went out of the house. A large number of people came together to see these wonders, and all who came were allowed to see the stones descending.

Saturday – The servant maid and one of the thrashers were struck. Some of the stones were rattling, and something like marks on several of them. The stones were not seen till they fell, and when they were taken up marks of them were on the floor as if they had been there from the year before. A large pole came right across the window without anyone visibly bringing it. Some people believed not, till they sent messengers to see, and to bring home some of the stones to their houses. A big stump of wood was taken up from the boiler to the house top, and fell in another place.

Sunday – A large number of people came together to see, and several of them cursing and swearing, and speaking lightly and blasphemously. Big stones fell on the loft of the house, but were not seen till they descended. An iron bar was struck out of the window, and another one bent as a packsaddle's hook; and the window was broken all to pieces. After dark the stones came into the beds, and window frames went to the loft, so that the family of the house were obliged to get up from their beds and go to a neighbour's house. Nothing but stones could be seen filling the house and surrounding it.

Wednesday Night – The barn and the corn as well as many other things were burnt; he (the spirit) was throwing stones every day, though not every hour. Sometimes the stones were thrown as fast as one could reckon them, most of which were river stones, and some of them weighing about seven pounds or more. Neighbours came together to pray to God in the house, and there was not much noise in the house that night. Many other things were done by the spirit, but at last he ceased.'

As a postscript to this account, Davies adds: 'There was a troublesome spirit of this kind now recently in the Vale of Towy, Carmarthenshire.'[22] Other examples of stone-throwing poltergeists can be found elsewhere in Wales, including at Bethesda in Gwynedd and at Llangunllo in Powys, and indeed from around the world.

Llangynog

A rather pathetic story comes from this village near St Clears. Many years ago, a woman called Mrs Thomas died, leaving behind her a young son, named William. Soon after her death, the heartbroken boy went out into a field near his home and there threw himself on the ground, weeping bitterly. Suddenly the spirit of his mother appeared, wearing a white dress, and she begged him not to cry.

'Your crying gives me pain,' she told him, 'and you need not be in trouble about the future, for there is plenty of food for thee.'

Whether this appeal to his stomach comforted young William is not recorded, but when he looked up, he saw the White Lady, his mother, vanishing. Ceredig Davies kindly gives us some clues as to when this incident took place, but maths was never my strong point, so I leave it to the intelligent reader to calculate. In 1911 he wrote: 'This W Thomas who saw his mother's spirit, died when a comparatively young man, but his son, from whom my informant obtained the account of the vision, lived till eighty years of age, and died about sixty years ago.' You have five minutes, no conferring![23]

Llanpumsaint

A fearsome ghost frightened a young man near Llanpumsaint in the 1820s. Youthful William Griffiths had been out courting and, 'having enjoyed the pleasure of love for some hours', as Ceredig Davies rather unfortunately puts it, he was returning home at about three o'clock in the morning. On his way he had to pass 'a place famous for its ghosts', the so-called Red Bridge of Glynadda. William did his best to hurry past this eerie spot, but he was not fast enough – the ghost appeared, 'in the shape of a big man'.

William ran away, but the ghost ran after him! It pursued him all the way to Llanpumsaint village, where, almost fainting, he made it to the house of Dafydd Llwyd, the blacksmith, who was fortunately working at his forge even at that late hour. The light coming from the forge may have prevented the ghost from approaching. At any rate, William was safe from its predations, but had to be taken home in a cart.[24]

Llansadwrn

Outside his house one night Evan y Gweydd (the Weaver) was accosted by a spirit, which asked him to do him a service. Evan agreed.

'That is a promise which must be kept,' the *yspryd* warned him, 'and thou shalt have no peace until thou hast performed it; name the time and sooner the better.'

'Three weeks to to-night,' Evan hazarded and with a curt reply, the spirit vanished. Well, come the appointed time Evan began to regret his promise to the terse apparition, so he barred his door and went to bed. But the spook would not be brooked – Evan had hardly got his head down, when he was violently upturned onto the floor. An invisible force then began to push him towards his front door, which was now standing wide open, and Evan had to grab his clothes and hastily put them on while so propelled. Outside he found the impatient spirit waiting for him. Evan was ordered to accompany him to a place called Glan-ty-Bedw and here he was directed to 'a very large stone', beneath which he found an iron chest. Now the bullying spirit told Evan he must carry this chest to Fanfach Lake, many miles away, and throw it in.

It was early Sunday morning when the weaver and the spirit passed through the village of Myddfe on the way to the lake, and the villagers, some of whom Evan knew, passed them on the way to church, but no one seemed to see them. At last they reached Llyn Fanfach and Evan threw the chest into the water. A thunderclap and lightning accompanied this action, and then Evan found himself carried through the air 'in a kind of half trance'. When he came to his senses, he found himself lying on the banks of the River Towy, not far from home. When he finally reached his bed, he remained there, unwell, for some time. (Another version of the story states that Evan had to throw an iron into the River Cothy near Edwinsford, as well as the treasure chest into Llyn Fanfach.)[25]

Nantgaredig

From this village between Carmarthen and Llandeilo was seen an apparition unique to this book – a ghost train. At about midnight, one year in the Age of Steam, a man named James noticed an engine passing along the line towards Llandeilo. He knew that no train was due through Nantgaredig Station at that time of night and assumed it must be a 'special'. He was curious enough to ask the stationmaster about it the following morning. But that worthy told him he must have been dreaming, for no engine passed through his station at midnight. A few days later a special train did pass through the station – and it had been booked by a large funeral party on their way to Llandeilo. James was convinced that his ghost train had been a portent of this melancholy 'special', an example of the Tolaeth moving with the times. [26]

Newchurch

Walking up the lane to Newchurch, a man named Davies encountered a 'great shaggy' Dog of Darkness. A practical sort of chap, Davies immediately lashed out at the dog with his stick. Any doubts he may have had that this was a corporeal rather than an incorporeal pooch were immediately dispelled when his stick struck the ground, having passed right through it. The *Gwyllgi* 'grinned terribly' but instantly vanished – so *kudos* to Mr Davies! [27]

Pendine

Down on the coast near the border with Pembrokeshire there is a cavern by the name of the Green Bridge Cave. It is said that long ago an old musician entered this cave, taking with him his fiddle and a lighted candle. Why he went in the first place is uncertain but one possibility is that he found the acoustics to his taste. What is certain, however, is that he never came out again. Having descended deep into its dark interior, his candle blew out, and he became lost. It is said that the sound of his fiddle can sometimes still be heard, emanating from the dank and chilly darkness. [28]

Pontyberem

There was once a man at Pontyberem who was pestered every night by a spirit who insisted on taking him out for little trips. The man would submit to being flown through the air by the eccentric spook, who would ask him how he would wish to be transported: 'Below the wind, in the wind, or above the wind?' If the man had answered 'above the wind', he would have been transported high above the clouds, gasping for breath and freezing in the upper atmosphere. The correct response was 'in the wind', for in this manner he would be pleasantly flown below the clouds, at the same sort of elevation as a glider. On one occasion, the man must have replied 'below the wind' because he found himself being transported a few feet above the ground and 'dragged through bush and briar' until 'his clothes were all rags'.

This 'above the wind, in the wind or below the wind' question was commonly made by spirits to mortals who had helped them in the disposing of treasure, and the same options were offered by fairies who either wished to reward or punish people whom they had encountered. Why this particular spirit was so keen to transport this man about the place is not known, nor where they went and to what purpose.[29]

Yscanhir/Yscarhir?

Both William Howells and Wirt Sikes tell of a bridge called Pont Cnwca Bach which was possessed by a *Bwgan* whose sole purpose was to frighten people off the bridge and into the stream running beneath it. Howell describes it as a 'grim spectre' with a 'ghastly smile' which announced itself by making rustling noises as if it was creeping up behind you, but Sikes, who may have done more research 50 years later, states that in fact it was never seen, nor was it felt in any tangible way.

'In crossing the bridge,' he writes, 'people were seized with "a kind of cold dread" and felt "a peculiar sensation" ... afterwards wandering away in a dazed condition'. They would come to their senses some distance from home and more often or not up to their knees in a bog. Needless to say, people would tend to avoid Pont Cnwca Bach at night.

Howells names the location of Pont Cnwca Bach as Yscanhir, and Sikes renames it Yscarhir. However, despite my best efforts, I have been unable to find any village, hamlet or house which corresponds with either spelling. Doubtless, a local reader will be able to put me right and I will be able to correct this anomaly in a later edition of *Haunted Wales*.[30]

[1]   Howells, 1831, p. 16.
[2]   Ibid, p. 20.
[3]   Ibid, p. 17.
[4]   Howells, 1831, p. 18.
[5]   Jones, Francis, 1954, p. 131.
[6]   Jones, Edmund, 1780, p. 87.
[7]   Ibid, p. 86.
[8]   Ibid, p. 95. See also Sikes, 1880, p. 220.
[9]   Jones, Edmund, 1780, p. 92.
[10] Ibid.
[11] Trevelyan, 1909, p. 196.
[12] Wilkins, 1879, p. 105. See also Davies, 1911, p. 166.
[13] www.bath.ac.uk/lispring/sourcearchive/ns3/ns3kb1.htm (Last viewed July 19, 2004).
[14] Jones, T G, 1930, p. 294, quoting from Peniarth Manuscript, MS 131.
[15] Jones, Edmund, 1780, p. 79.
[16] *Archaeologia Cambrensis* (1893), p. 159.
[17] Howells, 1831, p. 25.
[18] Davies, 1911, p. 168, quoting from *Old Llanelly* by John Innes, 1902, p. 145.
[19] Baring-Gould, 1905, p. 135.
[20] Davies, 1911, p. 189.
[21] Ibid, p. 166.
[22] Ibid, p. 152.
[23] Ibid, p. 165.
[24] Ibid, p. 168.
[25] Ibid, p. 149, translating from *Lloffion Adgof* by T Edwards, 1884.
[26] Ibid, p. 199.
[27] Howells, 1831, p. 22.
[28] Davies, 1911, p. 174.
[29] Ibid, p. 150.
[30] Howells, 1831, p. 21. See also Sikes, 1880, p. 144.

Llanrhidian

In 1691 an extraordinary book was published by one Richard Baxter. It was called *The Certainty of the World of Spirits* and was intended to convince the reader that ghosts and other supernatural phenomena existed, and that they were further evidence of the existence of God. This was the same theme as Edmund 'The Old Prophet' Jones's *A Relation of the Apparitions of Spirits etc*, which first appeared in 1780. Baxter's book is among the earliest to discuss Welsh folklore and contains within it a strange and disturbing account of a haunting in 'Gowersland' at a house called Llanellan (he spells it Llanellin).

The house belonged to a Lieutenant Colonel Bowen, who had been one of Cromwell's officers during the Civil War. Bowen was a wild sort of character and he led such a 'careless and Sensual Life' that he was sent out of England to Ireland. While in Ireland he sinned 'without Restraint', became an Atheist (very shocking in those days) and at last became 'hateful and hating all civil Society, and his nearest relations'. All this is told through a series of letters to Baxter. The hauntings took place during 1665 and the letters are dated just one year later.

While Bowen was enjoying his wild life in Ireland, he left his wife and family behind at Llanellan. One night Mrs Bowen was disturbed by loud, alarming noises, bangings on the doors or walls 'as if the whole House were falling in pieces', and 'the sound of Whirl-wind'. Mrs Bowen was in her bedchamber when these malevolent noises started and rather than give way to fear of them, she spent some time in prayer and then got into bed. Shortly after she saw 'something like her Husband' appear in the room. Clearly, it could not be Lt Col Bowen himself, because he was in Ireland, so what was it? It spoke to her: it asked whether it could join her in bed! Mrs Bowen prayed earnestly, told the apparition that it was not her husband and that it could not join her in her bed.

'What!' exclaimed the spectre. 'Not the Husband of thy Bosom? What! Not the Husband of thy Bosom?'

But it kept its distance. The rest of the night was spent in prayer with some other people but they were 'very often interrupted' by the pho-ney Lt Col Bowen. The next day, the apparition was still in evidence, as 'the Shadow of one walking would appear upon the Wall'. That night the haunting of Llanellan became truly horrible. The 'noise of Whirl-wind' came again, much louder than before, and was accompanied by eldritch howls and cries. On trying to get into bed, Mrs Bowen saw the impression of a body in the mattress and this was accompanied by 'the smell of a Carcase some-while dead'. This disgusting effect was added to by something invisible rolling from side to side. She and her servants resorted again to prayer but the spirit, or whatever it was, would not let them be. Strange cries were heard, and words they could not understand. Mrs Bowen felt something beneath her knees as she prayed, something like a dog which lifted her bodily off the ground.

The room was filled with 'a thick Smoak, smelling like Sulphur, darkening the Light of the Fire and the Candle' and the women were struck and slapped by the entity. By dawn Mrs Bowen and her servants had faces black from the smoke and 'Bodies swollen with Bruises'. During the day strange lights appeared in the house and in the fields around it and Lt Col Bowen's voice could be heard, calling as if to his hawks. Mrs Bowen did not stay in the house another night, she took her family to safer lodging. When the real Lt Col Bowen came to visit her from Ireland some time later he flatly refused to believe in the existence of his demon double, or any of the frightening events which had taken place at his house during his absence.

Mrs Bowen later joined her husband in Ireland, but in time he turned her and her children out and she was forced to borrow money to allow her to return to Wales. This information is given in a letter dated 1658. Baxter adds as a postscript that Bowen had 'immured himself in a small Castle [in Ireland], with one Boy who said, he oft rose in the Night, and talked as if some one were talking with him'. This is the last we hear of the troubled Bowens and the extraordinary case of the spectre husband.[1]

The Mumbles

There is a romantic legend attached to Oystermouth Castle. One of Wilkins's *Tales and Sketches of Wales*, published in 1879, concerns the castle's Norman overlord, the 'saturnine' Earl Neville. Neville was known for his cruelty, and on one occasion had imprisoned a saintly young monk for whom he had taken a dislike. This pious youth was locked up in a dungeon below the castle and there condemned to starve to death. To Neville's annoyance, the monk survived for many weeks longer than he had expected. The reason was that a young guard, impressed by his prisoner's piety, had been secretly hiding bits of food in hollow spaces he had carved in a wooden pillar supporting the dungeon's roof. Despite this kindness, however, the young monk's health failed and his suffering began to come to an end. Before he went to his salvation, however, he told the young gaoler who had been so kind to him that 'if any good man or woman, free of sin, should come to the pillar, and pray there, and pace around it nine times, his or her wish would be granted'.

Some time later Earl Neville took part in a raid in Ireland and brought home among his booty a lovely Irishwoman he had taken a shine to. He forced the poor woman into being his wife, an 'honour' she most certainly did not welcome. She was made thoroughly miserable by her fate, but so gentle and kind was she that all the servants grew to love and pity her. They called her the 'White Lady' because she was always dressed in spotless white. It was not long before the wretched White Lady came to hear of the 'Wishing Post' in the dungeon. She determined to give it a try. Taking the opportunity of the temporary absence of Neville from Oystermouth, his reluctant wife stole down to the holy gaol one night and there prayed fervently for deliverance from her unhappy state. As she prayed, she walked nine times around the Wishing Post, as she had been directed. The White Lady's prayers were answered; she was indeed released from her bonds – by death. The next morning, her body was found lying in her chamber, 'like a saint, with hands folded on her breast'.[2]

Ever after the White Lady was said to haunt Oystermouth Castle. An archaeologist writing in 1887 states that the haunted room was to be found two flights up within the great gatehouse.[3] I believe this is now open to the sky. According to an antiquarian writing in 1904, however, the White Lady appeared in the dungeon of the Wishing Post. The Wishing Post was still sanctified even in those days. The tradition he heard was that anyone sticking a pin in the pillar would be married within the year. J Ceredig Davies heard a slightly different version, more in tune with Wilkins's tale. Young people seeking a sweetheart walked round the pillar nine times, and then stuck a pin in it and looked at the wall – where they would see 'a lady in white'. In this way the pillar became full of pins, which the woman who looked after the castle in 1904 found very useful. She told the researcher that her mother and grandmother had been the guardians of the castle before her but that none of them had ever seen the White Lady and it was their belief that there was 'no such person'.[4]

The White Lady of Oystermouth Castle is not the only legend of the Mumbles. Another of its landmarks, the Mumbles Lighthouse, is also said to be haunted. The story behind the haunting is a mysterious one, hinting at dark deeds and the complicity of a supposedly holy man. Here it is, in all its intriguing obscurity, from *A Book of South Wales*, published in 1861:

'There is a legend that where the lighthouse now stands a holy monk, or a succession of holy monks, had charge of a small cell or chapel, tributary to one of the religious houses; and the legend tells of an aged monk who after sunset was telling his beads and looking across the waters to the opposite shore, when he perceived a boat rowing inwards. He watched it with the interest a lonely man always feels in the approach of fellow men, and seeing that it made direct for the small Mumble rock, he descended to the shore to give it welcome.

'The rowers drew in, and a man of grave aspect stepped on shore and gave the monk a sign, which he understood. He then caused a body to be brought up the path to a cave under the monk's oratory. The body was bravely dressed, like that of a man of high degree, and his still features were white as chiselled marble. The monk looking on him could not help saying, "So young and so handsome!" He was laid in the cave, and money was deposited with the monk for masses to be said for the repose of the soul. The boat rowed away, and the holy monk was faithful to his trust, and said double the usual quantity of "masses"; but to this day it is believed that the spirit of the poor murdered man cries from out that cave for Christian burial in consecrated ground.'[5]

Pennard

Perched above glorious Three Cliffs Bay on the Gower Peninsula are the ruins of Pennard Castle. The castle was said to have been built in Norman times by a captive Welsh sorcerer – in a single night! It was said that anyone foolish enough to spend a night among the ruins would be bewitched forever. A Carmarthen man was just that foolish, and paid the penalty. The banshee-like *Gwrach y Rhibyn* haunted the ruins and when she came across the man sleeping there she attacked him furiously, beating him and pecking him and clawing him with her talons, 'just as an eagle might have done'. He scarcely escaped with his life and was indeed 'bewitched' – which perhaps here means 'cursed' – for the rest of his days. For a startling description of the *Gwrach y Rhibyn*, see Llandaff, Cardiff.[6]

Rhossili

One of the best known haunted houses in South Wales is the old Rhossili Rectory. In common with Plas Teg in Flintshire and other celebrated haunted houses in Wales, I have been unable to find any early reports of it, however. The excellent Gower website explains that the house dates from 1850 but stands on an anciently inhabited site. 'Something unpleasant', it is said, would sometimes emerge from the sea and enter the Rectory at night, bringing a distinctly chilly atmosphere to the house. One man was so un-nerved that he fled the house in a panic – as he left, he heard a voice behind him saying, 'Why don't you turn round and look at me?' I wonder whether this rather plaintive request has anything to do with the apparition of a couple in Edwardian dress who are said to have been seen here one year between the wars? The otherwise respectable looking figures had thick, grey skin like elephant hide! Were they two afflicted people who lived here in self-imposed isolation?

The best known vicar of Rhossili was the Rev John Ponsonby Lucas, who served here from 1855 to 1898. It is said his ghost, mounted on a black stallion, can still be seen riding along the bay. A less benign ghost, that of a greedy squire called Mansell, also haunts the bay, thundering along the sands on stormy nights in a coach-and-four. Apparently, he once found a quantity of treasure on the beach and, having squandered it, is still searching for more.[7]

In 1823 a skeleton was found in Goat's Hole, one of the nearby Paviland Caves. Because it was stained red with rust, which had leached through the limestone, the skeleton became known as 'The Red Lady of Paviland'. Local people said the bones belonged to a woman who had become trapped in the cave by the rising tide while seeking for treasure. Goat's Hole had long been claimed as being haunted by her. The rather unavoidable fact that the skeleton turned out to belong to a male and clearly dated from the Stone Age did nothing to quell the tradition.[8]

---

[1]   Baxter, 1691, pp. 22 to 36.
[2]   Wilkins, 1879, p. 64.
[3]   Martin, 1887, p. 106.
[4]   *Bye-Gones*, March 1904, p. 304 and May, 1904, p. 342.
[5]   Hall, 1861, p. 343.
[6]   Trevelyan, 1909, p. 66. See also Hall, 1861, p. 350.
[7]   www.explore-gower.co.uk/rhossili_rectory.html (Last accessed July 21, 2004).
[8]   Hippisley-Coxe, 1973, p. 145.

Aberpergwm

In 1925 noted scholar D Rhys Phillips wrote and self-published one of the most comprehensive and enjoyable local histories I have seen, *A Romantic Valley in Wales... The History of the Vale of Neath*. In a note at the back of the book Phillips mentions a *revenant* at Aberpergwm. A squire of past ages having died, his widow remarried soon after – so soon after that the tenancy considered it indecent, not to say suspicious. This opinion may have been shared by the deceased squire, for after the marriage his spirit was often seen about the neighbourhood 'in the eerie hours of the night'. Perhaps he disapproved of the match, or perhaps foul play featured in his demise; unfortunately there is no record of anyone summoning up the courage to speak to the ghost, so we shall never know. [1]

I have been unable to pinpoint the exact location of the next tale, which is a very old one, but I guess it was in the vicinity of the Aberpergwm estate. The scene is 'a wild ravine' named Cwm Rhyd y Rhesg. A bridge spans or spanned this ravine and it was haunted. Every sixty years a headless woman was doomed to cross this bridge. One evening, Mary Lewis was making her way to Blaenpergwm farm and passed Pont Rhyd y Rhesg. To her horror, she saw the headless woman bearing down on her. 'Her dress was snow white, and a mantle of dazzling purity fell over her shoulders in Vandyke points' – actually she was rather beautiful, but this did nothing to dispel Mary's dread. The missing head detracted somewhat from her charm! Poor Mary hurried on to Blaenpergwm but the relentless White Lady followed her all the way, to within six paces of the farmhouse, and there, at last, she vanished.

Mary went into hysterics and collapsed at the farmhouse door. So complete was her nervous exhaustion that she appeared dead. By the time she showed signs of recovery, she had already been laid out for burial. It took her some time to gain strength enough to explain the reason for her shock. [2]

Afon Hepste

Somewhere along the stretch of this stream in Upper Neath there was a pool in which 'the spirit of a malefactor was doomed to dwell'. The spirits of wicked people were often con-signed to pools of water. We have seen this occur, for example, at Betws-y-Coed, Conwy, and Llanfor, Gwynedd. This spirit, however, was not absolutely tied to his damp cell, for 'whenever it sought relief it roamed abroad in the form of a frog'. [3]

Cwmavon

'Pencastell, hill of romance and tragedy, with its ancient camp on the summit, was once the abode of Hywel, a Welsh Chieftain, and Gwenllian, his beautiful daughter. Tradition has it that, hundreds of years ago, one of Fitzhammon's knights fell a victim to Gwenllian's charms, and swore to take her away as his bride. To achieve his purpose, attack was made on the Welsh stronghold. The fight continued till nightfall, with Gwenllian at her father's side, protected by his shield until he fell. Sooner than submit to the invader, and realising that all was lost, Gwenllian hastened away, under cover of darkness, to the River Afan below, to disappear into a pool, known since as Pwll Gwenllian. Near the pool at night, in times of flood, her spirit presides in misty white form, giving warning of the dangerous waters.' [4]

The above story comes from Martin Phillips's useful *The Folklore of the Afan and Margam District*, using an article from the 1929 transactions of the local history society. It bears some similarities to stories told at Kidwelly, Carmarthenshire – many legends seem to have been inspired by the Norman occupation of South Wales ('Fitzhammon' was a Norman, of course – see Newport, Newport).

The same article informs us that Gwenllian is not the only ghost created by the tragedy. Her father's spirit, too, does not rest. Hywel, and possibly some of his followers, are traditionally believed to have been buried under an 'immense boulder' called Y Gareg Fawr (Big Rock), near Pencastell Farm. Beside the Gareg Fawr, 'Hywel's spirit appears as an old man with head crowned, armed with sword, shield and battle-axe, and wearing a shattered breast plate.'

The boulder is also supposed to conceal hidden treasure, 'and there are visible signs (bored shot firing holes) of determined attempts having been made to remove or destroy it'. [5]

Cymmer

A man at Cymmer was approached by a ghost to help it dispose of some money. All in an instant, he found himself carried to Pontneddfechan, where he was to unearth the coins. Once this was done, he found himself brought back to Cymmer at the same breathtaking speed. The spirit then ordered him to throw all the money into the river, which he very reluctantly did, having first secured one guinea for his own use. After the spirit had disappeared, he made for the pub, 'with the intention of having a carouse'. As soon as he tried to spend the money, however, the ghost appeared again and forced him to throw the coin into the river along with the rest. The greedy man was later told that if he had asked the spirit for the money, he would have been allowed to keep it.[6]

Glyncorrwg

Court sessions up north in Wrexham revealed details of a haunting in Glyncorrwg. It was the Great Depression and work was scarce. A young man of Llangollen was prepared to travel all the way to Glyncorrwg to work in the bakery here but a few days later, he was back home, and the local authorities wanted to know why he felt he could throw himself on the county again when perfectly good work had been found for him elsewhere. It wasn't his fault, he said. He simply couldn't go on working there. 'Why?' he was asked. 'Because the bakery is haunted', he replied!

The young man told the court that he heard a repeated tapping at the bakery window shortly after midnight. It went on for about an hour. The same thing happened the next night but on this occasion he also felt a cold draught as if someone had walked past him. On his fourth night, he heard mysterious noises coming from the room next to the bake-house – on opening the door he found himself face to face with an elderly woman dressed in black. She drifted past him into the bake-house, regarded him for a moment, and vanished. The young man soon vanished, too – back up to Llangollen.

Rather decently, the owner of the bakery supported the young man and provided written testimony from other bakery workers describing similar experiences, including sightings of the old woman in black. In the event, the court decided to reinstate the young man's unemployment benefit.[7]

This interesting story comes from Russell Gascoigne's *The Haunting of Glamorgan and Gwent*. Mr Gascoigne also states that the Glyncorrwg Colliery was haunted by a woman in white who warned of impending disaster in the mine. In 1902, when she was seen in a tunnel waving her arms above her head, 300 colliers downed tools and refused to go back to work. The spirit was also believed to be heard screaming before an explosion but a canny mining engineer discovered that the sound was caused by coal gas escaping through thin apertures in the rock – left to themselves, however, such 'blowers' were likely to cause explosions, so the warning was nonetheless a real one.[8]

Glynneath (Glyn-Nedd)

D Rhys Phillips quotes the bard Carw Coch as claiming four spooks for the Vale of Neath - Sir Bwci Bal, Shon y Croen, Llwnc y Trothwy and Gwilwch Gwalwch. Of the first, says Phillips, there survived an old rhyme:

'Bwci Bal yn y wal,
Bwci Beto nesaf ato.'

'Bal the Ghost on a wall,
Beto the Ghost appears next.'

The addition of Bwci Beto increases the number to five. But there are more. A White Lady haunted the grounds of Rheola and the Gnoll had a White Lady who, in the first quarter of the 19th century, used to wander about at night crying out: 'Henry! Henry!' A Henry Grant lived in the Gnoll in 1810, so perhaps it was he for whom she called.[9]

In the 17th century a Green Lady used to visit Craig y Llyn, opposite Glynneath, every seven years. There was nothing in the least bit frightening about her; she would sit on a rock in her green robes, her green jewels sparkling in the sunlight, and peacefully pass the time making necklaces out of wild berries. She was particularly fond of the bright red berries of the rowan, or mountain ash, and could often be seen pottering from tree to tree filling up her apron with them. One day, a man stood staring at her, too nervous to approach, but she smiled encouragingly and beckoned him over. He timidly stepped over to her and she handed him a handful of rowan berries, which, thanking her politely, he put in his pocket. Then there was a sudden crash or bang and she vanished. The berries changed to gold coins.[10]

It is interesting that this Green Lady was partial to rowan berries, because there are many references in Welsh folklore to the rowan tree being hateful to supernatural beings, especially fairies and witches. It was the custom for Welshmen travelling on the moors and mountains to take with them a walking stick of rowan wood, or to twist together two twigs of rowan in the shape of a cross, and keep it about their person, as a talisman against witchcraft or fairy magic [11] (see also the story of the Goblin Well at Mold, Flintshire, and Pontrhydyfen, below, for other examples of its use). It is a very unusual detail that that the Green Lady, who so much more resembles a fairy maiden than a ghost, should have been impervious to the power of the rowan tree.

Margam

On Mynydd Margam above the village there once stood the so-called Bodvoc Stone, which commemorates the burial of a Dark Age worthy of that name. The stone, which was known to the locals as Y Maen Llwyd (the Sacred Stone) or Y Garreg Llythrenog (the Lettered Stone), is now preserved in the Margam Stones Museum. Legends attached to the stone included the belief that it covered a buried treasure and this treasure was guarded by the ghost of Bodvoc himself. The inevitable result of this superstition was that treasure hunters dug under the monument, and it fell over. For years it lay unregarded in a pool of water. When it was re-erected, iron railings were set up to protect it from further harm, but then it became a prominent target for Edwardian youths with revolvers! This is why it was taken off the mountain and put in a museum.

Despite its rough treatment, the Bodvoc Stone remains in a good state of preservation, possibly due to the fact that for the first thousand years of its existence it was regarded with a superstitious awe. The belief was that if anyone read the inscription on the stone, they would shortly afterwards die. Camden, in his *Britannia* of 1610, mentions this superstition and adds, with uncharacteristic irony: 'Let the reader therefore looke to himselfe, if any dare read it, for, let him assure himselfe that he shall for certaine die after it.'

Daniel Defoe went to look at the Bodvoc Stone in 1722, but claims he had no need to fear the curse, because the words were too weathered to read. This sounds like a fib – the inscription is still legible even now, centuries later. Perhaps the truth is that Defoe didn't dare risk it! You can take the risk for yourself by visiting the Margam Stones Museum at Margam Abbey, where the Bodvoc Stone is proudly on display among many other fine monuments of the period.[12]

A monk and a White Lady have been reported in more recent times as haunting Margam Abbey.

Neath (Castell-Nedd)

From *Cambrian Superstitions* of 1831, we have the following story, another which proves that ghosts can make you rich (unless you are a writer, of course):

'It was reported that a room in the mansion of a gentleman of Neath was haunted many years ago by an apparition, and that whenever the windows were opened, they would soon after close of their own accord; but one sabbath day, a servant girl lately entered into his service, and possessed of considerable fortitude, engaged to sit in the room while the family were at church, pledging that the windows should be open when they returned; she therefore entered the room, threw the *ffenestri* open and took her seat; but had not much time to deliberate, before the apparition came as a fine looking old gentleman, and sat on another chair; the heroine soon broke the silence by enquiring his business, when he desired her to inform her master, that if he would raise a certain quarry [ie flagstone] in the dairy, he would find a pot of gold, which, if taken away, he would never trouble them with his presence again: his request being complied with, he kept his word.'[13]

Pontrhydyfen

One of the most intriguing characters in Welsh ghostlore must be the so-called Benny'r Fiddler. Benjamin Williams, to give him his proper name, was a skilled maker of violins, who lived at Aberavon in the early years of the 19th century. He was often called upon to play at weddings and dances – and exorcisms. He was once asked to lay a ghost at Penhydd Farm at Pontrhydyfen. For the occasion, he took with him a special violin he had made himself; it had a back of rowanwood (a useful charm against the powers of evil) and mixed in with the varnish was a drop of dragon's blood! Tradition does not say where he acquired the latter ingredient. He used this magic violin to play 'a certain tune' at the haunted spot for three nights in succession, and this was sufficient to banish the ghost.

There seems no doubt that Williams was a real person. Martin Phillips describes him thus: 'Williams could write a beautiful hand, and no doubt his smattering of English and knowledge of about a dozen Latin words magnified him to Merlin-like proportions in the estimate of his fellows.' [14]

In 1848 it was reported that below the then productive Tewgoed colliery there was to be found a perilous pool in the river Afan which bore the name Pwll Gwen Marw, or Dead Lady's Pool. The pool was a cavity about fifteen feet deep which had been scooped out by the surging waters of the river, constricted to about a third of its normal width, as it foamed and thundered its way between two rocks. The sides of the Dead Lady's Pool were 'formed of shelving rocks, which would render it almost impossible for a person who once sank to rise again to the surface'. The Dead Lady herself could sometimes be seen hovering above the waters. She would appear to travellers and helpfully point out the footpath which avoided the dangerous place. There is no tradition to account for the presence of this warning wraith; possibly she was the spirit of a woman who had drowned here, or perhaps the ancient, good-natured spirit of the river itself.[15]

Port Talbot

A poltergeist made a young woman's life a misery for two years in the 18th century (the specific years are unrecorded). The girl was a maidservant in the house of a Mr William Thomas, of Aberavon. The *bwgan* would follow her about the house at night, putting out her candle and then striking her on the head 'as it were with a cushion'.

It delighted in pulling the clothes off her bed, especially on cold winter nights. This is a common trick of poltergeists, but rather uniquely, the Aberavon spook would also do the opposite – piling blankets on to the girl's bed on hot summer nights. One spectacular prank it played on her was lifting all the water out of a jar she was carrying and then spraying it all over the house. On another occasion it stole a quantity of stew, leaving the cooking pot empty over the fire.

The entity showed some moral sense by punishing the maidservant for greedily helping herself to some pilchards – which her master had told her would have been better left for the poor – by throwing them on a dung-heap before she had a chance to enjoy them. But it was no respecter of religion. It would cheerfully throw the big family Bible around and would often bother the maid while she was at prayer. Even visiting ministers who came to exorcise the spirit would find their sleep disturbed by loud bangs, a shaking bed and the occasional missile aimed in their direction.

Only once did it make itself visible. The maid had set out of the house before daybreak when her way was suddenly blocked by 'a thick darkness which was terrible to enter into'. She was tempted at first to turn tail and head back home, but she considered it wrong to yield to the evil spirit's machinations, so instead got down on her knees beside the hedge and prayed. After she rose up, the strange shadow dispersed and she boldly continued on her journey. This 'thick darkness' is interesting because it seems the entity had a particular aversion to light. It would chuck candles and candlesticks about and frequently turned its attention to an old lantern, which it would throw angrily about the house, although it never once broke it.

After two years of these disturbances, the poltergeist abruptly left the house – but first it found a voice. William Thomas thought he heard a female voice calling him while he lay in his bed. He realised it belonged to the poltergeist, and cried out into the darkness: 'In the name of the Lord Jesus what seekest thou in my house? Hast thou anything to say to me?' When the voice replied, Thomas recognised it as sounding very much like that of a deceased relative, but he also felt certain that this similarity was yet another trick. The voice demanded the removal of certain items from his home, but he refused to co-operate with what he considered a servant of the devil and bravely responded: 'Satan, I'll do nothing that thou biddest me any farther than my Bible gives me leave. I command thee, in the name of God, to depart from my house!' The stern words worked. Nothing more was heard from it...[16]

Poltergeist activity was also reported from Port Talbot in the 20th century. In the 1920s or 30s, the house of a Mr John Tossel in the since demolished Inkerman Row, Taibach, was plagued by a poltergeist which delighted in tormenting his family. Neighbours could hear the sounds it made, as of 'heavy furniture being moved about'.[17]

Martin Phillips tells us that a White Lady haunted the shell of Aberavon Castle: 'In snow white garb [she] haunted the ruins and the vicinity after dark, to the terror of the local inhabitants.' It has been suggested that she may be a Lady Margaret, one of the last occupiers of the castle.[18]

The same author also provides some very interesting information about the famous Morfa Colliery at Port Talbot. Victorian miners were superstitious folk, working as they did for hours on end in a dark, alien and dangerous world, and their belief in the *Tolaeth*, or omens of death, was very strong. The Morfa Pit was plagued with explosions and accidents and the miners there came to believe that it was haunted by many apparitions, all of which were said to appear as a warning of impending disaster. Among these was 'a strange man in oilskins who sometimes mysteriously appeared in the cage or on a journey of trams and would then suddenly disappear'. In addition, 'phantom trams were seen running wild in the pit drawn by a ghostly white horse'. These spectres were known as 'ghost trains'.

The *Tolaeth* also took the more usual forms of corpse candles and strange noises. There was also a supernatural smell, a not unpleasant odour which was said to emanate from an invisible 'death flower'. Most surprising of all is that the mine was also the haunt of a *gwyllgi*, or Dog of Darkness. But this variant was red in colour – perhaps if it had been black it would have been invisible among the coal! It was said to appear prior to an underground explosion and was known as the Red Dog of Morfa.[19]

Skewen

Neath Abbey was reported to be haunted by a ghostly monk. Tradition had it that the monk betrayed King Edward II to his enemies, dooming the king to a grotesque and horrible death in Gloucester Castle. At times the spirit of King Edward himself visited the Abbey, presumably to persecute the miserable monk. Legend has it that 'immediately the betrayer perceives his anointed king stalking through the ruins, he disappears, uttering the most blood-curdling shrieks'. Apparently the ghosts stopped being seen once oil works were established at Skewen.[20]

During the year 1758, John Abel found himself troubled by the spirit of his great-uncle, one Thomas Watkin Lleision. It took him some time to find the courage to speak to the spirit, but when he did so, it said: 'Thou must come to meet me, and fear no hurt.' The latter assurance was comforting, but by the time the appoint-

ment he had made with the spirit came round, John still had to drink 'two or three cans of ale' to fortify himself.

At length Mr Lleision's spirit guided John to the wall of a building and asked him to search it for twelve guineas that were hidden there. Once these were recovered, Mr Lleision told John to close his eyes and he disappeared, accompanied by 'a great noise, which ended like the sound of thunder'. One might have thought John would have been delighted with his unexpected windfall of twelve guineas, but in fact the incident upset him very much and afterwards he was unable to 'look steadfastly in any man's face', a characteristic which the Old Prophet, Edmund Jones, stated as common among ghost witnesses.[21]

D Rhys Phillips, writing in 1925, referred to the following interesting incident as being 'of modern occurrence'.

'A farmer's girl, repairing homewards at a late hour on a dark night, found that she was being followed by some ambling creature which presently caught her up and travelled by her side. She described it as an animal somewhat resembling a calf. Having reached the house, she reported the matter to her master, saying that "the devil had followed her". He flew to his gun and scoured the neighbourhood, but saw nothing. Next morning strange animal footprints were found leading to or from the house, which seemed to confirm the girl's story; and ever since, the track has been known as the Devil's Pathway (Llwybr y Cythraul).'[22]

This sounds something like a *gwyllgi*, the Welsh Dog of Darkness. A similar monster, with the body of a calf but the head of a dog, was seen at Rhosygarth, Ceredigion, and a mysterious calf, believed to be the Devil in disguise, appeared at Narberth in Pembrokeshire. Phillips says the 'Dog Demon', as he calls the *gwyllgi*, was not unknown in the Vale of Neath and usually appeared at night but also, unusually, on Sunday mornings as well.[23]

Tonna

In a house called Ty'n-yr-Heol there once lived a lady named Jenny Jones, famous for her skill on the harp. She won a prize at the 1883 Cardiff National Eisteddfod for the beauty of her playing. After her death it was rumoured around the town that 'an invisible figure', presumably the spirit of Jenny herself, 'came at night to play upon the harp in an upper room' where it was stored. Having heard this story, a harp-playing

(Above) Pembroke Dock, Pembrokeshire: The haunting of HMS Asp came to a head in this harbour. This engraving from Mr and Mrs Hall's *A Book of South Wales* was made just a few years after the haunting took place.

(Left) St Dogmael's, Pembrokeshire: The important Dark Age monument known as the Sagranus Stone was once used as a footbridge and was regularly traversed by a White Lady.
Picture: Fortean Picture Library

(Above) Llanychaer, Pembrokeshire: The row of standing stones bounding Parc-y-Marw, or Field of the Dead, had a very eerie reputation. People were so afraid of the White Lady who haunted them that a public footpath was diverted for nearly a mile off its course to avoid the site.

Kidwelly, Carmarthenshire: Kidwelly Castle is the subject of two ghost legends featuring beautiful women who died during the turbulent years of the Norman Conquest.

Llannon, Carmarthenshire: The parish of the Church of St Non (St David's mother) is the home of the Cyhiraeth, an invisible spirit which wails and moans to warn of coming calamities.

Oystermouth, Swansea: The White Lady of Oystermouth Castle was a virtuous Irishwoman kidnapped by a cruel Norman knight – and who chose death rather than a life as his wife. Picture: Alan Daulby

The Mumbles, Swansea: The spirit of a murdered man whose body was hidden in a cave somewhere beneath the Mumbles Lighthouse cries out to be buried in consecrated ground.

Pontypridd, Rhondda Cynon Taff: The confluence of the rivers Rhondda and Taff was the chosen place in northern Glamorganshire for spirits to dispose of their treasure.

Skewen, Neath Port Talbot: Neath Abbey is haunted by the monk who betrayed Edward II – and sometimes the spirit of the martyred king returns to persecute him.

Sker, Bridgend: The isolated Sker House has generated a number of ghostly legends, mainly inspired by the star-crossed Maid of Sker, who became the heroine of a novel by R D Blackmore. For years it was a ruin; when the photograph was taken in 2003 it was finally in the process of being restored – and was rather unromantically covered in scaffolding.

Llysworney, Vale of Glamorgan: The author explores the green lane from Llysworney Crossways, where roams a hideous spectre in the form of a dog with a man's head. Picture: Alan Daulby

St Donat's, Vale of Glamorgan: Arguably the most haunted house in South Wales, St Donat's Castle, now a college, boasts a long roster of ghosts, including the aristocratic Lady Stradling, the wild Matilda of the Night and a phantom panther which padded round the corridors at night.

Tongwynlais, Cardiff: The magnificent folly of Castell Coch stands on the site of a real medieval castle. Beneath both a treasure lies buried, which is guarded by ravenous, supernatural eagles and the spirits of the men they have killed attempting to retrieve it.

Ogmore, Vale of Glamorgan: Hidden treasure also features in the ghost story of Ogmore Castle, but this was guarded by a vengeful White Lady. A great deal of treasure also found its way into the River Ogmore which flows beneath the castle, disposed there on the behalf of troubled spirits. Picture: Fortean Picture Library

Cardiff, Cardiff: This engraving, made about the year 1860, shows how humble the now thriving city was in the period many of its ghost stories are set.

Taff's Well, Cardiff: In common with many of the healing and holy wells of Wales, Taff's Well was once resorted to by thousands of people but is now sadly neglected. And in common with many wells in South Wales, it was watched over by a female ghost, in this case a Grey Lady. Picture: Fortean Picture Library

Llandaff, Cardiff: The hideous Gwrach y Rhibyn brought a warning of imminent death to the landlord of the bizarrely named Cow and Snuffers pub.

Brynithel, Blaenau Gwent: An 1879 engraving by T H Thomas of Juan White, the spirit of a witch who led travellers astray on the mountainous wastes of Mynydd Milfraen.

Caerphilly, Caerphilly: The Gwrach y Rhibyn and a very weird Green Lady were the ghosts in residence of Caerphilly Castle, with its distinctive leaning tower. Picture: Fortean Picture Library

Monmouth, Monmouthshire: Many are the ghosts of this ancient border town. A woman crossing this impressive bridge over the River Wye encountered a phantom coach apparently fleeing an exorcism.

Redwick, Newport: Tom the Lord was addicted to cider, even after he died of excess of it. He would therefore surely have approved of this cider press set up as a monument in the village his tipsy spirit haunted. Picture: Alan Daulby

Llanfihangel, Monmouthshire: Indelible blood stains and a White Lady – old-fashioned ghosts for the very old world mansion of Llanfihangel Crucorney. Picture: Fortean Picture Library.

Tintern, Monmouthshire: A famous experiment in spiritualism took place among the beautiful ruins of Tintern Abbey when a medium claimed contact with a Saxon mercenary who died on the spot. The area is also said to be haunted by a monk and a murdered woman. Picture: Fortean Picture Library.

Llangua, Monmouthshire: One night 'a great number of officers and their ladies' were seen dancing round a mound where soldiers were buried after a battle. Picture: Fortean Picture Library.

Mongomery, Powys: The Robber's Grave, as it was in about the year 1900 (above left) and as it is today. The cruciform patch of bare grass which indicated the innocence of the executed man buried here has long gone.

(Right) Aberhafesp, Powys: In the porch of St Gwynnog's Church a man heard a grim voice prophesying the death of his friend. The prophesy came true all too soon.

(Below) Disserth, Powys: The graveyard of the beautifully situated Disserth Church was haunted by an angry ghost who referred to himself as 'a devil'.

Disserth, Powys: One Sunday morning Disserth Church was invaded by the apparition of a furious bull, which charged down the aisle, upsetting the congregation. Picture: Alan Daulby

Church Stoke and Hyssington, Powys: The most infamous of the 'bull ghosts' of the Welsh Borders was the Roaring Bull of Bagbury, which was not only enormous but especially horrible to look at, for it had no skin. After a mighty battle of wills with a group of clergymen in Hyssington Church (above right), its denuded spirit was finally 'laid' under a bridge at Church Stoke (above left).

Llanwddyn, Powys: Many ghosts of all shapes and sizes were 'laid' in the valley of the Vyrnwy at Llanwddyn. Now they are all submerged beneath the Llyn Vyrnwy reservoir – water with more than a dash of spirits! Picture: Fortean Picture Library

Partrishow, Powys: This grisly figure of Death in St Ishow's Church is said to have been painted in blood – and it can never be washed off. Picture: Fortean Picture Library

(Right) Llanthony, Powys: A White Lady was seen by two boys near Llanthony Monastery. The holy community believed this was no ordinary lady, however, but an appearance by the Blessed Virgin Mary, whose statue now stands to commemorate the event. Picture: Fortean Picture Library

(Below) Welshpool, Powys: One of the best-known accounts of ghosts revealing hidden valuables took place at Powis Castle, when an aristocratic phantom guided a humble but pious old lady to some important documents hidden in a closet. Picture: Fortean Picture Library

relative of D Rhys Phillips visited Ty'n-yr-Heol and asked whether he might be allowed to see the haunted harp. To his delight and astonishment, the then owner of the house insisted that he take it with him. He guessed that the man was pleased to pass on the neglected instrument to someone who could make use of it and that having it out of the house would end the rumours of the hauntings, 'which unnerved the domestics'![24]

[1] Phillips, 1925, p. 761.
[2] Croker, 1828, p. 263.
[3] Phillips, 1925, p. 580.
[4] Phillips, 1933, p. 29.
[5] Ibid p. 30, quoting from Richard, A J, 'Folk Tales of the District', *Transactions of the Aberafan and Margam Historical Society* (1929). See also Motley, 1848, p. 171.
[6] Evans, T C, 1885, p. 230.
[7] Gascoigne, 1993, p. 86.
[8] Ibid, p. 87.
[9] Phillips, 1925, p. 579.
[10] Trevelyan, 1909, p. 205.
[11] Jones, T G, 1930, pp. 29, 141 and 175.
[12] Phillips, 1933, p. 72.
[13] Howells, 1831, p. 27.
[14] Phillips, 1933, p. 54, quoting Morris, W M, *British Violin Makers*, Chatto & Windus 1904.
[15] Motley, 1848, p. 176.
[16] Jones, 1780, p. 96.
[17] Shanahan, 1963, p. 43.
[18] Phillips, 1933, p. 29
[19] Ibid, p. 66.
[20] Ibid, p. 579.
[21] Jones, NLW MS 16161B, p. 38.
[22] Phillips, 1925, p. 580.
[23] Ibid.
[24] Ibid, p. 579.

Rhondda Cynon Taff

Llantrisant

In Llantrisant there lived a man who was considered something of a prophet or seer. His name was Wil Harry Miles. Among Wil's many extraordinary claims was that he was visited every night by a pretty young ghost. In life she had been Betty Morgan, of Tal y Garn Fawr. Wil said that Betty's ghost would come to his window and awake him before retiring to the apple tree in the garden, where she would sit among the branches or recline on a big bough which extended horizontally above the grass.

'Wil declared that she was of a beautiful form, so much so that he felt inclined to give her a kiss,' Morgan Rhys tells us in the *Cambrian Journal* for 1855, adding: 'He was only restrained from doing so by the consideration that she was a ghost.'

We discover something interesting from Betty about the habits of ghosts – that they have two haunts, one for the daytime and one for the night-time. Betty told Wil that 'she dwelt by day above Aburthin, near Pontyfon, and at night in the town of Llantrisant'.[1]

A White Lady used to patrol a place called Rhiwsaeson, near Llantrisant. One evening a farm labourer was on his way home when he found the White Lady waiting for him.

'Your wife has given birth to a babe,' the *yspryd* informed him. 'Go and bring the boy to me at once, so that I may be saved.'

Hurrying home, the man found that indeed he had become the proud father of a bouncing baby boy. But he felt very uncertain about taking the infant away from its mother's breast and out into the cold night on the behest of a spook (and I'm sure his wife had something to say about it, too). He spoke to the parson who was attending and he told him that at the very least he should have the child christened before he did so. This the man did, and then decided to accede to the White Lady's request. When he brought his baby to her, however, he found her in a pitiable condition, crying bitterly. She told him that 'one of the conditions of her soul's redemption was the kiss of a new-born and *unbaptized* child'.[2]

Another White Lady, a young girl, was seen up on the mountain above Llantrisant by a shepherd. It was bright day, in fact the shepherd was sheltering himself from the heat of the sun in the shade made by a big heather-covered rock, and from here he watched fascinated as the white-robed girl went about scattering roses. This odd, but rather pretty, behaviour did not alert him to anything supernatural, however, and he waited quietly until the girl had gone. Then he left his shady nook and gathered up the roses.

'Oh, what beautiful flowers!' declared the sentimental chap, and then he decided to re-place them where they had been strewn. At that moment the girl appeared again. She treated him to a sweet, sad smile 'but never uttered a word'. After this strange encounter, the shepherd took the scattered roses home with him and put them in some water. In the morning he found the flowers had vanished – but in their place were three gold coins.[3]

Llanwonno

On the spot now occupied by a dark pool called Pwllhelig (which I am speculating is the Pwllhelyg in Llanwonno parish) a house once stood. The owner of this house was so evil, however, that retribution was visited upon him and his house collapsed into a crevasse made by a landslip, the hole left behind afterwards filling up with water by the bursting of a spring. A woman dressed as though for a funeral, in a long veil and black, trailing robes, was known to haunt the site of the disaster, and she could be heard muttering and moaning to herself. It was believed she was the widow of the wretch who died in the ill-fated house, but she was not to be greatly pitied, for indeed all she was hoping for was to recover her lost money and jewels. Early in the 19th century somebody made to speak to her, but she did not respond, 'only smiled sadly and wrung her hands, and vanished'.[4]

This tale bears similarities with that told of the Pool of Avarice, near Cwmbran, Torfaen.

Mountain Ash

In his *The Haunting of Glamorgan and Gwent*, Russell Gascoigne tells us that in 1737 a champion Welsh runner, Guto Bach, was so intent on beating an Englishman in a race that he died from exhaustion soon after winning. It is perhaps no surprise that such a hero should enter the stuff of legend – it is said Guto's ghost can still be seen running across the hills at midnight.[5]

Pontypridd

As we have seen before, the spirits of people who have hidden valuables during their lives were unable to rest after death unless the treasure was unearthed. In South Wales it was usually the case that the treasure must be disposed of by throwing it into a river. In northern Glamorganshire the confluence of the rivers Rhondda and Taff at Pontypridd was favoured by the spirits for this purpose. It was important to do as a spirit bade you when disposing of its treasure here (the temptation to keep the gold once found must have been very strong), and it was absolutely essential that it was thrown down with the current. If the valuables were thrown upstream, the careless mortal was often punished.

Such was the case of two unfortunates, a man from Treforest and a woman from Hafod, who were transported to Pontypridd for this purpose. The rivers were in flood and the sight of the raging waters unnerved them, so they hesitated and did not throw in the bags of treasure they had found as promised. For this they were 'badly beaten' during the night, so they hastened to make reparation the next morning. But in their confusion, they threw in the bags in such a way that they were carried upstream – and the furious spirit chucked them into the water along with them. They were swept away down the River Taff and nothing more was heard from them for two days, when they were found 'in a bedraggled condition' several miles downstream. Fortunately the bags of treasure had followed them and they were able to secure them before escaping the current. Once they had climbed up onto the riverbank, they threw the bags back in, downstream this time, and their unhappy adventure with the spirit was over.[6]

Four men were riding down towards Pontypridd one evening from Llantrisant when a fifth man on horseback began to ride near them. He had a 'dark disagreeable aspect' and said nothing to them, although he rode with them for a considerable distance, sometimes by their sides and sometimes actually in among them. They passed through a gate opening into a place called the Rhiw, but the gate made no sound as the stranger passed through. The men noticed, too, that his horse's hooves fell silent on the earth beneath. So unearthly did he seem, that none of the men dared speak to him. It was only after he had left them and they felt free to discuss the matter, that they discovered that only three of them had seen him; the fourth had seen nothing. This confirmed in the hearts of the other travellers that the strange rider must have been an evil spirit.[7]

'Rhondda Stonehenge'

Marie Trevelyan, in her *Glimpses of Welsh Life and Character*, published in 1893, records a story she heard from an old shepherd regarding an ancient haunting. I have chosen for its setting the so-called 'Rhondda Stonehenge', a bronze age burial site near Ferndale, for reasons I will explain below. But first, the story:

One day in the early years of the 19th century, a farmer's son named Llewellyn met a stranger who asked him his way across the high ridges of northern Glamorganshire. He said he had to pass the *cistfaen* and the Roman camp. A *cistfaen* is a Welsh word denoting a square, prehistoric burial chamber sometimes found within a ruined or robbed out cairn – a similar structure to that which contained the gold cape at Mold, in Flintshire. The stranger then quoted an old rhyme about the historic sites:

'Go up when you will on Michaelmas night,
On the grave of the Warrior there burneth bright
A weird looking light;
And the light strikes into the Roman Camp,
Like a ghostly lamp.'

One must hope this rotten piece of verse, as quoted by Trevelyan, is a poor English translation of a better one in Welsh. Anyway, it was enough to intrigue Llewellyn. The stranger, who had paused for a rest, then told the boy that his old nurse, who had made him familiar with the rhyme, also told him that ghosts were to be seen at the warrior's grave on Michaelmas, the night of the autumnal equinox (September 29th). He explained that in order to see the ghosts, one had to walk round the *cistfaen*, in the opposite direction to the movement of the sun, while repeating the lines:

'Pray let me come in,
To see who will win.'

Llewellyn pretended to be uninterested in the legend, but as Michaelmas approached, he found himself more and more curious about what he might see if he went to the ancient grave. On the night itself, the compulsion had become irresistible and he clambered up into the mountains where the *cistfaen* was to be found. It was like a summer evening and the view from the hill was so entrancing that Llewellyn lay back in the bracken and dozed off.

When he awoke, the evening had far progressed – 'the low-burning sunset looked like a distant camp-fire in wild wastes of heather, and the full moon like a golden ball arose above the dark ridges where frowning shadows lurked'. Llewellyn turned his head in the direction of the *cistfaen* and saw to his amazement that 'a strange and unearthly light' shone directly on the warrior's grave, just as the old rhyme had predicted. Not only that, but the light then struck off the stones and across to the site of the former Roman camp. Now the spell of the place really took its hold on Llewellyn, and almost without realising what he was doing, he approached the *cistfaen*, and began to walk around it, against the sun, as he had been directed. The fateful words tumbled from his lips:

'Pray let me come in
'To see who will win.'

Llewellyn's head began to burn and throb, he felt giddy, and then – horror of horrors – he realised that he was surrounded by ghosts!

'It was a terrible sight – a scene never to be forgotten. Haggard, hollow-eyed and wretched-looking ghosts crowded around him, peered into his face, stretched forth their long, bony arms to him, as if in entreaty. Was there no chance of escape? There was not! The ghosts jostled him unmercifully in their eager haste to reach the *cistfaen*, and in their hurry they dragged him with them. Then through the air a great battle shout rang, to which the ghosts responded with shrill unearthly cries, followed by sounds resembling the din of warfare. On that terrible uncanny battle-ground two ghostly warriors met and fought. The fight was desperate, and when the victor stood triumphantly over the prone figure of his ghostly adversary, wild and ringing cheers rent the air, after which the spirit crowds vanished as suddenly as they came.'

The unearthly light had dimmed and all around was still. Shivering with shock, Llewellyn climbed down the mountain in a daze. The next morning he was very ill and remained so for several weeks. He was never really well again. On hearing of Llewellyn's adventure, his father was convinced that the stranger he had met on the mountain was none other than the Evil One himself, tempting the boy to see sights which it were better for mortal eyes never to see. [8]

Where did this adventure take place? We may never know. Marie Trevelyan is notoriously vague about locations in her books, and she does not precisely set the scene for this old yarn. Writing of the old county of Glamorgan, Trevelyan describes the location as: 'Far away from the meadow-lands of the south, and just where the higher ridges, craggy steeps, and lofty peaks appear as sentinels to the grand mountain ranges of the north.' Knowing that the author lived in the Vale of Glamorgan, it is reasonable to suppose that she was referring to the land directly north, that which is now incor-porated into the new county of Rhondda Cynon Taff.

I have taken the liberty of choosing as the setting an extensive prehistoric burial ground known as the 'Rhondda Stonehenge', which can be found on Mynydd y Gelli between Gelli and Llwynypia. It is in approximately the right location and brings together several features from the story. Here is a recent description of the 'Rhondda Stonehenge': 'The site is basically a field full of stones with the remnants of modern shepherd's huts, field clearance piles, mixed in with the remnants of bronze age cairns.'[9] The square low walls of a *cistfaen* are still present and visible in one of the cairns.[10] Margaret Shanahan, in an article on 'Ghosts of Glamorgan', refers to Llewellyn as a shep-herd,[11] so the combination of shepherd's huts and a *cistfaen* is quite encouraging. In addition, there is a Roman camp not very far away on the Craig-y-Gilwern ridge above Ferndale, and there is another at Gelligaer.[12] It would be interesting to know whether there exists a record of the certain location of this extraordi-nary legend.

[1] Rhys, 1855, p. 70.
[2] Trevelyan, 1909, p. 199.
[3] Ibid.
[4] Ibid, p. 204.
[5] Gascoigne, 1993, p. 79.
[6] Trevelyan, 1909, p. 145.
[7] Jones, NLW MS 16161B, p. 51.
[8] Trevelyan, 1893, p. 380.
[9] www.megalithic.co.uk/article.php?mapref=SS975942 (Last accessed May 17, 2004).
[10] www.jharding.demon.co.uk/rhondda.htm (Last accessed May 17, 2004).
[11] Shanahan, 1963, p. 42.
[12] www.roman-britain.org/places/twynybriddallt.htm (Last accessed May 17, 2004).

Bridgend (Pen-y-bont ar Ogwr)

Between Bridgend and the village of Ewenny (just over the border in Vale of Glamorgan) a White Lady was seen. So frequent were her appearances that she gave her name to the spots she haunted – White Lady Meadow and White Lady Lane. She always seemed to be wringing her hands in distress. When one man was courageous enough to speak to her, she brightened up a bit, and she told him that if he wanted to help her, all he had to do was hold her tightly by both hands until she told him to stop, and then 'all her troubles would leave her'. The man was happy to oblige and took hold of her hands as requested. But then he heard the loud barking of a dog, which surprised him sufficiently for him to momentarily release his grip. The White Lady screamed: 'I shall be bound for another seven years!' and promptly vanished. Whether in time she found someone deafer or less afraid of dogs to help her is not recorded, so perhaps she haunts the lane and meadow still.

Marie Trevelyan mentions two traditions which claim to account for the White Lady. One is that she knew the location of some buried treasure but could never go to find it. The other was that she had committed some crime in a house which had once stood in the meadow and this had bound her to the place.[1]

Trevelyan sets another, similar story elsewhere in South Glamorgan, but without providing an exact location. In this case a White Lady asked a man to hold her tightly by the hand, but when a pack of hounds suddenly appeared and leaped up at him baring their teeth, he was so alarmed that he let go. The poor Ladi Wen moaned: 'I am lost for ever!' and was never seen again.[2]

We will encounter more such tales as we progress through South Wales.

Bryncethin

A particularly vivid account of a spirit approaching a mortal to dispose of some buried treasure comes from Bryncethin. The incident was considered 'quite fresh' in 1839, when it was recorded:

'A girl was going one fine summer evening for water to a well in a green pasture field, where there was a ruin of an old house. Suddenly something like lightning shot swiftly round her.

The girl was frightened, and returned home quickly. The next evening the same thing happened; but the girl now looking askance along the ground, as the brightness glanced round her, perceived the lower part of an antique female figure, having on high-heeled, peaked showes [sic], with immense buckles.

'She ran home in a desperate fright, and soon had all the neighbourhood about her. They persuaded her to go again, and ask the spirit in the Holy Name, what it wanted. This she did, and had to take a hoard from under a hearth-stone in the ruin, to the Ogmore [River]. The spirit had a very old-fashioned look, and was quaintly dressed; but made a most thankful curtsey when the hoard was thrown down the stream.'[3]

Llangynwyd

Llangynwyd is blessed with an extraordinary number of ghost stories, largely thanks to the researches of 19th century historian T C Evans and his son Frederick, who both published books on their home parish. The following dramatic tale was set down in T C Evans's book, *History of Llangynwyd Parish* in 1887, but another version appeared more than thirty years earlier in the 1855 volume of the *Cambrian Register*. To start with, here is the 1855 version:

The spirit of one Phil o'r Capel tormented a young girl named Shan because she had been careless in her duties while tending his deathbed. Phil's chief gripe was that Shan had been tardy about bringing him water when he asked for it. The poor girl was now suffering a punishment from beyond the grave for her slackness.

'Shan, I had but a small quantity of water from thee in my last hours,' the ghost told her after accosting her in the street, 'but thou shall have abundance now from me.'

At which point water began to pour all over her, 'so that it flowed from her like a river'! The punishment continued for days at a time, poor Shan spending her life constantly wet to the skin. In vain she would point out Phil o'r Capel to her friends and neighbours, but the spirit was invisible to all but her. There was no denying the existence of the water, however, and prayers were offered up that the punishment should cease. These proved to no avail, and Phil o'r Capel remained recalcitrant, the soakings continuing, until a clergyman of some gravitas took an interest. This was the impressively named Rev Priest Madoc, of Blaencorrwg.

The Rev Madoc bargained with the ghost. Phil agreed to stop tormenting Shan if she agreed to perform a task she had refused to do during his last illness. This was to recover a bag buried at a place called Sticl y Bauli and which contained the sum of half a guinea. Of course, Shan immediately fell in with the plan, and she made her way to the place where the coin was buried. Phil o'r Capel watched as she unearthed it and as soon as the gold was in her hand, both girl and spirit found themselves whisked away in a strong whirlwind and they were carried away through the air. At one point they passed over a sawing pit at a place called Craig Fach:

'The strength of the wind which Shan had raised drove the two carpenters from the saw-pit like chaff before it, so that they could not see the young woman concealing the piece of gold. After she had made the gold secure, Shan was carried back in the chariot of the whirlwind to the place from whence she had been snatched away.'

From this day, Phil o'r Capel left Shan alone, but he continued to bother people in the neighbourhood, in particular one Wil Howel, or Gwilym Hywel Bach. Wil claimed Phil's ghost forced him to take a 'good sized bag of gold and silver' from a place called Dol y Rhiolau and to throw it over the Pont Rhyd y Fen, and on another occasion to throw a chain over the weir of Ynys y Gwern in Cwm Nedd. The reason behind this latter task is unclear; it was either down to Phil o'r Capel's caprice, or perhaps Wil Howel's imagination.[4]

In T C Evans's version, the dying man, and subsequent ghost, is also called Phillip and the servant girl who treated him badly is called Catherine. Philip Thomas was an old pauper boarding at Pentre Farm House, near the parish church, and, as in the story above, the servant girl refused him a cup of water on his deathbed. After his death, Phillip's spirit tormented the family, throwing stones and on one occasion ordering the little daughter of the house to throw some drying clothes into the fire. He followed Catherine around and threw a pail of water over her. The cold-hearted servant girl never got a moment's peace. Volunteers guarded her bedside to protect her from Phillip's ghost, which made repeated attempts to strangle her.

Prayer meetings were held in Pentre and the Rev Parry, vicar of Llangynwyd, was asked to lead the prayers. Unfortunately, Mr Parry was terrified of the ghost and when he was told by Catherine that the angry pauper's spirit was standing right behind him, he shortly 'made himself scarce'! In time a less nervous clergyman was found, the Rev Jones of Glynogwr (Llandyfodwg), and his efforts were rewarded by the final departure of Phillip Thomas's spirit. A humorous poem describing this haunting was later written by one William David of Aberdare.[5]

Elsewhere in Llangynwyd, a spirit kept watch over a chest of treasure in the Old Castle. An elderly gentleman learnt of the hoard and made many attempts to secure it. Unfortunately, he was always foiled by the simple expedient of the spirit blowing out his candle! Obviously, this was in the days before electric flashlights; no doubt modern technology has since defeated the ghost.[6]

A servant at Hafod Farm was terrified by the continual appearance of a ghost. At last he summoned up the courage to speak to it and it asked him to go with it to a place near Neath to unearth 'a crock full of gold'. This man was luckier than many – he was made a present of the money. He used it to build a row of houses.[7]

Sometimes the 'hidden treasure' which binds a spirit to the earth is anything but valuable, as in the case of Phil o'r Capel, where a single coin was enough to prevent his spirit going to its eternal rest. One of the most trivial examples must surely be that from Gelly Siriol Farm. A ghost haunted Gelly Siriol, but no one knew why. It would lurk around at night and no stranger would be able to call after dark without the spirit accompanying them. And there was another mystery, although a much more mundane one – on a high shelf in one room there was a basket which no one had been able to fetch down to see what it contained. One day a very tall man named Sion Bifan Fawr visited the farm and a tenant, remembering the elusive basket, asked him to reach up for it. Sion stretched and stretched and brought it down for all to see. It contained nothing more than hazelnuts. Once the basket had been found and removed, however, the ghost also disappeared![8]

Edmund 'The Old Prophet' Jones writes that the 'wife of a preacher of the gospel at Llangynwyd, returning from market saw the apparition of a man, and informed her husband. The ghost commanded her to remove certain things from a barn and to cast them into the river. She would never tell what it was, nor who had appeared before her, but her husband supposed it was his own father, who had been excommunicated by the Rev Lewis Jones.'[9]

The parish church housed a ghost which would pronounce the names of those who were to die during the coming year. As we have seen, similar disembodied voices haunted the churches of Llangernyw in Conwy and Aberhafesp in Powys. These, however, spoke on Hallowe'en night, but the Llangynwyd voice delivered its list on New Year night.[10]

The parish was also haunted by a ghostly white horse:

'A butcher when riding on horseback one evening saw it looking at him over a gate near Cwmcorion. He did not wait to make investigation, but galloped homewards as fast as his frightened steed would go. Another man was driving through a lane near Llangynwyd on a moonlight night, when suddenly a milk-white horse appeared before him. The animal he was driving reared and snorted with fright, and the driver broke out into cold perspiration. The milk-white horse turned and after galloping some distance up the stony lane without making the slightest sound, took a high leap over the hedge and vanished.'

This passage appeared in *Household Words* for July, 1905, but no mention of the spectral steed is made by T C Evans or Frederick Evans.[11]

One of the better known legends from the parish of Llangynwyd centres on an old mansion named Cefn Ydfa. T C Evans, in his *History of Llangynwyd Parish,* devotes a whole chapter to the story of *The Maid of Ydfa,* but a more condensed history is supplied by Marie Trevelyan in 1893. In her *Glimpses of Welsh Life and Character,* Trevelyan explains that she took the details (and those of a similar story, from Sker, see below) from a curious little pamphlet bearing the title *The Cupid.* From this Trevelyan extrapolates the following:

'It [Cefn Ydfa] was occupied in 1700 by William Thomas, Esq., whose only daughter Ann – subsequently known as *The Maid of Cefn Ydfa* – born in 1704, was left an orphan and heiress to her father, who died in 1706. Miss Thomas became acquainted with William, commonly called Will Hopkin, who, though only a tiler and plasterer, was considered an excellent bard. A romantic attachment arose between Miss Thomas and the bard, and ripened into a

deep and passionate love ... When the young lady's feelings became known, her mother and the family tried to break off the connection between the rich heiress and the poor plasterer, who afterwards met clandestinely in the woods. These secret meetings were discovered, and Miss Thomas was kept prisoner in her room.

'Anthony Madock, Esq., sought the heiress's hand in marriage, but was refused. The young lady, aided by a servant, corresponded with Will Hopkin. Her letters were placed in a hollow tree in the woods, and the bard's were secreted there in return. This was discovered, and then writing materials were taken from her and she was urged to accept Mr Madock. When every means of communication with the bard had failed, Miss Thomas is said to have written to him on a sycamore leaf with a pin dipped in her own blood. She would then throw it to the winds. Ultimately, in 1725, she was compelled to marry Mr Madock. Their married life was a short and tragically painful one, for the young wife became insane, and her cries for the bard were said to have been heart-rending.

'The house where the "maid" lived is said to be haunted by her spirit, and although at the present time [ie 1893] it has been offered rent free, people will not live in it. The last to live there were disturbed by noises and strange apparitions. Will Hopkin lived fourteen years after the death of the Maid of Cefn Ydfa, but he never married, and his death was caused by a fall.'[12]

Convincing though this detailed history is, a recent author has poured scorn upon it. In his *The Folklore of (Old) Monmouthshire,* Roy Palmer says of the doomed lovers, Ann Thomas and Will Hopkin: 'In fact, both were fictional, and the words were written by Iolo Morgannwg to a tune previously called "Yr Hen Gelyn (the Old Enemy)".'[13] Iolo Morgannwg was a Glamorganshire-based bard particularly active in the first half of the 19th century.

Maesteg

A poltergeist once caused mayhem for the family of Duffryn farm. It practised the usual poltergeist habit of stone-throwing, but there was a more sinister aspect to this haunting. The entity was too lazy to carry out most of the acts of mischief and destruction itself, and instead it bullied the young son of the house into doing them. The *bwgan* appeared to the boy and told him that 'he had looked oftener in his face than ever his mother had done' – a very eerie remark. He then compelled the lad to perform all sorts of bad deeds, like letting the cattle out of their sheds and burning hayricks. If he dared to disobey, the boy was 'punished severely' – on one occasion he was thrown over the house and he landed in the branches of an oak tree! At last the evil spirit was removed by 'application of the Black Art'.[14]

Merthyr Mawr

Eerily isolated among a waste of sand dunes, its ancient walls smothered in creepers and hemmed in by trees, are the remains of Candleston Castle, a 14th century manor house once belonging to the Norman family of Cantelupes (the name referring not to a variety of melon but to the family crest of a running wolf, incidentally). Here there once stood a tall, elaborately ornamented cross which is now on display inside the nearby, and no less interesting, St Roque's Chapel. Despite the fact that it was a Christian monument, this cross was known as the Goblin Stone and it was avoided by the locals.

Marie Trevelyan, writing in 1909, tells of a traveller who unwisely chose to sleep under the Goblin Stone with the result that he was attacked by a whole gang of goblins which 'interlaced their grotesque arms around him and prevented him from moving.' They then tormented him all night by pinching, punching and poking him and laughing demonically in his ears. With the first ray of dawn, they vanished.[15]

In years gone by a ghostly wagoner and his team of horses could sometimes be seen crossing the wastes of Merthyr Mawr. This man had foolishly tried to cross the Afon Ogmore in a thunderstorm and he, his heavy load and his three horses were all swept away in the swollen river. The bodies of his horses were found some time later washed up on the beach, but his was never found. To see the wagoner wraith was considered very unlucky, a warning of death or shipwreck. A 'spectral taper', somewhat like a corpse candle, could be discerned leading the team across the sands.[16]

Newton Nottage

For several months one year in the 19th century the apparition of a tall man in antiquated costume would be seen standing and pointing at a sandhill near Newton Nottage. Eventually a local plucked up the courage to ask him, in the Holy Name, what he wanted there. The ghost replied that gold and jewels would be found in the mound he had been indicating and that these needed to be dug out and thrown down with the current of the River Ogmore. When the task was done, the tall man was seen no more.[17]

Sker

The aptly named Sker House has had a scary reputation for centuries. Its roots date back as far as the 12th century, and its 17th century walls are built on the foundations of a grange of Neath Abbey. The house stands in sombre isolation on 'a desolate waste of sands' near Porthcawl, a forlorn region which Alun Morgan describes as resonant with 'foreboding and loneliness'. This grim location alone may have been sufficient to inspire legends, but the fact that it had been steadily falling into decay for decades has surely helped. When Peter Underwood visited Sker House in 1978, it was 'almost in ruins', with 'a haunted appearance aided by the number of gaunt windows, devoid of glass and open to the sky'. Fortunately the house has since been rescued from total ruination by the local authority and has since been sold in a habitable state.

The legend of Sker House is said to date back to the 18th century, in a song composed by a Welsh harpist. *Y Ferch o'r Scer (The Maid of Sker)* recounts an unimaginative story of the unsuitable suitor variety, very similar to that of the *Maid of Ydfa* (see Llangynwyd, above) and the same doubts as to its origin may also pertain. In this case the lover is a harpist who, though celebrated for his artistry, is deemed by the maid's father to be too lower class to be admitted into the family, so he locks his lovelorn daughter away in her room, where, as is to be expected, she pines. The harpist makes a half-hearted attempt at abducting his beloved but gives up when things get too tricky – he hears the dogs bark, so runs away! The girl is thus doomed to a loveless marriage with a man chosen by her father, a marriage which she endures for nine long years before finally dying of a broken heart the day after hearing the song composed in her honour.[18]

R D Blackmore, who had connections with the area, published a novel, *The Maid of Sker*, in 1879, a year after his famous *Lorna Doone*. Perhaps wisely, however, he ignored the original plot completely and his *Maid of Sker* is set mainly at sea. Nevertheless, the book did a great deal to bolster Sker's legendary status and it wasn't long before the whispers started that the unfortunate maiden now haunted the house. She appeared, it was said, in the room in which she was imprisoned, and her materialisation was accompanied by the sound of clanking chains...[19]

Peter Underwood noted on his visit that local people still believed that 'a ghostly form' could sometimes be seen in a window on an upper floor, and that 'odd noises are heard there at night'.[20] In 2002 a BBC Wales camera crew explored the empty house one night for a television programme but, according to a BBC website, had to stop filming when 'a high-pitched noise filled the Great Hall'. According to the director, Dave Jones: 'Nobody could work out where it was coming from. The crew were checking all their equipment but just couldn't explain it.'

The medium they had taken along for company then cheered them up by telling them that they had 'disturbed something evil'. The result of this announcement was: 'Our lighting guy dropped his lamp with a deafening crash and we were out of the place in seconds.'[21]

Perhaps the sound was the *Cyhiraeth*, a kind of disembodied shriek, which is usually heard before a death. The *Cyhiraeth* was known to wail out warnings of shipwrecks round the coastline south of Sker. Alun Morgan's description of 'a ghostly wailing or shrieking sound that brings fear to the hearts of all who hear it' certainly tallies with the television crew's experience.[22]

[1] Trevelyan, 1909, p. 198.
[2] Ibid, p. 201.
[3] Redwood, 1839, p. 45.
[4] Rhys, 1855, p. 119.
[5] Evans, T C, 1887, p. 136.
[6] Evans, Frederick, 1912, p. 156.
[7] Evans, T C, 1885, p. 229.
[8] Evans, T C, 1887, p. 174.
[9] Jones, NLW 16161B, p. 60, quoted by Phillips, 1933, p. 53.
[10] Evans, T C, 1887, p. 151.
[11] *Bye-Gones*, August, 1905, p. 106.
[12] Trevelyan, 1893, p. 389.
[13] Palmer, 1998, p. 88.
[14] Evans, T C, 1885, p. 230.
[15] Trevelyan, 1909, p. 128.
[16] Trevelyan, 1893, p. 372.
[17] Trevelyan, 1909, p. 145.
[18] Trevelyan, 1893, p. 391.
[19] Morgan, Alun, 1974, pp. 23-4.
[20] Underwood, 1978, p. 170.
[21] www.bbc.co.uk/wales/ilovewales/sections/scary_places/skerhouse.shtml (Last accessed July 21, 2003).
[22] Morgan, Alun, 1974, p. 24.

Boverton

In 1839 an enjoyable little book was published bearing the title *The Vale of Glamorgan, Scenes and Tales Among the Welsh*; I don't believe it has ever been reprinted. The author was anonymous, but later identified as Charles Redwood, who divided his time between dusty law chambers in London and his beloved Vale, where he resided either at Cowbridge or at Boverton, near Llantwit Major. In his book, Redwood refers to his Glamorgan home simply as 'our village' but various clues strongly suggest that it is Boverton he refers to, rather than Cowbridge. The work is a collection of yarns and essays, often recollections of happy times spent with his intelligent nephew Davy, rambling around the hills and discussing local legends. There are many ghost stories.

As Redwood and Davy return from an inn where they have been listening to rustic tales of prophecy and divination, the youth announces: 'Strange things, uncle, are these stories; and so vouched for! There is our boy, Shanko, declares that as he was going with the wagon to the hills for coal, a little after midnight, through this very lane, he was pursued by the Phantom-lady, who, they say, promenades here every night, with her arms a-kimbo, and her tall, taper figure dressed in a scarlet bodice and large blue petticoat. Shanko set the team into a full gallop, and was terribly frightened. Had she got on one of the horses, as she is fond of doing, the Lord knows when they would have stopped.'[1]

Warming to his subject, Davy continues: 'Look, uncle, how often it happens that old rumours of certain places being haunted by spirits in unrest, get confirmed by the discovery there of human bones, belonging, no doubt to some one who had an untimely end and no Christian burial. This was the case at Pont-yr-ysbryd, where the spectres of a lady and a child had been frequently seen, – upon one occasion by a clergyman, in broad day-light, walking in the fields there. He heeded them little at the time, but presently went home, and fainted. Here, at length, some workmen in quarrying for lime-stone, found behind the hedge, two skeletons, answering in size the description of the spectres.'[2]

I cannot confirm the exact whereabouts of this Pont-yr-ysbryd (Ghost Bridge) but the indication is that it was in the neighbourhood of Boverton or Llantwit. Later in the book Davy refers to another haunting, the location of which is this time clear: 'When they were dismantling Old Boverton Place, one dark hazy day,' he says, 'a large shadowy female figure, dressed in deep widow mourning, of antique fashion, was seen passing from there ever and anon.'[3]

According to Marie Trevelyan, writing seventy years later, one of these workmen spoke to a 'very aged person' who informed them: 'Oh, she is Wissie, the King's widow. I've often seen her.' Trevelyan has an interesting theory regarding the identity of 'Wissie':

'In the reign of Richard I it [Boverton Castle] was the property of the Earl of Gloucester, whose daughter Hadwisa became the wife of Prince John. When, about ten years later, John divorced Hadwisa of Gloucester, so that he could marry Isabella of Angouleme, his wife, who has been described as amiable and affectionate, retired to the seclusion of Boverton Castle. According to local tradition, King John once fled from his barons, and was sheltered in Boverton Castle by the gentle woman he had wronged. May not this dark lady have been Hadwisa of Gloucester?'[4]

Colwinston

A horrible incident is played out over and over again in the vicinity of this village near Cowbridge. According to C J O Evans's *Glamorgan*, first published in 1938: 'Near Pwllywrach, a manor house outside the village, are the ruins of kennels where, it is confidently asserted, ghostly mastiffs, known locally as the "Hounds of Hell", bay at midnight, usually in the month of August. The story is, that the huntsman, having charge of a pack of hounds, left them unfed for several days whilst he was on a drunken carouse. On his returning to feed them, the hounds, maddened with hunger, tore him to pieces. That is supposed to have happened many years ago, but the baying of the hounds and the cries of the unfortunate huntsman are said to be still heard in the vicinity of the kennels.'[5] The story bears a vague resemblance to that of the squire of Borras Hall (see Wrexham).

A frightening entity preyed on travellers

along the Roman road which is now the A48. It lurked at the bottom of Crack Hill near the turning for Colwinston. Marie Trevelyan recorded two examples of its activities in her 1909 book *Folk-Lore and Folk-Stories of Wales*. Each story was related to her by people who had personal experience of the *bwgan*, and neither was known to the other. The first was an aged native of the district who had been returning home from Bridgend. In the autumn twilight, he began his ascent of Crack Hill –

'As he went upward he found walking unusually heavy work, yet the road was dry and hard, and particularly agreeable for walking. He therefore thought that either he was more tired than usual or lazy; so he tried to adopt a better pace, but could not. To make matters worse, night was approaching.

'When half-way up the hill something, he knew not what, seemed to spring upon his back, and afterwards pressed heavily into his shoulders. In the starlight he looked over his right shoulder, and saw a shape clinging closely to him. Being a strong man, he promptly endeavoured to shake it off, but it pressed heavier than ever. He felt great difficulty in proceeding on his journey, and the effort brought a "heavy sweat" to his forehead and face. When just at the top of the hill he groaned with agony, and so great was his distress, that he cried aloud: "O Lord, I pray Thee, deliver me of this burden!" While uttering these words he crossed his arms upon his breast. Instantly he was relieved of his load.

'Turning round to see if anybody had been playing a practical joke on him, he saw in the starlight a huge shape, which looked like "a great bundle" or a "fat, short man" enveloped in a dark wrap. The shape rolled rapidly down, and fell into a disused quarry at the foot of the hill. Immediately afterwards the sound of a loud explosion was heard, and from the depths of the quarry sparks of fire shot up and were scattered across the road. He hastened home, and when he related his experiences to an aged neighbour, the latter said he remembered his father telling a similar story of the "devil on the Crack".'

A very similar experience was had by Marie Trevelyan's second informant, an English railway engineer who was making his way to Cowbridge in a hired horse and trap. He was unaccompanied on his journey and was benighted by the time he reached the foot of Crack

Hill, but, with the carriage lamps lit, he was in a perfectly easy frame of mind. This, however, could not be said of his horse, which became very restless, 'snorting vigorously'. Suddenly something heavy landed in the back of the trap! The Englishman called out, assuming that someone had jumped aboard, but on receiving no reply, he whipped his horse to try and gain some speed. But the animal was now under the same burden as the solitary traveller in the previous account – 'it was hardly able to struggle upward, and toiled as if under a very heavy weight'.

At the top of the hill the horse staggered to a halt. The engineer jumped down and 'found the horse quivering, as if panic-stricken'. Then he looked behind him and 'saw in the fitful moonlight a monstrous bundle rolling downhill, where it fell into the quarry. It was followed by a loud explosion and sparks were scattered across the road.' It is easy to imagine his interest when, in 1896, he related his experience to Marie Trevelyan and she was able to then furnish him with the details of the local man's adventure.[6]

Cowbridge (Bontfaen)

There are many examples of phantom funerals seen in Wales, apparitions which precisely mimic a funeral to come. Usually the witness just happens to be in the right (or wrong) place at the right time; there is no particular reason why he should have seen the omen, although later on he may find himself one of the mourners. How horrible, though, to see the phantom of *your own* funeral – as did a farmer returning home from Cowbridge market one evening.

It was just before nightfall and in the gathering gloom he perceived a procession coming down the lane leading to his house. His horse, of its own accord, halted at the entrance of the lane to allow the people to pass. The farmer sat wondering as the mourners approached but we can only imagine his feelings when he suddenly recognised, immediately following the coffin, his own wife dressed in widow's weeds, supported in her grief by his eldest son!

The procession passed and then vanished and the farmer's horse, clearly in a state of repressed excitement, took the opportunity to bolt headlong down the lane, nearly bringing true this grim prophecy there and then. But there was not long to wait. A few weeks later the man developed a serious illness and he warned his family to expect the worst, describing to them his eerie experience. He died three days later.[7]

At an unnamed village near Cowbridge, there once lived a middle-aged bachelor and his two sisters. One of these ladies heard a mysterious voice calling below her bedroom window, but she stayed in bed and did not answer it. She heard the voice again the next night, so on the following morning she told her siblings about it. They advised her to reply to it if she heard it again. Well, on the third night she did hear it again, so this time she opened the window and looked out. Not entirely to her surprise, I suspect, she saw that no one was there. She called out into the night: 'What dost thou want?' and she was replied by a disembodied voice. It gave her a very strict set of instructions.

'Go down to the second arch of the gateway leading into St Quintin's Castle, Llanblethian, and there dig,' she was commanded. 'Thou wilt find buried in a deep hole close to an inner arch a crock full of gold pieces. It's no use to me now. Take it, and may the gold be a blessing to thee.'

The brother and sisters were happy to oblige and it didn't take them long to find the gold – and local gossip had it that it was a more than substantial sum. They were very lucky to have been allowed to keep it. In other cases of this type from Glamorgan, the gold had to be thrown away into the avaricious waters of the River Ogmore, to no benefit to the poor mortal who had to go to the trouble of digging it up.[8]

Llanmaes

According to Davy, the young hero of Charles Redwood's *The Vale of Glamorgan*: 'In the lane by Picketstone ... the farm-servants protested that they often saw a tall pedlar's ghost; but although there was some old rumour of a Scotch pedlar having been murdered there, they were scarcely believed, until immense large bones were afterwards found buried by the road-side.'[9]

Elsewhere at Llanmaes there is a track or lane bearing the grim name of the Gallows Way where ghostly dogs are said to prowl. Marie Trevelyan believes these are spirits of 'the faithful attendants of men who suffered the rigours of law on the Gallows Tree'. Weird noises, too, can be heard here at dead of night, including eldritch wailing, 'the sound of a lot of people running' and 'something heavy falling into the road'.[10]

Llanmihangel

At dusk a White Lady 'with a pale and careworn face and having an expression of intense pain' was sometimes seen rising out of a pool near Llanmihangel. Her name was Eleanor Dee or Ddu and she drowned here in the 15th century. She was supposed to have been a witch, but it is possible that she had been a lunatic, for round her wrist could be seen an iron ring with which, it was said, she had been restrained 'during moments of frenzy'. This ugly bangle earned her the sobriquet of The Ladye of the Ringe. Her appearance usually betokened a forthcoming death in the neighbourhood.[11]

Llantwit Major

It is quite hopeless to refuse when approached by a spirit demanding the usual treasure disposal service. The wife of a Llantwit tailor, for example, 'was haunted and teased by a spirit until she became mere skin and bone, for not choosing to take a hoard honestly to the Ogmore'.

For a goodly while, she had ignored the ghost in the hope she would be able to secure the hidden money for her own use but at last she was harried into consenting. A party of bell-ringers came across the lady in a distracted state near the church and she told them that, having agreed to take the money to the river, the spirit at once 'wafted her through the air so high that she saw the church-loft and all the houses, below her, as though she were in a balloon'. She was so confused by this sudden elevation that she accidentally threw the money upstream, instead of downstream as directed. This was an unpardonable error among the hoard-haunting fraternity (see Pontypridd, Rhondda Cynon Taff), and the spirit gave her a 'savage look' in consequence. Her task done, the poor woman was then ungratefully 'tossed into a whirlwind, and she knew not how in the world she had got back again'.[12]

One version of the story has it that the spirit was that of Barbara's (for that was her name) mother-in-law, who had given her a bag of gold on her deathbed to be divided up equally between several relatives. Only Barbara knew about the money, so she tried to keep it all for herself. Why the spirit should compel her to dispose of the funds in the River Ogmore rather than distribute them as originally intended is unclear.

An elderly resident of Llantwit told Marie Trevelyan that Barbara was convinced her mother-in-law still haunted her in the form of a crow and that she herself was present when a crow happened to fly down the chimney of Barbara's cottage: 'Barbara screamed with terror while the crow flapped its wings around her head and beat her unmercifully.'

When her neighbours offered to kill the bird, she cried out: 'Don't, don't! If you kill the crow you'll kill my mother-in-law, and I shall go to perdition.'

The crow flew out when the front door was opened. Trevelyan adds: 'People are living today who said that Barbara's children were "ghost-walked" or "ghost-ridden".'[13]

Adam de Frankton is credited with slaying medieval Welsh hero Llewellyn the Last, an act which filled him with remorse after he retired to the seclusion of Llantwit. Rather like Lawrence of Arabia or James Dean centuries later, he sought to cure his melancholy with the thrill of speed; not on a motorbike or in a sports car, of course, but on horseback. He was compelled to gallop at a wild pace through the countryside, until the inevitable happened and he fell and broke his neck. His death is recalled by the 'Frampton Horse', a ghost which is never seen but whose hooves can be heard thundering down the Frampton Road, the eerie record ending with the dull thud of de Frankton's body hitting the ground.[14]

A mysterious apparition which used to manifest in a field near Llantwit also seemed to recall some forgotten drama. At night a man dressed in black could be seen to 'ceaselessly toss away burning hay'. Margaret Shanahan, in an article on the *Ghosts of Glamorgan*, writes: 'No historical explanation has ever been offered, although several obvious possibilities present themselves.' I am afraid they are not so obvious to me – I can only think of one, that the poor man's hayricks had been set on fire and he was desperately trying to stop the blaze spreading. It was said that the same field was haunted by a huge, black hound, or *gwyllgi*, with eyes 'like coals of fire'. Perhaps it was his eyes which set the hay alight![15]

Not far away there was a stile known as the 'Big Man's Stile'. The Big Man was a 'a gigantic ghost', which could be seen sitting here of an evening, leaning on his elbow and 'gazing moodily to the west'. He was described as 'swarthy with coal black hair and fiery eyes' but who he was no one knew, although there might be a clue in the fact that the stile led to some old monastic buildings. The ghost has not been seen since the latter years of the 19th century.[16]

In reference to the Llantwit *gwyllgi*, Margaret Shanahan relates a story about a ghostly dog which used to accompany a salesman on his travels: 'His route was among the hills of this county, including a short-cut through a lonely wood, said by the local people to be haunted. He stated that the dog would suddenly appear beside him after he entered the wood, to walk in a companionable way with him until he was almost clear of the trees, vanishing then with what he described as "a sad, gentle canine smile". It happened many times and he sometimes kept his eyes closely on the creature to make sure it did not just disappear among the trees.'[17]

Llysworney

Charles Redwood, talking to his nephew Davy, recalled the appearance of a very unusual *gwyllgi*, half-human and half-hound, which haunted a narrow lane connecting the farm of Crossways and another place named Mousiad, which is no longer on the map. He had heard of the *bwgan* from Anthony, a farm-servant.

'Jenkin of Wilton, the farmer with whom Anthony lived, was returning home through that lane, flustered, from market one night, on a young mare, when she suddenly reared up perpendicular, and let him off, and then galloped home furiously, and stood trembling by the door. Off they all set to look for the old farmer; and soon found him on his back in the mud, hiccuping, and swearing roundly at the *gwyllgi* that had so frightened the mare.

'Indeed,' Redwood continues, 'Anthony himself met it on one occasion, in coming from courting of a Sunday night. At first he saw two large, bright, moonlike eyes, approaching. When it came up, the head and upper part seemed of human form, but the body and limbs like those of a large bright-spotted dog. Anthony aimed a blow at it with his hat, but felt nothing.'[18]

Today Crossways is a large, rambling house converted into flats. The lane leading from here to Wilton farm has become completely overgrown, with trees almost entirely enclosing it to form a long, green corridor of foliage. On the bright July day I strolled down the path I found it thoroughly delightful, with wild flowers in abundance and butterflies sporting along its margins. At night, however, I imagine there are few places more eerie...

Maendy

For several years in the early years of the 19th century a girl by the name of Elspeth John, in service at a farm at Prisk, between Maendy and Welsh St Donats, was tormented by a spirit. Appearing as a 'shadowy figure of a man in dark clothes', at first it did no more than stare at Elspeth, although this must have been unnerving enough. However, in time it began to pinch her and torture her with 'other molestations' so that she could get no peace. She became very depressed and the farmer and his wife became worried about her. At last she told them what was happening and they urged her to speak to the spirit; but for a long time she was too afraid to do so. It was grievous to the good people she worked for to hear her cries in bed and to witness 'the look of terror in her countenance' when the spirit assaulted her.

At last, following entreaties by her master, Elspeth spoke to the spirit. Her troubles now came to an end. The spirit told her that he had been 'waiting for her before she was born' but was powerless until she communicated with him. Now he guided her to an upstairs room, where she was directed to a floorboard under which was something he had hidden during his lifetime. What this was Elspeth never revealed, but she hurried past her employers, as requested, and once outside 'went like the wind', carried away up into the night sky by the spirit. Over a body of water, she wasn't sure which, but either a stretch of the River Ely, or possibly the fishpond at Hensol Castle, she was asked to drop her burden, which fell with a splash below. Then she was flown home in safety and the spirit told her: 'Now I shall have peace, and you shall have peace.' He never bothered her again.[19]

Ogmore

Ogmore Castle has always seemed part of Bridgend, but being to the east of the river, it belongs not to that modern county borough, but to the Vale of Glamorgan. Such are the vagaries of local government. Ogmore Castle was the haunt of a White Lady, who was said to guard the site of a hidden treasure. One bold fellow had the courage to accost her one night and he asked her to hand over the readies, or some words to that effect. The ghost guided him to a place in one of the towers and indicated that he should lift up a large floor-stone. He wasted no time in doing so and was rewarded by the sight of 'an old crock full of golden guineas'.

(Judging by pictures of 'crocks of gold' in fairytale picture-books I saw as a child, I always presumed a crock was some sort of small cauldron. In fact, the word means a large, earthenware jar – hence 'crockery'.)

The White Lady now gave the treasure-hunter a stern instruction: 'Take one half, and leave the remainder for me.'

The man was happy to oblige, and replaced the stone after gathering up his share. Unfortunately, he was not content with his good fortune. One night he came to the conclusion that there was no reason why he shouldn't have the other half of the treasure, too. So he returned to the tower, lifted the stone and filled his pockets with the remaining golden guineas. As he was stealing his way out of the castle, the White Lady appeared and accused him of stealing in a different way. The cheat feigned ignorance and denied any wrong-doing, but the White Lady was not satisfied. She made him remove his coat, and as he did so some coins spilled out, giving the game away.

Now, generally speaking these White Ladies of Wales are gentle creatures, even pathetic. But it is never a good idea to cross a ghost. This White Lady was furious with the ungrateful wretch and she began to attack him – with sharp claws! Her talons ripped his clothes and flesh alike and he cried out in agony and terror, but he could not escape her wrath. At last, battered and bleeding, he was allowed to flee. When he eventually made it home, he was accused of having been involved in a drunken brawl, which he denied, but at the time he would offer no explanation for his sorry appearance. Soon afterwards he became ill, with a disease no one could diagnose, and he wasted away until he was at death's door. Only in his last extremity did he explain what had happened to him. Then people began to refer to his fatal illness as 'the White Lady's revenge'.[20]

St Athan

West Orchard, near the village, is the site of an ancient castle called West Norchete. For many years – at least as late as 1863 – women who went into this field in the early morning to perform the very Welsh art of sheep milking would often see 'a very beautiful lady dressed in white going round and round', but none of them had a clue why. This seems a pity, for this White Lady was possessed of a legend worthy of a Waverley novel.

In the time of the Norman occupation of Wales, there lived at West Norchete Castle a Lady Berkerolles, whose husband, Sir Jasper Berkerolles, went off on the Second Crusade. She waited patiently for her husband's return, but when he did so her reward was to be accused, baselessly, of infidelity with the lord of East Norchete Castle, one Sir Gilbert D'Umphraville. Malicious persons whispered lies into the ears of Sir Jasper, so that he refused to listen to his wife's protestations of innocence and instead 'condemned her to a terrible doom'.

He dug a pit near the castle and into this buried poor Lady Berkerolles up to her neck, and there he left her to die a miserable death of thirst and starvation. It was absolutely forbidden to bring to the doomed woman so much as a crumb to feed her or a drop of water to quench her thirst. Her distraught sister begged Sir Jasper to allow her to visit her at least once a day, and this he agreed to, provided she take her no sustenance. The faithful sister carried out her mission every day and she chose the hour just after dawn as the time for her visit. On her way she would walk round and round, trailing her long dress in the dewy grass so that it would collect some moisture. From this scant supply of water, the tragic Lady Berkerolles survived for ten miserable days. After she had died, Sir Jasper discovered that she had been innocent all the time – and he went stark raving mad as a result.

The 'Ladi Wen' is presumably the apparition of Lady Berkerolles's sister, still carrying out her desperate task of collecting dew. Very unusually for a ghost, she was always seen just after dawn, rather than at night, but, of course, this makes perfect sense when one knows the legend. Traditional tales often get confused and embellished, however, which explains why local lore also claimed that the White Lady guarded a treasure under an old earthwork of the castle. But this ghost seems to have been that of the tragic Lady Berkerolles, rather than her sister. It was said she was happy to guide people to the hoard, but whenever she tried to do so, a white dog with red eyes would appear, rushing towards her and scaring her away. A woman who lived in the neighbourhood told Marie Trevelyan that if she ever passed this way at night, she would feel as though 'someone were pulling my gown'.[21]

A legend retold by Charles Wilkins in 1879 refers to a Lady Matilda Berkolles, who was buried alive. This Lady Berkolles was not a woman to be pitied, however; she was a power-hungry vixen who poisoned her husband. Her burial was different, too – she was thrown 'as a soiled thing in to her grave', which was then infilled as she struggled for breath. The place of her execution was Coity Castle, but the similarity with the West Norchete legend is intriguing.[22]

St Donat's

St Donat's Castle is situated down on the south coast of Glamorgan a few miles west of Llantwit Major. It is a very handsome place of great antiquity. Much of its fabric dates back to the 14th century and it stands on the site of an Iron Age hillfort. Today it is a college which reminded me of J K Rowling's 'Hogwarts' – a secluded and romantic castle with a strong suggestion of the magical about it.

A hundred years or so ago, however, St Donat's was fearfully haunted. The second volume of *Lord Halifax's Ghost Book* explains that a chap coyly referred to as Mr X came to exorcise the place, and he had to deal with a startling range of spooks. On reading the account one can only wish that it went into more detail, but its concise, unsensational style does at least lend it some believability. Here it is:

'The owner of St Donat's wrote to him [Mr X] and invited him to pay a visit to the Castle and investigate the phenomena which were giving such trouble. Mr X consented, and in due course arrived. He found that the principal manifestations were as follows:

(1) A panther was repeatedly seen by the household in the corridors.
(2) A bright light appeared nightly in one of the bed rooms, having the semblance of a large, glaring eye.
(3) A hag of horrible appearance was seen in the armoury.
(4) The piano, even when closed, was played by invisible hands.

'Having received this account of the manifestations, Mr X retired to the bedroom, in which the light had been reported, to pray and grapple with the Powers of Darkness. He requested the owner of the house to sit meanwhile in the hall, with the front door wide open, while the process of exorcism went on. After a while, as though to mark Mr X's triumph over the evil forces of the place, a great gust of wind suddenly blew out from the room where he was praying, swept down the main staircase and all

111

but carried the owner of the Castle into the garden. From that day and hour the ghostly disturbances completely ceased.'[23]

One ghost remained unaffected by Mr X's exorcism, however; that of Lady Stradling, who, until phantom panthers, big glowing eyes and other show-offs came along, had been the most celebrated at St Donat's. Her appearances are few and far between but when she does deign to appear, she always looks her best, draped in a 'long trailing gown of finest silk' and tottering about in a pair of high-heeled shoes. As she makes her elegant way down the Long Gallery or in and out of the chambers in Lady Anne Tower, her favourite haunts, the castle hounds spoil the effect by raising a din with their mournful howling, soon joined by all the dogs of the village and nearby farms. Lady Stradling, who was murdered by her family some centuries ago, makes her returns out of kindness, to warn the current family that misfortune, such as a death, is about to befall them. Perhaps this good-hearted, though gloomy, sense of duty spared Lady Stradling the attentions of the redoubtable Mr X.[24]

St Donat's Castle was also said to be one of several haunts favoured by a mysterious lady named Mallt-y-Nos, or 'Matilda of the Night'. At St Donat's she wandered about searching for the soul of a pirate named Golyn Dolphyn, who once kidnapped a medieval lord of the manor on his return from the Crusades. What connection Matilda has with Dolphyn, who released his prize once he had received a fat ransom, is a mystery, as is the reason why she should be searching for him at St Donat's. He was from Brittany and it seems unlikely he would ever dare visit the castle where he had caused so much trouble!

Whatever her purpose, Matilda is always seen at St Donat's wearing a hooded gown of 'dull green', although elsewhere in Glamorgan she wore an outfit of dark blue or dark red. The latter colour seems more appropriate, for legend had it that in life she was a hunting woman, so fond of riding to hounds that she once expressed the blasphemous wish: 'If I cannot hunt in heaven I would rather not go there.' Her wish was granted, for after her death her spirit was doomed until eternity to ride with the Cwn Annwn – a pack of unearthly hounds with connections to the Celtic underworld – and she could be heard mournfully repenting her vanity while galloping along 'on a fiery steed'.[25]

At the foot of the cliff below the castle an unfortunate pirate (*not* Golyn Dolphyn) suffered a slow and horrible execution. He was buried up to his neck in the sand to await drowning by the incoming tide. He still haunts the spot, and can be heard vainly rattling his cutlass.[26]

In the village of St Donat's there once lived a miser who, when he died, found he could not rest. So he returned from the grave and began to bother his housekeeper, much, no doubt, as he had done in life. This meek old lady was a Methodist, however, and when her fellow chapel-goers learnt of her situation, they forthwith held a prayer meeting in her house. While they were praying the old lady jumped up with a cry of 'There he is! There he is!'

Although they could not see anything, her friends did not doubt her word but instead urged her to speak with the spirit: 'Ask it what it wants,' they ordered, so timidly she did so. The reply she received they could not hear, but it soon became apparent that some instruction was being passed to the old housekeeper, for she shortly began to grope about above the hearth, with her scrawny arm up the chimney. In a cloud of soot, she produced a money-bag!

Here then was another example of the spirit-unable-to-rest-due-to-hidden-treasure scenario. Clutching the bag to her chest, the troubled lady scuttled out into the night and headed for the usual disposal place in South Wales, the Afon Ogmore. Some young men followed her but 'they saw her mount before them over the stile, into the road, without touching it, and whisk off, out of sight. No trace of her was then to be seen.' Sometime later, however, the old lady returned, wet and bedraggled but happy, for, having thrown the gold into the river, she had seen the shade of her former employer standing on the bank, courteously raising his hat to her. He troubled her no more.[27]

Southerndown

Dunraven Castle, a stately home of great history, was sadly demolished in 1963, making it one of the many 'Great Lost Houses of Wales'. It had been an important local landmark, standing on a promontory above Dunraven Bay and looking towards the village of Southerndown. It was a handsome, castellated edifice which, in the 1950s, boasted an extraordinary entrance hall, a glassed-in hothouse which created a real 'palm court' for visitors to wander through before reaching the inner rooms of the castle. It also had a ghost, a good account of which appears in a book written in 1926 by the Earl of Dunraven himself. Unfortunately, I have not seen a copy of *Dunraven Castle, Glamorgan* myself, but shall trust to the accuracy of the information drawn from it by Peter Underwood in his *Ghosts of Wales* (1978).

The apparition was of a small, frail woman with long grey hair and wearing 'a loose and flowing gown of pale blue', from which she earned the name The Blue Lady of Dunraven. The castle employees were aware of her and she was seen several times when the house was used as a makeshift convalescent home for soldiers during the First World War.

A nursing sister staying in the castle saw the Blue Lady in May, 1917. She was lying in bed preparing to sleep, when she noticed the room was feeling rather chilly. She decided to close the open window and sat up in bed, at which point she caught sight of the ghost, the actual cause of the draught, as it moved across the room from the door to the fireplace. As the nurse reached out for the lamp at her bedside, the figure disappeared. She saw her again the following August, but this time she was sitting in a chair by the fire, apparently warming her hands. On both occasions, the nurse recognised the strong scent of mimosa.

In February, 1918, the nurse got a room-mate, a Canadian, who two weeks after moving in, suddenly cried out one night: 'For God's sake, switch on the light!' It was, of course, the Blue Lady who had startled her. On this occasion she made her way from the door to the foot of the Canadian nurse's bed, before proceeding to the fireplace. The flood of light caused her to vanish, but when the English woman was lying awake an hour or two later, she reappeared, standing perfectly still and clear as ever, as if to show the nurse she was real and not just a figment of the imagination, as the Canadian nurse had convinced herself she was. This was the last time she was seen by either woman.[28]

On stormy nights, along the beach at Southerndown, blood-curdling sounds may be heard – the desperate wails of the heartbroken Thomas Wyndham. Unhappy though his spirit is, Wyndham's story is not one to inspire much sympathy. He was a 'wrecker lord', who made his living out of the deaths of others by luring ships on to the rocks and reefs around the coastline south of Bridgend.

One fateful night, having successfully brought a ship to grief by shining a light from an old, ivy-clad tower positioned above the treacherous rocks, Wyndham was horrified to discover that among the drowned was his only son. The boy had taken early passage in the ship with a view to surprising his family, and this was the result. He knew nothing of the tragedy until his men showed him the jewellery they had taken from the corpse. Wyndham, it is said, went mad with grief and would spend night after night staggering up and down the beach bewailing his lost son. Even after his own death, Wyndham found no rest and his melancholy cries can still be heard mingling with those of the gulls as they wheel above the storm-driven breakers as they crash against the rocks.[29]

There are alternative versions of the legend of the Wrecker of Dunraven. In others he is named as Walter Vaughan, a Lord of Dunraven, 'who had lost by extravagance his paternal estates'. In this version, he loses two children in a wreck he had caused.[30]

A third variant adds to the proceedings a desperate character called Matt of the Iron Hand. Matt's hand was chopped off as a punishment for theft, the order for the amputation coming from the Wrecker Lord himself when he was sitting as a magistrate. This does not prevent the wrecker from employing Matt – now armed with an iron hook where his hand once was – as one of his murderous minions. It is Matt who brings to the Wrecker Lord the evidence that his son has perished, a severed hand ornamented with a distinctive ring. Matt, delighted at the chance to take his revenge for his own loss, gleefully informs his master that he chopped the hand off himself, after first dispatching the boy, whom he found alive on the beach.[31]

Swanbridge

According to an article in a 1925 edition of the *Penarth Times*, the *Captain's Wife* restaurant gets its name from a haunting. It is a tale of star-crossed lovers, a Captain Winstanley and a young woman of good birth whose cruel father did not approve of her choice. Capt Winstanley found himself sent on a long voyage to Jamaica – secretly arranged by his love's disapproving father – and while he was away the unfortunate woman was married off to one Colonel Rhys. When Capt Winstanley eventually returned, he arranged a tryst with the lady, but alas they were discovered together and the enraged Col Rhys drew his sword. A hard-fought battle took place between the rivals, and Capt Winstanley was the eventual victor.

The captain hid the colonel's body and he and his ladylove ran away to sea together. But their fate was not a happy one. They fell victim to a mutinous crew on one of their voyages together and were burned to death in their cabin. Afterwards, it was said, the spirit of the remorseful 'Captain's Wife' returned to haunt the house she had shared with Col Rhys – now *The Captain's Wife* restaurant.

Russell Gascoigne, in his *The Haunting of Glamorgan and Gwent*, gives another version of this story, a rather more original one, and therefore possibly the true one. In this case the captain's wife dies of natural causes, a fever, while at sea. So as not to alarm the crew, the grieving husband hid his wife's body in a lead-lined box and kept careful guard upon it. Back in Swanbridge, he buried the box in a wood behind his house until a coffin could be made for his wife's body. However, when the coffin was delivered and the captain went to inter the box, he found to his dismay that it had gone. It seems that one of his crew, suspecting the box contained valuables, had seen where it was buried and had retrieved it for himself. The captain's wife, denied a Christian burial, was doomed to haunt the house.

In both versions of the tale she is said to appear either in a dress which is all white or one which is all black.[32]

[1] Redwood, 1839, p. 39.
[2] Ibid, p. 42.
[3] Ibid, p. 253.
[4] Trevelyan, 1909, p. 202.
[5] Ibid p. 53. See also Evans, C J O, 1943, p. 236.
[6] Trevelyan, 1909, p. 162.
[7] Ibid, p. 186.
[8] Ibid, p. 147.
[9] Redwood, 1839, p. 43.
[10] Trevelyan, 1893, p. 380.
[11] Evans, C J O, 1943, p. 301. See also Shanahan, 1963, p. 33.
[12] Redwood, 1839, p. 44.
[13] Trevelyan, 1909, p. 143.
[14] Trevelyan, 1910, p. 121. See also Shanahan, 1963, p. 40.
[15] Trevelyan, 1893, p. 379. See also Shanahan, 1963, p. 40.
[16] Trevelyan, 1893, p. 379.
[17] Shanahan, 1963, p. 40.
[18] Redwood, 1839, p. 41.
[19] Trevelyan, 1909, p. 148.
[20] Ibid, p. 201.
[21] Ibid, p. 197.
[22] Wilkins, 1879, p. 194.
[23] Halifax, 1937, p. 73.
[24] Redwood, 1839, p. 165. See also Sikes, 1880, p. 143.
[25] Trevelyan, 1909, p. 49.
[26] Shanahan, 1963, p. 38.
[27] Redwood, 1839, p. 46.
[28] Underwood, 1978, p. 29, quoting from Earl of Dunraven, *Dunraven Castle, Glamorgan,* 1926.
[29] Trevelyan, 1893, p. 367.
[30] Hall, 1861, p. 245.
[31] *Cambrian Quarterly* (1833) p. 527. See also Evans, C J O, 1943, p. 426. For another version see Wilkins, 1879, p. 280.
[32] Gascoigne, 1993, pp. 63-66.

Canton

Glamorgan folklorist T H Thomas heard an extraordinary adventure from a man who had been walking between Canton and Leckwith one night. He said he was joined by 'a silent man who dogged his footsteps and gazed at him imploringly'. What happened next is better told in his own words:

'He would not be shaken off. I called him names and threatened him. He only kept looking, looking at me, but said nothing. I got into a rage and said, "N'en o Duw, what do you want?" Tears ran down his face and he said, "I couldn't speak till you asked me in the name of God. I am dead but I cannot rest till my head is buried. I was boatman ... down by the Ely river, and my head is on the bank and devils do play football with it. If you come and bury it I shall rest."

'So I agreed to go in search of the skull and he took me down the river to a bend, just above the Taff Railway Bridge as is now, and there by a bluish light was a lot of people kicking football like hurrah with the poor man's skull. I thought I would go to them praying, and as I came to them they all flew away. So I took the poor man's head and buried it in a soft place, digging a hole with my knife, and the ghost he stood and looked at me, till he went out like smoke.'[1]

Cardiff (Caerdydd)

The ghosts of Cardiff are not as modern as you might expect from this increasingly modern city. An old-fashioned coach and four, for example, haunts the gateway to Cardiff Castle and has been seen in recent times. A man named David Brecon told of his sighting in a newspaper article printed in 1956. He said: 'Passing the walls of Cardiff Castle on a cold, frosty night, I heard a faint jingle of harness, the clatter of horses' hooves, the sound of bells and an Irish coachman's cry from the direction of Canton Bridge – a second later a coach and four passed me at a steady trot, swung left-handed through the Castle gate doors and all was gone from view.'

Mr Brecon was so fascinated by his experience, that he did some research and discovered that on November 10th, 1868, a man named Boyle heard the same thing while he was in the Castle's library, but on enquiring of the butler in the hall, he was told that no coach had come. On this and subsequent occasions, the appearance of the spectral coach seemed to herald a death, firstly of a member of the Hastings family, and then, in 1900 when it was next heard, of Lord Bute. Mr Brecon was unaware of any tragedy following his own sighting.[2]

According to Jack Hallam's *The Ghosts' Who's Who*, published in 1977, there are also two ghosts haunting the interior of Cardiff Castle. A former custodian told Hallam that he had seen what he believed to be the ghost of the 2nd Marquess of Bute. The marquess died suddenly after a banquet in his dressing room, a small chamber behind the library now converted into a chapel. Here stands a bust of the man, over the spot where he died, so it is no wonder that the custodian was able to recognise him. The young woman in a long robe he also saw remains an enigma, however.[3]

A mysterious lady dressed in grey haunts the neighbourhood of the castle. She has been seen walking along Queen Street, through Duke Street, past the castle and down to the bridge over the River Taff. Here she pauses and waves, or perhaps signals, across the river. Sometimes she turns her back to the river and waves up to one of the castle's forbidding towers. Was someone she knew imprisoned there? Since no one knows who she is, no one can say. Marie Trevelyan implies that the ghost was already defunct by 1909, when her book of folklore was published, but Peter Underwood places her very much in the present tense in his *Ghosts of Wales* published nearly seventy years later. Underwood adds the detail that the Grey Lady 'has been seen in daylight but usually appears towards evening'.[4]

A 'lady robed in black' used to haunt the old sea-lock in Cardiff, when the metropolis 'was a small and insignificant place'. This rather dramatic story is another collected by Marie Trevelyan:

'[The lady] appeared to be searching for something which she could not find. In the twilight she would go down to the sea-lock and return again, wringing her hands as she went. Mariners and others were quite aware of her visits, but felt afraid to address her. Sometimes she would stretch imploring hands towards people, and then go rapidly to the sea-level.

'At last one evening a skipper ventured to speak, asking what he could do for her. She asked him to take her out in a boat to the mouth of the River Ely. If he would he should be handsomely rewarded. Eager for gain, the skipper granted her request, and rowed to the mouth of the River Ely. Never had he ferried such a heavy cargo before. Every moment he feared that the weight of the black-robed lady would sink his boat. He was about to express his fears, when the lady said, "Land me quickly, and draw up the boat."

'He did so. The lady beckoned him to follow, and she led him into the woods far from the river. There she pointed to a stone, which the skipper lifted at her direction. In a crock under the stone there were gold coins. "I have found them at last. They are yours." Then she vanished. Many times the skipper went for the treasure, and by means of it grew rich. People wondered how he made his money, but his secret was not revealed until just before he died.'[5]

Duffryn House, near the town, has another ghost of some antiquity, that of a naval man, Sir Thomas Button, who found fame as an Arctic navigator during the reign of Good Queen Bess. The house itself isn't haunted, but Sir Thomas was reported, in the 1860s, pottering about in the flower-garden and – sensible ghost! – 'hovering over the beer butt in the cellar'.[6]

When alive, Sir Thomas was very fond of a white horse he named Cartouche. In his will he made Cartouche a pensioner of his estate, providing it with a field (Whitton Mawr) to graze in for the remainder of its life. Sadly, but rather beautifully, the beloved animal died the day after its master died. In the first half of the 19th century, a ghostly white horse, presumed to be Cartouche, would be seen in Whitton Mawr, sometimes quietly grazing, sometimes gambolling about and snorting. Local folk said the ghost's appearance was an omen, presaging a death in the family of Button.[7]

Llandaff

The road between Llandaff and Cardiff was frequented by a hideous apparition, 'a frog-woman', seen on moonlit nights. Local rumour had it that this was some unfortunate, deformed daughter of a 'high family', who had secreted her out of sight in the home of a Llandaff farm labourer, where, for a fee, she was cared for. She is described as moving like a frog – 'and her

croak was unmistakable'. The pitiful creature's days were ended when she fell into the River Taff, but for years afterwards the frog-woman's spirit was to be heard 'croaking and screaming for help to get out of the dark waters'.[8]

A striking visitation of the banshee-like *Gwrach y Rhibyn* was witnessed by a man at Llandaff in November, 1877. The man had been staying with a friend in the ancient cathedral city when he was woken at midnight by 'a frightful screeching and a shaking of my window'. He jumped out of bed and looked out into the night:

'Then I saw the *Gwrach y Rhibyn*... a horrible old woman with long red hair and a face like chalk, and great teeth like tusks, looking back over her shoulder at me as she went through the air with a long black gown trailing along the ground below her arms, for body I could make out none. She gave another unearthly screech while I looked at her; then I heard her flapping her wings against the window of the house just below the one I was in, and she vanished from my sight.'

That would have been more than enough for me, but the gentleman had courage enough to keep watching. In a little while the banshee-like creature reappeared and this time it went through the door of the building opposite, a public house rejoicing in the name of the *Cow and Snuffers*. That was the last he saw of it. The next morning, he was not surprised to learn that a Mr Llewellyn, who owned the *Cow and Snuffers*, had died during the night.[9]

Llanedeyrn

About the year 1756, Evan Gibbon was on his way home to a house called Ty'r Ffynnon, when he decided to make a stop on the way. It was already dark and the people at the house he called at warned him that his route took him past a place where a ghost had often been seen and which had become a terror to the neighbourhood. Mr Gibbon was determined to continue on his journey, however, but his friends were so in earnest that they ordered two servants to accompany him until he was clear of the haunted spot. Shortly, Mr Gibbon and the servants caught sight of the ghost – hanging about some distance away as if waiting to waylay them. Boldly, Mr Gibbon approached the apparition and found it to be that of a young woman with her hair plaited or tied up and wearing a style of petticoat old-fashioned even for the mid-18th century. She was sitting on a stile, apparently with the intention of blocking his way. Brave Mr Gibbon asked her, in the name of God, what she wanted with him.

The ghost showed him a weeding instrument which she required him to take away, and this she hung up in an ash tree. Mr Gibbon asked her where she was, and she replied: 'Sometimes in the clouds, sometimes on the earth, seventy years.'

After this the ghost and Mr Gibbon quarrelled, and she vanished in a spectral huff. Later Mr Gibbon went to retrieve the tool and he found that it was embedded in the bark of the tree – he realised that the tree had grown round it. He returned with a hatchet to hack it out and was accompanied by several curious people. When he had freed the weeding instrument, he found that it had all but rusted away and was now no bigger than his finger. The ghost, who was also watching, seemed satisfied at this and disappeared in a shining light.[10]

Llanishen

This area was haunted by a Grey Lady, whose base of operations appeared to be a holy well. Marie Trevelyan tells us: 'She was often seen, especially by drovers, who appeared to fascinate her, for she would follow them for a mile or so, and return to St Dene's Well, where people said she was held in bondage for having done many evil deeds' – presumably with drovers![11]

Pentyrch

A White Lady used to appear occasionally among the 'ancient monastic buildings' at Castell-y-Mynach (Monk's Castle). A man who saw her while working in the gardens said that 'her dress was as white as the driven snow, and her long black hair streamed over her shoulders'. In one hand she carried a bunch of forget-me-nots and with the other she beckoned to the gardener 'with fingers covered with rings which sparkled in the sunlight'. It is possible the charming apparition merely wanted some advice on the planting of forget-me-nots, but the gardener ran away in fright and begged his master and mistress to come and see her instead. 'There she is!' he cried, but she vanished. Local legend had it that the White Lady guarded the former monks' treasure.[12]

It was a Green Lady who haunted the slopes of Garth Mountain, overlooking Pentyrch. She,

too, had a habit of beckoning to men, but on the whole, they, like the gardener at Castell-y-Mynach, tended to ignore her. Two men who did venture to talk to her learnt something exciting. The Green Lady told them that she guarded 'hoards of treasure' and that the men could have it, if only they would undertake to free her from the bonds which held her there. She urged them to oblige her, because, she said, if they did not release her then, 'there would not be a man born for the next hundred years' who could do so. The men were cautious, however. They whispered together, unsure whether to believe this yarn. Then one of the men noticed that the Green Lady's slippers were dusted with gold-dust! But alas, they had dithered over their decision too long, for the Green Lady suddenly vanished – 'and for a long time after, her sobs and wailings were heard'.[13]

Roath

At Penylan a well was haunted by 'a woman dressed in sombre garments'. She hung about at twilight wailing and moaning. One evening in the early 19th century a Cardiff man accosted her with the words 'What dost thou seek?' and he was told that she sought release from her haunting. She told him that he could help her accomplish this – all he need do was hold her tightly round the waist, stay silent and not let go. Easy enough, you'd think, and possibly even fun, but after a short while the feeble individual let her go after feeling a sharp pain in his arm. The ghost was distraught, and ran away, crying: 'Two hundred years more before I shall be free!'[14]

A very similar story is told about Taff's Well, below.

Taff's Well (Ffynnon Taf)

Taff's Well seems better known now for its industrial estate than for its health-giving waters, but once upon a time the thermal spring which gives the area its name was a place of pilgrimage for rheumatism sufferers. 'Taff' is a corruption of Dafydd or David, Wales's patron saint, so this was presumably a holy well before its soothing properties became known. In days gone by the well was haunted not just by hobbling and complaining old ladies but also by a Grey Lady. Marie Trevelyan explains:

'A lady robed in grey frequently visited this well, and many people testified to having seen her in the twilight wandering along the banks of the river near the spring, or going onto the ferry

[!] under Garth Mountain. Stories about this mysterious lady were handed down from father to son. The last was to the effect that about seventy to eighty years ago [ie about 1830 or 1840] the woman in grey beckoned to a man who had just been getting some of the water. He put his pitcher down and asked what he could do for her. She asked him to hold her tight by both hands until she requested him to release her. The man did as he was bidden.

'He began to think it a long time before she bade him cease his grip, when a "stabbing pain" caught him in his side, and with a sharp cry he loosened his hold. The woman exclaimed: "Alas! I shall remain in bondage for another hundred years, and then I must get a woman with steady hands and better than yours to hold me." She vanished and was never seen again.'[15]

Tongwynlais

North of Cardiff can be found the extraordinary fairy-tale architecture of Castell Coch. Despite its medieval appearance, Castell Coch was built in 1870. However, it was raised upon foundations 600 years older. In a secret passageway constructed beneath this earlier fortress, a hoard of treasure was hidden and, legend has it, this was guarded by gigantic eagles which would rend apart anybody trying to get their hands on it. The treasure wasn't found when the Victorian Castell Coch was built, so the assumption is that it is still there.

Marie Trevelyan wrote in 1909 that: 'In certain seasons of the year, chiefly between October and March, these birds make fearful commotion in their retreat. They scream and shriek, causing terror to the dwellers in the country-side round the castle.' This implies that they, too, may still survive. Certainly, despite being interred by the medieval lord of the manor, Ivor the Little, these fearsome raptors were still defending their treasure as late as the 18th century, when 'a party of brave and fearless men' were beaten back by them. Tradition has it that they will continue to guard the hoard until Ivor the Little returns, King Arthur-like, together with a 1,200-strong army.

The treasure of Ivor the Little (I'm sure the poor man would rather have been remembered as Ivor the Great!) is not the only one buried at Castell Coch. A Royalist secreted some valuables somewhere in the castle during the Civil War, but was killed during the conflict before he was able to retrieve it. His ghost, described as 'a venerable gentleman in a full dress suit of the time of Charles I', was seen during the early 18th century wandering round a suite of rooms and the grounds outside, wearing a sorrowful expression. His perambulations would inevitably lead him to the spot where he'd buried his valuables, so it wasn't long before treasure hunters tried to get their hands on it. But – alas! – the over-protective eagles of Ivor the Little decided to guard this hoard, too, and they were foiled in their purpose.[16]

In his *The Haunting of Glamorgan and Gwent*, Russell Gascoigne has compiled some fascinating information about a haunted house – now demolished – called Greenmeadow. Built round the fabric of a 17th century farmhouse, Greenmeadow was an elaborate mansion, greatly extended for the benefit of the Lewis family. Many are the ghost tales Mr Gascoigne is able to relate about it. They include a red-headed man with a sword seen in the Oak Room, a former servant seen in the Blue Room and a hunchback in the cellar. In 1848 a Miss Martha Moggridge recorded how she and her bedridden sister were terrified by a ghost dressed in green livery and with a rapier by his side who entered their room in the dead of night and began to rap on the panelling as if searching for something hidden behind it. This mysterious apparition later disturbed the rest of one Captain Mostyn while staying in the same room.

The weirdest tale of all regarding Greenmeadow is that relating to an unknown, terrifying *something* which manifested along the tree-lined driveway leading to the house. Some musicians employed at a big party at the house in 1860 saw this 'shimmering apparition' as they began their journey home and dropped their instruments in dread. Their only description of it was that it was 'fierce, foul and awful'. It may have been this which contributed to the death of an old gardener at the house. Gwen Wyndham Lewis recalled that when she was a girl 'old Daniel' would regularly beseech her and her young playmates to stay away from a certain part of the garden. He would never explain why, but seemed frightened for them. Horrible to relate, one summer's morning Daniel was found dead, lying in the very spot he feared. The doctor said he died of heart failure – but that does not explain why his dogs were found dead alongside him.[17]

[1] Thomas, T H, 1904 (?), p. 12.
[2] Shanahan, 1963, p. 37, quoting from *Empire News*, May 6, 1956.
[3] Hallam, 1977, p. 29.
[4] Trevelyan, 1909, p. 196. See also Underwood, 1978, p. 42.
[5] Trevelyan, 1909, p. 203.
[6] Sikes, 1880, p. 143. For an earlier reference to this story see *Archaeologia Cambrensis* (1862), p. 113.
[7] Trevelyan, 1909, p. 183.
[8] Ibid, p 304.
[9] Sikes, 1880, p. 217.
[10] Jones, NLW 16161B, p. 55.
[11] Trevelyan, 1909, p. 196.
[12] Ibid, p. 199.
[13] Ibid, p. 204.
[14] Ibid, p. 203.
[15] Ibid, p. 195.
[16] Hall, 1861, p. 212. See Gascoigne p. 45 for a reference to an 1858 source for the legend. See also Trevelyan, 1909, p. 141.
[17] Gascoigne pp. 36-45.

Caerphilly

Abercarn

An invisible fairy called Pwca'r Trwyn lived at a farm near Abercarn. Its behaviour was so similar to what today we call a poltergeist that it deserves a mention here.

Its period of residence at Trwyn Farm was brief, from a few days before Christmas to a few days after Easter (about the year 1700). It first manifested itself by knocking on the front door at night. When the door was answered, there was nobody to be seen, but on one occasion a voice spoke out, which terrified the family, much to Master Pwca's amusement.

Later on it set up home in the oven and would talk to people. It was friendly when treated well. One evening it gently, though invisibly, caressed the man of the house, a Mr Job John Harry, on the toe. But it was a mistake to anger the Pwca. It gave a maid a good beating for being cocky and when a foolish individual named Thomas Evans actually tried to shoot the invisible entity, it pelted him with stones. The Harry family tried to protect Evans from the missiles but in vain – somehow every stone hit him while missing everyone else. Eventually, Pwca announced it was leaving and when asked where to, it piously replied: 'Where God pleases.'[1]

Bedwas

Henry Lewelin, a servant of Edmund Jones, was bringing some holy books to 'The Old Prophet', when he had occasion to pass by the Clwyd yr Helygan, an ale-house with an evil reputation.

The horse he was riding suddenly stopped still in the road. Lewelin urged it on, but it would not go; in fact, it drew backwards. And then he saw why.

Something very peculiar emerged onto the highway. It was 'a living thing round like a bowl [or ball], rolling from the right hand to the left, crossing the lane, moving sometimes slow, and sometimes very swift, swifter than a bird could fly, though it had neither wings nor feet; altering also its size. It appeared to be of a reddish colour with a mixture of an ash colour.' It appeared three times, and once or twice it rolled towards the horse as if searching for something – when he was later told of the adventure, the Prophet Jones suspected that it had been after the Bibles and prayer books. His servant was more fascinated than frightened by the creature but at length, deciding that it was not of this world and of evil intent, he spoke to it.

'What seekest thou, thou foul thing?' he demanded. 'In the Name of the Lord Jesus go away.'

On hearing the holy name, the object vanished, sinking into the ground beneath the horse's hooves.[2]

A schoolmaster named Henry Williams Hugh also had an unnerving encounter with something weird in Bedwas parish. He saw a man of 'somewhat odd figure' by a holly tree by a stile. Something about the man not only terrified Mr Hugh but also his dog, which ran away. The strange man suddenly became two men, confirming Mr Hugh's worst fears, and then vanished in 'a pillar of fire'. Mr Hugh's poor dog had been so frightened that it had run home and hid its head in a pot – doing so with such force that it got stuck, and its master was obliged to free it by smashing the pot with a hatchet.[3]

Bedwellty

It was formerly the custom to hold a wake in the house of a deceased person, to keep the relatives company through the long hours of the night. Ill-mannered people would often use these 'watch-nights' to get drunk and rowdy, with consideration neither for the dead nor for the grieving living. After the death of Meredith Thomas's child, two louts, Thomas Edward Morgan and Anthony Aaron, turned up at the watch-night, upsetting everyone by playing cards and swearing 'most horridly'. Suddenly the household was startled by 'a lamentable groaning noise' coming from outside the window. The family took this as a warning from the spirit world for the men to leave off their levity, and they were convinced for a time to settle down and stop their card playing. After a while the groaning ceased.

Growing bored, the men again took up their cards, at which point the groaning sound was renewed, and louder than before. Morgan and Aaron insisted that it was merely someone outside playing a trick on them, but they were too cowardly to go outside and confirm this for themselves. Others offered to do so, but when they found that their dogs cringed in terror at the sound, they lost heart, too. Now convinced that there was indeed some supernatural agency at work, Morgan and Aaron ceased their rowdy behaviour and never more caused trouble at another solemn watch-night.[4]

A vision of high weirdness was witnessed in July, 1760, by some people gathering in hay in Bedwellty parish. What was the vision of? A huge flock of sheep! For the benefit of readers who live locally and may wish to identify the site, I shall quote the passage describing the phantom flock's first appearance:

'The first sight they saw was the resemblance of an innumerable flock of sheep, over a hill, called Cefen Rhychdir, opposite the place where the spectators stood [a field called Y Weirglod Fawr Dafolog], about a quarter of a mile distant from them: soon they saw them go up to a place called Cefen Rychdir ucha, about half-a-mile distant from them, and then they went out of their sight, as if they vanished in the air.'

The vision returned half an hour before sunset, but even stranger than before, for this time some people saw one thing, some another. Many saw sheep again but others perceived them as swine, still others as a great pack of greyhounds. Weirdest of all, some people saw a host of naked infants! Edmund Jones put the whole thing down to an appearance of the Fairies, and he may have been right.[5]

Caerphilly

The extensive ruins of Caerphilly Castle are said to be haunted by a Green Lady, her name suggested by the colour of her dress. According to Wirt Sikes in his *Rambles and Studies in Old South Wales* (1881), she is 'a cross between a banshee and an elf' and he describes her as 'a sizeable woman, but light and airy in her style of getting over the ground, and good-natured in her disposition'. In *British Goblins*, published the previous year, Sikes credits her with a unique gift – 'the power of turning herself into ivy and mingling with the ivy growing on the wall'.[6]

According to an elderly informant of Marie Trevelyan's, the Green Lady is certainly more goblin-like than lady-like. Rather than being 'sizeable', she is 'a small person' but endowed with an 'enormously large head' boasting 'monstrous goggle eyes' which 'glared like great red moons'. The same venerable person also mentioned that the Green Lady is not the only haunter of the castle. Sometimes she appears in the presence of defunct members of the De Clare family, 'mailed and fierce', who patrolled the ramparts.[7]

The *Gwrach y Rhibyn* was another presence to be encountered at the castle, for she had a haunt nearby. This was 'the Caerphilly swamp', a damp patch below the fortress which had at one time served as a moat. Here, in the latter half of the 18th century, the horrible hag would be seen rising out of the water, droplets falling from her wings, talons and long hair and 'sparkling in the moonlight'.

'Each time she arose from the water she would wring her hands and moan, or utter a long-drawn wail, or a groan which was terrible to hear. Then, suddenly flapping her wings, she would fly to the castle and take refuge within its walls.'

In dry weather, when she had nothing to rise dramatically out of, the hag would wander up and down the Nant y Gledyr brook which flowed through her beloved swamp. The boys and men of Caerphilly were brave (or foolhardy) enough to watch out for the *Gwrach y Rhibyn* and try and catch her. What they would have done with her had they ever succeeded is anyone's guess, for they never did succeed.[8]

Edmund Jones refers to a room built into the ground wall of Caerphilly Castle which was supposedly inhabited by an evil spirit. Lads of the town used to play ball near this mysterious room – and invited trouble on themselves when they had the temerity to play on the Lord's day. Jones was told by 'an honest woman' who lived in a house adjoining the castle wall that in vain did she try to dissuade her son from playing ball on the Sabbath, until one Saturday night she heard sounds precisely mimicking those of ball playing, although there was no one to be seen. She woke up her son and made him listen, too.

'Awake, boy, to hear thy master playing ball!' she exclaimed.

The boy was much impressed: 'I will never go there again,' he said and neither did any of his fellows.[9]

Crumlyn

A chap who had buried something before he died found he could not 'pass over' until the item was uncovered. So his spirit press-ganged into service an old friend from Crumlyn and together they made their way through a dark and wintry night to the hiding place. This proved to be a huge stone, which the man quite reasonably pointed out he could not possibly lift. But the spirit egged him on and up it came light as a feather! The man was no doubt thrilled by his new-found power but disappointed perhaps to discover that the hidden 'treasure', the cause of all this bother, was nothing more than an old mattock, a tool used by the spirit when alive and gainfully employed.

Nevertheless, the recovery of the item, never mind how insignificant, caused great joy in the ether, for there came a light 'as great as if the sun shone'. The spirit now conducted the man to a nearby river, which soon received the mattock into its depths. The spirit, after politely seeing his friend home, went off to his eternal rest, but the man, I am sorry, if not surprised, to say, 'went out of his senses' for a good while after.[10]

One Mary M, standing on Crumlyn Bridge one evening, heard a weak, sorrowful voice passing up the river. 'O Duw beth y wnaf fi? (O God, what shall I do?)' it moaned. At first Mary assumed that this was the cry of someone in distress but inexplicably 'a great terror seized her ... so that she thought her hair moved, and she could not move forward or backward from the place where she stood'. Although she was rooted to the spot by this sudden supernatural dread, she was able to call out feebly to her sister – who had also heard the voice – for assistance. Her sister helped her into their nearby home, where she fainted. The Prophet Jones has an explanation for 'the lamentable voice'. He wrote: 'It was most probably the voice of some disembodied Spirit, who had lived – and died in sin, and felt the wrath of God for it; which will make all impenitent sinners cry at last!'[11]

Llanbradach

Charles Wilkins relates an interesting account of a haunted room in his *Tales and Sketches of Wales*, of 1879. He is imprecise as to the scene of his story, only referring to it as L———h. Fortunately, however, he furnishes some clues: the house is 'in the neighbourhood of Llanvabon', is not so very far away from Mountain Ash and there is a maid from Machen employed there. Llanbradach seems to fit the bill, as it is situated between Mountain Ash and Machen and, furthermore, belongs to the parish of Llanfabon.

The 'haunted room' was to be found at the top of a rickety, winding staircase in an old farm. The chamber was windowless but no light could be taken into it, because something invisible would always blow it out. The aforementioned maid from Machen laughed at the idea of a ghost and boldly entered the room for herself, armed only with a candle. She didn't stay in there long! Wilkins described her experience: 'It was very dark, awfully dark ... and a kind of ring began to gather round the light. She fancied two small keen eyes swept around, and there was a hum like that of voices in the distance. Then she distinctly heard something brush quickly by her, and in a moment a sound as of a puff of breath, and she was in the dark.'

Some time later, a stout old man with a distinctly cynical attitude towards ghosts happened to visit the farm and with him were two young men of equally practical dispositions, students of a Cardiff mining engineer. They, too, decided to investigate the haunted room – and got more than they bargained for. The first thing they noticed after they had climbed up the winding staircase and entered the windowless little room was that it was dark – very, very dark. It was 'a darkness that could be felt ... that was thick, and it could be smelt too'. For a while they were unable to see anything. The old fellow began to express mock disappointment and then one of the students exclaimed that he could see 'something like eyes' in the corner.

'We all looked, and even advanced a yard in that direction, when, as sure as I'm a living man, we all saw a pair of strange wild eyes that had a gentle movement of their own, as if something there was rocking itself to and fro! I looked keenly ... there they were slowly moving in our direction, and as they did so, a faint, far off moaning, not the hum of voices, but the sound of one in pain, was heard, and instinctively we backed in the direction of the door. I don't believe there was a coward amongst us, but there was a strange, supernatural kind of feeling about that [which] took away one's courage. It was worse than if we had entered a cave in Africa, and some stealthy panther or tigress was coming at you.'

The elder of the party, with commendable honesty and brevity announced: 'Don't like it. Let's go. Thank the Lord we have the light.'

But as they backed away to the door, something swept over them 'with an audible rustle' and their light was put out! The three men scrambled outside and wasted no time in making sure that the door to the haunted room was firmly secured.

'Shall we try again?' asked one of the young men.

'No,' replied his elder, 'we won't try it again. There is something uncanny in that room ... we are better off where we are.'

The little, dark room retained its secret. And may do still.[12]

Machen

Hilary Jones was a good old soul, a midwife of Machen, but she was unfortunately also rather too fond of a tipple. In 1773 poor Mrs Jones was found dead, drowned in a ditch by a forge, into which she had presumably stumbled when drunk. Soon afterwards her spirit started to appear to a young man, who, though terrified, was able to ask her what she wanted with him. As is so often the case, it was the recovery of treasure that she needed before she could rest, but in this case the 'treasure' consisted of an iron key and a purse containing fourteen pence. The young man had rather a long walk, follow-ing her to a field where the items could be found, but it was worth it, because she never bothered him again.[13]

Edmund Jones recounts that somewhere below Machen Hill (he is rather confused as to location) a wicked man named J W James was escorting a young lady, with the secret intention of debauching her as soon as he got the chance. He was foiled in his foul designs by a parade of increasingly alarming apparitions, a roster unsurpassed in any other story. The first to be seen was comparatively innocuous, 'the resemblance of a Boy'. But –

'while they were looking at it, they saw it put its head between its legs, and transforming itself into a Ball of Fire, rolling towards the top of the Hill; it being as easy for a Spirit to go up as well as to come down. Presently after they heard the jingling sound of Iron, with which they saw many Horses drawing a load; they went beyond Pont y Meister Bridge, and then turned to a cross lane leading towards a house where there was a man laying dead: when they went a little farther, they saw the earth cleaving and open-ing, and out of it came a Pillar of Fire, which waving in the air, singed the young woman's handkerchief of a yellow colour, which could never be washed out, but continued as long as any of the handkerchief remained.'

James, convinced all these visions were for his benefit, later confessed his evil intention towards the girl. What the young woman her-self thought is not recorded, but anyone who continues to use a handkerchief for months after it has been scorched by the fires of hell seems an unflappable sort of soul to me![14]

Risca

A *gwyllgi* in the form of 'a great Mastiff Dog' terrified William Jones on his way home one Sunday night from an alehouse. It initially ap-peared in the shape of a man, stalking along beside him, then, for another half a mile of the journey, it turned into the mastiff before trans-forming itself into 'a great Fire, as large as a small field' and making a noise like burning gorse. Jones was later told by godfearing folk that the appearance was a warning to him not to break the sabbath again, and he reformed his ways at once. A very similar apparition alarmed a much more respectable fellow in Aberystruth parish, however, so perhaps Jones was just unlucky (see Ebbw Vale, Blaenau Gwent).[15]

[1] Jones, 1780, p. 19. See also Sikes, 1880, p. 187.
[2] Jones, 1780, p. 29.
[3] Jones NLW MS 16161B, p. 7.
[4] Ibid, p. 14.
[5] Ibid, p. 11.
[6] Sikes, 1880, pp. 131-2. See also Hall, 1861, p. 327.
[7] Trevelyan, 1909, p. 204.
[8] Ibid, p. 68.
[9] Jones, NLW MS 790b, p. 109. 'This relation I had September 18, 1788,' writes Jones, dating this story – and presumably this part of the MS – to some time after the 1780 publication of *Apparitions*.
[10] Howells, 1831, p. 23.
[11] Jones, 1780, p. 23.
[12] Wilkins, 1879, p. 228.
[13] Jones, NLW MS 16161B, p.10.
[14] Jones, 1780, p. 32.
[15] Ibid, p. 32.

Merthyr Tydfil

An interesting account of a phantom funeral comes from Merthyr Tydfil. This one was heard but not seen. One of the witnesses described his experience in 1879:

'My wife was ill, and her sister and myself were sitting with her. We had left her in bed for a little while, and had gone downstairs, and were sitting by the fireside. It was midnight. The house was one of a long row. Not a hundred yards from our house was an old chapel with a graveyard in the rear, and access to the yard was had by means of an iron gate leading from the road. Well, we were sitting by the fire, I resting my head in my hand, when all at once there came a sound of distant singing, as at a funeral. At first it was faint, but gradually it increased in volume, and the steps of a great number of persons could be distinctly heard, with the rustle such as you hear when many are passing.

'I looked at my sister-in-law, and she as intently at me, and we both arose, went to the door, opened it, and looked out upon the street. Still we heard the singing and the rustle of a large crowd, but not a soul to be seen. The moonlight shone upon the street. The tramp continued up to the gate of the chapel of Bethesda, and then suddenly it ceased. That night my wife died, and a few days after that the funeral procession passed from the house to the graveyard of Bethesda.'[1]

I have only been able to find two other old ghost stories from Merthyr. This may be due to the fact that the area was one of the first to become industrialised, and the folklore and experiences of the original valley folk had been forgotten by the time scholars took an interest in recording them. Of course, it is also a fact that the new County Borough is a very small one.

At the northern end of the valley there were once several pools which had a sinister reputation. It was said that they lured people to commit suicide in them. One of these was the Black Pool of Cefn, which, according to an article on 'Ghosts of Glamorgan' by Margaret Shanahan, was haunted by a White Lady. Most White Ladies are gentle, even helpful, spirits, but not the Lady of the Black Pool. This fiend enjoyed luring people to their deaths. She would beckon to benighted travellers, who, enchanted by her beauty, would inevitably follow her. Her plan was to lead them into the pool, where she would chuckle maliciously as they struggled for their lives in the cold, black water. This habit is reminiscent of the spirit of Juan White which haunted the Brynithel mountain in the neighbouring county of Blaenau Gwent.[2]

I should point out that Shanahan takes as her source for the Lady of the Black Pool a book by a writer named Elliott O'Donnell. O'Donnell was a popular writer on the subject of ghosts who died in the 1960s. His books, most of which are now out of print, make fascinating reading, but it is not always easy to tell when he is stating facts and when he is resorting to his own imagination. The existence of this dangerous Ladi Wen should therefore be taken with a pinch of salt.

Edmund Jones's stories should also be taken

with a pinch of salt, but at least his tales are of certain antiquity, dating back more than 200 years. Jones tells of Hugh, a shoemaker of 'Martyn Tudvil', who was returning home from Pontypool when, on a lonely mountain, he saw a man walking a little way ahead of him. There was something sinister about this man, something that frightened Hugh inexplicably. Sometimes he remained ahead of Hugh, sometimes he was by his side, but he remained silent and Hugh found it impossible to speak; dread had robbed him of the power of speech. He reasoned with himself that there was nothing to fear from the stranger, that he was just an ordinary traveller like himself, but then he saw something which must have made him shudder – the man had hooves instead of feet! Then poor Hugh realised he had been joined in that lonely place by an evil spirit, but he lived to tell the tale to 'The Old Prophet'.[3]

[1] Wilkins, 1879, p. 207.
[2] Trevelyan, 1909, p. 10. See also Shanahan, 1963, p. 33, quoting from Elliott O'Donnell, *Dangerous Ghosts*, Rider, 1954.
[3] Jones, NLW MS 16161B, p. 28.

Blaenau Gwent

Abertillery

Imagine the shock of a sister finding her brother dead, a suicide, hanging by the neck. John Jenkins hanged himself in a hay-loft at his home near Abertillery and when his unfortunate sister suddenly caught sight of his dangling body she cried out in horror. Now imagine the shock of a neighbour of the Jenkins, a Mr Jeremiah James, when he looked out of his window at the sound of her voice and saw, not only the gruesome sight of the suicide, but also a weird humanoid thing coming out of the hay-loft and 'violently turning upwards and downwards topsy-turvy towards the river'!

It was, as Edmund Jones tells us, 'a dreadful sight to a serious godly man' and we can only be thankful that the bizarre but horrible object escaped the notice of the deceased's sister. I hope, too, that this lady did not read Jones's book, *A Relation of the Apparitions of Spirits*, for in it he callously states of the topsy-turvy thing that 'it could be no other but an evil Spirit going with his prey, the self-murderer, to hell'.[1]

Brynithel

The mountains around Brynithel between Abertillery and Pontypool were the haunt of a ghost which took delight in leading travellers astray. She was said to be the malevolent spirit of a witch called Juan White. A correspondent of Wirt Sikes identified this personage as having lived at an old cottage on Lasgarn Hill, near Pontypool. But it is Edmund Jones who has most to say about her. He described her as having 'the resemblance of a poor old woman, with an oblong, four-cornered hat, ash-coloured clothes, her apron thrown a-cross her shoulder, with a pot or wooden Can in her hands, such as poor people carry to fetch milk with'.

People who lost their way on the mountain would often catch sight of her some way ahead and would follow her retreating form, assuming her to be a local who knew the way. More often than not they were led into a bog. Juan had a habit of crying 'Wow-up!' which is an anglicised form of an old Welsh cry of distress, 'Wwb!' or 'Ww-bwb!' Sometimes only this cry was heard, from many different parts of the mountain, but Juan herself was not seen. Whether Juan made an appearance or not, the mountain itself would often defeat the traveller, for even those who crossed it regularly could find themselves confused and mysteriously unable to find their way, despite the fact that it is only a mile and a half long and half a mile broad. Edmund Jones himself was a frequent victim of its changing geography.[2]

Juan made a nuisance of herself over quite a wide range of the hills (see also Llangattock, Powys). One of Jones's best examples of her activities comes from a place he calls Milvre, but which the informative and interesting Blaenau Gwent website identifies as modern Mynydd Milfraen. One John ap John was making his way across Mynydd Milfraen before dawn when he heard a shouting coming from somewhere behind him. In the chill darkness, the sound seemed inexplicable and eerie, and became more so when, a little while later, he realised that it was coming from *in front* of him as well. He became really unnerved when he heard behind him the rattling sound of an approaching coach – even though it was impossible for a coach to make its way up there – and that this was accompanied by the dreaded 'Wow-up!'

'Fearing he should see some horrid appearance', John ap John quickly left the path and threw himself face down on the heather, so that he saw nothing at all of Juan White and her phantom coach as it went trundling past. Once the sounds had receded into the distance, he got to his feet and saw to his relief that dawn was breaking – 'also seeing some sheep before him, his fear went quite off'.[3]

Ebbw Vale (Glyn Ebwy)

A pathetic tale of the Victorian age explains the ghost of a young woman which has been seen carrying a baby along the millrace towards St John's Church. She was in love with a rich farmer's son who staged a phoney marriage ceremony in order to have his way with her. He soon abandoned the poor girl to pursue a romance with the daughter of a sea captain, unaware that she was already carrying his child. When the cruel youth's father found out about his 'wife', he insisted he marry her for real, but he refused, and went to the altar instead with his new fiancée. His father cursed him for his baseness and had nothing more to do with him. The wronged mother of his child pleaded with him in vain not to go through with the match, but he spurned her. She and her new-born baby were later found drowned in the millpond. The faithless lover suffered a similar fate – he was drowned at sea, leaving his new wife with a fatherless child.[4]

Ebwy Fawr

The valley of the Ebwy Fawr which runs through the heart of Blaenau Gwent features frequently as a location in Edmund Jones's *Apparitions of Spirits*. In the latter part of the 18th century, when Jones was writing, I imagine the valley was a lonely, enclosed sort of a place and sparsely populated.

Jones was on familiar terms with a family who lived in a house called Ty'n y Fid along the Ebwy Fawr. He tells several stories regarding this house and its immediate environs and they take place over three generations. The earliest concerns the house itself in the days when it was owned by one Walter Harry. Mr Harry had moved into the house after its previous owner, a weaver, had died. Rather annoying for Mr Harry, however, was the fact that the weaver, though dead, hadn't yet moved out. His spirit kept hanging round the place. The reason for this was the usual one – he had hidden some treasure in the house and couldn't rest until it was uncovered. The nature of this 'treasure' was more than usually pitiful, however – some 'bottoms of wool' hidden behind a wall.[5]

Some years later Ty'n y Fid became the property of a relative, Thomas Miles Harry. The house seems to have been situated in a particularly scary neighbourhood, for on two occasions Mr Harry encountered strange things when trying to get home. On the first, he was returning from Abergavenny one night when his horse shied, startled by something in the road which he could not see, and it bolted home, Mr Harry clinging on for dear life. When the horse came to a quivering rest within the safety of his yard, he wasted no time in dismounting. With trembling fingers, he began to remove his saddle, when a sudden movement caught his eye. He turned and then saw what it was that had frightened his horse – the gigantic apparition of a woman 'so prodigiously tall as to be about half as high as the tall beech trees at the other side of the yard'. Now it was his turn to bolt – straight into the house.[6]

On the second occasion, Mr Harry again found himself benighted on his journey home. He was just passing a house named Ty'n y Llwyn when he saw some little way off what appeared to be something on fire. He turned his gaze away from the fire for a moment, but when he looked back, there it was burning right beside him – and on his other side there stood a big, black hound! Mr Harry had no intention of tackling a Dog of Darkness and, since the mysterious fire prevented him from dodging past it, he hurried back to Ty'n y Llwyn. The people here knew him well enough to lend him a couple of servants to accompany him home. They as well as he, no doubt, were relieved to find that the *gwyllgi* had gone by the time they set out on their journey.[7]

Mr Harry's son also saw something weird on a road through Ebwy Fawr, as Edmund Jones relates:

'Lewis Thomas ... on passing through a field beyond Pont Evan Lliwarch Bridge, on the Bedwellty side of the river Ebwy Fawr, saw the dreadful resemblance of a man walking on his hands and feet and crossing the path just before him; at which, his hair moved upon his head, his heart panted and beat violently, his flesh trembled, he felt not his clothes about him; felt himself very heavy and weak although a strong lively man. He remembered it all his days, and was very ready to declare it, having been much affected with it.'[8]

Llanhilleth

The crawling thing which so terrified Lewis Thomas was seen elsewhere in Blaenau Gwent, near a place simply called The Farm, at Llanhilleth. At any rate, it was something very like it:

'Thomas Andrew ... coming home by night, saw, by the side of a wall, the similitude of a dark man, creeping on all fours, scraping the ground, and looking aside one way and the other, also making a dreadful noise; at which he was terribly frightened; for it was, to every one that will seriously consider it, a dreadful appearance.'[9]

[1] Jones, 1780, p. 8.
[2] Ibid, pp. 24 and 27. See also Sikes, 1880, p. 50.
[3] Jones, 1780, p. 6. See also www.blaenau-gwent.gov.uk/ (Last accessed July 26, 2004).
[4] Gascoigne, 1993, p. 20.
[5] Jones, 1780, p. 1.
[6] Ibid, p. 2.
[7] Ibid.
[8] Ibid, p. 3.
[9] Ibid, p. 28.

Torfaen

Cwmbran

A grotesque apparition was seen at Llantarnam, on the southern edge of Cwmbran, by a young man named Edward Frank. Edward could hear footsteps coming towards him as he was returning home one night, but at first, because it was dark, he could see nothing.

'Suddenly [writes Wirt Sikes] his way was barred by a tall dismal object which stood in the path before him. It was the ghost of a marvellous thin man, whose head was so high above the observer's line of vision that he nearly fell over backward in his efforts to gaze at it. His knees knocked together and his heart sank. With great difficulty he gasped forth, "In the name of God what is here? Turn out of my way or I will strike thee!" The giant ghost then disappeared, and the frightened Edward, seeing a cow not far off, went towards her to lean on her, which the cow stood still and permitted him to do.'

As Mr Sikes points out: 'The naïveté of this conclusion is convincing.'[1]

It is no surprise to learn that the above story was culled by Mr Sikes from the works of Edmund Jones. Nor is this the only one from Llantarnam (Llanfihangel-Llantarnam was an old and important parish when Cwmbran was still just a twinkling in a mine-owner's eye). The following yarn concerns a spirit still walking the earth because of a great wrongdoing committed during its life. Thomas Cadogan, for such was his mortal name, had been a major landowner but, in coveting more, had wickedly increased his holdings by cheating the widow of a neighbour.

The widow was enjoying an evening stroll when she was waylaid by the deceased Cadogan at a stile. So unexpected was his sudden appearance, that for a moment she quite forgot he was dead, and the spirit took the opportunity to quickly explain how he'd absorbed a parcel of her land by moving some boundary markers. He urged her to approach the new manager of the estate and insist on having them put back. Then he vanished, which reminded the poor woman that the gentleman was no longer living, and she 'was much terrified'. Nevertheless, she didn't forget to kick up a fuss about the boundaries the next day. Once they were restored, Cadogan rested easy again in his grave.[2]

Jones also refers to a fellow preacher, a Mr Thomas Edwards, who was plagued by an evil spirit while staying the night at a house called Pentrebach. All night, until cock-crow, the spirit made a 'squeaking noise' in his ear like that of a pig. Jones assures us that the pig is 'an unclean creature' and this is why the annoying spook chose to imitate one.[3]

To the north of Cwmbran, hidden somewhere among the nooks and crannies of the hills around Greenmeadow Community Farm, there is a mysterious pool of water. Called the Pool of Avarice, it sits in the bottom of a hollow caused by a landslip many years ago. It has a strange history, as described by the well-known Newport author, the late Fred Hando: 'On this site, so the shepherds tell, stood a great house. The mistress was basting a fowl with bacon. Outside the air was close; murmurs of distant thunder rolled among the hills. There was a knock on the door, and the humble voice of a poor cousin pleading, "Spare us a little food; we starve." The beggar was turned away with curses, but as he retreated, he was scared by a sudden violent movement of the mountain. He turned around, and, transfixed, saw the hillside lift, open, and crash over the house... At times, even now, the shepherds stand at the margin of the pool, and quail as they listen to the cries of the lost ones below, doomed by their avarice.'[4]

Panteg

At Panteg there once lived a woman named Marged yr Yspryd (Margaret of the Ghost). The poor woman had been jilted at the altar by a man who seduced her after making promises of marriage. It was the shock of this which people assumed had given her such a 'haunted' expression and which caused her to be seen muttering to herself after dark. But in time it came out that it was not to herself she muttered – for she was truly haunted!

The morning when Marged had suffered that insupportable humiliation in the gaily decorated church, she had fallen on her knees in despair and there and then, in front of everyone gathered, prayed Heaven that the man who had so wronged her should have no rest, in this world or the next. It was a moment of madness, but her cruel prayer had been answered and, though she knew it not, her seducer knew no peace.

A few years later he died but such was the nature of Marged's curse that his spirit was also unable to rest – and now it was haunting her. Having at last confided her unique problem to a friend, she was urged to speak to the spirit.

She agreed to do so and when, on her way home, she was met by the shade of her seducer, she stammered out some greeting. The spirit replied: 'Do thou forgive me, and God will forgive thee. Forgive me and I shall be at rest and never trouble thee any more.' Marged forgave him and then – strange to say – she and the spirit shook hands, and never more was she 'Marged yr Yspryd'.[5]

Pontypool

A coachman travelling one night near Trosnant was accosted by an unhappy spirit who demanded that he meet him in the same place a week later. The coachman reluctantly agreed and on the given night was taken by the ghost to a place near a nail works. Here he was commanded to shove aside some rusty metal and unearth a bright, new piece which the spirit had hidden while alive. The coachman's next task was to throw the bar of metal into Glyn Pond, between Pontypool and Hafodyrynys.

Glyn Pond must have provided the same function as the River Ogmore in South Glamorgan and the confluence of the rivers Rhondda and Taff at Pontypridd – it was a handy repository for spooks' money. A Mr Henry Jones, who lived at Pontypool in 1870, said that when he worked in the mine near Cwmynyscoy, he encountered a ghost in the pit itself. It, too, wanted some treasure unearthing and despite the best efforts of his fellow colliers, Jones was spirited away to the mountain, where he was instructed to dig under a pile of stones. Jones was transported through the air again. As they flew above Glyn Pond, he dropped the bar of gold he had found into its dark waters. The spirit thanked Jones for his help, but left him to walk home.[6]

As we have seen before, it does not need to be hidden gold or money that ties a spirit to the earth – worthless items had the same effect. Take the case of Francis William Watkin and William White. Watkin and White were lifelong friends – indeed when White died, he sought to continue the friendship even after his death. He rose from the grave and would appear to Watkin every chance he got. Fond though he undoubtedly was of White during his lifetime, this otherworldly affection was too much for Watkin. At last he plucked up the courage to speak to the spirit of his dead friend. White told him he should have spoken before. He said he could not rest because he had hidden two razors in the wall of a barn near Pontypool

127

and asked that Watkin remove them. After Watkin had recovered the razors, White's spirit stopped following him about.[7]

There doesn't appear to have been any reason for the next haunting recorded from Pontypool – unless it was just to scare an innocent couple silly. The victims were enjoying a walk in some woods west of Pontypool when they saw a woman approaching them, wearing a high-crowned hat and followed by a black dog. One presumes that the latter apparition was of the domestic rather than the *gwyllgi* variety. Anyway, when this strange woman drew alongside the couple she unexpectedly let out a loud 'Ooh!' and then, more unexpectedly still, 'rose up and did fly like mad over the trees ... until she was out of sight'.[8]

Tranch

Edmund 'The Old Prophet' Jones, the recorder of all the strangest stories to come out of South Wales, lived at the Tranch, just north of Pontypool. It is perhaps no surprise to learn that his own house was haunted. Jones and his wife came to the Tranch in 1740 and heard that the house was troubled by an evil spirit. Of course, this did not put off the indomitable Jones, maybe it even attracted him as being a fresh challenge – and the house rental was probably cheap. Nevertheless, the spook proved something of a burden. It was extremely noisy and usually made its presence known after ten at night. Its favoured form of disturbance was to make three successive sounds, as of blows, striking first of all the stable, then the door of the house, then somewhere inside the house, most often on the pewter dishes. It would also mimic the sounds of 'unclean' creatures such as pigs and weasels and once 'like a coughing of a horse above stairs'.

Jones's poltergeist never took on a visual form, unless a mysterious illumination can be described as a form. On one occasion, Mrs Jones was returning home – the Old Prophet being away – and she saw a light shining through three of the windows. The good woman was brave enough not to be kept from her home, however, and although she felt 'a disagreeable influence' around her when she went in, she bravely stirred up the fire to give a cheerful glow and nothing else affected her.[9]

Strange things, however, were seen in the vicinity of Jones's house. Jones himself saw the figure of a man with 'a little and deformed head' which went splashing into the water below a bridge.[10]

His servant, Henry Lewelin, had left his master's house late one night when he saw going before him the shadow of what he took to be a large man. But when he caught up with it, he saw that it was 'a dark thing without regular members'. Lewelin remembered that his father had met something similar when travelling by night on a lonesome mountain. He had said 'Nos dawch (Good night to you)' to the apparition, but on perceiving it to be other than human, he had qualified his greeting with: 'I was mistaken. No good night belongs to thee.'[11]

Mrs Jones had another adventure of her own one wild, stormy night while visiting a friend who lived over the mountain from Pontypool. She had intended to return to the Tranch the same evening but a terrific thunderstorm broke out, which produced such a deluge of rain that she decided travel was impossible, so asked her friend whether she might stay the night. To her surprise, her friend seemed reluctant to allow her to do so, despite the fact that she had stayed there on many occasions previously. Mrs Jones assured the lady that the spare room would do her very well, as it had always done, and then she discovered the reason for her friend's discomfiture.

'Dear Mrs Jones, what can I do?' wailed her hostess. 'For the last month it has been haunted by a ghost and we are too terrified to enter it.'

'Tut-tut!' replied Mrs Jones. 'Give me a Bible and a rush candle and I shall face Belial himself.'

The dauntless Mrs Jones was therefore allowed to stay, and so settled herself comfortably in the haunted room. She slept soundly until the small hours, when she was awakened by the appearance of 'a gnarled, withered-looking old man' – obviously the ghost. The candle was still burning and Mrs Jones could clearly see the apparition's unpleasant features as he approached the bed. The ghost seemed to recognise in Mrs Jones something of an adversary, for he challenged her with the words: 'Woman, your faith is in that candle!'

'Oh is it?' replied the doughty lady. 'You shall soon see!'

And with that she boldly blew out the light. In doing so, she apparently extinguished the ghost as well as the candle, her courage and good faith claiming a victory over the powers of darkness. She heard nothing more from the spook that night and it never again appeared in that house.[12]

Trevethin

One wonders whether 'The Old Prophet' some-how attracted these frightening Improbables to the region, for they only seem to have existed during his lifetime and been witnessed by friends, or friends of friends, or their servants. Here is one more example, something very grotesque indeed which frightened a dairymaid at a farm in the parish of Trevethin, near Pontypool. She saw it loitering by a holly tree one evening as she went to milk the cows. It was approximately the shape of a man but 'very big in the middle and narrow at both ends' and when the girl's dog approached it, it shot out a long, black tongue, scaring it away. With a heavy, earth-shaking tread, the monster marched off in the direction of a well suspiciously named Ffynnon yr Yspryd (Well of the Ghost), where it disappeared.[13]

Elsewhere in the parish, a man was woken up one night by someone pushing him hard in the chest. It was the spirit of his dead sister, seemingly with nothing better to do. This woman, when in life, 'was once thought to be ... virtuous and well disposed but afterwards was alienated from God, and gave to the lust of the flesh' – by which Edmund Jones means she had sex with someone she wasn't married to. Her brother wanted to know why she was disturbing his sleep, but she made no answer, merely groaning dismally. He tried again. He asked her where she was, and how she was getting on in her new afterlife. She replied that 'she was in a sore cold place, and that there was a sword over her head'. 'God give praise!' uttered her religious brother, but the miserable wraith replied: 'No, I will not.' Whereupon she vanished. The witness told Jones that he thought he saw, hovering in the background, 'R W J', the man with whom his sister had 'sinned against the Lord'.[14]

Another of Jones's correspondents, a tailor's assistant named John Llewelin, had a horrid walk home one night from Cwm y Gollen. He had just come to 'a deep hollow woody pit of ground' in a field called Mynach, when he was startled by a sound as if a big bird had flown out of it, 'but too strong and terrifying' to afford such a mundane explanation as that. Having been so alerted that something spooky was going on, John Llewelin then saw 'a bowl [ball] rolling before him' near the wood and this was followed by the appearance of a black dog. Fortunately, this was not one of the big Black Dogs of Welsh ghostlore, but a small 'cur-dog'. But alas, this was in turn followed by the latter sort – 'a great dog as big as any bear-dog'. This fearsome *gwyllgi* kept pace with John, and kept one eye upon him, so that the unfortunate fellow drew down his hat over his own eyes, so that he wouldn't have to look upon it.

His troubles were not yet over. The *gwyllgi* stood by the stile, blocking his way, so that he was obliged to crawl over a hedge. On the other side he saw 'first a calf then a hart skipping before him' and these, too, he took to be apparitions. Further on, he recognised a friend, a drinking partner, waiting for him and at first he felt very relieved to gain a companion on this terrifying journey – but then he recalled that this friend had been dead for two years! He dared not speak to the ghost, which fortunately vanished. At last, poor John saw the mysterious ball again, rolling before him, and this seemed to mark the end of the spectral procession. He arrived at his destination 'weeping and crying' and I'm not surprised![15]

[1] Jones, 1780, p. 37. See also Sikes, 1880, p. 176.
[2] Jones, 1780, p. 43.
[3] Jones NLW MS 16161B, p. 53.
[4] Hando, 1944, p. 29.
[5] Jones, 1780, p. 37. See also Sikes, 1880, p. 165.
[6] Palmer, 1998, p. 89.
[7] Jones NLW MS 16161B, p.22.
[8] Ibid, p. 21.
[9] Ibid, pp. 76-82.
[10] Ibid, p. 52.
[11] Jones, 1780, p. 30.
[12] Phillips, Edgar, 1959, p. 20. An incomplete version of the story appears in NLW MS 790b, pp. 119-120. This implies Phillips saw a fuller version, perhaps a MS held at Cardiff Free Library.
[13] Jones, 1780, p. 39.
[14] Ibid, p. 42.
[15] Jones, NLW MS 16161B, p. 18.

Bassaleg

A young maidservant of Graig y Saeson (now being unromantically developed as a business park) was met one night by the spirit of a man. The ghost told her he had long been waiting for the chance to speak to her.

'And now I have had it,' he said.

He told her he had hidden 'a handbill' in a heap of stones near Bassaleg and that he needed her to remove it. Otherwise, he told her, 'she should have no rest'. The unfortunate girl, so threatened, had no choice but to remove the bill as ordered, but she suffered for her kindness. After the spirit vanished, in 'a great flash of fire, with a great noise', she fell ill from an attack of the nerves. According to Edmund Jones, she died a scant three years after this 'infernal visit'.[1]

Malpas

At Malpas to the north of the new city of Newport stands the lovely old manor house of Pentrebach, its name ('Little Village') aptly describing its vast and rambling proportions. Approximately half the house is of Tudor age and the other dates from the 17th century. This latter portion boasts a grand hall which is something approaching 20 metres in length. This hall was once the haunt of a mischievous ghost, which took great delight in the sumptuous balls that were held there. During these glittering parties it would join in with a special party piece of its own. This consisted of shaking and shaking all the pictures lining the walls until they fell off, startling the guests underneath! Why it did this, nobody knew.[2]

Newport (Casnewydd)

A man who lived in Newport in the 18th century used a human skull 'to no good purpose', by which I imagine Edmund Jones, who tells us this story, means divination and other forms of low magic. At any rate, The Old Prophet considered him a man 'greatly estranged from good'. When this would-be wizard lay on his deathbed, who else should call to see him but the owner of the skull? A mysterious figure entered the dying man's chamber, skull in hand, and gave him such a furious blow to his head that it was heard by the servants below stairs. It also caused the wizard's nose to bleed. He died soon after.[3]

Jones tells another story regarding a skull – for a dare, an excise officer drinking in a Newport pub stole a headbone from the charnel-house and used it to amuse his fellow drunks. When he went to return it, however, a mighty wind, like a whirlwind, blew up around him, buffeting him from side to side and quite terrifying him. That night, at home, his cane, which hung in the room, beat 'dreadfully' against the wall in an eerie tattoo. His wife was convinced that this was done by some spirit, presumably that of the person whose skull he had abused, a theory which Jones fully supports. The excise officer vowed never to interfere with the bones of the dead again.[4]

Newport Castle is said to be haunted by its founder, the Norman baron Robert FitzHamon. He appears as a gigantic figure of a man with a fierce expression – perhaps a folk memory of his importance in the history of the oppression of the Welsh people.[5]

Redwick

A ghost after my own heart is Tom the Lord. Tom the Lord was the nickname of the lord of the manor, a man who lived 'not wisely but too well' and was especially fond of the cider brewed by one Farmer Thorn. On one fateful night of over-indulgence, Tom the Lord fell down drunk in a ditch and drowned in it. But Tom was too fond of his favourite tipple to let a little thing like death keep him from it, and his bibulous spirit staggered back from the grave to help himself to Farmer Thorn's cider. Farmer Thorn would find that in the early morning all the taps on his cider barrels would be open, and the cider dribbling out of them.

Not long after, Tom the Lord's ghost started to appear in the village. It would be seen sitting in a hedge opposite Rose Cottage, and where he sat the hedge withered and died away. The farmer placed a stile here (ghosts are fond of sitting on stiles) and he also took the precaution of leaving out a mug of cider every night. If he forgot Tom's drink, sure enough the cider taps would be found open and running again.

At last it was decided to lay the drunken ghost of Tom the Lord and the minister of the local chapel had a go at exorcising him. He was unsuccessful, however, because he lacked sufficient faith. Another attempt was made but failed for the same reason. At last, as Fred Hando wittily puts it, a 'mass attack' was made, with twelve ministers taking part, and Tom the Lord was finally laid to rest. [6]

St Brides Wentlooge

It is probably this St Brides Edmund Jones refers to in a previously unpublished story dating from 1773. A widow 'of considerable substance' (ie worth a few bob) was courted by one of her servants and she returned the young man's affections. Certain promises were made between them, but then another man, of a rather better standing in life, came to woo the wealthy widow and she neglected to mention the promises already made to her servant. When the former suitor heard of her intention to marry his rival, he 'fell sick of grief' and cursed the widow woman for her fickle nature. The poor young fellow died of a broken heart – or of frustrated ambition.

One evening, not long after this tragedy, the widow was sitting in the kitchen watching her maid-servants kneading dough, when she saw to her dismay the exact resemblance of the deceased young man come in through the door. The bold apparition strode right up to the horrified woman – and then sat down in her lap! When she cried out, the maids all turned and saw their mistress being dragged along the floor. They grabbed hold of her but the spirit – which they could not see – pulled even harder. One of the terrified maids slammed a door to prevent the widow being dragged outside. The weird tug-of-war then came to an end but they all heard 'a very loud dreadful scream'.

Soon afterwards a great many of the widow's cattle died and people began to whisper that God was exacting vengeance upon her for cruelly breaking her promise to her young servant. Her other suitor now deserted her and the widow ended up 'impoverished by great loss and detested by her neighbours'. Says the righteous Old Prophet: 'A warning to those that hear of it not to do the like.'[7]

Whitson

South of the city, close to the seashore, is the pretty village of Whitson. Here an old cottage, which served as the post office for many years, was haunted by one Eva Roberts. For some reason Eva's spirit would not rest, so the local clergy and villagers got together to lay her with the time-honoured ritual of bell, book and candle. When Eva's spirit popped up during the ceremony, the people, instead of asking what troubled it and whether they could help, chased the poor thing away. Pursued over the sea-moors by an angry mob, the beleaguered ghost ran as fast as its incorporeal legs could carry it until it came to a well in Maindee. Into this the spirit dived and the angry crowd gathered round muttering 'rhubarb-rhubarb' and probably beginning to feel a bit silly – after all, how do you catch a ghost, let alone hurt it? At length they wandered home, leaving Eva to her damp new home. The well became known as Ffynnon Eva and presumably she still haunts it. [8]

---

[1] Jones, NLW MS 16161B, p. 8.
[2] Hando, 1944, p. 36.
[3] Jones, 1780, p. 36.
[4] Ibid, p. 35.
[5] Palmer, 1998, p. 85.
[6] Hando, 1951, p. 68.
[7] Jones, NLW MS 790b, pp.112-4.
[8] Hando, 1958, p. 28.

Abergavenny (Y Fenni)

Case 73 in Sir Ernest Bennett's interesting *Apparitions and Haunted Houses: A Survey of the Evidence* (1939) centres on the Monmouthshire canal a few miles south of Abergavenny. Bennett quotes a letter he received from a Mr T James, of Cardiff:

'In the month of August, 1899, I and my wife and two children – a girl of twelve and a boy of ten – with a little girl cousin about six, were returning from a visit to a relative. It was a lovely evening, and we decided to walk home along the bank of the canal to avoid the dusty road. An arrangement had been made before we left home that an Aunt should walk to meet us on the canal side provided she had company.

'It was a delightful walk, and the children thoroughly enjoyed themselves, and were anxiously looking forward to meeting their kind Auntie. As we were getting nearer home, we had to pass under a rather gloomy arch; I had walked over the bridge hundreds of times, and had fished the canal there many times as a boy: but the place had a queer reputation of being haunted. I had never seen anything, and was quite sceptical about the rumour. It was about 8.30pm as we were passing through the archway, and the moon was fully up, illuminating the walk, and on each side of the canal the banks were wooded. The shrubbery of a large garden came down to the water's edge on our left and a small wood was on our right with sloping banks.

'We had walked about forty yards from the bridge with the children some fifteen or twenty yards in front of us, when we all distinctly saw a figure resembling a female. The appearance seemed to be gliding from us, and was clothed in black raiment, and seemed as if a shawl covered the head.

'The children at once shouted, "There's Auntie," and were about to run eagerly to meet her, but my wife and I said, "Don't go on, it cannot be your Aunt, as she is alone." It flashed through our minds instantly that it was some kind of an apparition, and we dreaded the children having a fright, so they came to us, and we walked slowly on. The uncanny thing still glided on in front of us, and at last suddenly vanished from our sight.

'My wife and I were not frightened, and the youngsters supposed it was a strange person. I am positive the spectre did not glide into the wood but simply, as it were, dissolved into thin air. I looked over the fence in the field after passing the wood, but there was nothing to be seen, and the moon was shining gloriously.

'We reached home at last and found Auntie and her Mother comfortably engaged in household duties. After the children had retired we spoke of our weird experience, and our relatives were greatly perturbed, as they also remembered that the place had a curious and ghostly reputation.'

Later, Mr James wrote back to Bennett to pinpoint the location of the sighting. He wrote: 'The exact spot was close to a bridge, on the canal over which the old highway from Pontypool to Abergavenny runs, some five and a half miles from Pontypool, and four and a half from Abergavenny. The old house is called Ty-Part.'

Mr James did not mention an old house in his first letter but it may be a clue as to the identity of the apparition, for no explanation was forthcoming from Mr James or his relatives. The grown-up daughter of Mr James, now a Mrs Cummins, vividly recalled the incident which took place more than thirty years before: 'I was a child of twelve at the time but have never forgotten the weird experience of seeing a woman appear suddenly in front of us, first walk towards us, then away, and disappear into nothingness before our very eyes. I was the first of the party to see the apparition, which I took to be my aunt coming to meet us, and was dashing towards her when my father called me back. It was the sudden disappearance as we watched her, which specially disconcerted me.'[1]

Caerwent

One of Edmund Jones's many bizarre and shapeless horrors was seen near Caerwent. About the year 1757, a carpenter named David Griffith was walking near the river when he suddenly heard an alarming sound in the air, 'like the braying of an ass', but with something more 'hellish' about it. Hardly had he recovered from this surprise when: 'To add to his terror, he saw a dark roller, rolling by his side.'

The 'dark roller' passed onto a hedge and made a terrible sound, as if it was tearing all the hedge to pieces. Poor Mr Griffith was so upset that he was hardly able to get himself home and when he did so, chose to spend the following fortnight in bed.[2]

Llanfihangel Crucorney

'I have rarely seen a more impressive hall,' wrote Fred Hando of Llanfihangel Court. 'The ceiling, with its late Seventeenth Century decorated plaster work; the great fireplace, surmounted by the strengthening arch; the floor, with its indications of changes through the centuries; the recesses, occupied by suits of shining armour – all made an interior of medieval charm.'

The yew-wood stairs boasted particularly interesting features, 'dark, sinister-looking blood stains'. There were three stains in all, one on each flight and one on the landing; they told of 'a quarrel, of drawn swords, of a swift thrust, and the thud, thud of a falling body'.

That such a house should *not* be haunted would be unthinkable, so it is right and proper to learn there are two ghosts. A White Lady was known to walk through the hall at night, descend the steps of the terrace and then make her way across to a wood, called the Lady Wood, presumably in her honour. She has not been seen for some time, but Hando learnt that the owner at the time of his visit (about 1950) had had a strange experience which might have been due to her nocturnal rambles. As the clock struck one he watched amazed as an inner door opened and closed of its own accord, immediately followed by the opening and closing of the exterior door. On another occasion he heard 'a prolonged scream' coming from the Lady Wood, but he was unable to see anything to account for it. It is interesting that the White Lady should choose the terrace as one of her haunts, for a skeleton was dug up here last century while some alterations were being made – and there was a bullet lodged between its ribs.

The second ghost of Llanfihangel Court is more unusual than the White Lady, and its origin just as obscure. A young visitor reported seeing a mysterious apparition in the White Room – 'a little green man with green eyes'![3]

(According to modern writer Russell Gascoigne, Llanfihangel Crucorney is the chosen haunt of 'The Lady of the Ringe', a spectre otherwise placed at Llanmihangel, Vale of Glamorgan.)[4]

Llangua

The tiny village of Llangua can be found nestling on the Herefordshire border just north of Grosmont. It possesses a very striking old house, formerly a coaching house called The *Monmouth Cap*. There are two legends to account for the name. One, told by Fred Hando, is that in a decisive battle in medieval France the forces of Monmouth wore caps stuck with leeks to identify themselves. The other, told by Mrs Leather in her *The Folk-Lore of Herefordshire*, is that the battle was actually fought in the village and that on its conclusion, The Duke of Monmouth 'held up his cap, the sign of victory'. I guess that in this version the battle was supposed to have taken place during the Civil War, but Mrs Leather does not make that clear. At any rate, this is the version pertinent to the ghost story, because the legend also states that after the fighting was over, the dead were buried in a mound near the River Monnow. The mound had a bare patch on its summit, on which the grass would never grow.[5]

This mound had an eerie reputation. As Mrs Leather has it: 'The children were not allowed to go near; the dead lay there.' One person who did go near was an old fellow named Tom Davies, whose job it was to mow the grass in the meadow in which the mound stood. One summer it was so hot that he decided to do his mowing by night and on this occasion he said he heard music coming from the mound.

'Looking up, he saw a band of soldiers on the mound, and a great number of officers and their ladies dancing round it; he threw down his scythe, and ran home through the river without stopping.'

When he told his neighbours, however, they laughed and said 'it was just the fairies, who were always there at midnight'.[6] There is a very close connection between the fairies and the dead, as we have seen before.

As an aside, I may mention that when Mr Hando visited Llangua in the 1960s, he learned from the owners that the *Monmouth Cap* was haunted. They told him: 'On two occasions, both quiet nights, my husband and I have both heard the rattle and squeak of a coach. With his hair standing up straight and stiff, our dog has howled, but when we opened the door we saw nothing...'[7]

Llanishen

According to Jacqueline Simpson in her *Folklore of the Welsh Border*, a man had a truly horrible experience one night in a church at Llanishen. She writes:

'A certain man had promised to watch all night beside a woman's newly-dug grave inside a church, but on the vicar's advice he had a Bible with him, and had a circle drawn round his chair. At midnight, in rushed a demon dog which dug up the corpse, skinned it and ate the body, but left the skin whole. The man hooked the skin and dragged it inside the protective circle, where the dog was not able to get at it. When dawn had broken and the dog had vanished, the vicar advised the man to burn the skin, "for evil spirits use those skins to appear to relatives of the dead person, and frighten them".[8]

This ghastly concept appears to be unique to Llanishen – let us hope so!

Magor

A schoolteacher named Matthews spent a horrible night in a grand house in this parish. Very unkindly, he was put into a room the owners knew to be haunted, one in which no one had ever been able to pass the whole night. He had hardly settled down to sleep when he heard a stirring in the corner of the room. Then he heard the sound of a man walking in his stockinged feet *above* the bed, 'rustling the bedclothes as he passed'. This happened three or four times. Then something more awful happened – Mr Matthews felt the ghost collapse onto his bed, with such force that he was thrown onto the floor, the bedclothes all about him. The next morning he was told that a man had died in that room, having fallen from a garret above.[9]

Mathern

South of Chepstow, squeezed between the Bristol Channel and the M48, stands the very grand manor house of St Pierre, now a golf and country club. So wealthy were the family of St Pierre in the reign of Henry V, that the King himself used to borrow money from them. Tradition has it that the crown jewels were once kept here as surety for King Harry's war loans. The house is quietly haunted by a Grey Lady of some antiquity and less quietly by a poltergeist which occasionally annoys guests in a bedroom in which a duel was fought in earlier and more romantic times.[10]

Monmouth (Trefynwy)

It is Mr Stephen Clarke we have to thank for this collection of ghosts from Monmouth and, indeed, for the records of many others from the county. Mr Clarke is an archaeologist and

heard all these stories first-hand, often while carrying out his digs and other investigations. The accounts originally appeared in the *Monmouthshire Beacon* in the years 1965 and 1966, and were then reproduced in a booklet entitled *Ghosts of Monmouth*. This booklet is now very hard to find (outside Monmouth, at least) and I am grateful to Mr Clarke for lending me his only copy to crib from.

A very unusual ghost was seen between the old Boathouse and Granville Street (which has since been flattened to make way for new buildings and a bypass). In life, this was a man who owned a sawmill with his brother, but died in an asylum. He was put there by his brother, who then became sole owner of the business. After his death, the dispossessed brother was often seen on the site of the sawmill, endlessly and monotonously chopping wood.[11]

On a ridge near White Hill, the distressing cries of a baby could be heard. The sounds emanated from a thorn bush, but the infant itself had long since perished. It was said the child had been murdered by a gypsy, who then hid its body in the bush.

White Hill is on the route of a phantom coach which trundles from Bailey Pit Farm to Wonastow Court. At its latter end the road is now a dingle through which a stream flows, but there is no reason why this should stop the coach from running. Another phantom coach charges down the Abergavenny Road 'on wild stormy nights'. At Rockfield it swings round a sharp corner and crashes into a wall, an echo perhaps of a real tragedy. Something not dissimilar frightened a man walking along Monnow Street late one night. He had almost reached Chippenham House when he heard a horse galloping up behind him. As the hoof beats passed him, 'he was faced by bright lights which stared into his eyes with intense brilliance'. The thing rushed past and then disappeared through the locked doors of a garage.[12]

In 1965, a Monmouth man recalled a spooky incident which happened in his childhood: 'One summer day, nearly thirty years ago, two friends and I set up a tent on the banks of the River Wye at Hadnock. During the evening we walked to the edge of the woods and, as boys do, laid a couple of makeshift rabbit wires. We walked back to camp and settled down to play cards. The game went on until after midnight, and then one of my friends suggested we should go to see if we had caught anything. It was a very clear night and although there was no moon the starlight was sufficient to see our way. We entered a field on the side of the wood when suddenly the figure of a lady appeared a few yards to our left.

'The apparition was of a hazy, bluish colour, almost transparent. Her long flowing dress was drawn in tightly at the waist and she wore what seemed to be either a tall hat or perhaps a high hair-style. She moved across our path. Her movements were quite silent, for she appeared to glide rather than walk and I do not recall seeing her feet. One of my friends was also watching her and we noted that she did not seem to have a face. But my other friend was obviously bewildered by our stares, for he could see nothing. As the two of us watched she faded away like a puff of smoke. Afterwards the two of us who had seen her compared notes and his description fitted mine but we could not understand why she should have appeared only to us and not the third member of the party.'[13]

The Buckholt Donkey haunts the Hereford Road. It's referred to as a donkey because of its huge size, but other descriptions suggest that it is actually a dog (and therefore a *gwyllgi*). Sometimes it is headless. Even more bizarre is the spectral cow which potters about a field on a farm just off the Abergavenny Road. It is seen first thing in the morning. It looks just like an ordinary cow – but if you try and touch it your hand goes straight through![14]

A fascinating account of an exorcism appears in Roy Palmer's *The Folklore of (Old) Monmouthshire*, another excellent source of ghost stories from the county: 'Old Mrs Pirrett lived in Monmouth whilst her husband was away fifteen years at the Peninsula War, and got her living by brewing, etc. She had to go and brew at a big house which stood where the Grammar School stands now, by the Wye Bridge. She had to go in the middle of the night, so as not to use the copper when the cook wanted it.

'She was crossing Wye Bridge shortly after midnight when a coach and four dashed past her, coachman and horses alike without heads, and rushed straight into the river. She went on as well she could, her knees shaking with terror, and went to the front door, the way she always had to get in at night. A clergyman came and opened it, in a bath of perspiration and said to her in furious tones, "What do you want here?" then, "Come in, for heaven's sake, quick!" As she passed towards the back of the house she saw a lot of gentlemen standing in a circle in one of the sitting rooms. And when she came to think of it she saw as how they must have been laying the ghost she met.'[15]

Tintern

About the year 1895, a psychic who was visiting the celebrated ruins of Tintern began to receive spontaneous messages from the troubled spirit of a Saxon soldier. He had been killed at Tintern while acting as a mercenary for the Norman invaders. He begged that the lady arrange two masses to be said for him, so that he might find peace. This the medium swiftly accomplished and the communications at Tintern ceased. However, ten years later, in a London seance, the Saxon's spirit got back in touch to express his thanks.[16]

According to Roy Palmer, the Saxon soldier is not the only spirit to haunt Tintern Abbey. A hooded monk dressed in grey has frequently been seen, kneeling as though in prayer.[17]

T H Thomas claimed that a road near Tintern was haunted by an unfortunate girl who was seduced and then cruelly murdered. The rapist 'thrust her alive down a chasm in the rock'. Her pitiful skeleton was discovered years later when the rock was blasted apart by lime workers.[18]

Tregare

When she was a young girl in the early 1900s, a 'Mrs E' was walking down a lane between Tregare and Penrhos when suddenly 'a large black dog appeared near a yew tree'. Mrs E told Stephen Clarke: 'It was a very large dog with curly hair, and walked close to my side. After a while I put out my hand to touch it, as I thought it would be better if I did. But as my hand went out to the dog it just wasn't there.'

In September 1905 Mrs E's grandmother saw 'a white form' near the entrance to Old Park Lane. It went through a gate and vanished near some ruined cottages. Both Mrs E and her grandmother believed that their respective brushes with the supernatural were warnings of impending deaths in the family, for shortly after each appearance they lost an aunt.[19]

Usk

Edmund Jones tells a tale of a cheating miller near Usk. Since it has never seen print before, I repeat it in full, making no apologies for the Old Prophet's quirky prose style:

'A very old man gave the following account to me of a miller belonging to Rhadri Mill, not far from the town of Usk in this county, who stole men's corn by taking an excessive toll; so that when he died he left much behind him. But [he] died before he could sign the will in which he had left much of his ill gotten goods to his brother, and a nephew of his. Therefore his wife, as wicked as he, having this advantage, kept them from the legatees; and his spirit therefore greatly troubled her. And altho [sic] she removed to five or six places seeking rest, but finding none, so that she came to have a very ghastly disagreeable look; yet the wretch would not part with her ill gotten goods, and those who had them afterwards soon spent them. But the trouble he gave was great and so often, that they conjured him into the Red Sea. After seven years he still returned, and was conjured again. The old man remembered his being conjured three times.

'A young woman of the neighbourhood going on business before day, met his apparition having as it were a bag of meal on his shoulders. She was so terrified at the sight, that she fell down in a swoon and could not rise. The family seeing her long a coming [?] went to look after her, and found her half dead. She lived but about two days after; yet declared what she had seen before her death.'[20]

Wolvesnewton

A manservant at Nantycelli farm was badgered by a spirit for the usual reason of hidden money. This one was more upfront than most. Having instructed the man to recover some gold guineas he'd hidden, he explained: 'I got this for some sows and pigs I sold at Usk market. I swore the devil should have the money before my wife laid hands on it.' Unfortunately, the man wasn't allowed to keep the money. He was made to take the coins to a place named Cae Byndra and there instructed to throw them over his head into the water.[21]

[1] Bennett, 1939, pp. 289-292.
[2] Jones, NLW MS 16161B, p. 17.
[3] Hando, 1951.
[4] Gascoigne, 1993, p. 19.
[5] See also details of the Robber's Grave, Montgomery, Powys, for a similar phenomenon.
[6] Leather, 1912, p. 45.
[7] Hando, 1964, p. 4.
[8] Simpson, 1976, p. 83.
[9] Jones, NLW MS 16161B, p. 69.
[10] Hando, 1958, p. 37.
[11] Ibid, pp. 7 and 20.
[12] Ibid, pp. 2, 4 and 20.
[13] Ibid, p. 3.
[14] Ibid, pp. 12 and 19.
[15] Palmer, 1998, p. 91.
[16] Halifax, 1937, p. 39.
[17] Palmer, 1998, p. 84.
[18] Ibid, p. 86.
[19] Clarke, 1965/6, pp. 4 and 6.
[20] Jones, NLW MS 790b, pp. 103-104.
[21] Palmer, 1998, p. 90.

Abbeycwmhir

'There is a story in Radnorshire,' writes John Ceredig Davies, 'that a palace [?] not far from the neighbourhood of Abbey Cwm Hir, was once haunted by a Spirit, which appeared in various forms and made such terrible noise that no one cared to live in the house for a long time.'

Eventually, some young blood, cocky because he'd just got married, faced up to the ghost. This turned out to be a good thing, because the spirit showed him a spot near the house where some gold was buried. The spirit was happy because it was now free to pass over into the afterlife, and the young man was happy because he had earned for himself a very handy wedding present![1]

Aberedw

In her 1894 book *From Snowdon To The Sea*, Marie Trevelyan relates some ghostly tales through the characters of two preachers wandering a lonely road at night and swapping stories to pass the time. We met them before at Llangollen, Denbighshire. In the following story, one of the ministers, 'Rhys', recounts how he was put up one bitterly cold winter's night by the deacon of Aberedw, who was also the village blacksmith. He says he woke up at about two o'clock in the morning and was surprised to hear sounds that suggested the blacksmith was still up and shoeing a horse in the smithy next door. He continues:

'I got up and looked out. Snow was covering the road, and the moon was shining. Down by the forge a man was standing while the blacksmith shod the horse. I thought it something important, or a man would never come to shoe his horse at such an untimely hour. Well, I saw the stranger remount his horse, and ride off, and when he was gone I saw a curious sight. In the snow, the marks of the horse's hoofs were the wrong way around. The smith had shod the horse backward. I didn't then tell the deacon a word about what I saw, but next time I went to Builth, I heard that another preacher had seen the same sight. I was told it was the ghost of Prince Llewelyn, who rode to the smithy at Aberedwy [sic] to have his horse shod backward in order to defeat the enemy.'[2]

Aberhafesp

As we have seen previously, it was once believed that certain Welsh churches became possessed of spirits on Hallowe'en night, disembodied voices which would spell out the names of those due to die during the following twelve months (see, for example, Llangernyw, Conwy). St Gwynnog's at Aberhafesp, a few miles west of Newtown, was just such a church. One Hallowe'en night 150 years or so ago, two men crept into the church porch and there huddled by the locked door in the hope of hearing the dismal roll call of death. The wait was a long and a cold one, but at about the hour of midnight one of the men distinctly heard emanating from the otherwise silent church the name of his friend! With a gasp of shock, he turned to his companion but found, to his relief, that he had fallen asleep and so had failed to hear the ominous voice. Waking his friend, he said: 'Let's go away, it's no use waiting here any longer.'

He did not mention what he had himself heard for fear of filling his friend's heart with dread. But in just a few weeks the grim prophesy was fulfilled. A funeral procession came to Aberhafesp from the opposite parish of Penstrowed. The nearest bridge across the Severn was many miles downstream, so it was decided to ford the river opposite St Gwynnog's Church. The man whose name had been intoned by the spirit volunteered to help carry the coffin over the river. The casket was placed on horseback and the man mounted behind it, leaning right over it to keep it steady as the horse waded across. And from that moment he was doomed. The corpse was that of a person who had died of an infectious disease, a disease to which he in due course fell victim.[3]

Abermule

A phantom horseman used to lurk around the so-called 'Captain's Bridge', which spans the railway and the River Mule between Abermule and Fronfraith Mill. The history of the ghost is obscure, but was thought to relate to a tragedy which occurred here, possibly to the mysterious Captain himself. An old lady related in the closing years of the 19th century how she had one night been passing by the Captain's Bridge when the ghost, mounted on a white horse, swept silently past her, and she could feel a rush of wind just as if there was a real horse and rider. The pair then disappeared 'as mysteriously as they had come'.[4]

Brecon (Aberhonddu)

The following is another story of the White Lady Needing Help class, but it's my favourite of the lot, because the details are so preposterous. I also like the fact that the ploughboy was so shy; few men in this day and age would resist a 'maiden smoothing her hair in the sunshine' and beckoning to him! The scene is a field three miles from Brecon, near Caer Bannau, which some believe marks the site of Bannium, a Roman frontier fort. The story was gathered by Marie Trevelyan.

'In the course of his work from day to day he [the ploughman] noticed a maiden robed in white, smoothing her hair in the sunshine, and beckoning the man to her. At first he took no notice of her, but as she repeated the signal he mustered up the courage to respond. The maiden told him she was a King's daughter who had sunk with a landslip into the ground. She could only be saved by a man who, without halting or looking round, would carry her to the nearest churchyard, and throw her down with all his might. The ploughman promptly picked her up, and ran with her to the nearest church. He was about to fling her off his shoulders when something tweaked his ears so violently that he looked round, and let his burden fall. The maiden flew into the air, lamenting that she must suffer more severely now, and wait another hundred years for a man with a more steady hand.'[5]

Another White Lady was to be found 'in the same neighbourhood, but a little nearer Brecon'. A farmer, apparently with nothing better to do, went to take a look at her and set off for her accustomed haunt. There indeed he found her, engaged in the peaceful occupation of scattering leek seeds. A handful of these seeds he received in payment for his curiosity, and he placed them in his pocket. He thanked the White Lady for her gift, but wasn't very grateful, because he threw most of them away. Perhaps, being a farmer, he considered his leek seeds better than hers. Silly man. When he got home he found the few seeds which had remained in his pocket had turned into gold.[6]

In the foothills of the high peak of Penyfan there was once a fine country owned by a cold-hearted princess. This princess had a suitor, but she told him that he was far too poor to marry her – if he could only procure some gold with which to swell her coffers, it would be a different matter. Her admirer, whom we may assume was as cold-hearted as she, found himself a rich man to murder and, having murdered him, brought his gold to the princess. She accepted the gold willingly but still did not accept the suitor's hand in marriage; she was rather put off by the fact that the spirit of the murdered man was haunting the place where her beloved had buried him. The would-be prince was commanded to go to the murder site and interview the ghost in order to find some way of laying it.

At the graveside, the killer discovered not one but two spirits, or the voices of them, at least. One voice in the darkness asked whether the innocent man's death was not to be avenged? Another voice replied that it would be avenged, but not until the ninth generation would that vengeance come. This was a long time ahead, so the relieved suitor returned to the princess and told her the good news. And they were married. Years passed and 'they multiplied and became numerous, while their town grew to be as it were another Sodom'. The prince and princess lived to an extraordinary age, so long that they were still alive to see their great-great-great-great-great-great-great grandchild. For this reason, they did not escape the curse as they had assumed, and they suffered along with everyone else. During a great feast, with all nine generations gathered in one place, they were all drowned in 'a mighty cataclysm' – the town sank into the ground and its place was taken by a lake, Llyn Syfaddon.[7]

Capel y Ffin

This isolated hamlet near the borders of both Herefordshire and Monmouthshire earned its place on the map when, in 1869, the self-styled Father Ignatius (née Rev Joseph Leycester Lyne) founded a monastery here. His intention was to 'afford the Church of England a house where men might consecrate together in prayer, praise and labour' and also 'to offer reparation to our Lord Jesus Christ for the insults He has received in our Church and country since the Reformation'. The Honddu valley in which he set up his community is now known as the Gospel Pass, largely because of the lovely ruins of Llanthony Priory further south. Kilvert, the humble schoolteacher whose diary became world famous, made friends with Father Ignatius and visited him several times.

One day in 1880 two apparitions were seen at Llanthony Monastery and Father Ignatius felt obliged to write to the local papers about them. Both had a religious aspect. In the first instance, the silver monstrance (a vessel which contains the sacrament) appeared outside 'the thick doors' of the tabernacle. That same evening four boys saw a white, glowing apparition in a meadow near the monastery. Although this vision was immediately claimed to have been a manifestation of the Blessed Virgin Mary, it bore a close relation to the White Ladies of Welsh ghostlore. The boys told Father Ignatius that they had seen 'the figure of a woman, dressed in a white alb, hands both raised, and from head and foot was a dazzling white light, oval shaped, shining round the body'. The figure moved through Abbot's Meadow, near the monastery, then entered a hedge 'and remained standing in it'. There, presumably, it disappeared.

Ignatius told the local press: 'These are extraordinary but absolute facts. That the two apparitions occurred the same day seems most marvellous, as though God intended one to corroborate the other.' [8] We must assume that the description of the female apparition was partly of his own imagination, for it is hard to imagine a Welsh boy of the 19th century using a word like 'alb', which I had to look up in the dictionary myself! (It means a long, white vestment, by the way.) Neither apparition was seen again. Llanthony Monastery did not last for very many years and the house was later taken over by the Arts and Crafts designer Eric Gill. I believe gravestones can be found in the nearby cemetery whose inscriptions were hand-cut by Gill in his own, still popular, Gill Sans typeface.

A Baptist minister at Capel y Ffin also had an encounter with a ghost.

'He was a hurdle maker,' he explained, 'and you could hear him tap, tap, tap, choppin' wood for his hurdles all about the place where he used to work.'

In an attempt to prevent his spirit from rising out of the grave, the minister and others interred the body and turned it over, so that it faced down. Then they reburied it. This method of confusing a wandering spirit was once used all over Europe. However, it didn't work – 'After we turned him, he came back seven times worse,' complained the exasperated minister.[9]

Disserth

Two hundred years ago a very alarming spirit kept the neighbourhood of Disserth in a state of dread. It belonged to Charles Lewis, a tanner,

who had cheated his friends and neighbours by using two different sets of scales when buying and selling his wares, so that he always got the best of a dishonest bargain. Having amassed something of a fortune, he suffered a fatal accident and was buried in Disserth churchyard. His malicious spirit could find no peace, however, and became a terror to travellers after dark. It particularly enjoyed leaping up behind riders on horseback and moaning in their ears: 'I am Charles Lewis of the light and heavy weights. Once I was a man, now I am a devil!'

At last the saintly old Parson Jones, vicar of Cefnllys and Disserth, was prevailed upon to tackle the *bwgan*. He and three other clergyman, after a great struggle, succeeded in trapping the spirit inside a large goose-quill, which was then stuffed inside a silver snuff-box, which in turn was tied to a rod of iron. The iron was sunk into a bog, and there Charles Lewis's 'devil' remains.[10]

A possible corruption of this story was recorded in 1910. It tells of the congregation of Disserth Church being rudely interrupted one Sunday by a fearsome spectre in the form of 'a raving mad bull with bloodshot eyes and clouds of breath coming out of his nostrils', which came thundering up the aisle. The combined prayers of the snowy-haired preacher and his flock defeated the *bwgan*, however, and it shrank smaller and smaller until it was the size of a moth. This was snapped up in a snuff-box and sunk in a pool. The spirit agreed not to return for another nine-hundred-and-ninety-nine years.[11]

Another brief tale which may have connections to the legend of Charles Lewis concerns a wagoner whose horses suddenly bolted up 'Disserth pitch'. As he struggled desperately with the reins, he happened to glance behind him – and saw 'two silent figures, cloaked and cowled' in his cart.[12] This sounds rather like the stories told about Crack Hill in Vale of Glamorgan.

Hyssington

Another spirit which manifested in the form of a bull haunted a bridge near this village on the Shropshire border. Rather horribly, the enormous animal appeared without any skin covering it and it used to roar and bellow continually. Because its favourite haunt was at a place called Bagbury, it was known as the Roaring Bull of Bagbury.

Needless to say, such a horror could hardly be allowed to romp about the countryside unchecked, so seven parsons gathered in the church to 'pray the devil down'. In the midst of their service of exorcism, the spirit (some say the Devil himself) burst into the church with such force that the 'walls were rent asunder and all the lights were put out'. (An alternative version says it swelled and swelled until it was so big it cracked the walls.) The parsons scattered in confusion, but plucked up the courage to try again on another night shortly after. This time the exorcism was successful and the Bagbury Bull was laid. Tradition has it that the spirit was buried 'under the second abutment of the bridge over the Camlad in Churchstoke village'. One version says that it was shrunk down until it could be trapped inside a snuff-box.[13] As well as the account from Disserth above, this yarn is almost identical to one from Trelystan (see below).

Kerry

Elias Owen tells an amusing story of a Kerry squire who returned to patrol the bounds of his former estate long after his earthly body had been consigned to its grave. The reason why he had returned to his mortal home was not known for some time because no one who had run into him on his nocturnal rambles had had the courage to speak to him. That the story has some truth to it may be divined from the fact that in his story Owen cautiously disguises the names of the *dramatis personae* by using their initials only:

'Among the most pronounced unbelievers in the apparition was the sub-agent of the estate, who thought that if his late master appeared at all he ought to appear to him, who had been so intimately connected with the estate. It would almost seem that the spirit heard, and felt the force of the remark made by his former sub-agent, for shortly afterwards, when the man was going up the steep road that leads from Kerry to Newtown, the squire appeared to him. Mr W was horrified at seeing Squire H approaching him, and would gladly have escaped from facing the spirit, but this was impossible, as his late master was evidently approaching to speak to him, so trembling in every limb, and his hair standing on end, he faced his employer's ghost and actually asked him why he visited the earth after death.

'To this question the squire vouchsafed the answer that he had defrauded the estate, and that certain trees were to be felled, which were specified, and the debt of honour paid with the proceeds, and then, said the ghost, when this is done I shall rest quietly in my grave! Furthermore, the ghost bade his old servant lie flat on the ground, with his face downwards, whilst he disappeared. The man obeyed the mandate, and when he got up there was no-one near. He reached home more dead than alive, and to many fond questionings of his careful wife he gave no answer, but she, shortly afterwards, ascertained the cause of her husband's great fright by listening to a conversation which she overheard between him and the head agent. The trees were felled and sold, and the debt paid, and no more did the squire trouble the peaceful vale of Kerry.[14]

A correspondent of *Bye-gones* in 1888 wrote: 'When I was a youngster an aunt of mine told me that if a person passed over Trefeen Bridge after midnight he or she would be sure to see three ladies sitting on the railing, dressed in green silk. For years after, if I passed over that bridge late, as I did many times, I used to put my nag at full speed and always felt relief when I had run the gauntlet. It is needless to say I never saw the ladies.'[15]

This appears to be the only place where more than one Green Lady manifest together. As we have seen (eg at Glynneath, Neath Port Talbot), Green Ladies tended to be kind-hearted, more fairy than phantom, so this young man probably need not have feared them.

Llandysilio

An evil spirit once took possession of Llandysilio church, to the great annoyance of the parishioners. When an antiquarian looked over the church in or about the year 1875, his guide told him about the terrible trouble they had in evicting the squatter:

'To such extremes had things come that it was resolved to send for a well-known and expert person to lay the Spirit. But the Spirit nearly overcame the expert, and the fight became hard and fast for a long time. The Ghost-layer came out often for fresh air – and beer. And then was plainly seen from his bared arms and the perspiration running down his face that there was a terrible conflict going on within the church. At last success crowned the effort, and the Spirit, not unlike a large fly, was put in a bottle and thrown into a deep pool in the River Vyrniew, where it remains to this day, and the church was troubled no more.'

As proof of the truth of the story, the antiquarian had pointed out to him places where the beams in the fabric of the church had become 'cracked at the time the Spirit troubled the church'.[16]

Llanerfyl

Close to the road between Llanerfyl and Llangadfan there is a clump of trees called Coed Bach. This was a very haunted spot. At midnight there was sometimes seen 'the shadowy figure of a dignified lady ... robed in a pure white trailing silk garment in graceful folds'. This 'very aristocratic ghost', as she has also been described, could be seen at midnight dancing in the road. This suggests rather a pretty sight, but it used to terrify the locals. Far more unpleasant were the 'agonising shrieks' which could occasionally be heard coming from the wood. What connection existed between these unnerving sounds and the dignified dancing lady is unknown. Possibly there was no connection; one writer believed that Coed Bach was haunted because several workmen were killed here when the road was being constructed.[17]

A man calling himself 'Cynvelin' wrote into *Bye-gones* to say that he had had a 'creepy' experience at Coed Bach on August 12th, 1897: 'On that precise evening I was engaged in a walking tour with a companion (a youth of seventeen), and we had left Llanfair town about eight o'clock with the intention of gaining the Cann Office hotel at Llangadfan ere closing time. The moon had risen by the time we reached Pont Llanerfyl, and we noticed as we crossed the bridge the dense ground-mist which spread like a shroud along the course of the river upwards towards Llangadfan. In spite of the bright moonlight the night was damp, clammy and sultry. Presently we were in that shaded part of the main road which runs through the thickets of the old dispaled [ie no longer enclosed] park of Llyssun.

'All of a sudden our attention was drawn to a rustling sound behind a hedge on the side overlooking the river, and where the noise came from we could discern a white flickering light. Then it died away. "Poachers," I whispered. "Jack o' Lantern," suggested the youth. We had only gone a few yards further before we were startled by another uncanny incident: right in front of us (some twenty yards ahead) appeared a vision of lighted windows. "The hotel. Never!" we both exclaimed – we were quite half a mile from Cann Office and, of course, out of

sight of it – but the lights disappeared as suddenly as they had appeared, and, for the remainder of our journey we had a veritable topic of interest, discussing the physical basis of the phenomena we had just witnessed. Our enthusiasm was somewhat damped upon reaching the hotel by the amused, incredulous air of the people to whom we recited our wonderful experience. I and my companion can vouch for the truth of the story.'[18]

Llanfair Caereinion

One winter's morning in the 1870s a 'mail driver' from Welshpool was terrified by a phantom horseman in the vicinity of Llanfair. He said the horseman appeared silently beside him, followed him for a while without saying a word and then as mysteriously disappeared. The mail man was so frightened that he turned round and refused to deliver the post to the outlying villages. The ghost may have been the 'notorious Yspryd Melin-y-grug' who was a well-known apparition in that neighbourhood. He was described as 'appearing after the fashion of a man, riding on a grey or white horse, crossing and re-crossing the road through the hedge'. The apparition was accompanied by 'a clanging, dismal sound of a chain'. The chains were supposedly 'prison chains', but it is unclear whether the bonds of a mortal prison were meant, or the metaphorical chains of the damned (such as those worn by Dickens's Jacob Marley).[19]

In 1884 Llanfair historian Edward Gittins made a list of all the ghosts in the parish. As well as the Yspryd Melin-y-grug, described above, and the Yspryd y Bryn-glas, described in detail below, he mentions two others:

'Yspryd y Derwteg – This ghost was of the mischievous goblin kind, which delighted to terrify people who kept late hours out; and was seen, or rather heard, only on the other side of the hedge of the old road leading to the house. It made no utterances, but showed its presence by making a rustling, unpleasant noise in the branches.

'Yspryd Coedygraig – This ghost had no head visible, but a body dressed after human fashion, a coat of the narrow-tail style with yellow buttons, knee-breeches, also with yellow knee-buttons. It walked in advance of persons about ten or twelve yards, and could never be overtaken, as it kept always the same distance off. It was supposed to be the shade of some departed person from the locality, having a message to some one or about something, yet unable to divulge its secret, for no one could get sufficiently near to speak to it.'[20]

Fifteen years or so ago I spent many of my evenings leafing through volumes of the invaluable old periodical called *Bye-gones,* which the then Clwyd County Library Sevice had been kind enough to let me borrow. By so doing I rediscovered many old tales and forgotten lore to fire the imagination. The one story which really made me sit up and take notice was the legend of the Bryn-glas ghost.

On February 18th, 1903, an antiquarian correspondent furnished some information on this ghost for the interest of his fellow readers. It was a very traditional sort of ghost story, concerning a family curse, but it was one certainly worth copying out. Then I continued to flick through the volume, making notes of other items of history and folklore which caught my eye, until a second heading for 'Yspryd Bryn-glas' appeared on March 24th. Another reader, seeing the previous entry, wrote in to say that his father had lived in Bryn-glas and had experienced there what today we would call poltergeist activity. This was even more interesting! *But there was more to come.*

A week later, a letter appeared, this time from a man then living in Oxford who had just received the previous entries in *Bye-gones.* He informed the editor that he was a member of the cursed family – and that the curse had come true! In elegant and mournful prose, Mr 'M W J' (only his initials appeared) informed the doubtless astonished readers of *Bye-gones* that for him the Yspryd Bryn-glas 'had a terrible significance' and that it was *to his own grandfather* that the ghost had intoned the curse. Suddenly a spooky old story, just like many others you will have read in *Haunted Wales,* had become real. Without *Bye-gones* or some other similar journal, this extraordinary saga would not have been told. So here it is, edited to an extent, retaining the stages in which a cosy old legend became an account of a poltergeist and then a true narrative 'of terrible significance'.

The first correspondent to *Bye-gones* set the scene by outlining the family history of Bryn-glas, stating that the two of most interest to antiquarians were the Devereux and the Joneses. He states that at the time of the appearance of the ghost, Devereux was the family in residence (although the initials 'M W J' imply that it was, in fact, the Joneses). Then he moves on to the haunting:

'This ghost made its appearance in the wood and hedge-row on the road-side near the house, in the form of a flickering light, and was always in the way when the master of Bryn-glas came home from Pool [ie Welshpool] or Llanfair. It always uttered in a dismal tone the warning and prophetic words "Dial daw, Dial daw (Vengeance will come)". It was believed that its message and the burden of its speech had reference directly to Squire Devereux, who, like other Welsh gentlemen of his day, partook of the good things of this life "not wisely but too well" – in fact this particular squire never quitted Llanfair town of nights without being more or less in a state of intoxication. This *yspryd* then had a special mission to perform (so the neighbours imagined) and if only someone would speak to it (they argued) and ask its message it would never more trouble the neighbourhood.

'Now, it is said, Squire Devereux at last mastered courage to do this piece of business himself, first fortifying himself for the task by sundry potations in the town, and, thus equipped, he went full of courage to the terrible thing, and asked for an explanation. But the apparition was too much for his nerves, and his voice gave way, and all he could say in reply to the dreaded "Dial daw" was "Pa bryd? (When?)" in a very hoarse whisper: to which the spirit replied, "Yn amser y gorwyrion y daw (In the days of the great-grandchildren it will come)". The voice after this was heard no more.'[21]

So much for Correspondent Number One. One can only imagine how M W J felt when he read this flippant account; an account, which, in all fairness, was intended to convey a folk tale, not something which might actually have occurred. Let us move on to the second correspondent:

'Prior to the [previous] highly interesting contribution I was certainly under the impression that I was the only individual living who had either heard of or known anything about the Bryn-glas ghost. My father, in the early part of his career, took up residence at Bryn-glas. This was evidently at a period when the manifestations of the supposed ghost were at their height, for by day as well as by night, the mansion was being subjected to intermittent storms of missiles, but whence they came or by whom sped, remained undiscovered, and apparently undiscoverable.

'Many's the night that my father, armed to

the teeth and on detection bent, kept vigil in an adjoining orchard, but on these particular nights neither goblin, ghost nor demon incarnate deigned, or, more probably dared, to put in an appearance, or continue the molestations. A certain yokel, whose veracity was regarded as unimpeachable, protested that at midday, in the light of the sun, he had seen the body of a wagon make a complete revolution, the wheels meanwhile remaining stationary.'[22]

The writer provided no satisfactory conclusion to these remarkable events, which appear to have had little to do with the grimly prophesying ghost outside the hall. But perhaps they were of no surprise to M W J. Now we shall hear from him:

'I have read with extreme interest the paragraphs relative to "Yspryd Bryn-glas". I have been acquainted with the story of the Yspryd these thirty years, my father having related it to me as long as that ago. Indeed, the Yspryd Bryn-glas has had for us a terrible significance, much as we, and I especially, feign to disbelieve in all matters superstitious; but in [the first] account of the Yspryd I hear for the first time of its colloquy with John Devereux. My grandfather, after his marriage to Miss Williams, of Llangyniew Rectory, lived for some year at Bryn-glas Hall, being at that time a man of considerable means and heir-presumptive to the Garth-lwyd Estates, his uncle, Mr Lloyd, having bred him in this belief, and he having lived at Garth-lwyd from childhood.

'Directly he took up his residence at Bryn-glas, strange phenomena manifested themselves, and the family was very much disturbed in consequence. My grandfather kept watch repeatedly in the full assurance, he being anything but a superstitious man, that the disturbances were caused by persons of mischievous or malicious intent, but ultimately he adopted a different view and became profoundly impressed by something which took place and of which he only had cognisance.

'I have always understood that the curse "Dial daw" was pronounced on my grandfather and his immediate descendants, that it was said they should be scattered to the four winds and find nameless graves in unknown and far distant lands, and certain it is with the single exception of my own father not one escaped the ban. The Far West, the battlefields of America, South Africa long years ago, each and all claimed a victim, and some died in absolute want and ignominy at our very doors. Disaster upon disaster speedily followed the pronouncement "Dial daw".

'Mr Lloyd was gathered to his fathers and laid to rest midst solemn pomp and sable woe, the tenantry were gathered together, as the custom then was, the will was read and lo! in the place of the name John Jones appeared that of Frederick Jones, his cousin. Five and twenty years ago, as a boy, I was walking to Welshpool, when an old man overtook me: he stopped and asked me if I belonged to the Garth-Lloyd Family. I told him I believed so. He said, "I see the likeness," and then, taking me by the arm – "Young man, I knew your grandfather, there is a curse on him, and all belonging to him."'[23]

So ends the saga of the Yspryd Bryn-glas. It should perhaps be pointed out that the final instalment was published on April 1st, 1903. However, M W J would have had to have been in collusion with the editor to have ensured publication on that date, and I cannot imagine *Bye-gones* stooping to April Fool pranks. An important point to mention, however, is that the 'Dial daw' curse visiting future generations is a staple of Welsh folklore (see, for example, Brecon). It can be found as a motif in various tales regarding wicked rulers, who imagine that they will escape the curse because it seems so far ahead, but, living to a great age, suffer along with all their descendants when the time comes. If the incidents occurred as M W J described them, it is reasonable to suppose that rumours of them could have become corrupted into a traditional story form when passed around and down by the Jones's uneducated neighbours. Is it possible such things could happen just a century ago? Could they happen now?

Llanfigan (Llanfeugan)

At this tiny hamlet near Talybont in Breconshire there once lived a happy young couple, engaged to be married. Tragically, shortly before the wedding day, the prospective groom was drowned and the young woman, Ursula by name, was devastated. She 'mourned excessively and continued to do so immeasurably' until the spirit of her beloved came to visit her one night. He sat on her bed and she felt his face – which was as cold as stone. The spirit told Ursula that she should no longer mourn for him, that it was God's will that he was where he now was (although he remained obscure on that latter subject). Then he left her. After this visit, Ursula was able to come to terms with her loss.[24]

Llangattock

Robert Williams, of Llangattock, near Crickhowell, became lost one night while making his way over the mountain which now forms the boundary with the new authority of Blaenau Gwent. Peering through the darkness, he was relieved to see some way ahead of him the figure of an old woman. He called out to her, hopeful that she would be able to direct him onto the right path, but he received no answer. Thinking that she might be deaf, he hurried to catch up with her but, old though she appeared to be, he found to his frustration that somehow or other she was able to remain ahead of him. In desperation, he began to run through the dark, never mind that he could hardly see where he was going, and the result was that he slipped up in a patch of boggy ground.

Lying in the wet, he heard the old woman laughing maliciously, and it dawned on him at last that this was no living person he had been following, but the sinister Juan White, a wicked spirit who loved to lead travellers astray. Angry and scared, he drew his knife, at the sight of which the apparition vanished. Cold iron will often drive off fairies, and it seemed to work in the same way with this malignant spook, too. Williams found that he been led into the middle of a dangerous bog, and he had to carefully pick his way back out of it before seeking his path home again.[25] (For more on Juan White, see Llanhilleth, Blaenau Gwent.)

Llangunllo

Poltergeists are scary things. More often than not their antics are harmless, even amusing, but on occasions the merely alarming becomes terrifying and eventually even life-threatening as its violent behaviour escalates. The Roberts family of Llangunllo, near Knighton, were lucky to escape with their lives when their resident spook's playfulness turned nasty.

The first clue they had that their farm was possessed of a new, invisible occupant, was when their servant-man, who had been threshing grain in the barn, burst into the house saying that something had repeatedly grabbed the flail from his hand and flung it into the hay-loft. The man of the house was away that day, so he told his tale to the wife and her maidservant, who found it highly amusing. Of course, they didn't believe him but, with much leg-pulling, agreed to accompany him back to the barn where they would 'protect' him. The three of them entered the barn, the man retrieved his flail from the hay-loft and the ladies settled themselves, one to do her knitting, the other to wind some yarn. Their hilarity was short-lived. The poltergeist turned its attention to them, yanking the things from their hands and throwing them all over the barn.

Terrified, all three hurried back to the house, but found no safety there – the poltergeist had got there first. The dishes on the dresser were moving about and some were thrown onto the stone floor, smashing at their feet. That night, the disturbances began in earnest. Keeping to their beds, they heard a terrible crashing and banging and they found the next morning that 'they could scarcely tread without stepping on the wrecks of crockery which lay about'.

From this time on, the family had no rest. The poltergeist continued to wreak havoc and the house became infamous – sightseers would turn up just to watch what it would do next. A man came over from Knighton with a view to exorcising the spirit for them, but the spook showed no respect, pulling the prayer-book from his hands and throwing it upstairs. Over the next few days it learnt the trick of throwing stones at people and, enjoying the success of this, it got completely carried away and ripped iron from the chimney and hurled this, too. After about three months, as its finale, it set the house on fire. The blaze proved uncontrollable and the house was burnt to the ground. For many years it stood a shell, a curiosity to the neighbourhood.

What happened to the unfortunate homeless family is not recorded, but the malignant nature of the supernatural attack may have been due to their own behaviour. It seems that the house was due to be inherited by the farmwife's brother, a soldier whom they believed had died some years previously in a far-off land. When her father died, her brother failed to claim his inheritance, so she and her husband took possession. But her brother was not dead, and by the time he returned home she and her husband had taken a great deal of time and money in restoring the house to a liveable condition. For this reason they absolutely refused to give up their home to him, or even share it. In response, the soldier offered to *sell* them the house – for a very modest fee of two guineas – this they also refused to do. Embittered and angry, he enlisted again and went to Ireland, warning his sister that she would have reason to repent her selfish behaviour. Perhaps in Ireland he truly met his end, and it was his vengeful spirit which wrecked the home that rightfully belonged to him.[26]

Llangynidr

From this village, situated a few miles west of Crickhowell, comes a tale of a spectre that was not only horrific to look upon but also aggressive enough to actually chase after someone unlucky enough to look upon it. The victim was a Wesleyan minister, Rev H Elwyn Thomas. Mr Thomas recounted his adventure to a Miss Estelle Stead, who wrote it up for a book called *True Ghost Stories*, published in 1936 (see Pwllheli, Gwynedd).

Mr Thomas explained that he had been preaching in the area of Crickhowell and was walking back to a friend's house at about a quarter to nine on a fine June night, when his attention was drawn to a peculiar figure standing a little way away on the banks of a canal. The canal ran parallel to the rather lonely road Mr Thomas was using, so he soon drew close to the figure, whom he presumed from his appearance to be some sort of beggar. So curious was Mr Thomas that he decided to stop and speak to the odd-looking character as he passed by. *This was a mistake.*

'Within half a yard of him [writes Estelle Stead] he saw a startling and dreadful sight, that of an old man over whose face the leaden-coloured skin was tightly stretched: the lips were thin and bloodless, and the half-open mouth toothless. Two piercing and semi-luminous eyes, set far back, stared at Mr Thomas...'

Perhaps most startling of all was the way the 'beggar' was dressed. Indeed 'dressed' is an inaccurate word to use – 'wrapped' would be more apt, for the thing's clothing consisted of nothing more than two filthy strips of bandage-like calico which were wound round and round its emaciated physique. The whole effect was that of an upright corpse dressed for the grave. Mr Thomas was so appalled that, by pure instinct, he actually ran away – although at this stage he had no inkling that what he had encountered was in any way supernatural, indeed he had been an 'absolute disbeliever in ghosts' until that night. After he'd run a good distance, his panic subsided and he staggered to a halt. He was perhaps a little embarrassed by his sudden loss of control, so he turned back But his heart gave a jolt of horror, for the hideous thing in calico was almost on top of him!

'By this time the wrappings had merged into a column of intense blackness, and there was nothing visible between the face and the ground. Raising his umbrella... the minister hit out blindly, only to encounter air, through which his umbrella easily passed.'

Realising now that his pursuer was not of this earth, Mr Thomas again took to his heels and there began a nightmare chase down the long and deserted stretch of road. At last, Mr Thomas reached a fork in the road, one arm of which he knew would take him into the centre of the village of Llangynidr. Knowing that safety was in reach, he paused and made the decision that, as a minister, he should try and speak to the thing. He turned to face it. However, as chance would have it, the spectre had broken off its pursuit. It was heading rapidly towards a wall bordering a churchyard. Here, by the lych-gate, it vanished among the foliage of an old yew tree. Mr Thomas gave out a shuddering sigh of relief and promptly fainted. It was two hours later before the poor man woke up, chilled to the bone, and it took him another hour to crawl to his friend's house, barely a quarter of a mile away.

Mr Thomas spent a week in bed 'laid up with a bad attack of nervous prostration', and it took a while before he was able to tell his friends what had happened to him. Remarkably, the ghastly appearance of the spectre, seemingly unlike anything human, was immediately identified as belonging to a real person, though one who was long deceased. This was a recluse 'lost to all personal sense of respect and decency' whose only garments were lengths of filthy calico, as Mr Thomas described, and who had lived in a cottage by the canal. After his death, the recluse was buried in his calico wrappings in a grave near where Mr Thomas saw the ghost vanish. The cottage remained untenanted and fell into ruin. [27]

Llanidloes

The area around Llanidloes was the haunt of the ghost of Lady Jeffrey, who would charge about the countryside in a fury. She was a wicked woman in life and her misdeeds prevented her from finding peace. In a ceremony identical to those we have encountered elsewhere (eg Llandegla, Denbighshire), Lady Jeffrey's angry spirit was persuaded to change her form from the variety of huge and horrible ones she usually delighted in, until she was small enough to be trapped in a bottle. This bottle was then 'cast into a pool underneath the Short bridge, Llanidloes, and there the lady was to remain until the ivy which grew up the buttresses should overgrow the sides of the bridge and reach the parapet'.

What happened subsequently, I shall leave to local lad the Rev Elias Owen to describe: 'The ivy was dangerously near the top of the bridge when the writer was a schoolboy, and often did he and his companions crop off its tendrils as they neared the prescribed limits for we were all terribly afraid to release the dreaded lady out of the bottle. In the year 1848, the old bridge was blown up, and a new one built instead of it. A schoolfellow, whom we called Ben, was playing by the aforesaid pool when the bridge was undergoing reconstruction, and he found by the river's side a small bottle, and in the bottle was a little black thing, that was never quiet, but it kept bobbing up and down continually, just as if it wanted to get out.

'Ben kept the bottle safely for a while, but ere long he was obliged to throw it into the river, for his relations and neighbours came to the conclusion that that was the very bottle that contained Lady Jeffrey's Spirit, and they also surmised that the little black restless thing was nothing less than the lady herself. Ben consequently resigned the bottle and its contents to the pool again, there to undergo a prolonged, but unjust, term of imprisonment.'[28]

Llansantffraid

Another strong-willed woman was Madam Godolphin and she lived at Llansantffraid in the 18th century. She was described as 'mean and eccentric'. On one occasion she presented her footman John with a well-picked bone to make a broth for his children. Having thanked her politely for her 'generosity', the disgusted John waited till she was out of sight and then threw it into the river. When Madam Godolphin later asked him whether he had made the broth, John, taking a sideways glance at the river, replied: 'Yes, madam, enough to last them as long as they live.'

Replied his self-satisfied mistress: 'That's right, there is nothing like good broth for growing children.'

Such a positive character was unlikely to rest easy in her grave, and after her death she was often still to be seen, attired in a black silk gown and sitting on a stile, with her little pet dog sitting beside her. In 1875 an old countryman named William rather vividly related: 'I once saw her ghost and I heard the rustling of her silk dress as plain as ever I heard a startled rabbit rushing over a bed of dried leaves in November.'[29]

Llanwddyn

Before the secluded valley of Llanwddyn was drowned to create the reservoir now called Llyn Vyrnwy, it was 'plagued' by a mischief-making entity called Yspryd Cynon. This *bwgan* centred its activities on a farmhouse of that name and became so 'savage' that 'people scarcely dared live there'. It was said that 'stones and slates from the tops of the buildings were hurled at the inmates in all directions'.[30]

A very famous personage was called in to lay the spirit, one Richard Morris, of Oswestry, who was known far and wide as 'Dic Spot the Conjuror'. Morris died in 1792, which gives us a clue as to when these proceedings took place.[31] Dic Spot conjured the troublesome Yspryd Cynon into a bottle or a quill (two versions are recorded), which he then placed under a large stone in the river below the farmhouse of Cynon Isaf. Ever after this rock bore the name Carreg yr Yspryd (Rock of the Spirit).

The conjuror put the following injunction on the spook, that it should remain under the stone until the water should work its way between the stone and the dry land. Another version of the injunction was that it should remain there until the river had dried up. Perhaps both were stated. At any rate, 'the poor Spirit was, by all appearances, doomed to a very long imprisonment'. However, as Elias Owen points out: 'Dic Spot did not foresee the wants and enterprise of the people of Liverpool, who would one day convert the Llanwddyn Valley into a lake fifteen miles in circumference, and release the Spirit from prison by the process of making their Waterworks.'[32]

An antiquarian writing in 1880, when the plans for the reservoir were gaining pace, archly noted: 'It is to be hoped that navvies of the Llanwddyn Water Works will not apply their pickaxe so heavily as to break the bottle, or it is to be feared the Liverpool Corporation will suffer much from damage committed by the ghost, for he must have gained a vast deal of strength after resting so many years.'[33]

Elias Owen recorded what actually did take place when the Scouse navvies arrived in Llanwddyn, their practical considerations clashing alarmingly with the traditions of the locals. He learnt the details from the then vicar of Llanwddyn, the Rev Thomas Henry Evans. I consider the following to be a classic of Welsh ghostlore and take pleasure in quoting it in full:

'The inhabitants of the valley knew the traditions respecting the Spirit, and they much feared its being disturbed. The stone was a large boulder, from fifteen to twenty tons in weight, and it was evident that it was doomed to destruction, for it stood in the river Vyrnwy just where operations were to commence. There was no small stir among the Welsh inhabitants when preparations were made to blast the huge Spirit-stone. English and Irish workmen could not enter into the feeling of the Welsh towards the stone, but they had heard what was said about it. They, however, had no dread of the imprisoned Spirit.

'In course of time, the stone was bored and a load of dynamite inserted, but it was not shattered at the first blast. About four feet square remained intact, and underneath this the Spirit was, if it was anywhere. The men were soon set to work to demolish the stone. The Welshmen expected some catastrophe to follow its destruction, and they were even prepared to see the Spirit bodily emerge from its prison, for, said they, the conditions of its release have been fulfilled – the river had been diverted from its old bed into an artificial channel, to facilitate the removal of this and other stones – and there was no doubt that both conditions had been literally carried out, and consequently the Spirit, if justice ruled, could claim its release.

'The stone was blasted, and strange to relate, when the smoke had cleared away, the water in a cavity where the stone had been was seen to move; there was no apparent reason why the water should thus be disturbed, unless, indeed, the Spirit was about to appear. The Welsh workmen became alarmed, and moved away from the place, keeping, however, their eyes fixed upon the pool. The mystery was soon solved, for a large frog made its appearance, and, sedately sitting on a fragment of the shattered stone, rubbed its eyes with its feet, as if awaking from a long sleep. The question was discussed, "Is it a frog, or the Spirit in the form of a frog; if it is a frog, why was it not killed when the stone was blasted?" And again, "Who ever saw a frog sit up in that fashion and rub the dust out of its eyes? It must be the Spirit."

'There the workmen stood, at a respectful distance from the frog, who, heedless of the marked attention paid to it, continued sitting up and rubbing its eyes. They would not approach it, for it must be the Spirit, and no one knew what its next movement or form might be.

At last, however, the frog was driven away, and the men re-commenced their labours. But for nights afterwards people passing the spot heard a noise as of heavy chains being dragged along the ground where the stone once stood.'[34]

The Rev Evans took great delight in collecting the ghost stories of Llanwddyn parish. There were very many of them, and he provides a fascinating list:

'Yspryd y pentre – This was the very troublesome one in the village, put down by prayer and fasting by certain divinities that met together for that purpose; and according to their instructions, he was placed in the sand below the foundations of Pont Dolwenith Bridge, there to remain till the bed of the river is dried up.

'Yspryd Ffynon Dwgan was put to rest by a person of that name under a large stone at the bottom of the well "Ffynon Dwgan" by Tynmawr. He is to remain there till the water wears a hole through that stone.

'Yspryd y Gro, a troublesome one, pelting passers-by with mud and dirt, is put down in the brook above Rhiwargor, and there to remain until the same is dry.

'Yspryd Llwyn y Famaeth, which appears in the form of a calf.

'Yspryd Ceunant Croesau, visible in all shapes.

'Yspryd Cefn Yspytty appears as alternate light and darkness.

'Yspryd Fedwddu has sometimes the appearance of a human without a head, a beautiful horse with a rider, a large bull, and as a greyhound.

'Yspryd Coed y Gyfyng, near Rhiwargor.

'Yspryd y Llan, in various forms, sometimes like a pack of hounds, and at other times in sheets of light.

'Yspryd Ceunant Pistyll, is the one that watches over the remains of treasures and relics of St Wddyn.'

If this alarming roll-call was not enough, Evans also mentions another in the parish capable of killing sheep and one on St John's Hill which forced night-bound travellers to hand over all their money! These latter two are more likely to be real-life criminals pretending to be ghosts but even so, this isolated parish seems to have been quite horribly haunted. Evans compiled his list in 1874, many years before Llyn Vyrnwy drowned a great portion of the parish. How many of these ghosts now lie under the reservoir, I wonder? I, for one, wouldn't wish to drink the water![35]

Even now we are not quite done with ghosts

from Llanwddyn. In 1904, a correspondent calling himself 'Cynon' related another in the pages of *Bye-gones*. I suspect Cynon was actually the aforementioned Mr Evans. Here's the story:

Many years ago, back in the good old days when pubs stayed open till midnight and often for longer, an old chap named Harry Parry was wending his way home from the *Powis Inn*, when he was accosted in the road by an old friend. It was indeed a very old friend, for he had been in his grave many a long year! Harry stared dumbfounded at his friend – Kynaston his name was – and then the apparition vanished. Harry did the only thing possible in such a situation, he returned to the pub! He sat in the *Powis*, imbibing a little more, a look of 'silent awe' on his face. At last he braved the journey home again.

He walked – or staggered – up Cedig Lane until he came opposite the mill pond at Ty-uchaf ; there he found Kynaston (deceased) waiting for him. What passed between Harry and the *yspryd* is somewhat obscure, because Harry was too scared to talk about it, 'lest the ghost should visit him with some terrible vengeance'. He did let on that Kynaston-as-was seized him and dragged him through the mill pond and across some fields, the result of this rough treatment being that he passed out. When he came to himself, he found he was in the old churchyard and standing over a certain grave. Here the spirit's 'last mission' was performed and it departed, allowing the bedraggled Harry to return home. His wife afterwards told the neighbours that when her husband came through the door, he 'smelt strongly of some sulphurous matter'![36]

Llanwnog

A man in Llanwnog took hold of his dead wife's hand and completed her will for her – altering it to his own advantage. Soon after, he married again, but if he looked for happiness in his new life he was much mistaken. From then on, he was literally a haunted man. Strange noises were heard in his house, doors locked and unlocked themselves and objects were broken. He moved house, but the trouble followed. It soon became apparent he was the at the centre of the haunting: 'Even in the chapel where he was a deacon, the man would suddenly stand up, appearing to be struggling with some unseen being. The atmosphere changed whenever he came near. His chil-

dren were disturbed...' Only when he had handed over to his late wife's relatives the money that should have been theirs in the first place, did the man know any peace again.[37]

Llanymynech

The border of Wales and England runs right through the centre of Llanymynech. In earlier days, I have been told, half the pubs in the village would be open on a Sunday (those in Shropshire) and the other half closed (those in Montgomeryshire) – indeed, one pub stood right on the border, and while one bar was closed, the other was doing an excellent trade! Perhaps this is a legend, but if so, it is certainly not the only one. One of the oldest and most famous ghost stories from Wales is set on the limestone escarpment which overlooks the village.

Here could be found the Ogof (Welsh for 'cave'), a tunnel in the limestone which may have been a mineworking dating from Roman, or even earlier, times. The whole area has been quarried since and I was unable to determine which, if any, of the many forbidding holes in the rock belongs to the following romance. Perhaps this is just as well, for the cave had a very sinister reputation. It was said you were in more danger approaching the mouth of the Ogof than you were approaching the crater of a live volcano – for 'whoever approached within five paces of it would inevitably be lost'!

There is a tale of an unfortunate fox being pursued by hounds on the hill and which found itself harried right to the Ogof's entrance. Rather than be consumed by the unknown terrors of the cave, however, it turned and leapt right into the middle of the pack – as if it preferred 'anything earthly, even an earthly death' to such a fate. Readers will be relieved to learn, however, that the hounds did not kill it – for its close proximity to the Ogof had tainted it with the uncanny. Its fur now bristled with numerous weird lights and it gave off a horrible stench; the hounds were content to leave well alone.

The Ogof was popularly believed to extend for many miles under the hills of Wales and Salop, from Llanymynech hill all the way to Chirk Castle. Once upon a time a fiddler named Iolo ap Hugh made a bet that he could enter the Ogof and 'dance all the way down the hill, and keep up a tune with his fiddle'. Iolo readied himself for this hair-brained expedition with seven pounds of candles and 'an immense quantity' of cheese. He was never seen again. Or rather, he was never seen again alive.

One misty Hallowe'en night after all hope had been lost for Iolo's safe return from the sinister cave, a shepherd wending his way homewards heard the pathetic scraping of a violin somewhere ahead of him in the dark. As he proceeded on his journey the eerie sound resolved itself into something resembling a tune and then the shepherd stumbled on the source of it – the yawning maw of the Ogof! There, framed by the jagged limestone, stood Iolo ap Hugh, faintly illuminated by a lantern slung around his neck. He was capering in the dark, scraping away at his fiddle with a feverish intensity. The shepherd, recognising him for the lost violinist, shouted his name again and again, but Iolo ignored him, continuing his lunatic prancing and playing without a pause. The shepherd began to feel a thrill of supernatural fear, and then the moon suddenly came out from behind a cloud and shone full on Iolo's face – 'distinctly and horribly'.

'His face was pale as marble, and his eyes stared fixedly and deathfully, whilst his head dangled loose and unjointed on his shoulders. His arms seemed to keep his fiddlestick in motion without the least sympathy from their master. The shepherd saw him a moment on the verge of the cave, and then, still capering and fiddling, vanish like a shadow from his sight ... he seemed as it were to skate into the cave, quite different from the step of a living and willing man, but he was dragged inwards, like the smoke up the chimney, or the mist at sunrise.'

This was not quite the last that was heard of Iolo ap Hugh. Many years later, the shepherd, now an old man, was sitting in old Llanymynech church one cold December Sunday when he and his fellow parishioners were suddenly startled by a burst of music coming from somewhere *underneath* the aisle. The congregation started up in confusion as the sound of the fiddle moved beneath their feet, continuing to the far end of the church before gradually dying away. The old shepherd recognised the tune; it was the same one he had heard Iolo ap Hugh play on that never to be forgotten All Hallow's Eve on Llanymynech hill. The parson of the parish took down the tune and recorded it for posterity. It was named *Farwell* (sic), *Ned Pugh* and the notation appears in the pages of the *Cambrian Quarterly* for 1829 – a unique artefact indeed.[38]

There are alternative versions of the above

legend. When it was recounted to a youthful Elias Owen in about the year 1846, the musician who entered the cave was described as a harpist and his name, like that in the title of the tune, was Ned Pugh. Ned Pugh boasted that he had walked through the Ogof (Owen calls it Ogo) down to the Lion Inn in Llanymynech, where, it is to be presumed, another cave entrance existed. His claim was scorned, so he laid a bet that he would be able to play a tune *en route* under the church the following Sunday. The wager was taken up and Ned entered the Ogo as promised. To everyone's amazement, the sound of his harp was later heard under church playing the tune later called *Farewell* (note corrected spelling) *Ned Pugh*, but Ned himself never emerged from the cavern.[39]

In 1871 a third version, dating from the 1850s, appeared in the pages of *Bye-gones*: 'A man playing bagpipes is said to have entered one of the caves, well provisioned with Welsh mutton, and after he had been in some time, his bagpipes were heard two miles from the entrance, underneath the small town of Llanymynech. He never returned to tell his story. The few bones that are found in the cave are supposed to be those which he had picked on his way.'[40]

As previously mentioned, Llanymynech stands right on the border between England and Wales. For this reason a County Stone was set up on the spot where three counties met, its three sides inscribed 'Denbigh', 'Montgomery' and 'Salop'. It was said that a spirit had been laid beneath this stone, but with insufficient skill, for at midnight the spirit would wander about. One man said that it smelt strongly of thyme, but as John Fewtrell, who recorded the story, points out, wild thyme grows all round the base of the stone. This is the second reference to the smell of thyme being linked to the supernatural (see Llanasa, Flintshire), but I am aware of no reason for this connection, other than the obvious rhyme with 'time'.[41]

Tradition has it that an old building called Siamber Wen (Sacred Chamber) had once housed a nunnery. It was haunted by at least two apparitions. A headless figure appeared in a bedroom and a woman dressed in 'a long, white flowing garment' was seen in the cellar. There was also a tradition of a shocking murder having taken place here. A nun was brought to the house to attend a woman in the last stages of labour. She was blindfolded and taken down many long passageways until she reached the room where the woman was to be delivered of her child. Three masked men were also present in the room and the nun was commanded to perform her duties in absolute silence; on no account was she to speak to the woman she was attending. All this secrecy convinced the nun that the child was to be done away with by the men, so after her duties were fulfilled, she tore off a small piece of the bed hangings so that the house could be later identified. The house was afterwards proved to be Siamber Wen and the skeleton of an infant was found under a slab in the floor of the kitchen.

The story is very similar to a classic of English ghostlore, that of Wild Will Darrell, who haunts Littlecote House at Hungerford in Berkshire. Darrell conveyed a blindfolded midwife to Littlecote to attend the birth of an illegitimate child, which he then immediately murdered. The midwife cut out a small piece of cloth from the bed curtains in order to expose the murderer. I believe there is hard historical evidence for the Littlecote version, however. [42]

The following exciting account of a phantom horse race took place in the vicinity of Llanymynech, on a road beyond a ford across the River Vyrnwy. Since the lady who features in the story had been returning from Oswestry Market, we can be confident that it occurred on the Montgomeryshire side of the river. The road leading up from the ford was enclosed for a stretch by woodland, making it rather a gloomy spot; ideal, in fact, for a haunting. A ghostly white horse with 'great blood clots' on its shoulders was known to charge up this road at a furious pace after dark. Those who had seen it said it was bridled and saddled but no one visible was riding it. On this particular Wednesday evening in the 19th century, our heroine had made many more purchases than usual, and as a consequence was much later coming away from market than she would have liked.

'She was most anxious to cross over the ford on her return before dark, being made timid by the stories she had heard, but night had set in before she came to it. Loaded as she was, she dreaded the crossing, and it was with difficulty she got her steed to enter the water, but when she had crossed, the spirited animal, smelling his stable, set off at a sharp canter. While she was incommoded by her load and the pulling of the horse, she distinctly heard behind her the terrifying sound of a furious galloping, and her steed, appearing to hear it also, set off furiously in the pitch darkness, and to her horror, glancing behind, she saw coming on at her flank the outstretched head and neck of the white horse.

'She was near the end of the wood, and as she emerged the sound of the spectre ceased, but her own animal raced on, only stopping at the gate of the farm, and backing to permit her to fling it open, and then raced for home, where he stood in the farm yard trembling with fear. The family had gone to bed, and only a man was up to attend to the horse, but in the morning she had a sound rating for riding so hard.'[43]

Llawryglyn

A very troublesome poltergeist bothered Gwernau Farm. In common with many modern accounts, the disturbances initially centred round a youngster, in this case a boy. T Gwynn Jones says: 'Articles were broken or torn in his hands or in contact with him.' A young servant girl was also a focus. On occasions her clothes would be seen standing up in the middle of a room as if worn by her, but would crumple in a heap if touched (I find this an especially eerie image). But they were not the only victims. The poltergeist also regularly tried to steal a hat belonging to a workman. He got so exasperated that he threw the hat on the ground with the words: 'Take it, if you want it!' The hat was torn to pieces in front of his eyes. After it tore a Bible, prayer meetings were held to exorcise the 'evil spirit'.[44]

Elias Owen also records a case of poltergeist activity at Llawryglyn, at a farm named Craig Wen. Loud and unexplained noises would be heard about the house, crockery would be smashed ... 'the dairy was greatly upset, the cream was found filled with dust, the cheese fell from the shelf into the milk; but the greatest sufferer of all was the mistress of the house, her dresses were all torn up, and her shawls as well.' The servant-girl told her mistress that she had seen the evil spirit. She said she had been walking through the cornfield when she had seen a mouse running before her. She had run after it but could not catch it and when they drew opposite the barn, the mouse had stopped *and laughed at her*, before disappearing into a hole!

However, 'an observant man' who visited the farm to see if he could get to the bottom of the disturbances was unimpressed with this evidence. He found it highly suspicious that the mistress of the house suffered most of the spook's attention and he quickly divined that it was the servant-girl herself who was responsible for the damage. When the servant-girl was sent away, 'the evil spirit went away with her'.[45]

Llywel

Some 'ghosts with a purpose' aren't too particular about whom they badger to ensure their eternal rest. The unquiet spirit of a suicide, a young woman named Anne Dewy, for some reason attached herself to a young man with whom she had had no previous connection. Not only would she meet him on the road as he went about his day to day business, she would even appear by his bedside. So frightened and so harassed was the boy that he fell ill. One day his cousin came to stay and was told of the unwelcome visitations. He was surprised to learn no attempt had been made to speak to the spirit, to find out what it wanted. This he strongly urged the ailing youth to do, assuring him he would be by his side as moral support.

After a visit to a pub to calm their nerves, the young men wandered about waiting for Anne Dewy to show herself. This she did, but only to her chosen one, the cousin seeing and hearing nothing. After an immediate return visit to the pub – followed by his exasperated cousin – the troubled youth determined to face his fear and this time he went out to meet Anne on his own.

He spoke to the spirit and it replied: 'Fear nothing; follow me'. The young man was led to a wall behind Anne Dewy's former home, where she had hanged herself, and here was shown, hidden among the masonry, a bag containing a great many pieces of gold. For a moment, it seemed all his earlier stress had been worthwhile, but to his disappointment the spirit told him he could not keep the money. Instead, Anne ordered that he do what all the ghosts of South Wales want doing in these circumstances – he had to throw it into the river. If only Anne had lived in a parish just a bit further north than Llywel, he might have been made a rich man! Ah well, at least his nights remained undisturbed from that day on and he was able to live a ghost-free life again.[46]

Machynlleth

Marie Trevelyan tells a fascinating account of a travelling preacher who spent the night in a crumbling old house in Machynlleth. The preacher, whom she names Richard Rhys (see also Aberedw, above, and Llangollen, Denbighshire), said that when he reached the town in about the year 1870, he found that he was unable to sleep in the deacon's house, as he had expected, but had to seek accommodation elsewhere:

'The house I had to put up in was very ancient, and I could see it would soon tumble down. Soon after supper the first night I went to bed early. My room I found to be very large – too big for a bedroom. In it was a neat four-posted bed, a good-sized round table of solid oak, and other furniture besides. Tired after the long journey I soon fell asleep, and suppose I must have slept for several hours, when a noise in the house disturbed me. At first I thought something had fallen to the floor in the next room, but by-and-by, when more sounds came, I could hear the tramp of many feet on the stairs. Suddenly the door of my room flew open, and in walked a troop of men. I could see them as plain as possible, because the moonlight was as bright as day. And what I thought most odd was that all the men were dressed as armed men of hundreds of years ago.

'One of the men planted himself by the chimney-piece, and the others stood before him. Although I was very fearful, I sat bolt upright in bed to look at them. Some were fierce-looking, others were milder, but all were armed, and all wore swords. The men seemed to be debating, and the leader was apparently giving directions, when one of the number rushed forward, and lifting his sword attempted to kill the leader. In the twinkling of an eye the head man sprang aside, and the assassin was foiled. Terrible noise followed, and I could hear the clatter of arms, and the clash of swords as the men crowded around the fellow, who had tried to slay their leader. Then, as strangely as they came in, they tramped out of the room, and I heard the sound of their feet going downstairs and out to the road.'

Rhys leapt out of bed and looked out, 'but all was as quiet as the grave'. The next morning when he told the deacon what had happened he confirmed that he had heard that the house was haunted. Years later Rhys learnt that the old dwelling he had stayed in was called the 'Parliament House' and that there was a tradition attached to it: 'There in 1402 Owen Glendower narrowly escaped being assassinated by Sir David Gain, the Fluellin of Shakespeare.'[47]

Ancient houses might well be supposed to have been the harbours of romance and tragedy over the years, but even the remotest parts of the Welsh countryside have their stories. An especially bleak and desolate part of the mountain wastes above Machynlleth, for example, is the setting for the legend of Catrin, a young woman who had lived happily in this out of the way place, setting up home in a tiny cottage with her husband, a young shepherd, until she died in mysterious circumstances one wild and stormy night in 1705.

The precise scene of the tragedy which befell Catrin and the subsequent site of her haunting may never now be located. It was somewhere high up on mighty Pumlumon between Llanidloes and Machynlleth in the vicinity of a place called Llechwedd Cwm Gwarchau and a small lake called Bugeilyn. It was recounted in the pages of the *Cambrian Quarterly* in 1829 by a man who had recently enjoyed a fishing trip in the area. In the company of a fellow angler and two shepherds named Evan and Lewis Jones, the anonymous author was making his way along the banks of the Rheidol when he spotted an attractive rill of water running past the ruins of a cottage. He suggested taking a look, but was astonished when Lewis Jones, 'his face contorted with horror and tobacco', absolutely refused to accompany him.

'In the name of heaven, sir, don't go!' he exclaimed (in Welsh). 'You will meet with white Kitty of the Grove Cave.'

'Meet with what?' asked the angler.

'With the evil spirit,' replied Lewis. The writer tried to ridicule the fears of the two locals but in vain. He writes: 'To attempt to convince the superstitious shepherds of the absurdity of their alarm, was useless; accompany us they would not, and remained behind. I firmly believe, if any of the sheep were to be lost on the rocks, Messieurs Evan and Lewis Jones would not dare to follow.'

His curiosity naturally piqued, the fisherman asked for the story of 'the evil spirit' and here is a condensed version of it:

In 1704 a young shepherd named Rowlant Humphrey married a maid named Catrin and they lived very happily together in their remote mountain home, tending their sheep and goats and 'a few dwarfish cattle' and every so often going to market in far Machynlleth. One autumn day, after they had been married for almost a year, Catrin set out on the nine-mile journey to Machynlleth to sell some poultry. It was a fine day and although Catrin was now five months pregnant, neither she nor Rowlant felt any trepidation about her travelling that distance alone; she had made the hike many times

before, she had her dog with her, and, besides, they were both looking forward to the purchases she would be able to make in preparation for the addition to their little family. However, as the day wore on the weather waxed stormy, and Rowlant began to look anxiously for his wife's return.

Catrin was still on the mountain when the storm broke. She had been in the company of some farmers' wives for the first part of the return journey, but they had long since left her to take the paths to their own homes. After a sudden flash of lightning and a deafening crack of thunder, the rain came down in torrents, 'such as the oldest shepherd never remembered to have been surpassed in furious descent'. Catrin did not return that night, nor any other night. The horrors of the storm were insufficient to prevent Rowlant and a friend from searching high and low on the desolate moors, even after 'the furious hurricane struck out their lights, and beat them to the earth'; but it was in vain.

The following morning at first light there came a violent scratching at the door of the cottage where Rowlant sat, sunk in a black despair. His companion opened the door, and in bounded Catrin's faithful dog. He leapt all over Rowlant, licking his face and whining pathetically. He then hurried back to the door and it was clear that he wished his master to follow him. Supported by his friend, the exhausted Rowlant staggered after the dog as it led them away over the mountain. Over the first hill he led them, between the crags of Gelli Gogo (The Cave of the Grove) and Bugeilyn lake, and then down along the banks of a stream until he came to the edge of a bog, whose deadly reputation 'they knew too well'.

'Upon the brink of the shaking soil, lay the little basket and its contents; and upon the treacherous maelstrom of death appeared a corner of the red cloak poor Catrin had been presented with, upon her marriage-day, by the now widowed Rowlant.'

Such a tragedy is not quickly forgotten. And it is not to be wondered at that the local people should have feared that the ill-fated Catrin should not rest easy in her grim, unsanctified grave. The anonymous correspondent to the *Cambrian Quarterly* adds: 'The legend is still told by the shepherds who affirm that, when the howlings of the storm are at their utmost fury, the apparition is seen riding on the whirlwind, attired in flowing white garments.'[48]

Meifod

Dolobran Hall, now a farm, boasts a tragic and romantic legend which features that staple of fiction, but rarely of fact, the headless ghost. Many years ago, the owner of Dolobran took a very pretty wife, perhaps too pretty. While he was away on fishing trips, she was being visited by an admiring gentleman from nearby Ystumcolwyn. One day, hubbie returned unexpectedly and the lover had to be quickly hidden. The lady concealed him in a small room, called the Lloft Goch (Red Room), in a disused portion of the house. This hiding place may not have been wisely chosen, for it proved impossible for the 'guest' from Ystumcolwyn to leave without being seen, and so he was forced to remain in this confinement for several days.

At last, the master of Dolobran made another expedition to the river. His wife rejoined her lover in the Lloft Goch and, since they were at their leisure, they lit a fire and prepared a meal. This was a mistake. The cuckold had not gone very far and he noticed the smoke rising from the chamber. This aroused his suspicions, and he returned home to find out why his wife was using an otherwise neglected part of the house. He barged into the Red Room, to find his wife alone. But it didn't take him long to find the lover, trembling in a closet!

A duel was fought and the master of Dolobran proved the victor. His wife's lover's body was dumped unceremoniously back in the closet. Ever after, the Lloft Goch became known as the Haunted Room of Dolobran. The ghost of the slain man made regular appearances here, and it was headless. Was he decapitated by the jealous husband in a frenzy of rage? The legend does not say so. However, there was certainly a lot of blood, the floor was stained with it – and it may be that the Red Room earned its name after this tragedy. Even as late as 1910, when this story was written down, the red heelmarks of the master of Dolobran were to be seen in the Lloft Goch – recording the very spot where he stood in his rival's blood while chucking his body back in the closet.[49]

Another version of this story sets the scene not at Dolobran but at Ystumcolwyn, and relocates the indelible bloodstains to the stairs. It was said that 'if one of the servants had to wash the stains away the hall would be troubled with dismal sounds during the night for weeks continually'.[50]

Marie Trevelyan recounts the following yarn about a holy ghost which saved the life of a preacher. It has something of the flavour of The Prophet Jones about it. The narrator is the same as that in stories from Aberedw and Machynlleth.

'In his age, my father was then over seventy, he preached one Sunday night at Meifod in Montgomery, and after service he had to go to Llanfyllin on the Vyrnwy, six miles away. It was a dark, wet, and windy night in December. My father, mounted on a merlyn, rode on very comfortably for two miles or more. Then the horse stood quite still. He tried to make it go on, but it would not. Then he heard a rustling noise in the hedge on the roadside. A minute later, a very tall gigantic figure appeared on the road. It stretched out its arms as wide as ever it could, and made a kind of barrier across the way. My father rode nearer to it, and implored it in the name of the Lord to speak. He heard a sound like the rushing of a flood, and then the phantom, without moving, said, "For your life go back."

'My father was so much astonished that he turned the horse's head, and rode back to Meifod. It was lucky he did, for next morning the news came to Meifod that about the time my father was stopped on the road, a man was attacked and murdered by a gang of highwaymen. If my father had ridden on, he would have shared the same fate. The spectre on the road was a warning from the Lord.'[51]

Mochdre

Once upon a time there lived at the Oak, a little house half a mile from Mochdre Church, two sisters, named Shukan and Bettan. Shukan was the eldest and so, in time, she was the first to die. As is so often the case between siblings forced into close proximity for many years, there was a great deal of tension between Shukan and Bettan. When the older sister was dying, Bettan was less than kind to her and Shukan, virtually with her last breath, told her that she would take her revenge by returning from the grave to 'trouble' her.

Not long after she was laid to rest in Mochdre churchyard, Shukan appeared at the bedroom window – and she was wearing her shroud. She rapped her bony knuckles on the glass and shrieked over and over again: 'Bettan, thee art worse than Judas! Bettan, thee art worse than Judas!'

Bettan was appalled, and begged her undead sister to leave her alone.

'Come with me to the churchyard,' rasped Shukan in reply. Bettan agreed and followed the angry *revenant* to Mochdre Church. Before they reached there, however, a cock crew at nearby Bronyllan Farm and Shukan, on hearing this warning of coming daybreak, immediately vanished. What her ghostly sister had intended for Bettan at the graveyard, she never discovered. Fortunately, that was the last she saw of Shukan.[52]

Montgomery (Trefaldwyn)

Around Britain there are various graves where the grass will not grow, usually because the person buried there had been murdered or wronged in some way. In other places there are 'footprints' composed of withered grass marking the spot where a wrongly condemned man stood before he was executed (such a site allegedly exists near Overton, Wrexham, for example, but the two expeditions I made to find them both proved in vain). In these cases the bare earth fulfils the same function as the more common indelible blood stains which mark the floors and panelling of some of our older mansions – they record for all time the death of innocents.

In the churchyard of Montgomery there was such a gap where the grass refused to grow. John Ceredig Davies describes the grave in *Folk-Lore of West and Mid-Wales*, and reproduces a sketch of it, but a fuller account was given by Christina Hole, in her *Haunted England*, which I reproduce here:

'In the early years of the 19th century a Mrs Morris lived at Chirbury with her daughter Jane. She was a widow who had been left very badly off, and it was locally thought that she would have to part with her estate in order to make ends meet. If this happened, a local man named Thomas Pearce hoped to acquire it, as it had formerly belonged to his ancestors. It seemed more than probable that he would have his wish until her brother introduced a Staffordshire man, John Newton, who was to act as her bailiff. After that things took a different turn. Newton was evidently an excellent bailiff for, in a little over two years, he restored her income to its old level.

'Perhaps because of this, or merely because he was a stranger and somewhat taciturn, he was rather unpopular in the district, and he made two powerful enemies for himself. One was Pearce, whose hopes he had thus dashed; the other was a young farmer named Robert Parker who was in love with Jane Morris. The girl preferred Newton, and the disappointed lover decided to revenge himself on his rival. He and Pearce met and devised a scheme for getting rid of the interloper. One dark November evening, about six o'clock, they set on Newton when he was returning form Welshpool, overpowered him, and brought him back to the town, where they accused him of highway robbery with violence. They were all well known and respected local men; he was a stranger and unpopular. Their evidence was enough to hang him, and he was duly executed in 1821 during a thunderstorm.

'At his trial he asserted his innocence and said that the grass would not cover his grave for a generation in proof of it. Nor did it. The place where he lies in Montgomery churchyard was clearly marked for many years as a sterile patch about the size and shape of a coffin. The Rev R Mostyn Price published an account of the matter in 1852 in which he says: "Thirty years have passed away and the grass has not covered his grave."

'Several attempts were made to break the curse by bringing new seeds and fresh soil, but they were all unsuccessful. In 1852 turf was laid down, and this did grow for a short time except over Newton's head, where it withered at once. A few months afterwards all the turf died, leaving the grave in the same state as before. By 1886, considerably more than a generation after the execution, the bare patch was smaller, but still there. Today it can be seen in the form of a distinct cross of sterile ground with the grass growing strongly round it. The "proof" of poor Newton's innocence has persisted for more than a hundred years, and is still there for all to see.'[53]

Christina Hole wrote these words in 1940. The bare patch had already shrunk down to a cruciform shape by 1911, when Ceredig Davies reproduced a sketch of it. Davies adds an interesting tradition, apparently refuted by Hole's account, that 'a curse seems to follow every one who attempts to get anything to grow on the spot'. He cites the example of someone who planted a rose tree at the head of the grave and who, for his trouble, 'soon fell sick and died'. Davies also assures us that Newton's accusers did not escape punishment for their false witness. One became a drunkard and the other 'wasted away from the earth'.[54] Today not only does grass cover John Newton's grave, but also a thriving rose-bush! His resting place is marked by a simple cross bearing the rather unfair legend of: 'Robber's Grave'.

A mile outside Montgomery, at a place called Weston Madoc, a 'wonderful apparition' was seen on December 20th, 1661. The sun was just setting as a company of men began to march across the common, two-abreast and numbering about five hundred in all. It was the height of the Civil War and the locals thought that it must be an army of Roundheads marching on Royalist Montgomery. Some of the spectators ran to the top of the hill to watch, and they were able to see that the army marched in three companies, with cavalry trotting between them. Their later testimony revealed that they were able to see it all in great detail. Nevertheless, they soon realised that something wasn't quite right – when they tried to get a closer look, the soldiers always seemed to be marching away from them, and they were unable to get nearer than about a hundred yards. Noticing a man high up on a house thatching a roof, they asked him whether he could see the army. But he could not! Nor were there any traces of the men and their horses having passed by.

The witnesses described the apparitions to the local Justices of the Peace, and the adventure was later recorded under 'Remarkable Observations' in a 1695 *History of Wales*. This book also stated that at the same time as the ghostly army was marching across one end of Weston common, a woman and six men at its other end were 'much terrified by the sight of a blazing star ... which seemed to hang just over their heads'. The woman fell off her horse at the sight of this UFO (or perhaps corpse candle) which was 'sometimes white and sometimes red, with a tail like an arrow'.[55]

It is also reported that after the battle of Montgomery, fought on the Shropshire border in September, 1644, the ghosts of the slain were seen to haunt the field of their death.[56]

Partrishow (Patricio)

Way down in the south of the county, near the border with Monmouthshire, can be found the secluded little church of Partrishow, which is dedicated to an early Welsh martyr, St Ishow (jokingly referred to by Fred Hando as the patron saint of hay fever sufferers!). Inside the church is a grisly mural of a skeleton. Once upon a time the skeleton was armed with a scythe, a spade and an hourglass, but these have been largely eradicated by continual scrubbing. In times past, in a bid perhaps to become immortal – for the image is clearly intended to represent Death – the villagers made many attempts to eradicate the skeleton from the church wall. But, alas for them,

it is painted in human blood – no matter how often it was scrubbed out, *it always returned*.[57]

Rhayader

Above the Carreg-ddu reservoir there was a lead mine named Cwm Elan, which was named after an important manor house whose site is now drowned beneath the waters. In the 1870s the superintendent of the mine was a Cornishman and, as a stranger to the area, had no idea that the old cottage he found to rent was a well-known haunted house. On his first night in his new home, he was disturbed by an unmistakable presence of someone else in the room, and he distinctly heard the rustling of a dress. As he lay breathlessly listening in bed, he could hear a table being moved and then the sounds of plates being placed on it. Then all movement stopped and 'a deathlike silence' fell upon the place.

These disturbances continued for some nights, but the superintendent, though becoming increasingly unnerved, told nobody about them. One night he spent the evening with some friends and returned home late. He very soon had the same uneasy feeling of not being alone and then he heard the rustling sound; this time it came from an empty room that had formerly been a bedroom. Suddenly the door of this room opened and to the superintendent's amazement, a little old lady walked out. She looked so real and solid that at first he did not realise that the intruder was a ghost. She held out towards him 'a long bony hand', which the superintendent took as a begging gesture. He placed a coin in her palm – and it fell straight through it! Then the apparition disappeared. The superintendent left the house the very next day. He was unable to discover any story which explained the presence of the busy little ghost.[58]

Trelystan

At Hyssington we learnt of a fearful spirit which took the form of a bull. Trelystan was once possessed of the same, or a very similar, monster. Interestingly, both villages share similar locations – Hyssington is a few miles south-east of Montgomery and is very close to the Shropshire border, Trelystan is a few miles south-east of Welshpool and is also very close to the Shropshire border. The legend of the Trelystan ghost is almost identical to that told at Hyssington:

'A ghost, in the shape of a great bull, was so bold that it used to appear in daylight, and became so terrifying that some parsons were fetched to read it down. Attracted by their appearance, the bull followed them, and they retreated towards Trelystan Church. Their reading was so potent that when they arrived there, the bull, which had been dwindling away, had shrunk so much that it could pass inside the door. By this time candles were needed, and while they were being procured the bull grew bigger and bigger till the walls began to burst. Luckily the candles arrived in time to save the church. The parsons read on, with might and main, the bull becoming smaller all the while until he was forced into a bottle, which was thrown into the Red Sea.'[59]

Until the early 1890s the crack in the beam caused by the bull was clearly visible. Unfortunately, after a thorough Victorian 'restoration', this and many other interesting features within the church were eradicated.[60]

Welshpool (Y Trallwng)

The ghost story of Powis Castle is one of the most famous from Wales, for two reasons. Firstly it centres on an important house, now a National Trust showplace with celebrated gardens which attract thousands of visitors every year. Secondly, the story is well attested; the witness was interviewed by a Methodist preacher, John Hampson, and the account of his interview was later written up in a book by a contemporary named Wright. The story was told to Mr Wright in 1780. Both John Ceredig Davies and Elias Owen quote this account in full in their own books and versions of it have frequently appeared in more recent anthologies. However, in essence it is little different from any of the other Ghost Reveals Valuables tales we have encountered before. A précis of it will therefore suffice.

The witness was an old lady who earned her living calling from house to house and spinning yarn of various kinds. One day she called at Powis Castle and was welcomed in by the steward and his wife who, along with the other servants, were looking after the house while 'the quality' were away in London. There was a great deal of work for her to do, and she was invited to spend the night so that she could get cracking again first thing in the morning. To her surprise she was shown into rather a fine chamber for one of her class, a ground floor room which was 'grandly furnished and had a genteel bed in one corner of it'.

The lady spent a little while getting used to her new surroundings and reading her little Welsh Bible. Her attention was suddenly drawn by the opening of the door and, looking up, she saw an opulently dressed man in 'a gold-laced hat and waistcoat' walking over to a window, on the sill of which he leant, his chin in his hand, for quite some time, uttering not a word. The woman guessed that the stranger was an apparition, and realised that she had been put in the haunted room on purpose. Her mind went back to when the servants showed her to her quarters, recalling how they all huddled together, each nursing a lighted candle! She later found that this was true – knowing that the lady was such a religious old soul, the servants decided to 'put the Methodist and Spirit together to see what they could make of it'.

The story now follows the usual course. The old lady was unable to summon up the courage to speak to the apparition, and it walked out of the room, closing the door behind it. Shortly, however, it returned and this time she spoke to it, asking it 'who are you and what do you want?' The spirit replied: 'Take up your candle, and follow me and I will tell you.' It then guided the brave lady out of the room and down to a small room or large closet. Here it tore up one of the floorboards and revealed to her a box hidden underneath it. Then it showed her a crevice in the wall where the key to the box was hidden. The spirit directed the woman to send the box and key to the Earl in London – he even knew the Earl's London address – promising that if this was done, he would trouble the house no more. He then vanished.

The old woman set up a holler which brought the servants running and she told them all that had happened. It transpired that the apparition had been making the room unusable for quite some time. The box and key were duly despatched to the Earl, with an account of the elderly guest's adventure. The contents of the box were never divulged, but the Earl and his family were so grateful to the religious old lady's good faith and courage in securing them that they made sure she was comfortably looked after all the rest of her days.[61]

There is, or was, another haunted house near Welshpool, Glanhafren. The origin of the haunting was obscure; all that is known is that there was a room here which was always kept locked because some horrible death had occurred in it, either through murder or suicide. In 1890 a local man recalled the years he spent living in this house, sleeping next door to the haunted room. Every night he and his brother would hear 'something like the footsteps of a big dog' pace inside the wall, where it would climb up to the ceiling before descending again down the other side. Even though no animal of any size could possibly squeeze in between the lath and the plaster, he pooh-poohed the suggestion that it might have been rats, because 'the thuds resounding from the steps were too heavy'. So often did the two boys hear the mysterious sounds, they grew quite accustomed to them.

This man also recalled the one occasion he got a chance to see inside the locked room. 'There was blood on one side of the walls,' he said, and he was told that countless attempts had been made to wash the gore out, but it had always reappeared.[62]

Ystradgynlais

Through the course of this book we have encountered many spirits which picked on some harmless mortal or other and proceeded to bully him or her into performing various tasks. Perhaps the most unreasonable and aggressive of these was the spirit of a large, well-dressed woman with a pale face which followed around the son of an Ystradgynlais innkeeper, Thomas Llewellyn. The apparition would waylay Thomas in narrow lanes, standing before him so that he had to squeeze past it – an eerie exercise, as you can imagine. At last he plucked up courage to ask it what it wanted with him. As usual, it was a money matter (are there no ghost accountants?). The sum was considerable, £200, but this was not to be a simple case of looking up a chimney, or under a stone, or behind some old panelling. This money was stashed in a house in Philadelphia, Pennsylvania – a whole continent away! Young Tom told the spirit that he was sorry, but that he really could not see how he could help.

'Meet me here next Friday night,' quoth the spirit. 'Meet me, I charge thee!'

But Thomas did not do so. He told his friends about his encounter and the parson also. They all agreed that discretion would be the better part of valour and that it would be better not to make his appointment. They all kept him company at the parson's house on the following Friday night, quite prepared to have it out with the spirit if need be, but since by midnight it had failed to appear, everyone agreed Thomas was out of danger, and the meeting was broken up. As they began to walk home, however, Thomas suddenly vanished. The angry spirit had him in its clutches! What happened next we can allow Thomas to say in his own words:

'The apparition carried me away to a river, and threw me into it, chiding me for telling the people of our appointed meeting and for not coming to meet her as she had charged me; but bade me be not afraid, that she would not hurt me, because she had not charged me to be silent on the subject; nevertheless I had done wrong to go to the parson's house. Now, said she, we begin the journey. I was then lifted up and carried away I know not how.

'When I came to the place [in Philadelphia] I was taken into a house, and conducted to a fine room. The spirit then bade me lift up a board, which I did. I then saw the box, and took it. Then the spirit said I must go three miles and cast it into the black sea. We went, as I thought, to a lake of clear water, where I was commanded to throw the box into it; which when I did there was such a noise as if all about was going to pieces. From thence I was taken up and carried to the place where I was first taken up. I then asked her, am I free now? She said I was; and then told me a secret, which she strictly charged me to tell no person.'

Thomas had been missing for three whole days and nights and when he returned he could scarcely speak. This, of course, helped him keep his secret, whatever that might be. The identity of the spirit caused some speculation, but it was soon remembered that a lady named Elizabeth Gething had departed Ystradgynlais for Pennsylvania, so it was concluded that the spirit must have been none other than she, more willing to trust a stout Welshman with her business than one of these newfangled Americans. [63]

[1] Davies, 1911, p. 156.
[2] Trevelyan, 1894, p. 103.
[3] Owen, 1896, p. 169.
[4] *Bye-gones*, July 1901, p. 149.
[5] Trevelyan, 1909, p. 200.
[6] Ibid.
[7] Rhys, John, 1901, p. 73.

[8] *Bye-gones*, September 1880, p. 113.
[9] Palmer, 1998, p. 91.
[10] Owen, D Edmondes, 1911, pp. 101-3.
[11] Palmer, 2001, p. 121.
[12] Ibid, p. 113.
[13] *Bye-gones*, July 1893, p. 116 and September 1896, p. 430, quoting from Charlotte Burne, *Shropshire Folk-Lore* pp. 107 and 642.
[14] *Bye-gones*, March 1887, p. 272.
[15] Ibid, February 1888, p. 43.
[16] Ibid, February 1875, p. 179.
[17] Ibid, September 1904, p. 405 and 415.
[18] Ibid, October 1904, p. 419.
[19] Ibid, July 1901, pp. 135 and 143, quoting from Gittins, 1884, p 323.
[20] Gittins, 1884, p. 322.
[21] *Bye-gones*, February 1903, p. 31.
[22] Ibid, March 1903, p. 41.
[23] Ibid, April 1903, p. 69.
[24] Jones, NLW MS 16161B, p.31.
[25] Jones, 1780, p. 24.
[26] Ibid, p. 53.
[27] Townshend, 1936, p. 181.
[28] Owen, 1896, p. 199.
[29] *Bye-gones*, October 1877, p. 302.
[30] *Bye-gones*, November 1880, p. 147.
[31] Ibid, July 1912, p. 248, quoting from *Gentleman's Magazine*, March 1792.
[32] Owen, 1896, p. 212.
[33] *Bye-gones*, November 1880, p. 147.
[34] Owen, 1896, p. 212.
[35] Evans, T H, 1874, p. 93.
[36] *Bye-gones*, December 1904, p. 450.
[37] Jones, T G, 1930, p. 33.
[38] *Cambrian Quarterly*, 1829, p. 40.
[39] Owen, *Montgomeryshire Folk-Lore*, p. 68.
[40] *Bye-gones*, November, 1871, p. 9.
[41] Fewtrell, 1879, p. 409.
[42] Ibid, p. 410. See also Hole, 1950, p. 85.
[43] *Bye-gones*, May 1903, p. 102.
[44] Jones, T G, 1930, p. 42.
[45] Owen, 1883, p. 147.
[46] Jones, 1780, p. 62. See also Sikes, 1880, p. 153.
[47] Trevelyan, 1894, p. 101.
[48] *Cambrian Quarterly*, 1829, p. 452.
[49] *Bye-gones*, June 1910, p. 229.
[50] Ibid, November 1880, p. 147.
[51] Trevelyan, 1894 p. 104.
[52] *Bye-gones*, September 1891, p. 168.
[53] Hole, 1950, p. 80.
[54] Davies, 1911, p. 273.
[55] *Bye-gones*, March 1874, p. 28 and May 1909, p. 66 , quoting from *History of Wales*, 1695.
[56] *Bye-gones*, December 1915, p. 199.
[57] Hando, 1944, p. 36, and Hando, 1964, p. 25.
[58] Palmer, 2001, p. 115.
[59] *Bye-gones*, August 1903, p. 157.
[60] Ibid, September 1903, p. 185.
[61] Owen, 1896, p. 204. See also Davies, 1911, p. 157.
[62] *Bye-gones*, December 1890, p. 521.
[63] Jones, 1780, p. 60. See also Sikes, 1880, p 157.

Index to Common Themes and Types of Ghost in the Gazetteer

TYPES OF GHOSTS

Poltergeists and Stone-throwers 30, 36, 37, 43, 50, 51, 53, 55, 57, 58, 62, 67-8, 68, 70, 71, 85-6, 89, 95, 103, 119, 128, 130, 134, 137, 142-3, 144, 146, 147, 150

White Ladies (Ladi Wen) 28, 34, 49, 54, 66, 69, 70, 74, 75, 79, 83, 86, 90, 92, 93, 94, 95, 97-8, 98, 101, 108, 110, 110-11, 114, 117, 122, 133, 138, 139, 141, 149, 152

Grey Ladies 28, 29, 43, 84, 115, 117, 117-8, 134

Green Ladies 66, 93-4, 112, 117, 120, 140

Ladies in Black 29-30, 93, 98, 106, 114, 115, 117, 132, 146

Horsemen / Coaches and Carriages 27, 40, 48, 50, 53, 54, 59m 60, 72, 79, 91, 98, 115, 125, 133, 134, 135, 137, 141

Monks, nuns and other members of the clergy 25, 90, 94, 96, 135

Phantom Armies and Soldiers 33, 48, 99, 120, 133, 135, 151, 154-5

Ghosts of Living People 49, 69, 71, 89

Humanoid but Weird or Grotesque 46, 47, 52, 72, 80, 81, 91, 109, 116, 119, 124, 125, 126, 128, 129, 133

Headless Ghosts 65, 66, 92, 153

Gwyllgi / Dogs of Darkness 37, 42, 47, 54, 70, 74, 76, 80, 84, 87, 96, 109, 122, 125, 129, 134, 135

Other Dogs 52, 65, 66, 68, 101, 106, 108, 109, 111, 120, 128, 129, 135, 146, 147, 157

Cats 72, 74, 111

Horses 66, 96, 103, 109, 116, 122, 128, 147, 150

Bulls / Cows / Calves 68, 70, 76, 96, 129, 135, 139, 147, 155

Pigs 48, 58, 66, 68, 85, 120, 127, 128

Birds 47, 53, 58, 109, 118, 129

Mice 66, 85, 150

Other Animals 85, 92, 120, 128, 129

Balls/Bowls or Cylinders 119, 129, 132

Without shape 82, 95, 135

Fiery Ghosts and Ghostly Glows 25, 27, 28, 29, 46, 47, 48, 50, 52, 54, 57, 60, 69, 72, 80, 101, 107, 109, 111, 112, 117, 120, 121, 122, 125, 128, 130, 134, 139, 141, 142, 147, 148

Corpse Candles 41, 78, 82, 96, 104, 155

Phantom Funerals 35, 74, 107, 123

Cyhiraeth 82-3, 105

Gwrach y Rhibyn 91, 116, 120-21

Other Omens or Prophecies (see also Curses) 40, 46, 54, 67, 71, 73, 82, 83-4, 87, 96, 97, 104, 112, 115, 116, 135, 137

Disembodied Voices 33, 40, 44, 47, 50-1, 54, 67, 68, 72, 77, 79, 84, 89, 95, 108, 113, 117, 119, 120, 121, 122, 124, 127, 131, 134, 137, 138, 141

Music 38, 60, 70, 85, 87, 96, 111, 133, 149

Smells 26, 52, 53, 63, 89, 96, 113, 148, 149

Indelible Bloodstains and other marks 48, 133, 141, 153, 154, 155, 156, 157

Skulls 28, 31-2, 130

Helpful or Generous Ghosts 29, 44-5, 54, 67, 85, 93, 95, 98, 112, 138

NAMED GHOSTS

BAGBURY, Roaring Bull of 139 / Sir Bwci BAL 93 / BERKEROLLES, Lady 111 / Bwci BETO 93 / BLACKBIRD/ BLACKBOURNE, Lady 34 / BODVEL, Sir John 50 / BODVOC 94 / BRENIN yr Allt 27 / Bwgan y BRYN 60 / Yspryd BRYN GLAS 141, 142-3 / Bwci BO 8 / BUCKHOLT Donkey 135 / BUTE, 2nd Marquis of 115 / BUTTON, Sir Thomas 116 / CADOGAN, Thomas 127 / CAPTAIN'S Wife 113-4 / Yspryd CEFN YSPYTTY 147 / CROEN, Shon y 93 / Yspryd CEUNANT CROESAU 147 / Yspryd CEUNANT PISTYLL 147 / Yspryd COED y GRAIG 147 / Yspryd COED y GYFYNG 147 / Yspryd CYNON 146-7 / DEE/DHU, Eleanor 108 / Yspryd y DERWTEG 141 / DEWY, Anne 151 / Yspryd DUNRAVEN, Blue Lady of 113 / EDWARD II, King 96 / ERILDA, Princess 42 / Yspryd FEDWDDU 147 / FFOWLER, Madam 32 / Yspryd FFYNON DWGAN 147 / FITZHAMON, Robert 130 / FLUELLIN 151 / FRAMPTON Horse 109 / GAIN, David 151 / GETHING, Elizabeth 157 / Ghost of DYFFRYN ALED 48 / GLENDOWER, Owen 151 / GODOLPHIN, Madam 146 / GUTO Bach 98 / Yspryd y GRO 147 / GWENLLIAN, Lady 51 / GWENLLIAN 83 / GWENNO 82 / GWILWCH Gwalwch 93 / GWYN, Catrin 151-2 / Bwgan yr HAFOD 67 / HUGHES, David 49 / JEFFREY, Lady 145-6 / JEFFREY, Old 34 / JONES, Jenny 96 / KYNASTON 148 / LEWIS, Charles 139 / Yspryd y LLAN 147 / LLANGOLLEN, Ladies of 39 / LLEISION, Thomas Watkin 96 / LLEWELYN, Prince 137 / Yspryd LLWYN y FAMAETH 147 / LUCAS, Rev John Ponsonby 91 / MAID of CEFN YDFA 103 / MAID of SKER 104-5 / MAIR Wen 67 / MALLT y Nos 112 / MARGARET, Lady 96 / MARY, Blessed Virgin 139 / MATHIAS, Lady 79 / MATILDA of the Night 112 / Bwci MELYN BACH y CWM 72 / Yspryd MELIN y GRUG 141 / MORGAN, Betty 97 / NEST 83 / Bwgan PANTYWENOL 62 / Bwgan y PARCIAU 50 / Yspryd y PENTRE 147 / PHIL O'r Capel 101 / PRENDERGRAST, Lady 53 / PRITCHARD, David 53 / PRYTHERCH, Morgan 85 / RED Dog of Morfa 96 / RINGE, Lady of the 108 / ROBERTS, Eva 131 / ROGERS, Dr 64-5 / SALISBURY, David 40 / STRADLING, Lady 112 / TAMBERLAIN, James Thomas (Hen/Old) 59 / THOMAS, Ann 103 / THOMAS, Phillip 102 / TOM the Lord 130 / TROTHWY, Llwnc y 93 / Pwca TRWYN 119 / VAUGHAN, Gwen 84 / VAUGHAN, Walter 113 / VYCHAN, Gruffudd ap R. ap Ph. 84 / WARRIOR Knight of the Blood Red Plume 42 / WHITE, Juan 124-5, 144 / WHITE Mary 67/ WHITE William 127 / WILLIAMS, Dr John 56 / WISSIE (Hadwisa?) 106 / WYNDHAM, Thomas 113 / WYNNE, Sir John 44 / YORKE, Pierce Wynn 48 / Yspryd YSTRAD FAWR 47

HAUNTED PLACES

Houses and Farms 25, 26, 30, 31-2, 32, 33, 35, 36, 37, 39, 41, 43, 45, 47, 48, 49, 50, 51, 55-6, 56, 60, 62, 63, 64, 65, 67-8, 69, 69-70, 70, 71, 76-77, 79, 81, 84, 85, 89, 91, 93, 94, 96, 102, 103, 104, 106, 112, 116, 118, 119, 125, 130, 133, 134, 136, 140-43, 146, 149, 150, 153, 156

Castles 25, 42, 43, 83-4, 89-90, 91, 95, 102, 104, 106, 110, 111-2, 115, 118, 120, 130

Churches and other Ecclesiastical Buildings 38, 40, 45, 46, 57, 67, 94, 96, 117, 133, 137, 139, 139-40, 140, 156, 78

Churchyards 75, 76, 77, 78, 154-5

Public Houses 35, 113, 116, 119

Bridges 34, 47, 68, 74, 79, 83, 86, 88, 106, 115, 121, 128, 132, 135, 137, 139, 140

Stiles 28, 109, 117, 119, 126, 129, 130, 146

Ancient Monuments 26-7, 29, 37, 46, 66, 75, 79, 80, 91, 94, 99, 104, 133

Roads and Lanes 25, 29, 30, 33, 34, 37, 47, 50, 51, 58, 59, 60, 72, 74, 81, 92, 96, 101, 106, 107, 108, 109, 116, 125, 134, 141, 145, 150

Crossroads 72, 79, 109

Wells 27-8, 82, 84, 117, 117-8, 129, 131, 147

Rivers, Canals, Pools and Lakes 34, 44, 47, 54, 66, 70, 92, 95, 98, 115, 116, 120, 121, 123, 127, 128, 132, 14-7

Trees 57, 62, 97, 119, 129
Caves 82, 87, 90, 91, 148-9
Coast 67, 90, 91, 104, 112, 113
**Mountains, Moors and other Wild
Country** 29, 37, 54, 60, 72, 79, 82, 83, 93,
94, 98, 99, 117, 120, 124, 144, 149, 151-2
Valleys and Woods 33, 34, 46, 47, 48, 53,
54, 72, 84, 109, 125-6, 128, 129, 133, 141

NAMED HAUNTED PLACES

Abbot's Meadow 139 / Aberavon Castle 95 /
Aberglaslyn Pass 54 / Aberhafesp Church
137 / Abermeurig 64 / Aburthin 97 / Alltisaf
85 / Allt y Crib 72 / Ardd Ddu, Yr 26 / Ash
Farm 26 / Bagbury 139 / Beaumaris
Grammar School 49 / Bettisfield Hall 32 /
Big Man's Stile 109 / Black Pool of Cefn 120
/Blaenporth Church 66 / Bodeugan 43 /
Bodvoc Stone 94 / Boncyn y Porthman 37 /
Borras Hall 35 / Borth Sands 67 / Boverton
Castle/Place, Old 106 / Broginin 69 / Bryn 60
/ Bryn yr Ellyllon 26 / Bryn Glas 140-3 /
Bwlch Pant y Groes 79 / Cadair y Bwgan 50 /
Cae Llwyngrydd 57 / Caerphilly Castle 120 /
Cae'r Yspryd 27 / Captain's Bridge 137 /
Captain's Wife Restaurant 113-4 / Cardiff
Castle 115 / Carnedd-ddew 46 / Castell Coch
118 / Castell y Mynach 117 / Cefen Rychdir
120 / Cefn Ydfa 103 / Cernioge Mawr 48 /
Cerrigydrudion Church 45 / Ceubren yr Ellyll
(Nannau) 57 / Ceubren yr Ellyll (Nant
Gwytheyrn) 62 / Chwythlyn 47 / Clochty
Gwenno 82 / Clwchdernog 51 / Coed Bach
141 / Cot's Moor 79 / Clwyd yr Helygain 119
/ Crack Hill 107 / Craig Ddu 60 / Craig y
Llyn 93 / Craig Wen 150 / Crugiau 65 /
Crumlyn Bridge 121 / Cymau Hall (Old and New) 33 / Cynon
146 / Deiniol's Ash 26 / Derwydd Mansion
84 / Devil's Nags 79 / Devil's Pathway 96 /
Disserth Church 139 / Dolobran 153 /
Duffryn 103 / Duffryn House 116 / Dunraven
Castle 112 / Erw 56 / Faenol 53 / Ffagnallt
31-2 / Ffrith 36 / Ffynnon Eva 131 / Ffynnon
yr Ellyllon 27 / Ffynnon yr Yspryd 129 /
Ffynnon Taf 117 / Foelas 48 / Gallows Way
108 / Gareg Fawr 92 / Gelly Siriol 102 /
Gernos 70 / Glanfred 69-70 / Glanhafren 156
/ Glas Fryn 28 / Gloddaeth 46 / Glyn Diffwys
47 / Gnoll 93 / Goat's Hole Cave 91 / Goblin
Stone 104 / Golden Lion, 35 / Graig y Saeson
130 / Green Bridge Cave 87 / Greenmeadow
118 / Gwernau 150 / Gwernydd 53 / Hafod
67-8 / Hafod Llwyfog 55 / Hafod Ucha 47 /
Hawarden Castle 25 / Henllys Hall 49 /
Hereford Road 135 / HMS Asp 30-31, 77-8 /
Holt Bridge 34 / Hyssington Church 140 /
Kidwelly (Cidweli) Castle 83 / Lady Wood
133 / Llandegla Rectory, Old 37 / Llandysilio

Church 140 / Llanellan 89 / Llanelly House
85 / Llanferc-Llawddog 78 / Llanfihangel
Court 133 / Llanfor Church 57 / Llangernyw
Church 46 / Llangynwyd Castle, Old 102 /
Llangynwyd Church 103 / Llanishen Church
133-4 / Llanthony Monastery 138 /
Llantysilio Church 40 / Llwybr y Cythraul 96
/ Llyn Nad y Forwyn 55 / Llys Bedydd 32 /
Lon y Bwbach 51 / Maenan Hall 47 / Milford
Churchyard 75 / Milvre 124 / Moel Arthur 29
/ Moelyllan 57 / Monachty 70 / Monmouth
Cap 133 / Montgomery Churchyard 154-5 /
Morfa Colliery 96 / Mumbles Lighthouse 90
/ Mynach 129 / Mynydd Milfraen 124 /
Nantycell 136 / Nant y Ffrith 33 / Nant y
Gledyr 120 / Nant y Weniar 34 / Neath
Abbey 96 / Newport Castle 130 / Oak 153 /
Ogmore Castle 110 / Ogof, The 148-9 / Old
Warren 25 / Oystermouth Castle 89-90 / Pant
y Manog 84 / Pantywenol 62 / Parc y Marw
75 / Partrishow (Patricio) Church 155 /
Pembroke Dock Churchyard 77 / Pencastell
92 / Penhydd 94 / Pennard Castle 91 / Pen
Parcau 65 / Penpompren 71 / Pentrebach 130
/ Pentre Farm House 102 / Pill Churchyard
76 / Pistyll Teilo 84 / Plas Draw 39 / Plas
Dyffryn Aled 48 / Plas Gwynant 55-6 / Plas
Newydd (Denbighshire) 39 / Plas Newydd
(Conwy) 48 / Plas Newydd (Anglesey) 50 /
Plas Teg 30 / Plas yn Rhiw 63 / Pont Cnwca
Bach 88 / Pont Glyn-diffwys 47 / Pont
Llanafan 68 / Pont y Gwendraeth 83 / Pont
yr Yspryd 106 / Pont yr Yspryd Gwyn 83 /
Pool of Avarice 127 / Pool of the Harper 70 /
Powis Castle 156-7 / Pribwll 48 / Pwll
Gwenllian 92 / Pwll Gwen Marw 95 /
Pwllhelig 98 / Pwllywrach 106 / Red Bridge
86 / Rhaeadr y Wenol 44 / Rheola 93 /
Rhosmeherin 72 / Rhossili Rectory 91 /
Rhuddlan Castle 42 / Ruthin Castle 43 /
Sagranus Stone 79 / St Dene's Well 117 / St
Donat's Castle 111 / St Pierre 134 / Sampson
Crossroads 79 / Shaft y Plentyn 72 / Siamber
Wen 149 / Sker House 104 / Stackpole Court
79 / Stepney Mansion 85 / Stradey House,
Old 85 / Swallow Falls 44 / Taff's Well 117 /
Tintern Abbey 135 / Trefeen Bridge 140 /
Trelystan Church 155 / Trewern 76-77 /
Trwyn Farm 119 / Twr 56 / Ty Felin 41 / Ty
Mawr 45 / Tymawr 36 / Ty'n y Fid 125 /
Ty'n yr Heol 96 / Valle Crucis Abbey 38 /
West Orchard 110-11 / White Lady Lane and
Meadow 101 / Whitton Mawr 116 / Wye
Bridge 135 / Yet Wen 72 / Ysgol Goch 81 /
Ystrad Fawr 47 / Ystumcolwyn 153

REASONS FOR HAUNTING

Guarding or Bound to Hidden Items 28,
29, 46, 49, 50, 51, 52, 54, 56, 63, 66, 68, 69,

76, 79, 85, 87, 92, 93, 94, 96, 98, 101, 102,
104, 108, 110, 11, 112, 116, 117, 118, 121,
122, 125, 127, 130, 136, 137, 147, 151, 157
Bound by a Person's Excessive Grief
65, 70, 56, 143
**Bound by Wickedness, Wildness or
Remorse** 25, 35, 39, 40, 42, 44, 47, 50,
51, 52, 53, 59, 92, 96, 98, 101, 112, 113,
113-4, 117, 126, 129, 139, 140, 145, 146
Murdered 26, 28, 34, 41, 47, 48, 51, 54, 67,
70, 71, 72, 78, 79, 83, 90, 106, 108, 112,
134, 135, 138
Died in Accident 30, 35, 70, 83, 134, 141,
152
Committed Suicide 33, 34, 124, 125
Seeking Revenge 34, 63-4, 101, 130, 131,
135-6, 144, 148, 153
Buried in Unconsecrated Ground 34-5,
57, 90, 106, 108, 114, 115, 152
Likes the Place they Haunt 39, 45, 130,
155
Appearing to Sabbath Breakers 65-66,
122
Appearing to Protect an Individual 38,
48, 59, 85, 153
Appearing at Time of Death 34, 65, 85
**Meddling in Mortal Affairs (see also
curses)** 25, 40, 124
**Needing to be Freed by a Mortal for
Unexplained Reasons** 74-5, 84, 101,
117, 118, 138

COMMON THEMES

Ghost Laying (Exorcisms) 25-6, 32, 34,
36, 37, 44, 47, 55, 56, 57, 58, 63, 68, 70, 71,
79, 85, 94, 95, 104, 111-2, 131, 135, 136,
139, 139-40, 140, 144, 145, 146, 147, 149,
150, 155-6
Transporting Mortals 34, 53, 85, 87, 93, 98,
102, 108, 110, 112, 127, 148, 157
Physical Attacks by Ghosts 37, 43, 50,
52, 53, 55, 58, 68, 80, 81, 82, 84, 86, 87, 89,
91, 98, 101, 104, 107, 110, 118, 119, 130,
131, 134, 157
**Death, Illness or other After-Effects of
a Ghostly Encounter** 48, 55, 60, 63, 77,
80, 81, 82, 91, 92, 96, 106, 110, 121, 130,
132, 136, 145
Protection Against Ghosts / Charms 28,
53, 58, 70, 87, 94, 134, 139, 144
Curses 31-2, 67, 98, 127, 138, 142, 154
Star-Crossed Lovers 26, 30, 103, 104
Witches 81, 108, 124-5, 144
Links to Fairylore 26, 27, 34, 37, 66, 70, 72,
75, 88, 94, 104, 119, 120, 133, 140